Charles & Camilla

PORTRAIT OF A LOVE AFFAIR

GYLES BRANDRETH

A former Oxford Scholar, President of the Oxford Union and MP for the City of Chester, Gyles Brandreth's varied career has ranged from being a Whip and Lord Commissioner of the Treasury in John Major's government to starring in his own award-winning musical revue in London's West End. A prolific broadcaster (in programmes ranging from *Just a Minute* to *Have I Got News for You*), an acclaimed interviewer (principally for the *Sunday Telegraph*), a novelist, children's author and biographer, his best-selling diary, *Breaking the Code*, was described as 'By far the best political diary of recent years, far more perceptive and revealing than Alan Clark's' (*The Times*) and 'Searingly honest, wildly indiscreet, and incredibly funny' (*Daily Mail*). He is married to writer and publisher Michèle Brown, with whom he founded the award-winning Teddy Bear Museum in Stratford-upon-Avon and co-curated the exhibition of twentieth-century children's authors at the National Portrait Gallery. He is a trustee of the British Forces Foundation, whose patron is the Prince of Wales, and a vice-president of the National Playing Fields Association, whose patron is the Queen and whose president is the Duke of Edinburgh.

CHARLES & CAMILLA

PORTRAIT OF A LOVE AFFAIR

Gyles Brandreth

Century · London

Published by Century in 2005

2 4 6 8 10 9 7 5 3 1

Copyright © Gyles Brandreth 2005

Gyles Brandreth has asserted his right under the Copyright, Designs and Patents Act, 1988
to be identified as the author of this work

First published in the United Kingdom in 2005 by Century
Random House, 20 Vauxhall Bridge Road,
London SW1V 2SA

Random House Australia (Pty) Limited
20 Alfred Street, Milsons Point, Sydney,
New South Wales 2061, Australia

Random House New Zealand Limited
18 Poland Road, Glenfield,
Auckland 10, New Zealand

Random House South Africa (Pty) Limited
Isle of Houghton, Corner Boundary Road & Carse O'Gowrie, Houghton, 2198, South Africa

The Random House Group Limited Reg. No. 954009

www.randomhouse.co.uk

A CIP catalogue record for this book
is available from the British Library

ISBN 1 8441 3845 3

Papers used by Random House are
natural, recyclable products made from wood grown in
sustainable forests; the manufacturing processes conform to
the environmental regulations of the country of origin.

Typeset by SX Composing DTP, Rayleigh, Essex
Printed and bound in Great Britain by
Clays Ltd, St Ives plc

Contents

There is love, of course.
And then there's life, its enemy.

Jean Anouilh (1910–87)

Dear Dad,

Happy 70th birthday.
I hope you enjoy this. Just
think back to the days of the
Macrae family impersonations of
the Royals! No one would dare
try Camilla!

Lots of love
Sheena
xxx

Preface

'The essential matter of history is not what happened,
but what people thought or said about it.'

F. W. Maitland (*1850–1906*)

On Saturday 9 April 2005, when Charles, Prince of Wales, married Camilla Parker Bowles, everything changed.

I began the research for this book eighteen months earlier, at the beginning of 2004, when 'Mrs PB' (as she was then known at Buckingham Palace) was a woman with an uncertain future – and a notorious past. She was the acknowledged mistress of the heir to the throne, but would she ever be – could she ever be? – his lawfully wedded wife? I concluded my research on 17 July 2005, coincidentally Camilla's fifty-eighth birthday, by which time the answers to those questions were known. 'Mrs PB' had become Her Royal Highness The Duchess of Cornwall, and the birthday of this newest member of Britain's Royal Family was marked by the unveiling of her official coat of arms and the hoisting of the national flag on public buildings throughout the land.

Camilla's coat of arms features the armorial symbols of two families: her new husband's and her father's. To the left of the central shield is a 'royal lion supporter'; to the right, a blue boar with golden tusks, a feature of the arms originally granted to the Shand family in the seventeenth century. Above the shield is an arched crown, which Camilla is entitled to use as the wife of the heir to the throne. Deliberately, though also entitled to do so, Camilla chose not to incorporate the Prince of Wales's motto, *Ich dien* ('I serve') in her crest. She is married to the Prince of Wales, she *is* the Princess of Wales, but she prefers to be known as the Duchess of Cornwall. She is fully aware that another, more famous, Princess of Wales has gone before her.

There are many who still remember Diana, Princess of Wales, in such a way that they find it difficult to give Camilla the respect that is her due. For example, while custom dictates that the Union Jack should be raised on the birthday of the wife of the heir apparent, in July 2005 some charged with this duty found themselves unequal to the task. In Cheshire, the mayor of Crewe and Nantwich said, 'After what Charles and Camilla did to Diana, there's no way we should honour her in this way.' In Lancashire, the mayor of Wigan declared, 'A lot of people still have very fond memories of Princess Diana, whereas until recently Camilla has been scorned as a royal mistress. To find that all of a sudden she's regarded as part of the Establishment and that therefore we are expected to fly the flag for her is something I do find rather hard to stomach. It's too soon.'

In truth, of course, it's too late. The deed is done. Charles and Camilla are man and wife, prince and consort. The Queen has accepted her new daughter-in-law as a full member of the Royal Family. The sovereign is happy for us to know that she took a 'keen personal interest' in the development of Camilla's coat of arms, which could only have been granted with Her Majesty's express approval. Like it or not, Camilla is now 'part of the Establishment'. Believe it or not, the woman once 'scorned as a royal mistress' now features on our postage stamps and, quite regularly, stands alongside the Head of State on the balcony at Buckingham Palace.

The transformation has been rapid and remarkable, but there is no denying it – and no turning back. In 2001, Mrs Parker Bowles was voted eighth on the list of Worst Dressed Women in the World and told that she packed 'the stylistic punch of a dilapidated Yorkshire pudding'. In 2005, the Duchess of Cornwall's dress sense was commended in London, New York, Paris and Rome and was cited by one previously critical fashion correspondent as being 'the epitome of graceful, dignified style'. Anna Wintour, editor of American *Vogue*, met her and was blown away. 'I couldn't take my eyes off her,' she enthused. 'She looked marvellous.' The vilified mistress, frequently described – even in the run-up to her wedding – as looking like a horse, is now saluted for her 'natural appearance', her impeccable grooming, her 'luminous' skin, her 'immaculate' hair ('the cut and colour both exactly right') and her charming manner. According to the *Daily Mail*, for years consistently hostile to Camilla, 'When she smiles', these days, 'she looks real: soignée, yes, but also approachable, almost soft to the touch.'

The Duchess of Cornwall now looks the part of a twenty-first-century senior royal: elegant yet real, regal yet approachable, 'soft to the touch'. She looks the part – and she plays it, too. The mistress who once lurked in the shadows, who spent years dodging the paparazzi, now faces the cameras willingly and on an almost daily basis. Where the Prince of Wales goes, the Duchess of Cornwall goes too. If you look at the Court Circular (published daily in *The Times* and the *Daily Telegraph*) or check out the Prince of Wales's website (www.princeofwales.gov.uk), I believe you will be surprised at the number and range of official engagements Camilla now undertakes in the company of her new husband. I have watched her on parade at close quarters and I can report that, on duty, she does what she does very well. Meeting both the general public and the run of those whom royals are required to meet – old soldiers, young people, mayors, matrons, farmers, firemen, politicians, patients – she is invariably friendly, interested, unaffected, unstuffy and ungrand. Over the years (as a reporter, as a politician, as a supporter of different charities) I have been alongside an assortment of royal ladies as they have gone about their official duties[1] and, from all I have seen, comparatively inexperienced as she still is, the Duchess of Cornwall is as good as any of them, and better than most. I have no doubt that one day, if Charles survives his mother, as he is likely to do, Camilla will be Queen – and a popular queen at that.

When I embarked on the research for this book, I knew very little about Mrs Parker Bowles. I had met her and warmed to her; I was friends with several people who were friends of hers; I knew what I had read (what no one could avoid reading!) in the press; but of her heritage – the extraordinary story of her Keppel and her Shand forebears and of their royal associations going back over several centuries – and of her own upbringing, and nature, I knew next to nothing. I have enjoyed the journey of discovery. The 'back-story' is more interesting than I had realised and helps to explain why she is where she now is, why she and Prince Charles are so at ease with one another, and why the rest of the Royal Family, once so resistant to her, have now accepted her as one of their own.

I began writing this book having recently completed an informal

[1] The Queen, the Princess Royal, Princess Alexandra, the Countess of Wessex, the Duchess of Gloucester, the Duchess of Kent and Princess Michael of Kent among them. (The Duke of Edinburgh once said to me, 'This name-dropping habit of yours is a bit irritating.' In the pages that follow, I shall try to confine my weakness for name-dropping – and my fondness for inconsequential anecdotes – to the footnotes. It will not be easy, but I will do my best, I promise.)

account of the lives and marriage of the Queen and the Duke of Edinburgh. I approached *Charles & Camilla: Portrait of a Love Affair* in exactly the same way as I had approached *Philip & Elizabeth: Portrait of a Marriage*, but the experience of writing the two books could not have been more different. In the case of the Queen and Prince Philip, not one person to whom I spoke was in any way guarded or ill at ease. With Charles and Camilla, almost everyone to whom I have spoken has seemed in some way anxious and careful to say only 'the right thing'. Several of my interviewees said to me, 'Whatever you do, please don't mention my name.' Others said, mid-conversation, 'This is where we go off the record.' As Lord Snowdon (once brother-in-law to the Queen and an admirer of Prince Charles) put it to me (on the day, as it happens, when he had been having lunch with 'Mrs PB' as she still was), 'I adore Charles, but it isn't easy talking about his life because there has been so much pain and hurt along the way. Why add to it?'

When I told Sir Michael Peat, private secretary to the Prince of Wales, that my aim was to write this book 'in a sympathetic, rounded, balanced and accurate way', he appeared amused. He gave me the impression that he thought it highly unlikely that any book on his master would turn out to be that. When, at Clarence House, I met with Paddy Harverson, communications secretary to the Prince of Wales, and told him I wanted my book to be as accurate as possible, he volunteered to 'check the facts' for me relating to any aspect of the story in the period from the royal engagement onwards, but he did not wish to go back into the past. 'Their Royal Highnesses don't want to rake over their first marriages. Understandably. They are looking to the future.' And the future for them, I reckon, looks bright. But the past, if you are to be King and Queen, is also, inevitably, part of the story. Charles and Camilla are the people they are today, in large part, because of their past – because of their heritage, because of their upbringing, and because of the long and often turbulent history of their extraordinary love affair.

Prologue

'If some great catastrophe is not announced every morning,
we feel a certain void. "Nothing in the paper today," we sigh.'

Paul Valéry *1871–1945*

I keep a diary and, in the run-up to the marriage of Charles and Camilla on 9 April 2005, I kept a 'watching brief' on developments, noting what I was hearing from Clarence House, Buckingham Palace and elsewhere, and recording the media's reaction to events.

Sunday 14 November 2004

World exclusive. Charles, Prince of Wales, is fifty-six today and, at last, at long last, has made up his mind to marry Camilla Parker Bowles. Maddeningly, I cannot share this intelligence with anyone (at least, not yet), but my source is reliable (as well as royal) and I understand the wedding will take place within six months. In the *Daily Mail*, the British newspaper that gives more time and attention to the royal family than any other, the columnist Richard Kay is telling his readers a very different story. According to Kay (usually well-informed), the fact that, ten days ago, Charles failed to turn up at a party in honour of Camilla's son, Tom, suggests that Charles, 'once again', is 'backing away from demonstrating unambiguous support to Camilla'. Not so.

Charles missed his future stepson's party only because he was obliged to fly to Abu Dhabi to represent the Queen at the funeral of Sheik Zayed, ruler of the United Arab Emirates. Duty comes first. That's the rule. Camilla knows that. Camilla now knows, too, that the waiting game is over. The heir apparent is about to demonstrate his support for his mistress without a trace of ambiguity. He is going to marry her, and damn the consequences.

After months of shilly-shallying, what seems to have triggered the decision were the seating arrangements for last Saturday's 'wedding of the year' at Chester Cathedral. Edward van Cutsem, twenty-nine, godson to Prince Charles, married Tamara Grosvenor, twenty-four, daughter to the Duke of Westminster. The guests of honour were the Queen and the Duke of Edinburgh, long-standing friends of the Westminsters, and Prince William and Prince Harry, long-standing friends of the van Cutsems.[2] Charles and Camilla should have been there as well, but they chose to stay away. Charles decided to pull out at the last minute in protest at the proposed seating arrangements. He was to be placed at the front of the cathedral, alongside his parents and sons, while his mistress was to be consigned to a pew six rows back on the other side of the aisle. Worse, the prince was expected to enter the cathedral by the west door, with the rest of the royal party, while Camilla was invited to arrive via the north door, along with the other 650 non-royal guests.

Charles and Camilla associate Chester with humiliation. The infamous 'Camillagate' tape was recorded when Charles was staying at Eaton Lodge as a guest of Anne, Duchess of Westminster. That was fifteen years ago, in December 1989, when Charles and Camilla were each married to other people and their affair was supposed to be a secret. Now, Diana is dead and Camilla is divorced, and Charles has decided that 'enough is enough'. He won't have his partner treated like this – with him coming in one door and 'protocol' requiring her to come

[2] Gerald, 6th Duke of Westminster, became a Knight of the Garter in 2003. His wife, Natalia, known as Tally, is the daughter of Gina Wernher (Lady Kennard), a childhood friend of both Prince Philip and the Queen. Tally's older sister, Sacha (married to the 6th Duke of Abercorn, KG), was, for a time, an intimate friend of the Duke of Edinburgh. Hugh van Cutsem and Prince Charles became friends at Cambridge and were so close that van Cutsem came to be nicknamed 'Prince Hugh'. Diana, as Princess of Wales, became estranged from the van Cutsems when she discovered that they were providing a 'safe house' in which Charles and Camilla could meet. Camilla's relationship with the van Cutsems became strained in 1999 when Emilie van Cutsem reportedly told Charles that Tom Parker Bowles had taken cocaine (see page 177) and that she was concerned about his influence over William and Harry, to whom she had become especially close since Diana's death. Camilla, apparently, responded by calling Emilie 'the Dutch cow'. Mark Bolland, assistant private secretary to Charles at the time, was said to have attempted to deflect the criticism of Tom by suggesting it was the van Cutsem boys whose behaviour should give cause for concern. Lawyers acting for the van Cutsems threatened action against Bolland, who denied the remarks attributed to him, and the matter was dropped. But the tension between the parties remained.

in by another. 'It's a nonsense, it's insulting,' Charles is said to have said last week, 'And I'm not going to put Camilla through it any more.' They live together as man and wife and Charles would like them to be treated as husband and wife. From next year, he hopes they will be.

Interestingly, I think his parents are relieved by his decision. 'It's been very messy, hasn't it?' one of the Queen's oldest friends said to me. 'The Queen likes things to be tidy and, despite what's been said, she isn't in the least bit vindictive. Since Camilla isn't going to go away, she may as well be welcomed. That seems to be the view.' The Queen, I am told, is happy for the situation to be, in her word, 'regularised'. The Duke of Edinburgh, apparently, is of the opinion that 'If they're going to do it, they might as well get on with it.' William and Harry, who are both very close to their grandparents, are equally relaxed about it. 'Great,' said Harry on hearing the news, 'Go for it. Why not?'

Wednesday 15 December 2004

The Swedish royal family is suing a major German magazine publisher over a total of 1,588 different stories the Swedish royals maintain are entirely without foundation: simply figments of the German journalists' fevered imaginations. It isn't easy being royal – even when you are dead. In today's *Daily Telegraph* there is a whole page devoted to Queen Victoria's relationship with her Scottish servant, John Brown. A letter, dated 1883, has just come to light in which Victoria speaks of her grief at Brown's death and of their 'warm and loving' friendship. Was there more to it than that? Apparently, we need to know. We *want* to know, that's for sure. There is something compelling about the private lives of princes and princesses. Peter Schaufuss, the Danish choreographer, has just created a ballet about Diana, Princess of Wales, in which Diana and Dodi perform a chilling 'dance of death', Charles is portrayed as a weak but devious fool, and Camilla is seen as a whip-wielding dominatrix in jodhpurs.

Over (several) drinks tonight, a royal godparent (who shall be nameless) tells me he had a very jolly lunch with Mrs PB and likes her. 'She's very county,' he says, 'very horsey. Doesn't take a good picture. Too like a horse herself. She must be an amazing screw. Like Mrs Simpson. Mrs Simpson was *fantastic*, apparently.' (How does he know? He doesn't. A girlfriend of Diana's told me that Charles is 'hopeless in bed – absolutely hopeless'. Well, he might have been 'hopeless' with Diana, but that does not make him hopeless overall . . .) According to my chum, Mrs PB was quite gossipy, but positive in all her judgements, except when it came to Sophie Wessex, who she described as 'very pushy indeed'.

Sunday 23 January 2005

The news of the engagement is about to break but, intriguingly, the newspapers haven't yet tumbled to it. This is providing satisfaction and amusement at Clarence House and Sandringham, where, by and large, the press is held in open contempt. *The Mail on Sunday* reports that Charles will be making an official visit to the United States in the autumn and is proposing to take Camilla with him. If you stop to think about it for a moment, you realise that Charles on an official visit with a mistress in tow is simply 'not on'. If Charles takes Camilla to the US, she will be his wife by then.

I understand the broad details have all been agreed: everything was settled with the Queen over Christmas. Indeed, we might already have had the announcement had it not been for the New Year brouhaha over young Harry being photographed at a fancy dress party wearing a Second World War Afrika Korps uniform. Pictures of Harry, sporting a swastika armband, have been splashed on front pages around the world. 'Why on earth hasn't Charles cut short his holiday with Camilla?' thunders the *Mail* on its front page. 'Because he's trying to play it down' is the answer, and not turn a drama into a crisis. From what I've seen of Harry at close quarters, he's typical of any number of his Eton contemporaries. He is nineteen. He drinks, he smokes, he's toyed with drugs; he's got a feisty girlfriend; he's got an adolescent temper too. He is also sporty, determined, kind-hearted, thoughtful, caring and good with babies and young children. My friend Jim Davidson (Cockney comic, professional jack-the-lad and unlikely friend of the Wales family) thinks there's nothing wrong with Harry that time and 'a spell at Sandhurst won't sort out'.

Jim is founder of the British Forces Foundation. Charles is patron. 'I love Charles,' Jim said to me. 'I don't swear in his presence, of course, unless it's part of the act. He invited me to speak at the Beaufort Hunt Ball. I did my usual stuff. Poor bugger, he sat there with his head in his hands. He said to me afterwards, "Thank God you were funny." I stayed at Highgrove . . . You should have seen us at breakfast. I had eggs and bacon. Charles hand-picked his own muesli, bless him. The boys were there. I wish the public could have seen them. They were all over each other. He's a fantastic dad. His sons adore him, you can tell. I love Camilla too.'

I said to Jim, 'She's not really your type, is she?' 'I don't know,' he said. 'She's a lot prettier than that ghastly picture of her they keep printing in the papers. . . . And she's so kind. And she's great for Charles. The boys can see that. I tell you, eventually the country will love her for loving him. If they want to, they should get married. Of course they should.'

Friday 11 February 2005

It's out. It's official. The *Bristol Evening News*, which circulates in the area around Highgrove, has the best headline: 'Tetbury Man to Wed'.

The first opinion poll (from YouGov) has 65 per cent of respondents saying the couple should be free to marry, compared with just 40 per cent in 1998. Only 7 per cent of those interviewed want to see Camilla as Queen, however; 47 per cent don't reckon she should have any title at all; 6 per cent 'don't know'; but 40 per cent are content for her to have the title 'Princess Consort'. I know that Charles believes that, when people get to know her, they will warm to her and that by the time of his coronation – which may be fifteen and could be twenty years away – what Camilla is 'called' will no longer be an issue.

For now, the only issue is to avoid all echoes of the late Princess of Wales. The 'home team' – Charles, Camilla, Sir Michael Peat (Charles's private secretary), Paddy Harverson (communications secretary) – know full well that the press will want to run pictures of Charles and Camilla alongside pictures of Charles and Diana, and they are determined to make it as difficult for them as possible. There will be no formal engagement pictures; there will be no pre-nuptial interviews; there will be no 'kiss' on the Palace balcony. Indeed, it is all going to happen in Windsor rather than London, with a brief blessing at St George's Chapel, attended by the Queen, following a civil marriage in the castle, courtesy of my 1994 Marriage Act.[3]

The hope at Clarence House is to play this as a relatively low-key family affair, but the media will make mischief if they can. Joanna

---

[3] As an MP, I introduced a private member's bill enabling civil marriages in England and Wales to be conducted in venues other than register offices. It has proved a popular piece of legislation, though when, on local radio, my wife heard me being described as 'the acknowledged expert on the Marriage Act', she nearly fell off her bunk.

Lumley, who knows them and is bound to be a guest at the wedding,[4] calls and says, 'Charles and Camilla are so "right" together, even the *Daily Mail* will have to come round in the end. They've been through so much as a couple, they're bonded. When you see them look at each other, even across a crowded room, there's an electricity between them, a complete connection: *whoosh!* It's very, very powerful.'

Sunday 20 February 2005

Pace Miss Lumley, the media in general – and the *Mail* Group in particular – have not yet come round. The *Mail on Sunday* is having a field day. According to today's paper, the Queen is 'furious', Charles is 'close to tears' and Camilla is 'stressed out' and turning to yoga to calm her nerves. Charles once said to me, 'The papers simply make things up', and when I tried to protest silenced me saying, 'Believe me, they invent things – all the time.' I do believe him. Today's newspapers are jam-packed with fanciful fabrication. According to one, the Queen has 'no desire to see Camilla before the wedding', Charles has been 'ordered' to end the wedding reception by 6.00 p.m., and Her Majesty is 'dismayed at Camilla's engagement ring'. None of this is true.

The Queen has no problem with Camilla's engagement ring. It is a square-cut diamond with three diamond baguettes on either side on a platinum band. It is a family heirloom, last worn by Queen Elizabeth The Queen Mother. The Queen is quite content for Charles to give it to Camilla. The wedding ring is likely to be made from a nugget of Welsh gold that has supplied the wedding bands of several generations of royal brides, including the Queen Mother, the Queen, her sister, Princess Margaret, and her daughter, Princess Anne. The Queen is said to have said last week, 'There is very little [of the nugget] left, of course. There wouldn't be enough for a third wedding.' That I do believe.

I also believe that the Queen wanted a wedding reception that was

[4] She was. Joanna Lumley is an ideal celebrity friend for Charles and Camilla. She is the same age as Camilla and relates well to Charles's range of interests, from organic farming to life's spiritual dimension. Her father, like Camilla's, had a military career; she understands the aristo set; she, too, has had her travails with the press. She also manages to be enthusiastic, encouraging and positive at all times – for which Charles and Camilla are grateful, given the amount of 'negativity' they feel they have to contend with. And Joanna is good with royalty: she manages to be intimate without being intrusive, she is very friendly but never over-familiar. She treats Charles as a prince and Camilla as a consort worthy of respect as well as affection.

'not too elaborate'. Given the number of guests and the time of day, from the outset the plan was for simple finger food and a 6.00 p.m. finish. There has been one cock-up, however, and the Queen was not amused. She is a stickler for detail and, unfortunately, no one studied the small print of my 1994 Marriage Act. If Windsor Castle is to be given a licence as a venue for civil marriages, couples other than Charles and Camilla will also be able to apply to get married there. Since much of the Castle is open to the public anyway, I do not think that creates a problem, but the Castle authorities feel otherwise and, consequently, the civil wedding has been switched from the Castle on the hill to the Guildhall in the town. The Queen is not inclined to be seen going to the civil wedding in the High Street. She will give her blessing to the couple when the Archbishop of Canterbury gives his: in St George's Chapel. The word 'fiasco' is now appearing in the headlines, Charles's wedding plans are said to be 'in ruins' and Camilla is dubbed, disparagingly, as 'the town hall bride'.

Charles has not been reduced to tears, but he is frustrated – and, to use his phrase, 'a bit depressed' by all the negative coverage. Camilla is not 'stressed out': she seems remarkably cool, calm and collected under the circumstances. Her life is changing: she now has an armed protection officer at her side, she can no longer pop out to the shops as she used to do, she has to watch what she says and how she looks at all times. She is taking her grooming very seriously; she is having fun extending her wardrobe; she says she wants to 'enjoy her wedding day' but she knows it will be 'nerve-wracking'. When you meet her, she seems both calm and grounded. Her deep voice helps: she sounds like the steady character she is. On first acquaintance, I think her voice is the major surprise: it's a smoker's voice, of course, but velvety and soothing rather than rough and rasping. (The other surprises are that she is much smaller than you would imagine and really rather pretty.)

Camilla was introduced to the joys of yoga by one of Charles's favourite health gurus, Dr Mosaraf Ali, who is off this week to the foothills of the Himalayas with a group of National Health Service doctors who want to learn about complementary medicine. The trip is being funded by Charles. Says Ali, 'People don't have any idea how much the prince does for complementary medicine.' Camilla has been to India with Ali and what's attractive – and very English about her – is that she accepts that herbal remedies, homoeopathy, yoga, massage, iridology and the rest have tangible benefits without buying into all the New Age gobbledygook that can go with it. She is doing yoga to reduce her stress levels, to lower her blood pressure, to improve her posture and she feels the better for it, but you won't catch her indulging in the mystic musings that Charles is prone to. Dr Ali says they are both fit people because their diet is good and they take plenty of exercise. He also believes passionately, as those who know them well all do, that they are 'good people'. He says, 'I don't understand these vendettas and accusations . . . People who oppose this marriage should be careful about hanging on to past resentments.'

Some, evidently, cannot let go. I wrote a positive piece about the wedding for last Sunday's *Telegraph*. This Sunday, the paper's readers offer their verdict. Under the headline, 'Damn them and damn the monarchy', Henry Hughes of Bideford in Devon writes: 'Gyles Brandreth's sycophantic article makes no mention of another side, a sense of justice, no recognition that many people who have difficult marriages soldier on out of a sense of obligation to the vows they made.' A. V. Cotham from Southwold in Suffolk says, 'Gyles Brandreth may well be right in forecasting a happy ending for Prince Charles and Camilla Parker Bowles, but isn't it a little hard on the country to have such a fussy, extravagant and endlessly opinionated man on the throne, with a wife who will endlessly encourage him?' The last word goes to G. Evans, a not-so-loyal subject from North Wales: 'Now is the time for the Duke and Duchess of Parker Bowles to move abroad permanently, leaving Prince William as heir. What an outpouring of joy and affection for the monarchy there would be.'

Thursday 24 February 2005

The press hostility is unremitting. The front pages all tell the same story in their own way: 'A bloody farce' (*Daily Mirror*), 'Wedding shambles' (*Evening Standard*), 'Humiliated' (*Daily Mail*), 'Queen snubs Charles wedding' (*Daily Telegraph*). Even the Americans are getting in on the act. 'Queen to skip Chuck nups' is the headline in the *New York Post*. It's all nonsense, of course. The only mix-up has been over the location for the civil ceremony, which, wherever it happens, will be over in fifteen minutes in any event. The Queen will be at the blessing, which for her – a woman who is serious about her faith – is what counts. I understand (from a member of her family) that she *is* irritated by the way it is all being played out in the papers, but only because she knows that the drip-drip-drip of negative publicity – however unfair – has a corrosive effect. She worries about it because of the slow but inevitable damage it inflicts on the standing of the monarchy. Charles is not 'in despair' as the papers claim, but he is infuriated by the way everything *appears* to be getting out of hand and he is concerned about the effect all this 'beastliness' (as he calls it) will have on Camilla. Camilla is reportedly 'dismayed and bewildered'. She is certainly apprehensive. She has wondered, out loud, if, on her wedding day, she is going to be booed in the streets.

Sunday 27 February 2005

On it goes. Yesterday's *Telegraph* claims 'Wedding fiasco deepens hostility to Charles'. The paper's YouGov poll shows only 31 per cent of those surveyed want to see Charles as King. Twenty-three per cent think we should abandon the monarchy at the end of the Queen's reign, while 42 per cent advocate skipping a generation and allowing William to succeed his grandmother as sovereign. Today's *Mail on Sunday* is particularly malicious. Its lead story claims, 'Prince Charles has delivered an astonishing attack on the British people, accusing them of "torturing" him over his affair with Camilla Parker Bowles.' The paper quotes Charles saying, 'I thought the British people were supposed to be compassionate. I don't see much of it.' What the *Mail on Sunday* does not make clear is that these sentiments were expressed – in private, off-camera, to the BBC reporter Gavin Hewitt – some *seven* years ago! This isn't 'news'. It's personal vilification. Charles is on his way to Australia, New Zealand and Fiji, via a visit to the tsunami victims of Sri Lanka, shaking his head wanly at the ways of the British media. Camilla is spending time with her hairdresser, her dressmaker, her children and her sister. She said to someone at Clarence House this week, 'Will the nastiness ever end?'

Wednesday 2 March 2005

Prince Charles is in Perth where a sixty-two-year-old grandmother kissed him on the mouth and explained, 'I love him to bits and hope Camilla won't be jealous.' (It's a rum life being royal.) In London, I see Camilla at the memorial service for Princess Alexandra's husband, Sir Angus Ogilvy. She is seated with the royal party and looking really good: she has lost weight and gained confidence. Her smile is sustained and unforced. Her only sign of insecurity is her habit of holding on to her hat. Given the years she has had to spend hovering in the shadows, she is entering into the limelight with considerable assurance. She is very chatty and, if she is 'sunk in depression' as some papers claim, she is certainly making a magnificent fist of hiding it.

I have lunch at St James's Palace with the Duke of Edinburgh who is in very mellow mood. When Lord Howard of Rising reminds him of the saying that 'when a man marries his mistress it creates a vacancy', His Royal Highness chuckles obligingly and mutters, 'Don't, please.' When I tell him that I am responsible for the 1994 Marriage Act, HRH laughs out loud and says, 'I might have guessed'. He adds, 'At least it's settled and that's good.' He is frequently impatient with his son, and has major reservations about the way he has handled his life, but now the wedding is happening he wants it to go well, for everybody's sake, notably the Queen's. He cares about her, and his grandchildren, and about the role of the monarchy. He also knows that the tide of popularity rolls in and out and that the wisest course is to do what you believe to be right and ignore the press who, as he puts it, 'are simply out to make mischief'. I remind him of one of his best jokes – 'If you see a man opening the car door for his wife, it's either a new car or a new wife' – and ask him if he is planning to use it in his father-of-the-groom's speech on 8 April. 'I shan't be saying a word,' he says, firmly.

Thursday 31 March 2005

Will he even be there? Of course, he will be – but because the Duke is going to be in Germany the night before, sundry papers have had fun speculating: 'Will Philip miss Charles and Camilla's big day?' As Charles says, 'If they haven't got a story, they make one up.' The truth is that the plans for the wedding are now proceeding quite smoothly (clothes sorted, music chosen, invitations sent), but, according to the newspapers, everything is in a state of 'turmoil'. The latest line being run is that the Queen is so unhappy about Camilla that she plans to 'bar her' from the Buckingham Palace balcony. I don't think so. There is nothing mean about the Queen. She has accepted Camilla as a fact: now the marriage is happening, she wants it to work.

Charles, of course, does not always help himself. At an official photocall at the Swiss ski resort of Klosters today, Charles, with both his sons, faced a phalanx of reporters and photographers and, within range of a microphone, muttered 'Bloody people'. This whispered aside has been transformed into the headline, 'YOU BLOODY PEOPLE!', on the front page of the London *Evening Standard* where Charles is described as 'bad-tempered' and 'petulant'. William and Harry get a much better write-up – deservedly. Charles arrived for the photocall, disgruntled, mumbling, 'I hate doing this.' He asked his sons, 'Do I put my arms around you? What do we do?' 'Keep smiling,' said William, wisely. From the press pack, the BBC's Nicholas Witchell called out an innocuous question and Charles muttered, 'I can't bear that man, I mean he is so awful, he really is . . .'

Tuesday 5 April 2005

Pope John Paul II has died. His funeral is on Friday. Charles and Camilla have been obliged to postpone their wedding by twenty-four hours. 'Can anything *else* possibly go wrong?' asks the *Daily Mail* gleefully on its front page. On page three the newspaper provides a 'Diary of disaster' detailing the alleged embarrassment, humiliation and catastrophe the paper claims has dogged the royal couple since the announcement of their engagement. At Clarence House, the couple remain remarkably sanguine. They don't watch television. They try to avoid reading the newspapers. Happily, they are surrounded by people who wish them well.

Saturday 9 April 2005

It's happened. They've done it. Charles and Camilla are man and wife. I think Nic Paravicini [Camilla's former brother-in-law, who features in the pages that follow] was spot-on. 'This is one of the great love matches,' he said this morning. 'Everyone talks about young love, but this is enduring love of a kind that is rare and wonderful. They are two good, decent, nice people who make each other happy. Camilla provides that deep comfort every man needs, especially someone in his position. She is a rock: a kind, warm-hearted, feet-on-the-ground person. Their relationship is something good and strong to see.'

Inevitably, some will be never be reconciled. There are several members of the synod of the Church of England who simply do not believe that a divorced man married to a divorced woman can ever become supreme governor of the established church. Today's order of service included the General Confession taken from the Book of Common Prayer (Charles is nothing if not a traditionalist) so that Charles and Camilla (along with the rest of the congregation) acknowledged their 'manifold sins and wickedness' and sought God's forgiveness 'with hearty repentance and true faith'. The Confession gave the press the excuse for a churlish final fling. The *Daily Express* described the couple's public act of repentance as 'too little, too late'. The *Daily Mirror* filled its front page with a picture of Charles and Camilla sporting a cuckold's horns and devil's tails, under the stark headline: 'We have SINNED'.

In the streets of Windsor, the crowds were not vast, but they were sympathetic and good-humoured. As the couple arrived at the Guildhall for the civil marriage, I heard one half-hearted 'boo'. It came from a middle-aged man who was quickly hushed by those around him. Inside St George's Chapel, as the guests arrived for the service of blessing and dedication, there was a sense of nervous excitement. 'So far, so good,' says Camilla's father, Major Bruce Shand. 'I'm terribly relieved it's finally happened,' says the actor Timothy West, who is reading Wordsworth's 'Ode on Intimations of Immortality' during the service. I only hear one dissenting voice. It belongs not to a guest, but to an army officer, on duty at the Castle. He loved Diana: he has not met Camilla, but 'the very idea' of this marriage is repugnant to him. He sees Camilla's sister, Annabel Elliott, 'looking like the cat that got the cream' and he cannot bear it. 'The whole Shand family look so pleased with themselves,' he says, with distaste. The other people I know – here as guests – take a different line. Richard E. Grant is a huge fan of Camilla's: 'She is so firmly unneurotic, such a calm, kind, compassionate, human person . . . She doesn't seem to have any lah-di-dah airs and graces.' Stephen Fry says it's 'all delightful, simply delightful – she adores him and he adores her . . . The history has been unfortunate, but the history of humanity is full of star-crossed lovers who have found life difficult.'

The day was not easy for Camilla. She was nervous (understandably) and she was suffering from sinusitis (which nobody knew). Her head was throbbing. But she looked wonderful – exactly right – and there was something endearing about her moments of awkwardness. Outside the Guildhall, she knocked her hat with her hand. Outside St George's Chapel, she held on to her hat for fear the wind was going to whisk it away. It was touching, too, to see Charles helping her find her place in the order of service, holding her hand to display the ring, whispering to her, 'You're doing so well.'

The reception was a triumph. Everyone was happy – really happy: the atmosphere was bubbly, good-humoured, good-hearted. When Charles ended his speech with the words, 'Down with the press!'

everybody cheered. When William gave Camilla a congratulatory kiss, it was not cursory: it was done with real affection. When Charles thanked 'my darling Camilla who has stood with me through thick and thin, and whose precious optimism and humour have seen me through', there were tears in many eyes. Charles also paid tribute to 'my sons' ('they would be annoyed if I called them my children') and 'my dear mama' for meeting the bill for the occasion. The Duchy champagne flowed freely and the much-mocked 'finger food' went down a treat.[5]

The Queen's speech stole the show. She gave the marriage her unqualified seal of approval. She did not speak for long, but what she said was funny, apt and profoundly touching. The wedding coincided with the Grand National and the Queen began by saying she had two important announcements to make. The first was that Hedgehunter had won the race at Aintree; the second was that, at Windsor, she was delighted to be welcoming her son and his bride to 'the winner's enclosure'. She said, 'They have overcome Beecher's Brook and The Chair and all kinds of other terrible obstacles. They have come through and I'm very proud and wish them well. My son is home and dry with the woman he loves.'

Sunday 10 April 2005

The wedding gets a good press, and rightly so. I exchange e-mails with Andrew Motion, the poet laureate, who has written a perfect poem for the occasion that has pleased Charles and Camilla very much. It is called 'Spring Wedding':

> I took your news outdoors, and strolled a while
> In silence on my square of garden-ground
> Where I could dim the roar of arguments,
> Ignore the scandal-flywheel whirring round,
>
> And hear instead the green fuse in the flower
> Ignite, the breeze stretch out a shadow-hand

[5] The sandwiches included smoked salmon on brown bread, roast venison with Balmoral redcurrant and port jelly on white bread, and egg and cress on granary. There were potted shrimp bridge rolls and mini Cornish pasties; scones with Cornish clotted cream and Duchy strawberry jam; lemon tarts, caramel banana slices and miniature ice-cream cornets. For other wedding details, from the frocks and the flowers to the wedding cake, see Appendix C on pages 333–7.

To ruffle blossom on its sticking points,
The blackbirds sing, and singing take their stand.

I took your news outdoors, and found the Spring
Had honoured all its promises to start
Disclosing how the principles of earth
Can make a common purpose with the heart.

The heart which slips and sidles like a stream
Weighed down by winter-wreckage near its source –
But given time, and come the clearing rain,
Breaks loose to revel in its proper course.

I am going to finish my book now, go right back to the beginning and trace this story from its source.

Chapter One

A Heritage and Its History[6]

'Good God, who would have thought that we three whores should
have met here!'
> The Countess of Dorchester, mistress of King James II, on
> encountering the Duchess of Portsmouth, mistress of King
> Charles II, and the Countess of Orkney, mistress of King
> William III, at the coronation of King George I, 20 October 1714

This business of royal mistresses goes back a long way. In 955, one
thousand and fifty years before Charles, Prince of Wales, married
Camilla Parker Bowles, Charles's Saxon kinsman, Edwy the Fair, great-
grandson of Alfred the Great, became King of the English. On the very
day of his coronation, at Kingston upon Thames in January 956, Edwy
was caught *in flagrante delicto* with his mistress – and her mother. The
young King (barely sixteen, but wonderfully handsome by every
account) had slipped away from the coronation banquet to pleasure
himself with the two ladies and was discovered by, of all people, St
Dunstan, then Abbot of Glastonbury, later Archbishop of Canterbury,
'wallowing between the two of them in evil fashion, as if in a vile sty'.
The King was determined to marry his mistress – as kings sometimes are
– and, in due course, he did. But, sadly, the story does not have a happy
ending. Ælgifu, Edwy's mistress-turned-wife, was a kinswoman: the
marriage was deemed uncanonical; Edwy was deemed a fine lover but a
poor leader; Ælgifu was banished; Edwy was overthrown. In October
959, he died, in Gloucester, almost certainly murdered. He was

[6] In the first draft of this book, I borrowed my chapter titles from the novels of Barbara
Cartland and Jilly Cooper, two popular writers who feature as themselves in the course
of the story. On reflection, however, I decided it was more appropriate to base my
chapter titles on the novels and plays of Ivy Compton-Burnett (1892–1969):
Edwardian domestic dramas, heavy with unspoken family secrets.

succeeded by his younger brother, known as Edgar the Peaceful, whose reign was long and stable, who enjoyed at least two wives and many more mistresses, and who has a unique place in English history as the only king to have fathered two saints.[7]

The coronation of King Edwy is not a bad place to start our story – it sets the tone, in some ways – but the coronation of King George I is probably better, simply because, by chance, it includes a brief and telling moment that serves to introduce us at once to the kith and kin – and certain of the characteristics – of each of the central characters in the 'Charles and Camilla' saga.

That moment – when the Countess of Dorchester, aged fifty-seven, the Duchess of Portsmouth, sixty-five, and the Countess of Orkney, fifty-seven, came face to face in Westminster Abbey on 20 October 1714 – brings together three unusual and gifted women who, between them, not only served three of Prince Charles's more interesting ancestors as lovers and friends, but who also, intriguingly, have direct connections with both Lady Diana Spencer *and* Miss Camilla Shand.

The Countess of Dorchester's line – 'Good God, who would have thought that we three whores should have met here!' – was to the

---

[7] Edgar the Peaceful was so-called because his reign, 959–75, was free from war. He was succeeded by Edward, his only son by his first wife, Æthelflaed. In 978 Edward was murdered at Corfe Castle on the orders of his stepmother, Ælfthryth, Edgar's second wife, who wanted power for herself and her son, who became Ethelred II, known as 'The Unready' – from the Saxon word 'unraed', meaning 'lacking counsel' or 'un-advised'. Shortly after Edward's murder miracles began to be reported from the site of his tomb and by 1001 he was declared a saint and martyr. Edgar the Peaceful also had a daughter, Edith, by his mistress, Wulfryth, a novice at Wilton Abbey. Wulfryth eventually became Abbess of Wilton and Edith – several times rejecting the possibility of a life at court – became celebrated for her piety, her service to the poor and her love for wild animals. She died, aged twenty-three, in 984, and reported miracles at her tomb quickly established her cult. By 997 she was known as St Edith of Wilton. Her feast day falls on 16 September. A key figure throughout this period of English history is another saint, Dunstan (909–88; feast day, 19 May), the Benedictine monk and reformer, whose life was truly remarkable and whose legacy includes what was said to be Queen Elizabeth The Queen Mother's favourite 'Noël Coward story'. In 1915 a home, named after St Dunstan, was founded in London to care for those blinded in war. Many years later, in the late 1960s, Noël Coward, playwright and royal favourite, was visiting his friend, the actor Laurence Olivier, in Brighton. Looking out of the window on to the Brighton promenade, Olivier's young son, Richard, spotted two dogs having protracted inter-course and, innocently, asked Coward what the dogs were doing. 'It's very simple,' said Coward. 'The poor dog in front is blind; and the kind dog behind is pushing her all the way to St Dunstan's.'

point, and typical. It was said to be heard, and intended to be repeated.[8] The countess was a caution. Her claim to fame is that she was the mistress of King James II and bore him a daughter, in 1679, and a son, in 1684. Her claim to the King's attention was not her beauty, which was negligible (she had a squint among other blemishes), but her wit, which was considerable, and often caustic. (During George I's coronation, when the Archbishop of Canterbury formally asked the congregation for the people's consent to the King's crowning, she turned to her neighbour and whispered loudly, 'Does the old fool think that anybody will say no to his question when there are so many drawn swords?')

James II had many mistresses and two wives. His first wife was a commoner, Anne Hyde, the daughter of a lawyer – albeit an ambitious lawyer who became Lord Chancellor and Earl of Clarendon. In 1660, when Anne fell pregnant by James, then Duke of York, he was pressed into marrying her by his older brother, King Charles II, recently restored to the throne, who took the view that James 'must drink as he has brewed'. (I reckon that is a line with which the present Duke of Edinburgh would have some sympathy.) Over eleven years, until her death, aged thirty-four in 1671, Anne Hyde bore James eight children. Only two survived: two daughters who, in time, became Mary II, wife of William III, and Queen Anne.

Two years after Anne Hyde's death, Catholic James married Catholic Mary of Modena, daughter of an Italian duke – though rumoured (by malcontent Protestants) to be the bastard daughter of the Pope. Mary was fifteen; James was forty. He liked them young. Indeed, most of his many mistresses (in his prime, he was insatiable[9]) were in or barely out of their teens – at least, at the start of the

[8] Such lines are. Not long ago, at a party given in honour of the present Marquess of Bath, I was spotted across the crowded room by Mrs Cynthia Payne, the celebrated London 'madam'. As she sailed towards me, for all to hear she cooed, 'Gyles, I haven't seen you in *ages!*' (Of course, we had only met once before – and then in a radio studio, not her salon.) Mrs Payne – like the Countess of Dorchester – has a way with men. She told me, 'I can do anything with a man, until he's despunked.' The Countess of Dorchester – like Mrs Payne – had a way with words. She claimed not to be able to explain James II's infatuation with her. 'It cannot be my beauty,' she said, 'for he must see I have none, and it cannot be my wit, for he has not enough to know I have any.'
[9] His taste in women was catholic: if they were willing, he was able. Charles II remarked on both the quantity and quality of his younger brother's conquests, noting the number of them and how plain their faces often were. The King encouraged the joke that James was given his mistresses by his priests as a penance.

relationship. His longest-serving mistress was Arabella Churchill, daughter of the original Sir Winston Churchill and sister of John Churchill, who became the 1st Duke of Marlborough. Arabella was seventeen when she was appointed maid of honour to the Duchess of York and so caught the Duke of York's ever-roving eye. Their affair lasted twelve years, straddling both of James's marriages, and she bore him four children, including a daughter, Henrietta, who married Henry, 1st Baron Waldegrave, and was a grandmother, six times removed, of Diana, Princess of Wales. (Diana's direct forebears included not only James II's longest-serving mistress, but also two, if not three, of Charles II's favourite mistresses. As she said once, when grumbling about Prince Charles's affair with Camilla, 'You would have thought I'd have seen it coming.')

In due course, James tired of Arabella (well, she was pushing thirty) and turned his attentions to a younger, fresher maid of honour, who may not have been gorgeous, but was certainly game. When she was still fifteen, Samuel Pepys described her as 'none of the most virtuous, but a witt'. Catherine Sedley (1657–1717) was held to have inherited her ready way with words – and her easy manner between the sheets – from her father, Sir Charles Sedley, baronet, playwright and *roué* about town. For several years, James adored Catherine. When he became King, he made her Countess of Dorchester. She gave him two children – or, at least, he believed they were his children. The boy, James Darnley, almost certainly was. The girl, Katherine Darnley, almost certainly wasn't – though she liked to feel she might have been. Her mother told her: 'You need not be so proud for you are not the King's but old Grahame's daughter.' Colonel James Grahame (1649–1730) was the King's Keeper of the Privy Purse.

In time, in exile, in old age, James II came to regret his former incontinence. 'I abhor and detest myself,' he said, 'for having lived . . . so many years in almost a perpetual course of sin.' The Countess of Dorchester had no such regrets. James II's squinting mistress went on to marry a one-eyed Scottish soldier serving in the army of James's successor, William III. Sir David Colyear, later Earl of Portnore, was said to be a good man and the Countess of Dorchester determined to be a good wife. She bore her husband two sons. When they were of age, she told them, 'If anybody call either of you the son of a whore, you must bear it, for so you are, but if they call you bastards, fight till you die; for you are an honest man's sons.'

The second in the triumvirate of 'whores' on parade at Westminster

Abbey for the coronation of George I was the most senior, both in rank and years. Louise de Kéroualle (1649–1734) was a favourite mistress of King Charles II – perhaps *the* favourite. As he approached the end of his life, Charles begged his brother James to ensure 'that Nellie might not starve', but of Louise he said, 'I have always loved her, and I die loving her.' Nell Gwyn was an actress, an orange seller, the proverbial tart with the heart of gold, pretty and witty, but she was not a lady.[10] Louise de Kéroualle came from a Breton family of quality. She may not have had beauty,[11] but she had breeding – and brains. She arrived in London in 1670 as one of the maids of honour to Charles's youngest sister, Henrietta, Duchess of Orleans. Louise was not yet twenty-one, a committed Catholic and a virgin. The King was forty and a serial womaniser. He was nicknamed 'Old Rowley' after a notorious goat that grazed and rutted on Whitehall green. For almost a year young Louise resisted Old Rowley's lascivious entreaties – and then she succumbed, during Newmarket race week, encouraged to do so by assorted courtiers (who wanted a happy sovereign) and possibly even by Louis XIV of France (who may have regarded her as a potential French spy). Word that she had at last given in to the King quickly spread. John Evelyn noted in his diary: 'The fair lady was bedded one of these nights and the stocking flung after the manner of a married bride.'

Louise was not the King's wife, but she was now his recognised mistress and, within ten months, gave birth to their first child, Charles Lennox, 1st Duke of Richmond – another forebear of Diana, Princess of Wales, and the father of Anne Lennox, who married William Anne van Keppel, 2nd Earl of Albemarle and direct forebear of Camilla Shand.

Louise gave Charles every attention: that's what these men want. Gilbert Burnet, Bishop of Salisbury, recorded at the time: 'She studied to please him and observe him in everything.' Charles gave Louise a fine title, handsome apartments and a liberal allowance. She was extrava-

[10] Actresses weren't: that was part of their charm. (It still is. To this day, theatre people like to quote their favourite maxim: 'It's not "adultery" on tour.') Charles II was generous to Nell Gwyn – her son by him was made Duke of St Albans and she might have become Countess of Greenwich had the King not died before the honour was bestowed – but it was not until Queen Victoria knighted Sir Henry Irving in 1895 that the acting profession was accorded any degree of 'respectability'.
[11] She was another one with a cast in her eye. Nell Gwyn dubbed her 'Squintabella'. She also nicknamed her 'the weeping willow' because of Louise's trick, when crossed, of dissolving into tears.

gant, but she had a taste for what John Evelyn called 'the riches and splendour of this world' which the King admired, shared and was willing to fund. Evelyn visited the Duchess of Portsmouth's apartments and marvelled at what he found: 'the new fabric of French tapestry, for design, tenderness of work, and incomparable imitation of the best paintings, beyond anything I had ever beheld . . . Japon cabinets, screens, pendule clocks, huge vases of wrought plate, tables, stands, chimney furniture, sconces, branches, braziers, &c . . . all of massive silver, and without number, besides of his Majesty's best paintings.' Visitors to the Duchess of Cornwall's apartments at Clarence House – wonderfully refurbished for her by Prince Charles – come away equally overwhelmed. An uncharitable handful even echo John Evelyn's lament that the 'riches and splendour' on view were 'purchased with vice and dishonour'.

The Duchess of Portsmouth – like the Duchess of Cornwall – was a controversial figure. At court, she was a deft operator who out-manoeuvred her rivals with some skill. In the streets, she was held in open contempt. She was a Catholic and did not hide the fact. Once, famously, Nell Gwyn's carriage was jostled in the street by an unruly crowd who thought it was Louise de Kéroualle on board. The actress turned the jeers into cheers when she thrust her head out of the carriage window and roared, 'Do not hurt me, good people! I am the Protestant whore!'

Charles II, of course, was a married man. His wife was Catherine of Braganza, a pleasing, pretty, pliant princess of Portugal. They married when she was twenty-three and he was thirty-one. She adored him: he ignored her. He liked her well enough, but he never pretended to be in love with her (whatever 'in love' means) and the marriage cost her dear – in terms of her health, which was poor, and the humiliations heaped upon her, which were many. At first, Catherine protested when Charles attempted to install a favourite mistress – Barbara Palmer, Lady Castlemaine, already the mother of one of his children and shortly to be the mother of another – as one of her Ladies of the Bedchamber, but, over time, she had little choice but to give up the unequal struggle. The King was King and he would have his way. Over the years he fathered at least thirteen children (none by his wife), including three sons by Lady Castlemaine – among them, Henry, 1st Duke of Grafton, another direct forebear of Diana, Princess of Wales – and, possibly, a daughter, Mary Crofts, by one of the earliest (and unluckiest) loves of his life, Lucy Walter. Lucy ('brown, beautiful, bold, but insipid', according to

John Evelyn) met Charles in The Hague when he was sixteen and she was a couple of years older. She died, in Paris, probably of syphilis, in 1658, two years before Charles became King. She was certainly the mother of Charles's first child, James, later Duke of Monmouth. The paternity of her daughter, Mary, is more doubtful – which is a pity because Mary Crofts married one William Sarsfield, another forebear of Diana, Princess of Wales.

The third in our trio of 'whores' is, possibly, from our point of view, the most interesting. Elizabeth Villiers (c. 1657–1733) introduces us to William III (1650–1702) who introduces us to Arnold Joost van Keppel (1669–1718) who introduces us to a long line of notable Keppels, culminating in Alice Keppel, mistress to Edward VII, and Camilla Parker Bowles, mistress and wife to Charles III and stepmother to William V.[12] And, only fifteen paragraphs in, we are also about to get our first whiff of rumoured royal homosexuality . . .

William III and his wife, Mary II, succeeded Mary's father, James II, and, uniquely among British sovereigns, reigned jointly. The couple were cousins. Charles I and Henrietta Maria of France were their grandparents. William was the son of another Mary, sister of Charles II and James II, who had married another William, the head of the House of Orange, the 'Stadtholder' of the Dutch Republic. Mary II was the daughter of James II by his first wife, Anne Hyde, who had died in 1671, when James was still Duke of York, and Mary only nine. She was only fifteen when she was married to her cousin, William, at St James's Palace, on 4 November 1677, his twenty-seventh birthday. By several accounts, the poor girl wept and cringed as William led her away to the bridal bed, his uncle Charles II bellowing after, with lubricious glee: 'Now nephew to your work! Hey! St George for England!'

It seems, in fact, that William, unlike his uncles, was not highly sexed. He was not strong (he suffered from asthma); he was not tall (he

[12] Actually, who knows what the future holds? In any event, even if Charles and William do succeed to the British throne, they may choose to reign under different names. A sovereign may choose to be known by whatever name he or she pleases. When the present Queen succeeded her father, on 6 February 1952, almost as the news was broken to her, her private secretary asked her what name she wished to use as Queen. 'My own name, of course,' she told him, 'Elizabeth.' Her father's first name was Albert: he reigned as George VI. Edward VII's first name was also Albert. Edward VIII used the first of his seven Christian names while King, but, by his family, was known by the last of them, David.

was four inches shorter than his wife); he was not especially handsome (he was mildly hunchbacked), though, if Abraham Raguenau's fine portrait of him as a young man is to be believed, he had a kindly face: pleasing, pale and a little effeminate. William and Mary's marriage turned out to be a good one. Despite its inauspicious start, Mary came to be devoted to her husband. While her claim to the English throne was stronger than his, she was younger than he was, and a woman, and content to support her husband and refrain from officious interference in matters of state. She said as much: 'He comes to my chamber about supper time upon this condition, that I should not tire him more with multiplicity of questions, bur rather strive to recreate him, over-toil'd and almost spent, with pleasing jests, that might revive him with innocent mirth.' That is what these princes want. That is precisely what Prince Charles felt Princess Diana was never able – or willing – to provide.

Mary's devotion to William notwithstanding, he was nonetheless unfaithful to her – not serially, as his uncles would have been, but certainly, or almost certainly, with Elizabeth Villiers. Elizabeth was the daughter of Colonel Sir Edward Villiers of Richmond and Frances Howard, daughter of the 2nd Earl of Suffolk, governess to the princesses Mary and Anne. Elizabeth's elder brother, Edward, later became Master of the Horse, while Elizabeth and her sister Anne joined Mary as maids of honour at the time of Mary's marriage to William of Orange in 1677. Three years later, in 1680, Elizabeth was generally acknowledged to be William's 'mistress', but what precisely they got up to together nobody is entirely sure. Sex was generally assumed to be part and parcel of their relationship, but was it? Certainly no late eighteenth-century equivalent of St Dunstan caught them in the act. Mary, encouraged by mischief-making courtiers, did once set about spying on her husband and was distressed to discover him leaving Elizabeth Villiers's apartments in the early hours of the morning. However, he told her, emphatically, 'What has given you so much pain is merely an amusement: there is no crime in it.' She was ready to believe him – and perhaps she was right to do so. Some years later, when they were joint sovereigns, and the rumours of the King's affair with Elizabeth Villiers continued, John Evelyn recorded that 'the impudence of both sex being now so great and universal, persons of all ranks keeping their courtesans so publicly, the King had lately directed a letter to the Bishops, to order their clergy to preach against that sin'. If William had been guilty of the sin himself, would he have called on the bishops to orchestrate its public denunciation?[13]

It is possible (isn't it?) that William was drawn to Elizabeth's mind and company rather than her body and bed. The great Jonathan Swift declared she was 'the wisest woman I ever saw'. (Swift is also our source for the information that Betty Villiers was yet another royal mistress with a squint. 'I always forget myself and talk of squinting people before her,' he said, 'and the good lady squints like a dragon.') Whatever the truth about its exact nature, whether or not 'the act of darkness' ever took place between them, or whether, like Jimmy Carter, the King committed adultery but only 'in his heart',[14] William's intimacy with Elizabeth Villiers continued, off and on, until Queen Mary's unexpected death on 28 December 1694, when, abruptly, it stopped.

Mary died of the smallpox, aged only thirty-two, reportedly leaving a letter for her husband, apparently containing 'an admonition to the King, for some irregularity in his conduct'. William was devastated by his wife's death. According to Bishop Burnet of Salisbury, 'He turned himself much to the meditations of religion and to secret prayer.' Closeted with his friend John Tillotson, Archbishop of Canterbury, 'He entered upon solemn and serious resolutions of becoming, in all things, an exact and exemplary Christian.' William now set about his prayers at least twice a day, wore a lock of Mary's hair and her wedding ring next to his heart, and abandoned altogether his relationship with Elizabeth Villiers. He had already taken care of his friend financially; now she took care of herself. Within a year of Mary's funeral, Elizabeth was married to one of her own cousins, Lord George Hamilton, a soldier and a gentleman, fifth son of the 3rd Duke of Hamilton. Within a year

---

[13] One of several reasons why I am ready to believe that the Duke of Edinburgh has not been unfaithful to Elizabeth II is because of the open way he is and was critical of his own son's infidelity to Diana. Prince Philip has enjoyed close friendships with women not his wife – what the French call *amitiés amoureuses* – but playful friendships are different from illicit liaisons. . . . Aren't they? Certainly, I believe Elizabeth II thinks they are. The Queen invites Philip's carriage driving companion, Penny Romsey, to stay – regardless of the rumours. Even more generously, Mary II signed patents transferring 90,000 acres of James II's former Irish estates (worth £5,000 a year) to Elizabeth Villiers.

[14] During his first presidential campaign in 1976, Jimmy Carter admitted to *Playboy* magazine: 'I've looked on a lot of women with lust. I've committed adultery in my heart many times. This is something God recognises I will do – and I have done it – and God forgives me for it.' The doyen of American newscasters, Walter Cronkite, told me that Carter was 'the wisest President I ever met, the most intelligent' – and, since Franklin Roosevelt, Cronkite had met them all. Mrs Carter simply said, 'Jimmy talks too much . . .'

of the marriage, William had created Hamilton: Earl of Orkney, Viscount of Kirkwall and Baron Dechmont. By every account, the Orkneys were a contented couple and, despite her age (she was approaching forty at the time of her marriage), Elizabeth promptly presented her young husband (he was some nine years her junior) with three children in quick and happy succession.[15]

William did his best to rise with dignity above the rumours of his relationship with Elizabeth Villiers. He was more troubled by the rumour of his alleged homosexuality. Princes are prey to this kind of thing. Prince Charles has often been subject to the accusation: Princess Diana, as we shall see, was one of those in part responsible for spreading the slur. Charles's sister-in-law, Sophie, Countess of Wessex, famously assured readers of the *News of the World*: 'My Edward is not gay.' And Charles's father, the Duke of Edinburgh, told me he was once accused of having an affair with Valéry Giscard d'Estaing, the former President of France. What are we to believe?

In the case of William III, while several of the authorities I have consulted assert his homosexuality as a matter of fact, I am inclined to think, on balance, he liked men for their companionship rather than their bodies. The notion that William was homosexual has taken root partly because of his appearance and manner ('He had a thin and weak body,' according to Bishop Burnet, 'and delicate constitution . . . his senses were critical and exquisite . . . he spoke little'), partly because of his heritage (he was brought up by strong women), partly because of the company he kept (we are about to meet his 'favourites'), but principally because Bishop Burnet's detailed and vivid account of William contains this sentence: 'He had no vice, but of one sort in which he was very cautious and secret.'

It is an intriguing sentence. Some historians take it to be a reference to Elizabeth Villiers and other mistresses besides, women he enjoyed (if he did) with rather more discretion than his uncles enjoyed their assorted conquests and concubines. Others take the sentence to be a clear (if coded) reference to the King's favourites: the Earl of Portland and the Earl of Albemarle. Apparently, Bishop Burnet confided to a

---

[15] If Elizabeth had been having a full sexual relationship with William, it is perhaps surprising they had no children. Elizabeth was fecund and William was fertile: Mary had no children, but at least one miscarriage. Elizabeth went so far as to admit to her husband that she had been 'on very good terms with a certain person' but did not wish to hear 'any reproaches or insinuations on that score'. I am happy that she should have the last word.

friend that 'some things' were 'too notorious for a faithful historian to pass over in silence'.

That William was close to Portland and to Albemarle is not in doubt. In different ways and at different times in his life, no one – certainly no man – was closer. When William was young, William and Portland were boon companions. When he was older, William and Albemarle were all but inseparable. But were they lovers? Who knows? As one of the present Duke of Edinburgh's alleged paramours once put it to me, 'Unless you are in the room, under the bed, with a lighted candle, who knows what goes on?'

We do know that Hans Willem Bentinck (c. 1649–1709), later 1st Earl of Portland, once shared William's bed for sixteen nights in succession, but that was in 1675 and specifically to help 'draw off the fever' when William had smallpox. He put his own life on the line in consequence. Bentinck was devoted to the Prince of Orange. He joined his court as a page of honour, was quickly advanced to the post of Gentleman of the Bedchamber, and was soon acknowledged as the prince's personal secretary, principal counsellor and most intimate friend. In 1689, when William and Mary ascended the English throne, Bentinck received his reward: at a stroke he became Baron Cirencester, Viscount Woodstock and Earl of Portland. (As a senior courtier once informed me, without a trace of a smile: 'The sovereign is the fount of all honour. Inevitably, those closest to the fount get splashed the most.') For more than twenty years, in peace and war, at home and abroad, Bentinck was at William's side, but, as far as I can tell, there appears to be no evidence of any substance to suggest anything untoward in their personal relationship – just rumour. (And royalty is used to that.)

We know that William was married, and contentedly, *pace* his friendship with Elizabeth Villiers. We know, too, that Bentinck was a marrying man. He had three wives in all: his second wife was Anne Villiers, Elizabeth's younger sister. There is nothing in his history to suggest a strain of bisexuality. Is the same true in the case of Bentinck's only real rival for William's affections, Arnold Joost van Keppel, 1st Earl of Albemarle?

Keppel was twenty years Bentinck's junior. He was younger, better looking, more gregarious, readier to please. Unlike Bentinck, he was open and playful, well-mannered and warm-hearted. He was also, apparently, a flatterer in a way that Bentinck resolutely refused to be. Like Bentinck, he was Dutch and came from an old and established family, a descendant of Walter van Keppel (1179–1223), lord of Keppel in the Low Countries. His parents were Oswald van Keppel and Anna Geertruid van Lintelo. In 1688, when he was nineteen, he accompanied William to England as one of his pages of honour. In my biography of the Queen and Prince Philip I wrote, casually, in a footnote that William was bisexual and 'brought sixteen-year-old Arnold Joost van Keppel with him from Holland to England as his catamite'. That is what I had heard: that is what I repeated. I now think I was wrong.[16] There is plenty of hearsay: there is no evidence.

Keppel was boyish in appearance and engaging in manner. He had the bloom – and charm – of youth. William was forty-one in 1691; Bentinck was forty-three or possibly forty-seven (his date of birth is disputed); Keppel was just twenty-two – and that year made a particular impression on his sovereign by the fortitude he showed when he broke his leg in a fall while out hunting. 'That is such a good lad,' said the King, 'he withstood terrible pain.'

By the mid-1690s Keppel had supplanted Bentinck as William's foremost favourite. He was probably not as able, and certainly not as conscientious, as his older rival, but he was now the personal aide and confidant to whom the King turned most frequently and first. The King ennobled his young friend in 1696, making him, aged not quite twenty-seven, Baron Ashford, Viscount Bury and Earl of Albemarle. Rumours abounded. William was aware of them. He was saddened and perplexed by them. He said, very much as Prince Charles might have done in similar circumstances (I think you can hear the present Prince of Wales in William's tone and turn of phrase): 'It seems to me very extraordinary that it should be impossible to have esteem and regard for a young man without it being criminal.'

Again, there is no evidence that the 1st Earl of Albemarle was gay, except in the traditional sense of the word. Indeed, John Miller, in his

[16] And I apologise. It is all too easy to libel the dead: they have no redress. I have just finished reading *Portrait of a Killer* by Patricia Cornwell. I have met Ms Cornwell; I like her (indeed, in a wholly futile way, I fancy her), but I am alarmed that readers of her book – and she has readers by the million – will come away from it believing that a fine British artist, Walter Sickert (1860–1942), was also the multiple murderer Jack the Ripper, simply because she says so. Sickert, incidentally, like Bentinck, was three times married. Bentinck, however, was undoubtedly more buttoned up. I reckon Sickert's approach to such matters was more in accord with the Keppel tradition. Sickert maintained that he held 'blessed monogamy' in high esteem, but he also believed it should be 'reasonably tempered by the occasional caprice'.

scholarly account of the life and times of William and Mary, insists 'Keppel was heterosexual to the point of being randy'.[17] In 1701, a year before the King died, Keppel, aged thirty-two, married Geertruid Johanna Quirina van der Duyn, daughter of the lord of St Gravemoer, governor of Bergen-op-Zoo and Master of the Buckhounds to William III. When, recently, I told one of Camilla's friends about my researches into Camilla's grandfathers-ten-times-removed, she laughed uproariously and said, 'Are you telling me one was a randy bugger and the other was master of hounds? That sounds par for the course.'

The Albemarles had just two children: a son and a daughter. The son was born at Whitehall on 5 June 1702, and named William Anne, after the late King, who had died in March (with Albemarle at his side), and the new Queen, Anne, who had been crowned in April. He was baptised in the Chapel Royal: Queen Anne was his godmother. As a young man, as soldier and a courtier, he prospered. In 1717, aged fifteen, he was appointed captain and lieutenant colonel of the Grenadier company of the Coldstream Guards. In 1718, he succeeded to his father's titles and estates. In 1737, he was made governor of Virginia (not that he ever went); in 1727, the year in which George II succeeded George I, he was appointed aide-de-camp to the King; by 1739 he was a brigadier general; by 1744 he was colonel of the Coldstream Guards. On 16 April 1746, at the Battle of Culloden, the last battle fought in Britain, he was a commander of the first line. In 1748, he was appointed both commander-in-chief in north Britain and ambassador extraordinary and minister plenipotentiary to Paris. This time, he went. In 1749, he became a Knight of the Garter. In 1750, he was made Groom of the Stole. In 1754, he was sent again to Paris, where, unexpectedly, aged fifty-two, he died. He lived life to the full – and spent to the hilt. Horace Walpole called him 'the spendthrift earl' and said that the British Embassy in Paris was 'kept up for his benefit'.

[17] 'Randy' is also the word used to me by one of their friends to describe some of the members of 'the Parker Bowles set' in the early 1970s. It is a delicious (and useful) word, not as much used in this century as in the last. Its etymology is obscure. According to the *Oxford English Dictionary*, its first use in the sense of 'wanton, lustful and lewd', as opposed to its earlier meaning of 'aggressive, loud and coarse', was around 1847. 'Gay' has meant 'merry and bright' since the fifteenth century. It has been used as a euphemism for 'homosexual' for less than a century. Prince Charles, like his grandmother, is one of those who regrets the way the new meaning has eclipsed the old. Queen Elizabeth The Queen Mother liked to say, 'In my day, when someone referred to "a gay dog" you knew exactly where you were. Now we're all confused.'

According to Walpole, when Albemarle was married, in 1723, he had '£90,000 in the funds' and his wife brought him £25,000 more. By the time of his death, the bulk of this fortune had been 'squandered', and Albemarle died 'without leaving a penny for his debts or for his children, legitimate or illegitimate, who were many'.[18] George II conferred a pension of £1,200 a year on his widow.

William Anne, 2nd Earl of Albemarle, was married, you will recall, to Lady Anne Lennox, daughter of Charles Lennox, 1st Duke of Richmond and bastard son of Charles II by Louise de Kéroualle, Duchess of Portsmouth. These Albemarles, William Anne van Keppel and Anne Lennox, had a total of fifteen children: eight sons and seven daughters. It is from this family that our Camilla, Duchess of Cornwall, is directly descended.

It is an interesting family, with some colourful members. William Anne's eldest son, George, 3rd Earl of Albemarle (1724–72), followed in his father's military footsteps, with almost as much success, in terms of rank and honours achieved, though, arguably, with less real distinction. As a young man, he narrowly survived the Battle of Culloden where he was fired on, at point-blank range, by a Highlander who, seeing his elaborate dress, mistook him for the commanding general. His near-contemporary James Wolfe, the hero of Quebec, dismissed him as 'one of those showy men who are seen in palaces and the courts of men . . . He desires never to see his regiment and wishes that no officer would ever leave it.' Nevertheless, George prospered. He became an MP, a Privy Counsellor, an aide-de-camp to the King, a general, a Knight of the Garter and governor of the island of Jersey. In 1762, Britain declared war on Spain and Albemarle was sent, with a force of ten thousand troops, to the West Indies to capture Havana from the Spanish. He succeeded and was rewarded by the Crown to the tune of £122,000, money he used to acquire a fine family seat at Quidenham in Norfolk. His conquest of Havana was controversial,

[18] Horace Walpole (1717–97) was a noted collector (of art and gossip), a writer (a pioneer of the 'Gothick' novel), a raconteur and a prolific correspondent. In 1776, in a letter to the Countess of Upper Ossory, he wrote, 'The world is a comedy to those that think, a tragedy to those that feel' – a line that might well serve as an epigraph to this book. Horace was the bachelor son of Sir Robert Walpole (1676–1745), Britain's chief minister between 1721 and 1742. In 1741, in a celebrated speech to the House of Commons, he coined the phrase 'the balance of power'. Horace's elder brother was Sir Edward Walpole, whose illegitimate first-born daughter, Laura, married the Reverend Frederick Keppel in 1758.

however. His treatment of the local people was reckoned harsh. He banished the Bishop of Havana to Florida for making appointments without his approval and attempted to extract contributions from the local merchants which the government back in Britain denied his right to levy.

Three of Albemarle's brothers were also involved – to a greater and lesser extent – in the aftermath of the siege and capture of Havana. His brother Augustus (1725–86) was a naval commander of note who served under Admiral Hawke during the Seven Years War and helped destroy the French fleet at Quiberon Bay, so saving Britain from invasion. In 1762, Augustus was second in command of the fleet sent to Havana, and he and another brother, who was a general officer on the staff, each received a reward of £25,000 for their endeavours, leading to the charge that – the humiliation to Spain notwithstanding – 'the expedition was mounted solely to put money into the Keppels' pockets'. Worse, back home, it was even suggested that a fourth brother, Frederick Keppel (1729–77), a clergyman of no especial note, was appointed Bishop of Exeter solely as a consequence of Albemarle's victory at Havana.

In fairness to Frederick, it seems he was promised his mitre before the news from the West Indies reached London. He appears to have been quite adroit in securing advancement for himself in any event. He was chaplain in ordinary to both George II and George III. He also became Dean of Windsor and Registrar of the Order of the Garter, prompting the comment that 'all things are crowded into three or four people's pockets'. He was, apparently, a genial soul, fond of fine wine and good living, but also concerned for the needs of the poor. He could afford to be: he married well. When he died, at Christmas 1777, stout with the dropsy, he was buried in St George's Chapel, Windsor, near the altar where, in 2005, the present Dean of Windsor assisted at the blessing of the marriage of his kinswoman, Camilla – who, like her forebear, and her new husband, Charles, appreciates the finer things of life and shares their concern for the needs of the poor.

Frederick became a bishop and, in due course, Augustus became an admiral and a viscount. His naval career was sustained and distinguished – though briefly blighted in the late 1770s, during action against France, when he was accused of 'neglect of duty' and tried by court martial. The case was politically and maliciously motivated and not only was Keppel found not guilty, he was also pronounced by the court to be 'a judicious, brave and experienced officer'. Briefly, he became a national hero. Bonfires were lit in his honour. Joshua Reynolds painted his portrait at least six times. He was appointed First Lord of the Admiralty.[19]

'General George', 3rd Earl of Albemarle, married in 1771, aged forty-eight. He died a year later, his wife, in the interim, having given birth to a baby boy, William Charles, who succeeded him as 4th Earl aged only five months. He grew up to become yet another Keppel who would do service to his sovereign, though, in his case, more on the hunting field than the field of battle. He was Master of the Buckhounds and Master of the Horse, in which capacity William IV invested him as a Knight Grand Cross of the Hanoverian Order in 1833. Unlike his father, grandfather and great-grandfather, the 4th Earl of Albemarle was not made a Knight of the Garter. Instead, and most improbably, given that he had no known connection with anything Scottish, he was offered Scotland's highest order. At the time, the Duke of Sussex reported to a friend: 'You will laugh when I tell you that the King took Albemarle by surprise, and has made him a *Knight of the Thistle*. I do not think the members of the House enjoyed it, but it could not be helped.' King William, of course, was the original 'Silly Billy'.

William Charles Keppel, 4th Earl of Albemarle (1772–1849), had two wives and, by his first wife, Elizabeth Southwell, daughter of the 20th Baron de Clifford, nine children, three of whom predeceased him, including his eldest, another William, who died aged only nine in 1804. When Elizabeth died, aged forty-one, giving birth to her ninth child, William Charles sought consolation (as men will) and soon found himself a second Countess, in the younger, livelier shape of Charlotte Hunloke, daughter of a Norfolk baronet. Charlotte has become a legendary figure within the Keppel family. When William Charles died, as the dowager countess she was soon nicknamed 'The Rowdy Dow'. She took to gambling and frittered away much of the family fortune. She held on to Quidenham, but its finest features – its silver, its gilt, its

---

[19] There are parallels to this story in Prince Charles's family. Charles's paternal grandfather, Prince Philip's father, Prince Andrew of Greece, a senior officer in the Greek army, was subjected to a court martial in 1922. The trial was politically motivated and, as with the case of Augustus Keppel, sprang from a disagreement between officers as to the best course of action to take at a critical moment of battle. Both Keppel and Prince Andrew were on trial for their lives. Prince Andrew, unlike Keppel, was found guilty. His life was spared, but he was condemned to 'perpetual banishment' and escaped from Greece to France, taking his entire family with him.

mahogany doors, the celebrated Reynolds' portraits – all went to assuage her creditors.[20]

William Charles's second son, Augustus Frederick Keppel (1794–1851) became the 5th Earl in 1849, by which time he had been declared insane and only had eighteen months left to live. His was a colourful, if troubled, life. He joined the Foot Guards. He fought at the Battle of Waterloo. He was briefly MP for Arundel. He died, childless and intestate.[21] He was succeeded, as 6th Earl, by his younger brother, George Thomas Keppel (1799–1891), who lived a long life and a good one.

This George had been brought up largely by his grandmother, the Dowager Lady de Clifford, who, at the time, was governess to Princess Charlotte of Wales, only child of the Prince Regent and heiress presumptive to the British Crown. Charlotte was a spirited girl ('hot-tempered, ill-mannered and hoydenish, like her mother, Caroline of Brunswick', according to one account) and endeared herself to George Keppel, three years her junior, by 'tipping' him liberally. In May 1816, aged twenty, she married Leopold of Saxe-Coburg, later King of the Belgians, not her father's first choice. The Prince Regent had fancied the Prince of Orange as a prospective-son-in-law. Charlotte, wilful and beautiful, fancied Crown Prince Augustus of Prussia. Leopold was a compromise – an ill-fated one, as it turned out. Charlotte died in childbirth in November 1816, a young death that prompted an

[20] The Albemarles managed to hang on to Quidenham until 1948, when it became a Carmelite monastery. It is a beautiful place, both peaceful and rich in historical and royal connections. Boudicca, queen of the Iceni, is said to be buried nearby. Edward VII came on a visit in 1907. The original hall, the Tudor-style mansion acquired by 'General George', 3rd Earl of Albemarle, was transformed by William Charles, 4th Earl, who added substantial wings to the building. It was transformed again by the 7th Earl, Camilla's great-great-grandfather, who added the Georgian facings that remain to this day. You can visit the monastery on a private retreat. Contact the Guest Mistress at Quidenham, Norwich, Norfolk NR16 2PH. The nuns are lovely people and, care of the Sewing Department, accept commissions for embroidery work. I also recommend the wonderful artwork of Sister Deirdre, who, on request, will gladly show you her portfolio.
[21] He was married in 1816, by special licence, to Frances Steer. When he died, Frances took, as her second husband, Lt. Col. Peregrine Francis Cust, son of Sir Brownlow Cust, 1st Baron Brownlow, and forebear of Peregrine Francis Adelbert Cust, 6th Baron Brownlow, lord-in-waiting and friend to Edward VIII (and Mrs Simpson) and key player in the 'Abdication crisis' of 1936. (You will have gathered by now that, over several hundred years, members of exactly the same families are meeting one another, running off with one another, even marrying one another – and giving service, where possible, to the Prince of Wales or sovereign of the day.)

outpouring of national grief comparable, in its way, with that felt at the time of the death of Diana, Princess of Wales.

Young George Keppel had spirit, too. Not academic (his headmaster at Westminster School pronounced him 'unfit for any learned profession'), he joined the army aged fifteen and was commissioned in time to be present at the Battle of Waterloo and, 'ragged and footsore', to march with the victorious troops to Paris. He became the 'travelling Keppel' and his adventures, over the years, took him to India, Baku, Astrakhan, Moscow, St Petersburg, the ruins of Babylon and the court of Teheran. He published several accounts of his travels and, as a consequence of them, became a Fellow of both the Geological Society and the Society of Antiquaries. At home, he served his country and his sovereign. He was twice an MP; he was private secretary to Lord John Russell during his premiership; he was a royal equerry in attendance on Queen Victoria on her wedding day. He lived to be ninety-one and kept his wits about him till his dying day. He was an enthusiastic raconteur, though his style was not to everybody's taste. In 1857, the *Gentleman's Magazine* noted that 'his voice is loud, confident and somewhat overbearing.'

In 1831, George married Susan Trotter, daughter of Sir Coutts Trotter, 1st Baronet. They had five children: four girls and a son, William Coutts Keppel (1832–94), great-grandfather of Camilla, known through most of his life as Viscount Bury. His was another Keppel career that combined public duty with royal service. He was a soldier, a member of parliament, and, briefly, under-secretary of state for war; he was also an aide-de-camp to Queen Victoria, and, for seven years, Treasurer of Her Majesty's Household. He took a keen interest in religion (in his late forties he became a Roman Catholic), in homoeopathy, and in the Empire in general and Canada in particular. In 1855, in Saskatchewan, he married Sophia, second daughter of Sir Allan Napier McNab, prime minister of Canada. William and Sophia had ten children, seven daughters and three sons, including: Arnold Keppel (1858–1942), 8th Earl of Albemarle, soldier, MP, aide-de-camp to Edward VII, and lord-in-waiting to George V;[22] Sir Derek Keppel

---

[22] He married Lady Gertrude Egerton, kinswoman of the sisters Lady Meg and Lady Alice Egerton, friends and ladies-in-waiting to Elizabeth II. Lady Meg married 'Jock' Colville when he was private secretary to Princess Elizabeth. This is the way it goes. (As we shall see, another of Elizabeth's private secretaries, Robert Fellowes, married Lady Jane Spencer, the older sister of Diana Spencer, and herself once spoken of as a possible Princess of Wales.)

(1863–1944), GCVO, KCB, CIE, CMG,[23] who served Edward VII, George V and George VI in a variety of capacities, from equerry-in-ordinary to Master of the Household; and the Hon. Lt. Col. George Keppel (1865–1947), about whom we need to know much more, not only because he is a character of almost music-hall comicality, but also, and more significantly, because he allowed – perhaps even encouraged – his wife, Alice, to become Edward VII's last and longest-serving mistress.

It is worth remembering at this point that, until quite recently, kings and princes *expected* to have mistresses. Queen Victoria and her husband, and Elizabeth II and her father and grandfather, are the exceptional ones in the matter of marital fidelity. It is worth remembering, too, that infidelity can lead to unintended consequences. For example, as we shall see, it is quite possible that Camilla and Charles are cousins, both direct descendants of Queen Victoria. Camilla's grandmother was born on 24 May 1900. Nine months earlier, in the late summer of 1899, the then Prince of Wales and Alice Keppel were certainly lovers. Edward VII may have been Camilla's great-grandpapa. It is possible.

Of course, if Edward VII is Camilla's great-grandfather, then George Keppel is not – in which case Camilla is not a direct descendant of Charles II, after all. In any event, we can, at least, be certain that Charles, Prince of Wales, is not directly descended from Charles II because we know that Old Rowley had no legitimate offspring.

Neither Charles II nor William III produced heirs. By Mary of Modena, James II did produce a son, but, since he also contrived to lose the throne in the same year that his son was born, much good it did him.[24] By Anne Hyde, James did have two legitimate daughters: Queen Mary II, who died childless, and Queen Anne – poor Queen Anne: 'Brandy Nan', fat, foolish, gout-ridden, greedy, but generous, too, and

---

[23] VD too, since he was awarded the decoration of the Royal Naval Volunteer Reserve Officers' Decoration. GCVO is Knight Grand Cross of the Royal Victorian Order; KCB is Knight Commander of the Order of the Bath; CIE is Companion of the Order of the Indian Empire (now gone), and CMG is Companion of the Order of St Michael and St George.

[24] James II was forced to flee the country at the time of the so-called 'Glorious Revolution' of 1688. His son, James Stuart, 'The Old Pretender', 'reigned' in exile, as 'James III', from the time of his father's death in 1701 until his own in 1766. Had it been a real reign, it would have been the longest in English history. He was 'succeeded' by his sons, 'Charles III', who 'reigned' from 1766 to 1788, and 'Henry IX', 1788–1807, who became a cardinal and so (we assume) died without issue.

possibly gay[25] – who became pregnant (by her husband, Prince George of Denmark) on seventeen occasions, and suffered sixteen miscarriages and stillbirths and the death of her only surviving son, a little Duke of Gloucester, when he was just eleven. Prince Charles, though related, is not a direct descendant of any of these. He is, however, a direct and legitimate descendant of James I, father of Charles I and grandfather of Charles II and James II, through James I's daughter, Elizabeth (wife of Frederick, King of Bohemia), and *her* daughter Sophia (wife of Ernest Augustus, Elector of Hanover), and *her* son who became George I.

And it was with the Coronation of George I, you will recall, that we began. If Prince Charles is sometimes depicted as a figure of fun – and he is, and he knows it, and it hurts him, as we shall discover – George I was a wholly ludicrous figure who didn't give a damn. He was loud; he was preposterous; he wore a ginger wig. He was German; he arrived in England speaking no English; he spent most of his thirteen-year reign in Hanover, where he felt at home. He had a wife, whom he despised, and kept locked up in a castle (on suspicion of adultery), and mistresses, several of whom were as unpopular and improbable as he was. (Two of them were especially notorious: a squat stout one, Sophia von Kilmansegg, and a tall thin one, Ermengarda Melusina von Schulenberg, ennobled, respectively, as the Countess of Darlington and the Duchess of Munster,[26] but known at court, respectively, as 'The Elephant' and 'The Maypole'.)

The Countess of Orkney, Betty Villiers, one of our trio of 'whores' at the Coronation of George I in 1714, happily lived long enough also to be a star attraction at the coronation of his son, George II, thirteen years later. According to Lady Mary Wortley Montagu, who was there, Lady Orkney 'indisputably' drew the greatest number of eyes. Now seventy, she was a sight to reckon with: 'She exposed behind a mixture of fat and wrinkles, and before a considerable pair of bubbies a good deal

[25] The rumours abounded. Were the likes of Sarah, Duchess of Marlborough (another forebear of Diana Spencer), and her Lady of the Bedchamber, Abigail Hill, simply her close companions, or were they her lovers, too? And how about Anne's older sister, Mary: did she also have lesbian tendencies? What was the nature of her friendship with Lady Frances Apsley? Anne sent Frances a series of sentimental letters that are intriguingly suggestive and infuriatingly inconclusive.

[26] He also created her Duchess of Kendal. She was his favourite and bore him three children. According to Sir Robert Walpole she was 'in effect, as much Queen of England as any ever was'. Indeed, George treated her very much like a queen: he was unfaithful to her, notably, late in his life, with Anne Brent, the dark daughter of the Countess of Macclesfield, generally known as 'The Sultana'.

withered, a great belly that preceded her; add to this the inimitable roll of her eyes and her grey hair which by good fortune stood directly upright, and tis impossible to imagine a more delightful spectacle.'

George II, as Prince of Wales, had planned to marry one Lady Diana Spencer – forebear of the Lady Diana Spencer who married the present Prince of Wales. According to Horace Walpole, the young prince was short of funds:

> Old Sarah Duchess of Marlborough, ever proud and ever malignant, was persuaded to offer her favourite granddaughter, Lady Diana Spencer, afterwards Duchess of Bedford, to the Prince of Wales, with a fortune of an hundred thousand pounds. He accepted the proposal, & the day was fixed for their being secretly married at the Duchess's lodge in the great park at Windsor. Sir Robert Walpole got intelligence of the project, prevented it, and the secret was buried in silence.

In the event, George II (the last English monarch to have been born abroad, the last to lead his troops into battle, the last to be buried in Westminster Abbey) married Caroline of Ansbach, an impressive individual (intelligent, tolerant and strong), a patroness of the arts and a knowledgeable plantswoman, whose gardener, with her encouragement, invented the ha-ha. King George loved Queen Caroline. He admired and trusted her. He even allowed her to select his mistresses for him.

George and Caroline were married in 1705, when they were both aged twenty-two. It was a further twenty-two years before George succeeded to the throne. At the coronation, the magnificence of the Queen's appearance must have rivalled the absurdity of Lady Orkney's. According to one witness, 'She had on her head and on her shoulders all the pearls she could borrow of ladies of quality at one end of the town, and on her petticoats all the diamonds she could hire of the Jews and jewellers at the other.'[27]

George II was contentedly promiscuous throughout his marriage and, at his death, *hundreds* of assorted locks of hair were found among

---

[27] The witness is John, Baron Hervey of Ickworth (1696–1743), a favourite of Queen Caroline, whose *Memoirs of the Reign of George II* give an often spiky, sometimes spicy, account of life at court. In fairness to Queen Caroline, she was obliged to borrow jewellery because her father-in-law, George I, had apparently distributed most of the jewellery he had inherited from Queen Anne among his German family and favourites.

his possessions. After a long reign (thirty-three years), because his own unloved son ('Poor Fred') had predeceased him ('I have lost my eldest son, but was glad of it'), he was succeeded by his grandson, George III – known, in his time, as 'Farmer George' because of his enthusiasm for model farming; known to us as 'Mad King George' because of Alan Bennett's celebrated play about the King's heart-rending descent into madness.

George III broke with royal custom: he was promiscuous before marriage but continent within it. As a young man, he was rumoured to have had an affair with a Quaker girl called Hannah Lightfoot – and was even said to have gone through a form of marriage with her. (There was supposed to be a child of this union, a boy who was shipped off to South Africa and brought up in Cape Town under the name George Rex. It seems unlikely.) More certainly, George had a dalliance with Lady Sarah Lennox, another of the descendants of Charles II and the Duchess of Portsmouth and, consequently, another kinswoman of Camilla.

Just as Prince Charles, in his twenties, loved Camilla, but 'knew his duty' and married someone else (pressed to do so, he would say, by his formidable father, Prince Philip), so Prince George, in his twenties, loved Sarah, but knew his duty and married the girl his formidable mother (Augusta of Saxe-Coburg-Gotha) selected for him. Charlotte Sophia of Mecklenburg-Strelitz was seventeen and no beauty, but she was chosen as George's bride-to-be and he accepted his lot. The young couple were married within hours of their first meeting, and, while George pined for Sarah, and throughout his long life wrestled with his carnal appetites, he was wholly faithful to his wife. And Queen Charlotte was dutiful, too: she bore her husband fifteen children – including, of course, another George, Prince of Wales, Prince Regent and eventually George IV, probably the most libidinous king in English history.

I once asked the distinguished theatre director Sir Peter Hall why he had been married so many times. 'Because,' he said, 'as soon as it isn't all right, it's all wrong.' This seems to have been the approach adopted by George IV. He would adore a girl until he didn't – and then he would immediately move on. He had a particular penchant for actresses. He fell in love with Mary Robinson watching her play Perdita in *The Winter's Tale*. Until she succumbed, he plied her with presents and sent her love notes, signing himself 'Florizel'. In due course, his love letters fell into the public domain. He was not a judicious lover. He was rapacious, voracious and ever hungry for more. The one sustained love of his life was Maria Fitzherbert, a Catholic and a widow. She tried to resist him, but he would have his way. (He was the Prince of Wales, dammit! 'I am the Prince of Wales, dammit!' Prince Charles once shouted at Diana.) In December 1785, in a secret ceremony, the priapic prince and the young widow were wed. The service was conducted by an Anglican clergyman, released from a debtors' gaol and promised a bishopric in the next reign. George loved Mrs Fitzherbert – at his death he asked for her picture to be buried with him, 'placed right upon my heart' – but he was not faithful to her. He had other mistresses – actresses, courtesans, daughters of the aristocracy, the wives of friends – and, in due course, another wife. Under the Royal Marriages Act of 1772, his marriage to Mrs Fitzherbert, contracted without the King's consent, was invalid. In 1785, urged by parliament to marry a proper, Protestant, princess, he agreed to marry his cousin, Caroline of Brunswick.

George IV was a man of taste (he created Brighton Pavilion; John Nash was his architect of choice); Caroline of Brunswick was not to his taste. Her body was misshapen, her face was unappealing, her teeth were black, her breath was acrid. Famously, at their first encounter, George gasped, 'Pray get me a glass of brandy, I am not well!' He was drunk when he married her and drunk when the marriage was consummated. Caroline gave birth to just one child by George, a daughter, Charlotte, who blossomed briefly and then died in childbirth in 1817.

George and Caroline lived apart for almost all their married lives. He set her up in a mansion on Blackheath, where the reputation for high living and loose morals, which she had brought with her from Brunswick, was consolidated. Her licentiousness and self-indulgence were held to rival his. The Prince of Wales was said to have had at least two, and possibly six, illegitimate children. The Princess of Wales was said to have had at least one. When 'Prinny', fat and fifty-eight, eventually succeeded to the throne, at his coronation he had the doors of Westminster Abbey barred against her. His mistresses were well represented in the congregation. His wife was not. Nineteen days later she was dead.

George IV died in 1830. 'He was,' said the Duke of Wellington, 'the most extraordinary compound of talent, wit, buffoonery, obstinacy and good feeling.' He had reigned as Regent for nine years and as King for ten. He left no heir. His one legitimate offspring, Princess Charlotte, was dead. His eldest brother, Frederick, 'The Grand Old Duke of York', had died in 1827. He was succeeded, therefore, by his second brother, William, 'Silly Billy', 'The Sailor King': bluff, blunt, occasionally out-rageous, often outspoken, odd in appearance (a small head on a large body: a radish on an onion), odd in manner. There was something endearing about him, too. Encountering a shy young man at a reception, he said, 'Come, we are both boys, you know.' Though he lived for a while at the Brighton Royal Pavilion, he had little time for the Prince Regent's fabulous art collection. 'It seems pretty,' he said. 'I dare say it is. My brother was very fond of Knicknackery. Damned expensive taste, though.' He spoke as he found. He once said, 'I know no person so perfectly disagreeable and even dangerous as an author.'

He was sixty-five when he became King. The diarist (and clerk to the Privy Council) Charles Greville, encapsulated the public response to his accession: 'Never was elevation like that of King William the Fourth. His life has been hitherto passed in obscurity and neglect, in miserable poverty, surrounded by a numerous progeny of bastards, without consideration or friends, and he was ridiculous from his grotesque ways . . . King George had not been dead three days before everybody discovered that he was no loss, and King William a great gain.'

Charles Greville's nice observation is a timely reminder of the fickle-ness of public favour. One day, you're up; the next, you're down. The day after, you may well be up again. The Queen and Prince Philip are keenly aware of this: over a lifetime they have seen the 'popularity' of the monarchy ebb and flow. They have, as Prince Philip put it to me, known adulation ('in the early 1950s, such adulation – you wouldn't believe it') and derision ('page after page of negative coverage, day after day') and, as a matter of deliberate policy, have tried to rise above it, or, rather, tried to keep it in perspective – neither being too easily seduced by the adoration, nor overly downcast by the contempt. Prince Charles understands the theory, but he is less robust than his parents. He knows he shouldn't mind too much what people think on any particular day, but he does. He cares. He wants to be liked; he'd like to be loved. When, once, at Buckingham Palace, I said to the Duke of Edinburgh, 'What you do is amazing!', he raised an eyebrow and harrumphed. When, at Highgrove, I said to the Prince of Wales, 'What you do is wonderful!', he said, 'Do you think so? Do you *really* think so? A lot of people don't seem to.'

William IV's character and history provide us with another timely reminder: that, when it comes to their relationships with women, very few princes have behaved like gentlemen. As a boy, aged thirteen, William was sent to sea. When the Keppels joined the navy, they arrived as officers. When William enlisted, he joined as a humble midshipman. On the express instructions of his father, George III, 'no marks of distinction' were shown to him: 'The young man goes as a sailor.' William was a true sailor: he saw active service in the American War of Independence; he also took to the traditional naval pursuits of drinking, gambling, brawling and whoring. The navy life seems to have encouraged what his older brother Frederick called 'his natural inclination for all kinds of dissipation'. As one of his biographers neatly put it: 'He acquired the sexual habits of a tom cat.' From Hanover, in 1785, when he was twenty, he reported to his brother in England that there were no women of quality to be enjoyed locally, so that he was obliged to have it away 'with a lady of the town against a wall or in the middle of the parade'. He yearned for home: 'Oh, for England and the pretty girls of Westminster; at least to such as would not clap or pox me every time I fucked.'[28]

William did settle down, eventually. He left the navy. He became the Duke of Clarence. He set up home, in Bushey Park, with a handsome and popular actress, Dorothy Jordan. (Her actual surname was Bland – wholly inappropriate, given her colourful career and character: she was Irish, four years his senior, and already the mother of several children by two previous liaisons. She was also, by all accounts, great fun. 'Her smile,' wrote the critic William Hazlitt, 'had the effect of sunshine, and her laugh did one good to hear.') William, Duke of Clarence, and Dorothy Jordan had twenty-one years and ten children together. William was a caring and conscientious father: he as good as gave his children his surname – they were called FitzClarence – and he certainly gave several of them right royal Christian names: George, Mary, Frederick, Augustus, etc.

William and Dorothy's domestic idyll eventually came unstuck. They were bedevilled by debt; her beauty and popularity were waning;

---

[28] The word comes easily to royal sailors. When it is used by the present Prince of Wales, it usually has an edge of anguish or anger to it. By contrast (at least in my hearing), the present Duke of York uses it quite casually, in a relaxed, everyday sort of way. Recently, discussing the devastation brought to the beautiful island of Phuket by the tsunami of December 2004, the Duke of Edinburgh took me to task for pronouncing the island's name as 'Foo-kay'. In his flying days, he used to stop off on the island when piloting himself to Australia. 'It's Phuket, pronounced Fuck-it. Particularly appropriate, of course, since it's become a honeymoon destination.'

he decided to seek a wife with a fortune. He did not find it easy. He was a royal duke, but he was also middle-aged, stout, preposterous and the father of ten children. Dorothy Jordan's story ended sadly: she died, in poverty, in France, in 1816, aged fifty-five, forced abroad to evade her creditors. In time, William was more fortunate. Most of the women of fortune and quality in whom he was interested were not interested in him. Eventually, in 1817, the year of Princess Charlotte's death (and, incidentally, of Jane Austen's death, too) he found an heiress – a Miss Wykeham – who both took his fancy (a 'dear sweet angel', he called her) and, more to the point, was ready to accept his hand. Unfortunately, parliament and the Prince Regent were having none of it. With Princess Charlotte dead, the Duke of Clarence was suddenly closer to the throne than ever he – or anyone else – had expected him to be. A bride of royal standing – with good breeding prospects – needed to be found. Enter the plain but willing, kindly and continent Adelaide, daughter of the Duke of Saxe-Meiningen. William was fifty-two, Adelaide was twenty-six. In its own way, the marriage really worked.

I have recounted William's story this fully, not only as a further reminder that the love-lives of heirs to the English throne have often been fraught, but also because I want to quote one of William's 'outbursts' and one of his letters. They have a resonance with our story – and the pain that is at the heart of it.

First, the 'outburst'. One day, in a public place (in an inn, in fact; William did not stand on ceremony), at the time when his older brother, George, the Prince of Wales, had publicly parted from his wife, Caroline of Brunswick, the Duke of Clarence turned and, out of the blue, addressed a lady he did not know. 'My brother has behaved very foolishly,' he told the astonished stranger. 'To be sure he has married a very foolish, disagreeable person, but he should have made the best of a bad bargain, as my father has done. What do you think, Madam?'

Now, the letter. At the time of his betrothal to Adelaide, William wrote, plaintively, to the eldest of his ten children: 'The Princess of Saxe-Meiningen is doomed, poor, dear, innocent young creature, to be my wife. I cannot, I will not, I must not ill use her . . . What time may produce in my heart, I can not tell, but at present I think and exist only for Miss Wykeham. But enough of your father's misery.'

There, in essence, at the beginning of the nineteenth century, we have all the elements of the dilemma that faced Charles at the end of the twentieth. Charles found a 'doomed, poor, dear innocent young creature' to be his wife. At the time, he, too, vowed 'not to ill use her'; he, too, loved another; he, too, did not know what 'time' might 'produce in his heart'. And when Diana, in his eyes, turned out to be 'a bad bargain', he did not make 'the best' of it – as his father would have done. He allowed the 'misery' to overwhelm him. Was he right? Was he wrong? Why is he as he is? And is the way he is – and the way he has behaved with Camilla, and the way he behaved towards Diana, from the day he met her until the day she died – tantamount to a foolishness that has perhaps even jeopardised the future of the British monarchy. 'What do you think, Madam?'

Chapter Two

A Family and Its Fortunes

'The real test of a man is not how well he plays the role he has invented for himself, but how well he plays the role that destiny assigned to him.'

Jan Patocka (1907–77)

Legend has it that, in the early summer of 1971, when Camilla was still twenty-four, and Charles was twenty-three, the star-cross'd lovers met for the first time at a polo match at Smith's Lawn, in Windsor Great Park. It had been raining. Charles had been playing polo, hard. His shirt was damp. His hair was wet, slicked down with rain and sweat. He was stroking the mane of one of his ponies when a young woman, in green Wellington boots, brown corduroy trousers and dark green Barbour jacket, came quietly to his side and said, 'That's a fine animal, sir.' Charles turned and smiled his shy smile, as the girl introduced herself. 'I'm Camilla Shand,' she said, 'I'm so pleased to meet you.' He noticed at once that when her mouth smiled, her eyes smiled too. He liked that. 'I'm so pleased to meet you,' he replied. The attraction was instant – and mutual – and sufficiently evident – and exciting – to embolden Camilla to come up with what must be one of the most arresting come-on lines in the long history of seduction: 'You know, sir, my great-grandmother was the mistress of your great-great-grandfather – so how about it?'

When, more than thirty years later, I asked Camilla if there was any truth in the story – whether, in fact, she had ever said any such thing – she pulled a face, then laughed, then shook her head and backed away. I am afraid I did not have the courage also to ask her whether she believes Edward VII was in fact her great-grandfather. She probably doesn't, but many do.[29]

[29] Many also believe, incidentally, that Queen Victoria was not actually the daughter of her supposed father, Edward, Duke of Kent, fourth son of George III. If they are right

Edward VII first came into contact with the Keppels when he was Prince of Wales. He was a wayward Prince of Wales. His mother, Queen Victoria, came to the throne with the promise, 'I will be good'. She was not a libidinous, drunken, spendthrift as, in their way, each of her Hanoverian uncles had been. But she liked sex and she adored her husband, Albert of Saxe-Coburg-Gotha. 'He is perfection in every way – in beauty, in everything . . .', she said. Victoria and Albert were both twenty when they married at St James's Palace in February 1840. 'Gratifying and bewildering' is how Victoria described her wedding night. The young Queen was wild about her consort. He was the perfect lover. Of one memorable night, she wrote: 'His excessive love & affection gave me feelings of heavenly love & happiness, I never could have *hoped* to have felt before! He clasped me in his arms, and we kissed each other again and again!' Albert was her first cousin, her mother's brother's son.[30] To another cousin, another young Victoria, in capitals of ecstasy, the new bride wrote: 'YOU CANNOT IMAGINE HOW DELIGHTFUL IT IS TO BE MARRIED. I COULD NOT HAVE DREAMED THAT ANYONE COULD BE SO HAPPY IN THIS WORLD AS I AM.'

The marriage of Victoria and Albert was both blissful and fruitful. Nine months and eleven days after their wedding night, their first child was born. 'It is a princess,' announced the Queen's 'physician accoucher'. 'Never mind,' murmured Victoria, 'the next will be a boy.' It was. Forty-six weeks after the birth of Princess Victoria, known first

– and Victoria was actually sired by the Duchess of Kent's secretary and alleged lover, Sir John Conroy – then neither Victoria, nor Prince Charles, are direct descendants of Alfred the Great or William the Conqueror, or James I or George III, as we had all supposed. Camilla, of course, if she is not descended from Edward VII, *is* descended from Charles II. Come what may, Charles is not descended from Charles II. If it turns out also that he has no full royal lineage prior to Queen Victoria, then you could argue that Camilla's royal pedigree is actually some two centuries older than Charles's. In future, sadly, the advent of DNA-testing is likely to take all the fun out of this sort of speculation. Meanwhile, if you want a summary of the remarkably convincing case against the Duchess of Kent and her secretary, I recommend Chapter 2 of A. N. Wilson's wonderful book *The Victorians*.

[30] Or was he? Prince Albert's paternity has also been called into question. His father was supposedly the 'syphilitic, promiscuous and unintelligent' Duke Ernest of Saxe-Coburg, but perhaps he was actually one of the young Duchess of Saxe-Coburg's several lovers – namely Baron von Mayern, a chamberlain at the Coburg court. 'If the suspicions about both Victoria and Albert are well-grounded,' writes A. N. Wilson in *The Victorians*, 'this means that many of the crowned heads of Europe are descended jointly from an unscrupulous Irish soldier [Conroy] and a German Jew [von Mayern].'

as 'Pussy', then as 'Vicky', on 9 November 1841, along came Albert Edward, Prince of Wales, known as 'Bertie' within the family and, later, as 'Teddy' and 'Tum-Tum' by the world at large.

Bertie was a problem Prince of Wales. Almost all of them have been. He was a particular challenge to his parents, who were devoted to one another, and wanted their eldest son to be as Prince Albert was (sober, serious, intellectual, industrious) and not as Bertie's great-uncles had been (idle, indulgent, extravagant, promiscuous). Albert's maxim was, 'Never relax, never relax, never relax'. Bertie, from adolescence onwards, appeared to do little else.

As we shall see, in the late 1960s, as Charles turned twenty, his great-uncle, Louis Mountbatten, encouraged the young Prince of Wales to 'sow his wild oats' and even, on occasion, lent him his country house for the purpose. A century before, the then Prince of Wales's father ('Albert the Good', as Victoria termed him) took a very different approach to his son's youthful indiscretions. In 1861, when Bertie was still nineteen and stationed, as a young officer, with his regiment in Ireland, an obliging young actress, Nellie Clifton, was slipped between his sheets. The Prince Consort was not amused. In fact, he was appalled. He wrote to his son, upbraiding him, and warning him of the potential consequences of his folly. There might be blackmail. There might be bastard issue. The woman in the case might drag the heir apparent through the courts: 'Yourself crossexamined by a railing indecent attorney and hooted and yelled at by a Lawless Mob!! Horrible prospect, which this person has in her power, any day to realise! And to break your poor parents' hearts!'

What broke Victoria's heart, of course, was Albert's death, only a few weeks later, that same year. Albert may have died of cancer, or of typhoid. Victoria attributed her beloved's demise to the anguish he had been caused by the behaviour of their son. 'Oh, that boy,' she wailed, 'much as I pity him I never can or shall look at him without a shudder.'

In the fullness of time, forty years after his father's death, Bertie turned out to be rather an impressive King, a skilful diplomatist and, for nation and Empire, a figurehead of surprising stature and authority. As a man, he was not tall (five foot seven inches) and he was stout (two hundred and twenty-four pounds at his heaviest), and, though he lived to be nearly seventy, he did not treat his body as a temple. He ate (five hearty meals a day); he drank (copiously); he smoked (constantly, both cigarettes and cigars); he took little exercise (except of the horizontal kind). Like the present Prince of Wales, he was particular about his clothes and took care with his appearance: he liked to look his best for the ladies.[31] Like the present Prince of Wales, his reign was a long time coming – Bertie was sixty when he became King, Charles is sixty in 2008 – and the waiting in the wings was often a frustration to him. Like Charles, also, Bertie had a complicated love-life. Unlike Charles, however, Bertie, on the whole, seems to have enjoyed it.

Charles's love-life has often been fraught and frequently been unhappy. Charles's early girlfriends (at least, the two who have gossiped to me) say they found him somewhat uneasy and awkward as a young man. Not so Bertie. Charles's first marriage was doomed, almost from the start. Bertie was undeniably blessed in his. Charles had one mistress and his love for her caused him much soul-searching and heartache, and, ultimately, cost him his marriage, and, to an extent, his reputation. Bertie, by contrast, had mistresses galore. His wife endured them. His friends entertained them. His people – as and when they heard of them – appeared to accept them as part and parcel of 'Good Old Teddy'. Sir John Fisher, First Sea Lord at the time of Edward VII's death, reflected: 'How *human* he was. He could sin "as it were with a cart-rope", and yet could be loved the more for it!'

On 10 March 1863, Bertie, aged twenty-two, married Princess Alexandra of Denmark, who was just nineteen. She was beautiful: tall, svelte, soft-eyed, kind-hearted, aptly described by Queen Victoria as 'one of those sweet creatures who seem to have come from the skies to help and bless mortals'. 'Alex' really was quite saintly. She had her frailties, of course (she could appear a little vacant, she had a stubborn streak, she was chronically unpunctual, she became increasingly hard of hearing), but chief among her many strengths were her conscientiousness in her public duties and her tolerance of her wayward husband.

Queen Alexandra, as she became after almost forty years as Princess

---

[31] Diana, Princess of Wales, was sometimes irritated by her husband's sartorial fastidiousness – which is odd, given the time and attention she gave to her own appearance. She also found Charles's taste in clothes a bit on the tweedy side. By contrast, Camilla, who is much less concerned with her own appearance (check out those gardener's fingernails when you meet her), is quite comfortable with her husband's 'look'. Charles cares about his appearance: Edward VII was obsessive about his. He also insisted on correct dress in those around him. When Lord Rosebery arrived at an evening party at Buckingham Palace in trousers rather than knee breeches, the King said, 'I presume you have come in the suite of the American ambassador!' When his secretary, wearing a tail coat, was ready to join him on a visit to an art exhibition one morning, the King upbraided him: 'I thought everyone must know that a *short* jacket is always worn with a silk hat at a private view in the morning.'

of Wales, has a special place in England's royal history. Victoria's husband, as Prince Consort, pioneered the idea of a Royal Family engaged in active 'good works' and service to the community. 'Alex' was the first princess to give expression to Albert's ideal. What Camilla will be finding herself doing more and more of (visiting the sick; cheering the needy; heading up an assortment of charitable organisations), what Diana did with such apparent ease (bringing glamour and a magic touch to lives lacking both), Alexandra did first. Before Alexandra, only one thing was really expected of a royal princess: that she should be fertile – ready, willing and able to produce robust royal heirs.[32] Alexandra broke the mould; she was much more than a brood mare: she was a striking public figure who devoted her long life (she died in 1925, aged eighty) to community service and charitable endeavours.[33]

Alex was a good woman, but a poor time-keeper. She habitually kept her husband waiting. 'Keep him waiting,' she said, 'it will do him good.' On one occasion, not long after Bertie's accession as Edward VII, she and the King were expected to receive a series of deputations together at twelve noon. According to an eye-witness,[34] 'The King sat in the Equerries' room drumming on the table and looking out of the window with the face of a Christian martyr. Finally at 1.50 pm the Queen came

[32] She delivered, though not all her children were robust. The youngest, Alexander John Charles Robert Albert, died the day after he was born. The oldest, Albert Christian Victor Edward, Duke of Clarence, died of influenza, aged twenty-eight. He was devoted to sex and polo and, such was his reputation, there were those who were ready to believe he was the notorious Jack the Ripper who murdered and mutilated prostitutes in London in 1888. Alexandra's second son became George V. Of her three daughters, the eldest, Louise Victoria Alexandra Dagmar, became Princess Royal, married the Duke of Fife and lived to be sixty-four; Victoria Alexandra Olga Mary never married, but lived to be sixty-seven; and her youngest daughter, Maud Charlotte Mary Victoria, married Prince Charles of Denmark (later to become King of Norway), and died in 1938, a few days before her sixty-ninth birthday.

[33] In 1913, to mark the fiftieth anniversary of her arrival in Britain, she founded Alexandra Rose Day to support work in hospitals. The sick were her special concern and there are touching accounts of her visiting the poorly and the dying and giving comfort in much the same way as Diana would do almost a century later.

[34] Sir Frederick 'Fritz' Ponsonby who, following a family tradition, spent his life in royal service. His memoir, *Recollections of Three Reigns*, is stuffed with memorable anecdotes. Famously, he advised Edward VIII, when he was Prince of Wales, not to become 'too accessible'. 'The Monarchy must remain on a pedestal,' Ponsonby insisted. 'If you bring it down to the people,' he told the young prince, 'it will lose its mystery and influence.' The prince disagreed – and we know what happened to him.

down looking lovely and quite unconcerned. All she said was, "Am I late?" The King swallowed and walked gravely out of the room.'

The King put up with the Queen's tardiness, because the Queen put up with everything else. Bertie was greedy and incorrigible. He ate, he drank, he gambled, he womanised – and all to excess. Alex put up with the lot. Famously, on 6 May 1910, as the King lay dying, the ever-patient Queen even allowed his final and most enduring mistress – Alice Keppel, Camilla's great-grandmother – to come to say farewell at his bedside. Queen and mistress kissed and shook hands, and, with extraordinary generosity, Alexandra said to Alice, 'I am sure you always had a good influence over him.'

Undoubtedly she did. In many ways, Bertie was a spoilt child and Mrs Keppel could soothe his temper, smooth his ruffled feathers, and tease and coax him out of his sulks and ill humour. 'The King is a funny man,' observed the Duchess of Sutherland, towards the beginning of his reign, when Mrs Keppel had only been on the scene for a couple of years, '– a child, such a much pleasanter child since he changed mistresses.' Prince Charles is not a traditional 'spoilt child': he found his childhood challenging and, as we shall see, believes he is, to some extent, still recovering from it. He is not a spoilt child, as Edward VII was, and he is not a self-indulgent playboy, as Bertie was as Prince of Wales, but Charles does have a temper, can be irritable, is known to sulk – and Mrs Parker Bowles has long been adept at coping with what she described to a friend as 'his moods and funny ways'. Bertie had a difficult relationship with his parents; Charles has a strained relationship with his. Bertie had Queen Victoria for a mother – imagine it! – and the restless, exacting, deeply serious, Germanic Prince Albert as a father – who died when Bertie was barely out of his teens. Charles has Elizabeth II and Prince Philip as parents and, when younger, felt his mother was not as 'motherly' as he would have wished and his father was often absent and, when present, was both harsh and forbidding. Mrs Keppel was a mother to Bertie, as well as a lover, companion and friend. I think Prince Charles (who is interested in psychology) would acknowledge that, in his life, Camilla has fulfilled much the same role as her great-grandmother fulfilled for Edward VII.

In certain cultures, of course, both Mrs Keppel and Mrs Parker Bowles would have been stoned to death as adulteresses. In Britain, however, one ends up at the sovereign's deathbed and the other marries the heir to the throne. They may both have broken the seventh commandment, but, in her time and in her way, each also did her best to abide by the first rule of good mistressing: don't flaunt yourself – and keep out of the wife's way.

Mrs Keppel's behaviour on the day of her lover's death was not typical of her. She had recently spent seven weeks on holiday with him: she was truly devoted to him and appalled at the prospect of his dying. She was also anxious about what her position might be after his death. She arrived at Buckingham Palace and behaved badly – or, at least, hysterically – and, immediately after the King's demise, began to put it about that, at the dying sovereign's bedside, Queen Alexandra had as good as forgiven her, had 'fallen upon her neck and wept with her' and had promised that she would be 'looked after'. 'Mrs Keppel,' said Viscount Esher, in the aftermath of the fateful day, 'has lied about the whole affair ever since, and describes, quite falsely, her reception by the Queen.'

According to Esher – who got it from Sir Francis Knollys, the King's secretary, who was there – the Queen did not kiss Alice or make any promises to 'look after her'. The Queen and the mistress did shake hands and Alexandra said 'something to the effect' that Alice had always had a good influence over him, but there was no embracing or collaborative weeping:

> The nurses remained close to the King, who did not recognise Mrs K. and kept falling forward in his chair. Then she left the room with Princess Victoria [the King's daughter] almost shrieking, and before the pages and footmen in the passage, kept on repeating, 'I never did any harm, there was nothing wrong between us,' and then, 'What is to become of me?' Princess Victoria tried to quiet her, but she then fell into a wild fit of hysterics, and had to be carried into Freddy's [Sir Frederick Ponsonby's] room, where she remained for some hours; altogether it was a painful and rather theatrical exhibition, and ought never to have happened. It never would only she sent to the Queen an old letter of the King's written in 1901, in which he said that if he was dying, he felt sure those about him would allow her to come to him. This was written in a moment of weak emotion when he was recovering from appendicitis.

According to the King's doctor, Sir Francis Laking, the Queen did kiss the mistress, but only at the dying King's insistence. When Mrs Keppel arrived, the King was conscious and fully recognised her. 'You must kiss her,' he told his wife. 'You must kiss Alice.' When the King relapsed into unconsciousness, the mistress began to sob and the Queen hissed to the doctor, 'Get that woman away.' Later, when the King had died, Alexandra told Laking, 'I would not have kissed her if he had not bade me. But I would have done anything he asked of me. Twelve years ago when I was so angry about Lady Warwick,[35] and the King expostulated with me and said I should get him into the divorce court, I told him once and for all he might have all the women he wished, and I would not say a word; and I have done everything since that he desired me to do about them. He was the whole of my life and, now he is dead, nothing matters.'

When Edward VII died, for a while nothing seemed to matter to anyone anywhere. Royal deaths can have that effect. On 20 May 1910, the poet Wilfrid Scawen Blunt, then seventy and less sentimental than most, noted in his diary: 'Today the King was buried and I hope the country will return to comparative sanity, for at present it is in delirium. The absurdities written in every newspaper about him pass belief . . . In no print has there been the slightest allusion to Mrs Keppel or to any of the 101 ladies he has loved, or to his gambling or to any of the little vices which made up his domestic life. It is not for me or perhaps any of us to censure him for these pleasant wickednesses, but his was not even in make-believe the life of a saint or of an at all virtuous or respectable man, and according to strict theology he is most certainly at the present moment in hell. Yet all the bishops and priests, Catholic, Protestant and Non-conformist, join in giving him a glorious place in heaven.'

Charles will get good obituaries, mark my words. (I know: I have already read some of them; one I have written myself.) Camilla, too, will almost certainly get a better press when she is dead than the one she has – on the whole – received to date. Charles is not very like his great-great-grandfather. Camilla, I think, is very like Mrs Keppel. She looks like her. Take a look at the photographs and you will see what I mean. Mrs Keppel in her thirties – in her prime – has very much the look of Camilla at the same age. Alice is the more obviously beautiful of the two, but the family resemblance is unmistakable – in

[35] Daisy Maynard, Countess of Warwick (1863–1938), was Bertie's mistress for nine years, from 1888 to 1897. She did not love him as Alice would love him (she even complained that she found him 'boresome as he sat on a sofa holding my hand and goggling at me'), but she was fond of him, fond too of the royal life, and, for a while, he was obsessed by her. When the affair ended, Alex was certainly relieved. 'The Princess has been an angel of goodness throughout all this,' Bertie acknowledged at the time, 'but then she is a Lady, and never could do anything that was mean or small.'

the nose, in the set of the eyes, in the shape of the shoulders and the bosom. If you look at a picture of the older Alice – taken in the 1930s, when she and her husband had moved to Italy, to the Villa dell'Ombrellino on Bellosguardo, above Florence – the similarity is even more striking, although Alice's hair, once chestnut, has now turned to white, in a way, we can presume (hopefully, but safely, I think), Camilla's never will. Sir Harold Acton[36] was one of the Keppels' Italian neighbours and an admirer of Alice: 'A fine figure of a woman, as they used to say, more handsome than beautiful, she possessed enormous charm, which was not only due to her cleverness and vivacity but to her generous heart. Her kindnesses were innumerable and spontaneous.'

Mrs Keppel and Mrs Parker Bowles were evidently two of a kind. Here is one of Mrs Keppel's biographers, Theo Aronson, summarising what Alice had to offer Bertie: 'She was attractive enough to interest him sexually; entertaining when he was bored, patient when he was cantankerous, sympathetic when he was ill, unobtrusive when he appeared in public. In his company she was amusing, even-tempered, uncomplaining.' From all I have seen and heard, this is precisely what Camilla offers Charles.

There were differences, of course. I get the impression Mrs Keppel had a bigger personality and a grander manner. She also drank. Sir Harold Acton said 'none could compete with her glamour as a hostess' and suggested 'she could have impersonated Britannia in a *tableau vivant* and done that lady credit.' Sir Henry 'Chips' Channon gave a dinner party in her honour in November 1943 and noted in his diary: 'She looked magnificent in black sequins and jewels, and her fine white hair and gracious manners are impressive: she is so affectionate and grande dame that it is a pity she tipples, and then becomes garrulous and inaccurate in her statements.'[37]

[36] Many years later, in 1984, Sir Harold Acton (1904–94), aesthete and historian, entertained Charles and Diana when they visited Florence. Charles was bowled over by his first experience of the city; 'moved to tears', he said. He confided to his diary, 'My head and my heart are reeling from the sheer concentration of unadulterated beauty.' Diana said it was 'interesting'.

[37] Henry Channon (1897–1958) came from Chicago, but from the 1920s was a leading figure in London society, becoming an English MP, a generous host (spiking the drinks with drugs to help the party go with a swing) and a waspish diarist. 'Chips' liked to feel he knew everybody who was anybody – and, broadly speaking, he did. His diary entry for 19 November 1943 continues: 'Cecil [Beaton] told us that he had been to see the

Mrs Keppel died of cirrhosis of the liver on 11 September 1947, some eight weeks after the birth of her great-granddaughter, Camilla. She was seventy-eight. She would have appreciated her obituaries: they referred to her royal past with the utmost discretion. *The Times* revealed that she had belonged 'to the intimate circle of the Edwardian court', but little more. Nine weeks after her death, on 22 November 1947, aged eighty-two, George Keppel died. 'Always the most courteous of men,' said their daughter, Violet, 'it was as though he were loth to keep her waiting.'[38]

George Keppel is the Andrew Parker Bowles of Edwardian England. Keppel, like Parker Bowles, was a soldier and a gentleman. His younger daughter, Sonia, said that, kind-hearted and spontaneous, 'he was easily pleased, easily appeased, willing to believe the best of everyone. He was what the French call *bon public*, an optimist.' He was also what the French call a *mari complaisant*. In some ways, he was more fortunate than Andrew Parker Bowles. Keppel remained married to his wife – and contentedly so – for fifty-six years, and, when he died, received friendly obituaries that referred neither to his own reputation as a ladies' man nor to Alice's long love affair with the King. Inevitably, Parker Bowles will not get off so lightly, although he may be recognised for three of the qualities *The Times* obituarist admired in Keppel in 1947 (and which the present Queen, I believe, admires in Parker Bowles today): good looks, perfect manners and 'benign geniality'. While Elizabeth II has

Queen, who told him that the Buckingham Palace balcony has become unsafe; they want to use it for their victory appearance [at the end of the war], and are ordering cement.' Cecil Beaton took many wonderful photographs of Queen Elizabeth: he also took a striking photograph of Sonia Keppel, Alice's younger daughter – not surprisingly it was Camilla's grandmother's favourite portrait of herself. Someone very close to Camilla said to me recently, 'I do hope you'll make it clear in your book that Camilla isn't some sort of jumped-up interloper. Her family has been moving in royal circles for years.'

[38] Violet Keppel (1894–1972), later Mrs Denys Trefusis, once said, 'Across my life only one word will be written: "waste" – waste of love, waste of talent, waste of enterprise.' In 1973, Nigel Nicolson, the son of Harold Nicolson and Vita Sackville-West, published his celebrated account of his parents' relationship, *Portrait of a Marriage*, including his mother's journal of her love affair with Violet Trefusis. Violet's relationship with her own mother is brilliantly explored in *Mrs Keppel and Her Daughter* by Diana Souhami. Violet published her own memoir, *Don't Look Round*, in 1952. It is more evocative than revealing. When Alice was dying in her villa in Italy, Violet tried to cheer her up. 'Look at the view from your window,' she said to her mother. 'Surely you love nature?' 'Yes,' replied Alice, 'the nature of the Ritz.' Mrs Keppel spent the war years in London, living – and living it up – at the Ritz Hotel in Piccadilly.

never had an easy relationship with Camilla, she has always had a soft spot for Andrew Parker Bowles.

In one respect, Andrew Parker Bowles is more fortunate than George Keppel. One of the artist Lucian Freud's late, great paintings is of Parker Bowles, unbuttoned, in mess kit, relaxed, feet crossed, in a leather arm chair. It is a formidable portrait of a middle-aged soldier who looks both likeable (he is a friend of Freud's) and like a man who has led an interesting life. The photographs I have seen of George Keppel, by contrast, make Camilla's great-grandfather appear faintly ridiculous. It is probably the upswept waxed moustache (curled with tongs, daily), the ramrod posture, the overelaborate flower in the button-hole. 'One could picture him waltzing superbly to the strains of "The Merry Widow",' reflected Sir Harold Acton. Harold Nicolson nicknamed him 'Paw Paw' and likened him to a character in a French farce. George and Alice's daughter, Sonia, was, understandably, more generous. 'At their wedding,' she wrote in her own memoir, 'the combined beauty of my father and mother had been sensational. In an age of giants he stood six feet four inches high, and in his Gordon Highlander bonnet, at nearly eight feet. Like her, he had eyes of bright blue. But whereas she had chestnut hair, his was black. And his magnificent breadth was a foil to her slender figure.'

The Hon. George Keppel was the third son of the 7th Earl of Albemarle, the direct descendant of William III's favourite, Arnold Joost von Keppel, who became the first Earl back in 1696.[39] George had seven sisters ('all forceful and clear-cut', according to their niece, Sonia, 'like black-and-white silhouettes') and two brothers: another Arnold, who became 8th Earl, inherited the family estate, and was ADC to both Edward VII and George V, and Derek, knighted for his services, over many years, to George V, as Duke of York, Prince of Wales and King.[40]

[39] When, in Italy, the Hon. George saw Harold Acton's mother reading a biography of Oscar Wilde, he murmured, 'A frightful bounder. It makes one puke to look at him.' Acton, a lifelong aesthete, later reflected, 'Fortunately Mrs Keppel had enough humour to spare. Did she ever remind him that he was descended from William III's minion who was created Earl of Albemarle for his *beaux yeux*?'
[40] These included not beating him at tennis. In his *Recollections of Three Reigns*, Sir Frederick Ponsonby gives a chilling account of a game of tennis he and Keppel played with the King. The King was accustomed to having his tennis partners 'kowtow' to him. When Keppel and Ponsonby played a normal game, 'the King sulked and refused to try after the first set'. Eventually the courtiers coaxed the King back into a good humour, but the story is yet another reminder that nobody is ever completely 'normal' with a monarch.

King Charles II, c 1665,
artist unknown

Louise de Kéroualle,
later Duchess of Portsmouth,
c 1672, artist unknown

King William III, 1677,
after Sir Peter Lely

Arnold Joost van Keppel,
1st Earl of Albemarle,
c 1700, by Sir Godfrey Kneller

Four generations: the future George V,
Queen Victoria, the future Edward VII
and the future Edward VIII, 1899

Alice Keppel, with her husband,
George, at the races, photographed
for *The Tatler*, 1909

King Edward VII at Lady Savile's house party at Rufford Abbey, with Alice Keppel
standing behind him, third lady in from right, 1906

George and Alice Keppel, with their elder daughter, Violet, 1907

Alice Keppel and her daughter Violet, on a postage stamp in 1995, ten years before
Mrs Keppel's great-granddaughter, Camilla, made her postage stamp debut

Alice Keppel, photographed in 1906, for an article in *The Sketch* in which she was described as 'the most fascinating woman in England'

Camilla's mother,
Rosalind, on her pony,
with her brother, Harry,
and her parents, Roland
and Sonia Cubitt, 1930

Camilla and her
sister, Annabel,
as bridesmaids, 1952

The Shand children:
Camilla, Mark and
Annabel in 1952

The Windsor children:
Anne and Charles
in 1954

King George VI's last Christmas, 1951: *standing*, l – r, the young Duke of Kent, Princess Margaret, Princess Alexandra of Kent, the Duchess of Kent, the Duke of Gloucester, Princess Elizabeth, the Duke of Edinburgh, the Duchess of Gloucester; *seated*, Queen Mary, George VI with Princess Anne, Queen Elizabeth with Prince Charles; *front row*, Prince Richard of Gloucester, Prince Michael of Kent, Prince William of Gloucester

George, when he married Alice Edmonstone in 1891, was twenty-six, a young lieutenant with a booming laugh and a certain charm, but very few prospects.

Alice Edmonstone was twenty-two when she married George. He called her 'Freddie' because her middle name was Frederica. She was born in Scotland, at Duntreath Castle, by Loch Lomond, the ninth and final child of Sir William Edmonstone – whose namesake and forebear, the original Sir William Edmonstone, had been given the estate by King Robert III of Scotland (c. 1337–1406) on his marriage to the King's daughter, Mary. (Oh yes: there is plenty of royal blood coursing through Camilla's veins.) The nineteenth-century Sir William had married another Mary, Mary Elizabeth Parsons, the daughter of the governor of the Ionian Islands. Sir William was a naval officer as well as a Scottish nobleman; he met Mary on the island of Ithaca, where she had been born, and transported her, as his wife, from her Ionian idyll to his ancient castle. 'From Ithaca to Kelvinside! What an odyssey!' said their granddaughter, Violet. 'How she must have loathed and resented the indefatigable rain, the sulphurous fogs, the grim bewhiskered elders.' Alice's younger daughter, Sonia, said: 'I cannot remember my maternal grandmother. My grandfather was born two years before Napoleon's retreat from Moscow and was much older than she was, and was nearly sixty when my mother was born. My grandmother had been brought up in Greece. Throughout her life apparently she preserved a fascinatingly nymph-like quality, rather oddly reproduced in some of her daughters.'

By all accounts, Alice was the liveliest and prettiest, as well as the youngest, of the Edmonstone girls. Her own favourite sibling was her brother Archie, 'beloved Archie', only eleven months her senior, whom she regarded as 'my twin'. 'They seemed to complete one another,' said Violet. 'My mother all dynamism, initiative, and, yes, virility, my uncle all gentleness, acquiescence, sensibility.' When Admiral Sir William Edmonstone died in 1888, young Archie succeeded to the family title and estate, and Alice, the only remaining unmarried daughter, set about finding herself a husband.

She found George Keppel and she married him, for love not money. He was a soldier: you joined the army for glory, not remuneration. He was the third son of a none-too-rich earl, with seven sisters: his allowance from his father was a modest one. On his marriage, a generous aunt settled £5,000 on him in trust and Alice's 'beloved Archie' stumped up a further £15,000 – 'or thereabouts or the securities representing the same'. These were handsome sums, certainly sufficient to maintain a respectable and quite comfortable late-Victorian lifestyle, but they did not represent a king's ransom. And Alice and George wanted to live well. They wanted not just the good life but the best life: they set their crampons on the Everest of high society and did not rest until they reached the top. How did they do it?

'Throughout her life,' said Sonia Keppel of her mother, 'mama was irresistibly attractive to bank managers.' In the early years of her marriage she was particularly close to one Ernest William Beckett, senior partner of Beckett & Co., bankers of Leeds. Beckett was also MP for Whitby and destined to become 2nd Baron Grimthorpe. He was Yorkshire through and through. He was also the husband of a young American wife, Lucy Tracy, who died in childbirth in 1891, leaving him with three infant children and a gap in his bed. We do not know – we were not in the room with a lighted candle – but we believe that Mr Beckett and Mrs Keppel were lovers. Certainly, their friendship coincided with the Keppels' move from a good house in Wilton Crescent to an even better house in Portman Square; equally certainly, it coincided with the birth, in June 1894, of Alice's first daughter, Violet. In later life, Violet had a range of theories about who her father might have been, but she told her lover, Vita Sackville-West, it was probably Beckett, and Beckett's grandson said that Violet 'undoubtedly had the Beckett nose'.

According to Alice's most thorough biographer, Diana Souhami, 'Mrs Keppel viewed adultery as sound business practice, a woman's work':

> In 1914, on holiday in Spain with the young Winston Churchill and his wife Clementine as guests of Bertie's erstwhile financial adviser Sir Ernest Cassel, she advised Clementine to further her husband's career by finding herself a rich and influential lover. She inferred it would be selfish to desist and offered to recruit one.

Unquestionably, Mrs Keppel had a reputation as a 'goer'. In September 1901, nine months after Edward VII's accession, Lady Curzon, wife of George Nathaniel Curzon, Viceroy of India, reported in a letter to her husband:

> Mrs Favourite Keppel is bringing forth another questionable offspring! Either Lord Stavordale's or H. Sturt's!! Lord Stavordale is going to be married off to Birdie Stewart as Mrs Keppel made a

promise to Lady Ilchester [Lord Stavordale's mother] to allow him to marry at the end of the summer! Jenny said people were seriously disgusted at the goings on of the King – his pursuit of the Keppel and daily visit there in his green brougham.[41]

In fact, Alice Keppel had no further children after Sonia, who was born in the summer of 1900, and whose father was – well, who was he? He might have been Giles Stavordale, later 6th Earl of Ilchester (family name: Fox-Strangways), who did indeed marry Helen 'Birdie' Stewart, only daughter of the 6th Marquess of Londonderry, in 1902. He might have been Humphrey Sturt, Baron Alington, friend of the Prince of Wales and near neighbour of the Keppels in Portman Square. (The Keppels lived in style at No. 30; the Alingtons lived in splendour at No. 38.) He might have been the Prince of Wales himself, who called on his 'little Mrs George' for tea and sympathy, and sometimes for dinner as well, with noticeable regularity. Sonia, after all, did call her own autobiography, *Edwardian Daughter*.[42] Sonia's father could have been one of several of Alice's gentlemen callers. He could even have been – hold your breath! – George Keppel. Why not? He was married to Alice; he is named as the father on Sonia's birth certificate; and, most tellingly, according to Diana Souhami, Sonia 'had the Keppel nose'.

According to Sonia Keppel, her parents were devoted to one another: theirs was 'a companionship of love and laughter'. Evidently, they had 'an understanding': each of them took lovers and neither of them complained. It may not be how we would choose to order our domestic lives (I am speaking for myself: I am wholly middle class,

---

[41] It is interesting to me that Lady Curzon believed her husband would be interested in this tittle-tattle. I was brought up on stories of Curzon's high-mindedness, unapproachability and pomposity. His parliamentary manner was likened to that of 'a divinity addressing blackbeetles'. He was notoriously grand, claiming on one occasion not to know what a napkin ring was for. When it was explained to his lordship that not everyone had fresh linen at every meal, he expressed amazement at the revelation, murmuring, 'Can there be such poverty?'

[42] It is a delightful book, first published in 1958. It begins: 'Mamma used to tell me that she celebrated the Relief of Mafeking [on 18 May 1900] sitting astride a lion in Trafalgar Square. And that I was born a fortnight later . . .On the day of my birth, Papa, and other anxious friends, smothered the road outside our house with straw, whereby to deaden the sound of traffic. For this was an age of chivalry, of putting women on pedestals. Mamma was adored in the Edwardian circle in which she moved, and, had she so wished, I feel sure that she could have decreed that her particular pedestal should have been made by Fabergé.'

completely a creature of my middle-of-the-road middle-England 1950s upbringing), but we need to accept (*pace* the spurious indignation of the *Daily Mail*) that there are other people, not like us, for whom it is overall loyalty within a relationship that matters, rather than strict sexual fidelity. From what I have seen of the world, this play-away-as-you-please-but-stay-true-to-my-heart code of sexual conduct works most successfully within the (male) gay community and the upper echelons of the aristocracy.

Prince Charles's great-uncle, and mentor, Dickie Mountbatten, Earl Mountbatten of Burma, was married for thirty-eight years to Edwina Ashley, the granddaughter of Bertie's (and Alice's) great friend and astute financial adviser, Sir Ernest Cassel. Mountbatten loved his wife dearly, but nonetheless, as he told a friend, 'Edwina and I spent all our married lives getting into other people's beds.' Just as Prince Charles's great-grandfather, King George I of Greece, a happily married man, allowed himself 'an occasional relaxation' at Aix-les-Bains, on his annual French holiday away from his queen, so Sonia Keppel, Camilla's great-grandmother, also happily married, allowed herself to spread her 'gift of happiness' (the phrase is Violet's) among her circle of male admirers.

If my father, or grandfather, had played the field I don't think I'd want you to know. If my grandmother or great-grandmother had 'slept around' (as we used to call it) I think I would be keeping the secret well under wraps.[43] Not so Camilla. Friends who have known her since her schooldays report that, even as a teenage girl, Camilla talked enthusiastically about her great-grandmother and took familial pride in Alice Keppel's achievements as a determined (but discreet) sexual mountaineer. (These are the same friends who, in a chapter or two, will be reporting to us on Camilla's own sexual adventures from the mid-1960s onwards.) This is relevant to our story, not because I am suggesting there is a promiscuity gene and it forms an essential part of Camilla's family's DNA (though there may be and it could); more, because I am conscious that in many families there are patterns of behaviour that recur – and do so, not because they are 'inherited', but

---

[43] I have to say, it's most unlikely. My maternal grandmother was a missionary: when Bertie was enjoying what he called his 'small Mrs George dinners' in Portman Square, she was travelling through India on a donkey, with hope in her heart and a bible in her hand. At the same time – the turn of the twentieth century – my paternal great-grandmother, another religious zealot, was dissipating the remains of the (small) family fortune building a chapel in North Wales.

because they form part of the family 'tradition'. The children and grandchildren of Mafiosi become criminals, not because they are intrinsically bad people, but because that is what members of Mafia families do. Members of the family of the writer Ernest Hemingway commit suicide, not only because they are genetically prone to depression, but also because suicide is 'allowed' among the Hemingways: it is what Hemingways do.[44]

In the 1970s Camilla Shand was a 'goer' who made a play for the Prince of Wales. In the 1890s Alice Keppel was a 'goer' who did the same. Bertie, as Prince of Wales, knew the Keppel brothers, especially the older two, knew their father, the 7th Earl of Albemarle, and was particularly fond of their great-uncle, Sir Henry Keppel (1809–1904), younger brother of the 5th Earl, a sportsman (in his youth, not infrequently 'hard up for tin'), an Admiral of the Fleet and the celebrated author of A *Sailor's Life Under Four Sovereigns: His Personal Journal Edited by Himself*, published, in three volumes, in 1899. 'Dear little Sir Harry', as Bertie termed him, was just five foot tall and almost a national hero. He had seen service in the war against China (1842), in the naval brigades before Sebastopol in the Crimea (1854) and, in the 1860s, in command of a seven-nation force, returned to the China seas to fight pirates. He was a character, and a charmer, and, in retirement, a regular yachting and racing companion to the Prince of Wales.

It seems it was at the races – at Sandown Park[45] – that Bertie and Alice Keppel enjoyed their first *tête-à-tête*. He had, apparently, already 'noticed' her on a previous brief encounter: as colonel-in-chief he had recently inspected the Norfolk Yeomanry: 'the delectable Alice' had been on parade as one of the officers' wives. At Sandown, Alice was

---

[44] I first began thinking about this when a friend – the actor and raconteur Kenneth Williams – took his own life in 1988. Although he kept this out of his autobiography (and from his mother), he told me that he knew (which his mother did not) that his father had committed suicide and consequently he believed he had 'permission' to do the same. Suicide and Ernest Hemingway is one of the themes explored in a brilliant book by the American psychiatrist Kay Redfield Jamison: *Touched by Fire: Manic-Depressive Illness and the Artistic Temperament*, 1993.

[45] The racecourse at Sandown Park, near Esher in Surrey, was founded in 1875 and has been popular with racegoing royalty ever since. It was a favourite course of Queen Elizabeth The Queen Mother, who was especially happy when her escort for the day's racing was the then chairman of Sandown Park, one Andrew Parker Bowles. Bertie and Alice had their first close encounter at the races; Charles and Camilla had theirs on the polo field. Horses play a prominent part in this story.

accompanied, not by her husband, Lt. Col. George, but by another admirer, Sir John Leslie. According to Leslie's granddaughter, the writer Anita Leslie, just as her grandfather was about to present Mrs Keppel to the prince, he was assured that they had already met. 'Then,' according to Anita, 'in the most gracious way possible, H.R.H. gave Leslie to understand that his presence was no longer required. Whimsically, my grandfather used to describe that certain look – blending shrewd appraisement and admiration – that crossed the Prince's face as his eyes travelled over Mrs George Keppel's lovely face and fashionably curved figure.'

Just as there are varying versions of precisely where and how Charles and Camilla first clapped eyes on one another (the protagonists themselves say they 'can't really remember'), so too with Bertie and Alice. The story handed down by Sir John Leslie is generally accepted as the truth, more or less, but, in her memoirs, *Not All Vanity*, the indefatigable hostess Baroness Agnes de Stoeckl maintains that it was she who first presented Mrs Keppel to the Prince of Wales – at a small luncheon party in the South of France. The baroness thought the prince would be 'amused' by Mrs K.

What is certain is that by 27 February 1898, Bertie and Alice were friends. That was the evening when the Prince of Wales first came to dine at 30 Portman Square and when, between the prince and the Keppels – in the telling phrase of Sir Philip Magnus, Edward VII's official biographer – 'an understanding arose almost overnight'.

Bertie was fifty-six; Alice was twenty-nine; George was old enough to understand the workings of the world. The heir apparent became an habitué of 30 Portman Square. Some thought that, following his accession in 1901, as King-Emperor he might choose to be more circumspect. Not so. Bertie was at ease with his 'little Mrs George' – in her bed, in her drawing room, at her dining table. He particularly enjoyed playing bridge with her. He enjoyed playing with her children, too. Violet and Sonia called him 'Kingy' and, such was his devotion to their mother, he appears to have allowed them a familiarity that he probably denied his own children. 'Sometimes', Sonia recalled, Kingy 'came to tea with Mamma' and was still in the house when little Sonia was brought down from the nursery at six o'clock:

On such occasions he and I devised a fascinating game. With a fine disregard for the good condition of his trouser, he would lend me his leg, on which I used to start two bits of bread and butter (butter side down), side by side. Then, bets of a penny each were made (my bet provided by Mamma) and the winning piece of bread and butter depended, of course, on which was the more buttery. The excitement was intense while the contest was on. Sometimes he won, sometimes I did. Although the owner of a Derby winner, Kingy's enthusiasm seemed delightfully unaffected by the quality of his bets.

The Keppel girls were understandably hazy about Kingy's role in Portman Square – and beyond. Not long after his accession, Violet, who turned seven in 1901, enquired, 'Mama, why do we call Grandpapa "Majesty"?' The girls were instructed always to curtsy to the King. Sonia, six years her sister's junior, did her best, 'but sometimes,' she confessed, 'I made mistakes.' She was small and she was shy: 'I dared not look higher than beard-level so played safe and curtsied to the cigar and rings. Sir Ernest Cassel, too, had a beard and wore rings and smoked cigars; so, more often than not, he came in for the curtsy.'

In the Keppel household, Sir Ernest was worthy of honour, in any event. In King Edward's too. Cassel (1852–1921) was a German-born Jewish financier of genius – and integrity. (Well . . . by the standards of these things. He arranged loans for the governments of Egypt, Argentina, Brazil, Uruguay and China; he was a huge investor in copper, iron, shipping, the railways and the arms industry.) He was wily, worldly, wise, witty, generous and philanthropic. He made millions and he gave away millions. He worked wonders with the Prince of Wales's finances. He was nicknamed 'Windsor Cassel' in consequence, and when he was knighted, in 1899, many a wag repeated the sally about 'the importance of being Sir Ernest'.

Ernest Cassel was a friend of the Prince of Wales over many years and a friend to Alice Keppel, too. Sonia said she was forever in awe of him and 'came to rely on him as a living form of gilt-edged security'. He gave the little girl charming little presents (for example, at Easter, a jewelled egg from Fabergé: I'd have curtsied, too) and was even more generous to her mother, providing her with palatial accommodation in Paris and Biarritz when she travelled to France to holiday with the King. He may have given her cash: he certainly gave her financial advice (she was interested in money: 'she was fascinated by the power of capitalism', said Sir Harold Acton) and, more to the point, he gave the King the kind of financial advice that allowed His Majesty (not a 'natural' with money himself) to 'look after' his mistress as he would wish to. For example, on one occasion, Bertie 'took care' of Alice's dress bill – to the tune of £5,000; on another, the King presented Mrs Keppel with shares in a rubber company – shares which, over time, earned her some £50,000. On the day Edward VII died, Sir Ernest went to Buckingham Palace to bid farewell to his old friend, taking with him an envelope containing £10,000 in banknotes. The following day, the King's secretary returned the banknotes to Cassel, with an accompanying note of his own: 'I presume they belong to you and are not the result of any speculation you went into for him.' According to Anthony Allfrey, author of *Edward VII and his Jewish Court*,[46] the money was 'the fruit of a quite exceptionally lucrative investment' and – worth around £500,000 in today's money – quite possibly intended for Mrs Keppel.

Sir Ernest maintained his benevolent interest in the Keppel family until his death. When Violet was married to Denys Trefusis, in 1919, Sir Ernest was there. When Sonia was married to Roland Cubitt, in 1920, Sir Ernest sent what Sonia described as 'a fat cheque'. (Interestingly, Alice, preferring gifts in kind to cash in hand, told her daughter that 'cheques were vulgar', so Sir Ernest's money was 'transformed into a long stole and muff of Canadian sables, which I did not particularly want.') When it came to their creature comforts, the Cassel connection was a key factor in the life of George and Alice Keppel and their daughters. It played a part in the life of their great-granddaughter, Camilla, too.

In 1878, Cassel married a young Scotswoman, Annette Maxwell, who died of tuberculosis in 1880, leaving Ernest a baby daughter, Maudie, to bring up on his own. Maudie, the light of her father's life, grew up to marry Wilfrid Ashley MP (a grandson of the great Earl of Shaftesbury) and it was Wilfrid and Maudie's daughter, Edwina, who, in due course, married Dickie Mountbatten, the last great-grandson of

---

[46] Published 1991. The King had a number of Jewish financiers in his circle of close friends – to the dismay of the traditional court. At the time of the accession, Winston Churchill wondered, 'Will he sell his horses and scatter his Jews . . .?' He did neither. Having won the Derby and the St Leger in 1896 with Persimmon and in 1900 with Diamond Jubilee, Persimmon's brother, he went on to win the Derby again in 1909 with Minoru. And to the Jewish bankers who had lent him money as Prince of Wales he continued to lend respectability as King. Cassel, in fact, while born Jewish, was a Catholic convert. At her behest, he promised his wife on her deathbed that he would change his faith to hers in the hope that they might meet again in heaven.

Queen Victoria to be born in her lifetime and later, of course, great-uncle to Prince Charles. Maudie died, prematurely, in 1911. Wilfrid remarried, inevitably, soon after. Edwina (whose godparents had included the King:[47] he had hoped she would be called Edwardina!), aged seventeen, went to live with her grandfather at Brook House, his mansion in Mayfair. When Sir Ernest died, Edwina inherited some £2.3 million. When Cassel's sister died, Edwina inherited Brook House and yet more money. When her father died, she also inherited her parents' country house: Broadlands, near Romsey in Hampshire. Broadlands is where she and Dickie Mountbatten began their honeymoon in 1922; it is where Princess Elizabeth and the Duke of Edinburgh began theirs in 1947. It is also where Camilla and Charles made love at the beginning of their life-long romance.

When Edward VII died, Sir Ernest Cassel remained on cordial terms with Queen Alexandra and with the new King, George V. He was no longer an intimate at court, but he was in no sense ostracised. As his granddaughter Edwina's biographer, Janet Morgan, puts it: 'Sir Ernest had been a dazzling star in the Edwardian constellation. He was not extinguished when King Edward was removed but from that time his light did not burn as vigorously.' Mrs Keppel, on the other hand, left the country.

'Why does it matter so much, Kingy dying?' Sonia asked her father, the day after the King's death. George Keppel hugged his bewildered daughter. Alice was upstairs, in bed, gazing blankly into the middle distance, apparently unable even to recognise her own children. 'Poor little girl!' said George. 'It must have been very frightening for you. And for all of us, for that matter. Nothing will ever be quite the same again. Because Kingy was such a wonderful man.'

He was indeed. Through Bertie's good offices, George had been

---

[47] Sonia Keppel's godparents, incidentally, included Grand Duke Michael of Russia and his wife, Countess Torby. In 1916, their daughter, Countess Nadejda (Nada) Torby married Georgie, younger brother of Princess Alice of Greece (Prince Philip's mother) and older brother of Dickie Mountbatten. In 1917, Nada's older sister, Anastasia (known as Zia) married Harold Wernher, for a while considered the richest catch in England. Both the Mountbattens and the Wernhers were generous to Prince Philip when he was a boy, helping to pay for his education and upkeep. The Wernhers' three children included a daughter, Gina (born 1919), whose own daughters include the present Duchess of Abercorn (once rumoured – I think erroneously – to be the mistress of Prince Philip) and the present Duchess of Westminster, the seating arrangements for whose own daughter's wedding in 2004 triggered the marriage of Charles and Camilla. This is a small world.

introduced to the King's yachting friend Sir Thomas Lipton, tea planter and grocery magnate. Over many years, George was employed by Lipton's Buyers' Association at a handsome salary. In the aftermath of the King's demise, Alice and her daughters set off on a trip around the world, beginning with a three-month sojourn as guests of Sir Thomas Lipton at his tea plantation in Ceylon. 'No young lady's education is complete without a smattering of Tamil,' Alice said to Violet, by way of explanation.

In the event, after their time together in Ceylon, Alice continued east – sailing on to China with her brother, 'beloved Archie', and his family – while the girls, plus governess and nanny, were despatched back to Europe to take advantage of educational and cultural opportunities available to them in – of all places – Munich. The family was not properly reunited until the beginning of 1912, when Alice returned to London – to a new address, 16 Grosvenor Street, a Georgian mansion even more magnificent than 30 Portman Square had been. 'In these spacious rooms,' according to Sonia, 'Mama had all the scope she needed to demonstrate her matured taste and knowledge.' Mrs Keppel was herself again. 'The hostess,' said one of her appreciative guests, the young Osbert Sitwell, 'conducted the running of her house as a work of art in itself.'

Grosvenor Street remained the Keppels' base until 1924 when George, in his sixtieth year, and no longer retained by Sir Thomas Lipton, and Alice, now fifty-five and tired of London (and a little tired of life – and certainly tired of the English winter), upped sticks (and Meissen china and the rest) and removed themselves to L'Ombrellino, their fabulous villa in the hills outside Florence. They kept a toehold in London – a furnished suite at the Ritz – but London no longer had the same hold on them. Edward VII was long gone; Sir Ernest Cassel was dead now, too; there was even a Labour government, under Ramsay MacDonald ('whoever he might be'). The glittering Keppel world was not any more what it once had been. Besides, Violet and Sonia were now married and no longer requiring a parental home. (At least, that was the theory.)

The story of the love-life of Camilla's great-aunt, Violet Keppel, is a gripping one; heart-rending, too. Violet was in love with Vita Sackville-West, but she married Denys Trefusis. It ended in tears. Alice and George were not amused. Having an affair with the King of England is one thing; having a Sapphist in the family, quite another. Alice did not approve of her daughter's behaviour, nor did she welcome the scandal it provoked. 'Things were done much better in my day,' lamented the late King's mistress. Diana Souhami, in *Mrs Keppel and Her Daughter*, retells the story of Violet's affair with Vita[48] – and its unhappy aftermath: the failed marriage; the heartache; the talk of divorce and separation; the thoughts of suicide; the 'solution' of a sort brought about by Denys's death, aged only thirty-nine, in 1929; Violet's troubled life thereafter; her sad decline ('Approaching seventy, Violet looked eighty'; 'With a single glass of champagne she could appear completely befuddled'); her eventual death, in her mother's bed, in the parental home, at L'Ombrellino, in March 1972, aged seventy-seven. 'I'm alone, so alone,' she kept repeating, towards the end.

The story of the love-life of Camilla's grandmother, Sonia, is less dramatic, but it ends unhappily, too. Sonia met her husband-to-be at the end of the First World War, shortly after the signing of the armistice in November 1918. Sonia was eighteen, and as happy as a lark: Roland (Rolie) Cubitt was rising twenty and a young officer in the Coldstream Guards. 'The first time I saw Rolie,' Sonia recalled, in 1958, eleven years after their divorce, 'he filled me with alarm as he was wringing the nose of a very pretty girl, at a party.' Rolie was a party animal. According to Sonia, his 'greatest charm was his gaiety. With his bright eyes and inexhaustible capacity for enjoyment, he looked like an alert fox terrier, eager for exercise. He did not mind where he got it (in the ballroom; out of doors) as long as his light feet could tune in to the steps of his friends.'

Rolie belonged to a family of heroes. He was the fourth of the six sons of Henry Cubitt, 2nd Baron Ashcombe. All three of his older brothers were killed in action during the First World War. Rolie was heir to a barony and to a fortune established by his great-grandfather, Thomas Cubitt (1788–1855), builder.

'Old Tom Cubitt' came from nowhere (Buxton, near Norwich) and

[48] First revealed, of course, by Vita's son, Nigel Nicolson, in his *Portrait of a Marriage*. At the amazing and moving memorial service for Nigel Nicolson at the Guards Chapel in December 2004 – we should all have the Band of the Grenadier Guards to play us out – I reflected that many of us in the packed congregation were there, not only because of our love and admiration for Nigel, but also because, to us, he represented our last link with an inter-war world we never knew but wished we had. He was Vita's son: he had known Virginia Woolf. (When I was in my early twenties, and just down from Oxford, Malcolm Muggeridge kindly introduced me to Leonard Woolf. It's not quite the same, is it?)

nothing (he was the son of an impoverished farmer[49]) and ended up as a man of property and means, and an architectural guru and adviser on construction to Prince Albert, the Prince Consort. (This family cannot keep away from royalty!) Tom left Norfolk as soon as he was able, working first as a journeyman carpenter and then travelling to India as a ship's carpenter. He returned to London in around 1809 and quickly established a thriving business as a master carpenter. Soon after – with a view to keeping the men in his employ permanently occupied – he branched out into house-building and property speculation. He bought land and he built houses on it. He started by building a handful of villas in Highbury. Next he developed a row of houses by Newington Green. Soon he was owning or leasing land and building property – fine property – across the length and breadth of London, from St Pancras to Clapham Park. Working with the Dukes of Bedford and Westminster, he masterminded the creation of some of central London's best-known streets and squares, from Bloomsbury to Belgravia. He created Eaton Square. He was responsible, too, for the creation of Queen Victoria's favourite home, Osborne House on the Isle of Wight, and for the remodelling and restoration of Buckingham Palace. He was the foremost builder of his time and he made a fortune. When he died his will, running to 386 chancery folios, was the longest on record.

Tom Cubitt was rich and famous in his day. He was also reckoned a good man. In 1854, a year before his death, when his premises at Thames Bank were burned to the ground, his first words on hearing the news were, 'Tell the men they shall be at work within a week and I will subscribe £600 towards buying them new tools.' Tom Cubitt was a decent employer, a hard worker, a generous benefactor and a visionary. He was much admired by the Prince Consort and Queen Victoria who hoped to see his worth recognised with a peerage, and would have done had his death not intervened.

Tom had twelve children and his eldest son, George, succeeded him

[49] Jonathan Cubitt (1760–1806) must have done something right, because Tom was not the only achiever among his sons. Lewis Cubitt designed the Great Northern railway terminus and William Cubitt became Lord Mayor of London, president of St Bartholomew's Hospital and was the instigator of the public subscription to create a memorial to Prince Albert on his death in 1861. (This William Cubitt is not to be confused with another William Cubitt of Norfolk, his kinsman and near contemporary, a civil engineer whose claims to fame include the building of the Berlin waterworks, the construction of the Great Exhibition buildings of 1851 and the invention of the treadmill.)

as head of the family business. George Cubitt (1828–1917) continued his father's good work, as builder and philanthropist, and, in due course, received his father's reward. In 1892, he was created 1st Baron Ashcombe. Tom Cubitt had been a farmer's son, of humble stock, poorly educated, born without prospects. He brought his son up as a gentleman. George went to Trinity College, Cambridge. George, as well as running the family firm, served as a Conservative MP for thirty-two years. He also did his bit in the service of his sovereign, as a Privy Counsellor, as Honorary Colonel of the 5th Battalion, Royal West Surrey Regiment, as Deputy-Lieutenant of Surrey and Middlesex. He did his bit as a family man, too – or, rather, his long-suffering wife, Laura (a clergyman's daughter), did. She bore him nine children: four girls who survived into adulthood; two girls and two boys who died in infancy; and one son, Henry, her youngest child, who succeeded to the family title, business and estates and who continued the family's upwardly-mobile social trajectory. Henry Cubitt (1867–1947) was educated at Eton College and Trinity College, Cambridge. He, too, was a Conservative MP for fourteen years. He was also Colonel of the Surrey Volunteer Regiment, Honorary Colonel of the 4th Battalion, The Queen's Royal Regiment, Honorary Colonel of the Surrey Yeomanry, and Lord-Lieutenant of Surrey from 1905 to 1939. He was invested as a Companion of the Order of the Bath.

Tom Cubitt was high-minded and humble. Henry Cubitt, 2nd Baron Ashcombe, was high-minded and grand. He and his wife – he had married a colonel's daughter, Maud Calvert – were also deeply conservative. The Ashcombes had dignity and gravitas. The Keppels had neither. When Sonia, still in her teens, first went to visit her prospective parents-in-law, she did at least do her best to look the part: 'My skirt was several inches longer than the fashions decreed (Nannie had let it down specially); my hands were encased in white cotton gloves [the Ashcombes required ladies to wear gloves in the house at all times]; and, with a big effort of renunciation, my nose was practically free of powder.' Sonia was wholly unnerved by her reception at Denbies, the Ashcombe family seat at Dorking (built, of course, by Tom, the farmer's son):

> The old butler ahead of us threw open a door and announced us, and by this time I was so nervous that my hand trembled as I shook hands with my hostess. As we sat down to tea I took a furtive glance at the room which was dominated by three life-size full-length portraits of

Rolie's dead brothers. . . . Nearly all the furniture in the room seemed to be late Victorian and was upholstered in railway-carriage plush . . . A large Victorian plate-glass looking-glass surmounted the chimney piece in which I saw the whole party sombrely reflected . . . Just before dinner, a housemaid brought me a pair of elbow-length, white kid gloves. 'His Lordship's compliments, miss, and will you please wear them.'

Lord Ashcombe was a Christian and a gentleman. He led his household in family prayers every morning. On Sundays, he attended church twice, and, at Matins, sat in the Choir, in a white surplice, surrounded by his surviving sons and the male members of his staff. He was courteous to Sonia – charming, even – but he did not want his son – his heir – to marry the daughter of the late King's mistress, let alone the younger sister of a young woman who was rumoured to be an hysteric and a lesbian. He did his best to discourage the match.

Alice Keppel was not sure it would work either. 'It isn't that I don't like Rolie,' she told her daughter. 'I think he's very nice. But if you marry him, you'll marry into a world you've never known, and I'm not at all sure that you'll like it.' But the young lovers were determined – and they had allies. Among the number of Sonia's distinguished godparents was Mrs Ronald Greville, Maggie McEwan as was, friend to royalty and neighbour to the Ashcombes. According to Sonia, her godmother's intervention was decisive:

As Lord Lieutenant of Surrey, Lord Ashcombe had had some differences with Maggie and for years neither he nor she had attempted to bridge the intervening two miles between Denbies and Polesden.[50]

[50] Mrs Greville, daughter of the brewing magnate William McEwan, lived at Polesden Lacey in some style. In 1923, she lent the house to Prince Charles's grandparents, the Duke and Duchess of York, for their honeymoon. Cecil Beaton (who photographed the Yorks – and Sonia Keppel) described Mrs Greville as 'a galumphing greedy, snobbish old toad who watered at her chops at the sight of royalty'. Violet Keppel's lover's husband, Harold Nicolson, described her as 'a fat slug filled with venom'. Queen Elizabeth was more charitable. When Mrs Greville died in 1942, the Queen wrote to Osbert Sitwell: 'She was so shrewd, so kind and so amusingly unkind, so sharp, such fun, so naughty.' She left all her jewellery – including Marie-Antoinette's diamond necklace – to the Queen, 'with my loving thoughts', and a bequest of £20,000 to Princess Margaret. As Harold Acton observed – apropos the fact that the food served by Mrs Keppel at L'Ombrellino was conspicuously more lavish when a Rothschild was being entertained – 'unto everyone that hath shall be given'.

So, one day, with considerable surprise, he heard that Maggie was in her Rolls-Royce, outside his front door, demanding to speak to him . . . Mystified, Lord Ashcombe had gone out to behold a chauffeur and footman on the box of the Rolls, and Maggie inside it, formally dressed for the occasion. When he had politely invited her into the house, she had answered: 'No, thank you, I only called to tell you that I do not consider that your son is good enough for my god daughter.'

The Ashcombes bowed to the inevitable. As Violet's lover, Vita Sackville-West, noted, they were 'very old-fashioned and apt to cut up rusty at any provocation'. They hated the idea of a Cubitt–Keppel alliance 'because of little Mrs George and all that', but they went along with it. Poor Henry Ashcombe was even obliged to meet Alice Keppel face to face to negotiate an appropriate marriage settlement. 'Little Mrs George' was noted for her skill at bridge: it seems she was a dab hand at poker, too. Mrs Keppel said, 'If we give Sonia a certain figure, will you give Roland the same?' He found himself saying he would and was then staggered when he discovered the amount. Having agreed to 'ante-up' (in Sonia's phrase), he expressed the hope that the costly marriage would last. 'My dear Lord Ashcombe,' replied Mrs Keppel, 'neither you nor I can legislate for eternity.'

The marriage did not last, but the wedding took place in the Guards Chapel at Wellington Barracks on 16 November 1920. The bride and groom were young and full of hope. 'Dreamily' was how Sonia recalled listening to the canon who conducted the service 'pronounce the beautiful words setting out the three purposes of marriage . . . "for the procreation of children . . . for a remedy against sin . . . for the mutual society, help and comfort that the one ought to have of the other . . ."' The canon was officiating alone because the Bishop of Guildford, who had been expected, simply failed to show. Later, when it transpired that the good Bishop, by mistake, had gone instead to a mothers' meeting, Lord Ashcombe murmured, 'Jumping his bridges a bit.'

But only a bit. Nine months later, almost to the day, on 11 August 1921, at 16 Grosvenor Street, London W, the Hon. Rosalind Maud Cubitt, the first of Sonia and Rolie's three children, was born. She was, of course, a beautiful baby. She was also destined, one day, to be a mother herself: the mother of the Duchess of Cornwall, the mother, possibly, of our next Queen. Camilla was born at King's College Hospital, London, on 17 July 1947, a fortnight after the publication of

Sonia and Rolie's decree nisi and only weeks before the deaths, in turn, of Alice Keppel, Henry Ashcombe and the Hon. George Keppel MVO.

For some time after George's death, according to Harold Acton, Italian tour guides would point out L'Ombrellino and explain that its owner had been a distinguished old English gentleman, with bristling moustaches and perfect posture, 'the last lover of Queen Victoria'. George's elder daughter (or whoever's daughter she was) inherited the villa, but not its contents. To Violet's near-desperate dismay, Sonia insisted that virtually all of them – pictures, porcelain, wall-hangings, carpets – be put up for sale. Early in 1949, from London, Sonia wrote to Violet to recommend two possible auctioneers in Florence – and to share some family news:

> Whichever we decide on should start his catalogue soon. Rosalind had another sweet little daughter, Annabel, on Feb. 2nd & both are v. well.

> Camilla is lovely.

Chapter Three

Daughters and Sons

'As the family goes, so goes the nation
and so goes the whole world in which we live.'

Pope John Paul II (1920–2005)

On 10 July 1947 – as Christian Dior launched his 'New Look' on London and the government cut the tinned-meat ration to twopence-worth a week[51] – Buckingham Palace issued the following statement:

It is with the greatest pleasure that the King and Queen announce the betrothal of their dearly beloved daughter The Princess Elizabeth to Lieutenant Philip Mountbatten, RN, son of the late Prince Andrew of Greece and Princess Andrew (Princess Alice of Battenberg), to which union the King has gladly given his consent.

According to press reports, 'There had been an air of expectancy all day'. Before the news broke, the princess was seen looking 'particularly happy' – despite a heavy downpour – as she arrived with her parents at White City to attend the Royal International Horse Show: 'As she climbed the steps to the royal box she positively beamed.' Outside Buckingham Palace, crowds, apparently 'thousands strong', stood under umbrellas and cheered the good news.

Exactly a week later, on Thursday 17 July 1947, across town, in London SE5, the sun shone brightly on King's College Hospital,

---

[51] The post-war recession was biting hard. Austerity was the order of the day. The Chancellor of the Exchequer, Hugh Dalton, announced reductions in petrol and tobacco imports and ordered newspapers to revert to their wartime size: four pages. Dior's 'New Look' (the hourglass shape: soft shoulders, hand-span waists and billowing skirts below the calf) was condemned by junior trade minister, Harold Wilson, as 'irresponsibly frivolous and wasteful'.

Denmark Hill, when, just before 7.00 a.m., Camilla Shand was born.[52] There was, naturally, no cheering in the streets, but there were announcements in the newspaper and much positive beaming in the family. Camilla was certainly a lovely baby. She had handsome parents and came from colourful stock.

Rosalind Cubitt and Bruce Shand met at the end of the Second World War. They were married, midweek and relatively quietly, on 2 January 1946. She was twenty-four, tall, slim, pretty, with a slightly beaky nose and gently hooded eyes. He was three weeks short of twenty-nine, a young major in the 12th Royal Lancers, a war hero with an MC and bar, and three years in a German prisoner-of-war camp, to his credit.

Rosalind was essentially conventional. Her Keppel grandparents may have been on the rackety side, but her father and mother remained married throughout her childhood and did their best to bring her up in the traditional manner of the English upper crust. They wanted for nothing (when Sonia insisted on selling off the furnishings at L'Ombrellino she was only recently divorced): they lived, during their marriage, in unostentatious comfort, near Marble Arch, at 20 Hyde Park Gardens. Rolie, who succeeded as 3rd Baron Ashcombe in 1947, was pretty typical of his time and type and class. He was an officer and a gentleman when the phrase meant something – and in his case it meant Eton, Sandhurst, the Coldstream Guards and a gently roving eye for the ladies. His other recreations were hunting and polo. His clubs were the Turf, Buck's and the Guards. Sonia was a dutiful wife and a

---

[52] The Royal Obstetrician and Gynaecologist, Sir William Gilliatt, had his consulting rooms at 108 Harley Street, W1, but preferred his patients to give birth at King's where he founded the department of obstetrics and gynaecology and became vice-president of the hospital in 1945. King's College Hospital was founded in 1840 at Lincoln's Inn Fields and within two years was treating some 1,300 patients in 120 beds – with staff instructed to keep bed occupancy to a maximum of three patients per bed. The hospital pioneered midwifery as a specialism and enjoyed royal favour from the start. In the 1840s, by royal permission, the men's ward was named Victoria and the women's ward, Albert [sic]. When the hospital moved to Denmark Hill, Edward VII laid the foundation stone. The Duchess of York visited the children's ward in the late 1920s and inaugurated 'the Princess Elizabeth cot'. Despite my best endeavours, I have been unable to discover whether baby Camilla slept in it or not. However, I can tell you that the hospital now boasts a Gilliatt Ward, a Mountbatten Ward, a Golden Jubilee Wing (recently opened by the Queen) and is looking forward to the possibility of a visit from the Duchess of Cornwall. 'I'm sure we can find something to name in her honour,' a spokesman told me.

loving mother. She had two children after Rosalind (two boys, Henry and Jeremy) and, though her manner was gay and her tone could be sharp,[53] she knew sadness in her life (her younger son died in 1958, aged only thirty) and loneliness, too, and coped better with both than her more notorious (and much sadder) sister, Violet. She liked to call herself 'an unrepentant blimp', but, in fact, she accepted the world as she found it. She was a survivor. She dedicated her own memoir, *Edwardian Daughter*, 'To My Darling Daughter Rosalind Shand' and of her daughter's daughter, Camilla, she said, 'I simply adore her.'

Bruce's parentage was more exotic. The Shands, like Rosalind's forebears the Edmonstones, hailed from the south-west of Scotland. However, the Shands, unlike the Edmonstones, had neither an estate nor a title to their name. On 5 June 1809, Camilla's great-great-great-grandfather, Alexander Garden Shand, went some way towards remedying at least part of the lack by marrying an heiress, Isabella Morton, whose dowry included a useful estate in Banffshire. Alexander and Isabella had a son, named Hugh Morton, after Isabella's father, but, unhappily, this Hugh failed to succeed to his grandfather's estate because Isabella predeceased Alexander and Alexander did (as men sometimes do) and formed a passion for his housekeeper – marrying her on his deathbed and, effectively, dispossessing his son.

Hugh Morton Shand, however, born in the year of Napoleon's defeat (1815; and dying in the year of Bismarck's fall, 1890), was a man of spirit, with a sense of adventure and ambition. He joined the army; he went to India; he established a lucrative trading company; he returned to London, and, having made his fortune abroad, by way of investment at home acquired a complete terrace of houses at the western edge of Kensington. Edwardes Place wasn't Eaton Square, and Shand was no Cubitt, but, having come from Scotland with nothing, within a generation he established himself and his family as people of property and standing. In 1857, aged forty-two, he married a widow of thirty-five, Edrica Faulkner, born in Florence (two years after Florence Nightingale), the daughter of an itinerant portrait painter. Hugh and

---

[53] When I met her she struck me as very grand and 'county'. It was 1964: she was living at Hall Place at West Meon in Hampshire and I was a pupil at Bedales School nearby. During the general election campaign that October, as the school's 'Conservative candidate', I made it my business to call on all the grand houses in the neighbourhood. The gentry (e.g. Mrs Cubitt) were invariably welcoming: interested and (I now realise) amused. Others on whom I called (e.g. Sir Alec Guinness who also lived nearby) were not.

Edrica had three sons in quick succession: the first, Alexander Faulkner Shand (1858–1936) Camilla's great-grandfather, born nine months to the day after his parents' wedding.

This Alexander had spirit, too, but, in his case, his sense of adventure led him to test the boundaries of English society rather than to explore the further reaches of the Empire. He was educated at Eton and Peterhouse College, Cambridge; he read for the Bar but did not practise as a barrister; he was intellectual, but he was not ascetic. Far from it. He smoked and drank and probably experimented with narcotics. He moved in circles that might best be described as both Bohemian and radical. His friends included three exact contemporaries of note: Sidney Webb (1859–1947), Beatrice Potter (1858–1943) and Constance Lloyd (1858–98). Sidney and Beatrice married and, together, became a radical force to reckon with, as economists, as social reformers, as founders of the Fabian Society and pioneers of the Labour Party. Alexander Shand and Constance Lloyd were briefly engaged and it is not clear which of them called it off. Alexander was drawn to Constance by her beauty and her intellect: she was tall, with wavy chestnut hair, dazzling blue-green eyes and a fine figure; she could read Dante in Italian and cared for music, painting and mathematics. Perhaps not unsurprisingly, she did not marry Alexander: she married Oscar Wilde.[54]

Alexander's eventual marriage may have been more prosaic and less overtly tragic than Constance's, but it was not necessarily happier. On 22 March 1887, Alexander Shand, aged twenty-eight, married Augusta Mary Coates, aged twenty-seven, a pleasant looking, softly spoken, mild-mannered doctor's daughter from Bath. She came from a good, professional, middle-class background that included several generations of doctors, bankers, merchants, justices of the peace.[55] Her people

[54] On the night they first met, Wilde told his mother, 'By the by, Mama, I think of marrying that girl.' The attraction was instant, but eventually it wore thin. According to Constance's brother, Wilde was unsympathetic when she tried to tell him about the unhappiness of her upbringing. Her father died when she was young; she had a strained relationship with her mother. Wilde was not interested: 'He could not be bothered with people who went back to their childhoods for their tragedies.'

[55] I have discovered that Camilla's great-great-great-grandparents and mine were neighbours and friends! Augusta's parents were Charles Coates MD, FRCP, and Sarah Hope, daughter of Samuel Hope JP, a member of a well-respected Liverpool shipping and banking family. Samuel Hope was a contemporary and friend of Dr Joseph Brandreth, founder of the Liverpool Infirmary and inventor of 'Brandreth's Pills', a patent medicine that cured *everything*.

were sound. Unfortunately, Alexander Shand was not. Augusta was conventional and religious. By contrast, her husband was a man who wanted to push boundaries, both intellectually and in terms of his personal conduct. His intellectual legacy is probably his work as a pioneer in the field of social psychology. In 1914 he published *The Foundations of Character, Being a Study of the Tendencies of the Emotions and Sentiments*. The book makes heavy reading now, but its central theme is relevant to our story: the balance between instinct, sentiment and emotion on the one hand and the pressures of society on the other – particularly when the 'system of emotional tendencies' is 'centred about some object'. His personal legacy is certainly more obvious.

Alexander's and Augusta's marriage was fraught, but fruitful. Their claim to fame – until the advent of their great-granddaughter as a potential Queen of England – was undoubtedly their celebrated son, Philip Morton Shand (known as P. Morton Shand, 1888–1960), writer, raconteur, *roué*, author of *A Book of Wine* (1926), *A Book of Food* (1927), *Bacchus* (1927), *A Book of French Wines* (1928) and *A Book of Other Wines (than French)* (1929). Yes, he was into food and drink – and other men's wives – and all in a big way. He had a huge appetite for work as well as pleasure, and an eclectic range of interests. He was a world authority on traditional apples and on modern architecture. He founded the Fruit Group at the Royal Horticultural Society. He translated (from the German) Walter Gropius's seminal *The New Architecture and the Bauhaus*. He was a friend of Gropius and the other leading figures in the 'modern movement' of architecture in the 1920s and 1930s, notably Le Corbusier and Wells Coates. He was a friend, too, of the young John Betjeman who loved him for one work in particular: *The Architecture of Pleasure: Modern Theatres and Cinemas* (1930). Betjeman described him as 'a man of compelling charm'. Others were less persuaded, calling him cantankerous, opinionated, arrogant, obdurate and 'casually anti-Semitic' in the manner of the upper middle classes of his day.[56]

P. Morton Shand was clever and contrary. At school (he followed his father to Eton and Cambridge) he won prizes for German and Divinity.

[56] This last accusation is interesting, given Shand's admiration for the Jewish Austrian playwright, Arthur Schnitzler, at least one of whose plays he translated. It may, of course, have been the erotic undercurrent in Schnitzler's evocation of demimondaine Vienna, rather than his tracts on anti-Semitism, that caught Shand's imagination. Shand is a man of contradictions and difficult to pin down – though he may be, in due course, in a biography by William Whittam.

At King's College, he was remembered for his 'daring neckties' and 'mercurial temperament'. At his death, in 1960, the college magazine recorded: 'His detestation of port was well known; whisky he considered a poison fit only for persons of depraved tastes; and he was really offended by the more vulgar forms of ugliness.' On post-war architecture, he and Prince Charles would have found common cause. He described London in the 1950s as 'a nightmare of hideous and shoddy Americanised buildings'. He feared that, when championing Gropius, Le Corbusier and the rest of the modernists, he had not foreseen what contemporary architecture would become: 'the piling up of gigantic children's toy bricks in utterly dehumanised and meaningless forms'. 'It is no longer funny,' he bleated towards the end of his life, 'it is frightening.'

As a young man, he showed brilliant promise,[57] but he was profligate with his gifts – and with his family's money. His way with wine, with women, and with his parental allowance, were such that eventually he and his father fell out. John Betjeman's daughter, Candida Lycett Green (a good friend of Camilla's, as it happens), echoing her father, described Shand as 'kind and perceptive'; the high court judge presiding over the third of his divorces described him as 'peculiarly shameless'. Alexander Shand was on the judge's side. For several years, Alexander refused to speak to Philip – his only son. He even cut him out of his will and decreed that if any grandchildren decided to give financial assistance to their spendthrift father they, too, would be disinherited.

I own a 1937 edition of Who's Who. It is a collector's item:[58] described as 'the coronation issue', it opens with a portrait of the King who was never crowned. It also records the death, on 6 January 1936,

[57] 'Whom the gods wish to destroy they first call promising.' Cyril Connolly, *Enemies of Promise*, 1938. Connolly knew Shand, whose greatest gift was possibly as a raconteur. Connolly recognised the problem: 'For most good talkers, when they have run down, are miserable; they know that they have betrayed themselves, that they have taken material which should have a life of its own to dispense in noises upon the air.'
[58] Like the memorabilia created for Charles and Camilla's wedding dated 8 April 2005. When the wedding was postponed to 9 April because of the funeral of Pope John Paul II, bidders on ebay, the internet auction site, ran riot. Souvenir mugs, designed to retail at £5, were changing hands at more than £70. However, Steven Jackson of the Commemorative Collectors Society believes that those who snapped up the items dated 8 April at inflated prices may have made a mistake. He believes that, in the long run, items bearing the correct date may prove the more valuable because manufacturers will have produced more with the wrong date than the right one.

of Alexander Faulkner Shand and features a two-inch entry covering the life and career of Philip Morton Shand. What is interesting about the entry, for which Shand himself provided the information, is not so much what is included (*Address:* 15 Ladbroke Grove, London W.11. T. Park 4836) as what isn't. Shand records that he was married, in 1931, to Sybil Mary Sissons, elder daughter of the late R. J. Sissons of Weybridge. True. He also states that he has two daughters. True, too. However, he makes no mention of any of his previous wives – including the mother of one of these daughters. Nor, and somewhat more significantly, does he acknowledge in any way the fact that he has a son: Bruce Middleton Shand, born 22 January 1917, Camilla's father. The *Who's Who* entry reflects a sad truth about Bruce's childhood: it was as if, to his father, he did not exist.

P. Morton Shand was – like so many in this story – a notable Lothario.[59] He was married four times and had girlfriends – ranging from established mistresses to one-night stands – by the dozen. In 1916 – at St Peter's Church, Hammersmith, on 22 April, nine months to the day before Bruce's birth – he married his first wife, Camilla's grandmother, one Edith Marguerite Harrington, later known as Margot. Not much is known about this lady. She did not feature in his life for long.

Margot appears to have been a respectable girl, definitely 'middle class' in 1916, but with forebears of much humbler origin. At the turn of the nineteenth century, her great-grandfather's family were farm labourers living in Essex. Her grandfather, Henry Harrington, moved to London in the 1850s to better himself, and his son, George, born in 1865, is reported to have worked for a time in a tyre factory and later as a book-keeper and accountant. On 4 August 1889, at St Luke's in Paddington, George Harrington married Alice Edith Stillman. To Denis Harrington, eighty-five in 2005, a former foreman in a spark plug factory, now living in quiet retirement in Cardiff, this Alice is 'my old gran'. Denis Harrington's father and Bruce Shand's mother were brother and sister. Mr Harrington can still picture his grandmother: 'Her hair was swept back into a bun and she was always in her pinny. She was a tall, rather big lady with a ruddy face – not pretty but countrified, I suppose you'd call it – and I suppose that's where Camilla Parker Bowles gets her looks from.'

[59] 'A gay libertine, a seducer of female modesty, a debauchee. The character is from Rowe's *The Fair Penitent*.' Brewer's *Phrase and Fable*, 1896. (Rowe's other work includes the first biography of Shakespeare and a popular drama called *The Ambitious Stepmother*. He was appointed Poet Laureate in 1715 and is buried in Westminster Abbey.)

Alice Keppel has long loomed large in Camilla's personal iconography. Not so her other great-grandmother, Alice Harrington. Bruce Shand says, 'I don't think I ever met my mother's mother. I certainly don't think I was ever taken to see her.' Shand describes his childhood as 'rather *mouvementé*' – full of incident and uncertainty. Camilla's father, Bruce Shand – like Charles's father, Prince Philip – came from a broken home. Shand's parents split up when he was quite small, and virtually disappeared from his life – as happened to Prince Philip. Bruce was largely brought up and cared for by his father's parents – much as Philip was by his mother's mother and his older sisters and their husbands. Bruce Shand was sent to Rugby ('a school I heartily disliked') and joined the Royal Military Academy at Sandhurst when he was eighteen. Prince Philip was sent to Gordonstoun (a school, he would say, that was the making of him) and joined the Royal Naval College at Dartmouth when he was eighteen.

Major Shand and the Duke of Edinburgh both suffered fractured childhoods, endured domestic dislocation throughout their formative years and had parents who, by accident or design, were more absent than present. Neither talks about this much, nor complains about it ever. They are of a comparable age and of a similar, stoical disposition. Prince Philip says, 'That's what happened. That's life. You just have to get on with it.' Major Shand says, 'Family splits happen in lots of families. Nothing I can do about it now, I'm afraid.'

Prince Philip respects the memory of his parents and, for all their frailties and failings, evidently still has admiration and affection for them both. In this regard, with Bruce Shand, it is a different story. Indeed, in his *Who's Who* entry (I am looking at the 1988 edition), Major Shand acknowledges that he is the son of the late P. Morton Shand, but makes no reference to the existence of his mother. Bruce was born at the start of 1917, the year of Passchendaele and of the United States' entry into the First World War. By 1919 – the year of Scapa Flow and the Treaty of Versailles – his parents were already separated and on their way to divorce.

Both remarried almost at once. P. Morton Shand's second wife was a Frenchwoman, Alys Fabre-Tonerre, by whom he had his first daughter, Sylvia, born within weeks of the wedding. Margot's second husband was a man called Tippet – whose first name was either Herbert or Charles. Bruce Shand has only a vague memory of him – though he gets an honourable mention in the major's military memoirs. Tippet, according to his stepson, 'although not a regular soldier, had fought with gallantry in the 1914 war and had retained a taste for the army, with considerable knowledge of its uniforms, history and traditions. Perhaps some of this rubbed off on me.'

From about the age of four, both of Bruce Shand's parents largely disappeared from their son's life. His grandmother, Augusta, oversaw the rest of his upbringing; his grandfather, Alexander, financed it. His father might be a Lothario and his grandfather a Bohemian, but his grandmother – a straightforward, some say 'straitlaced', Christian lady – simply wanted her grandson to become an uncomplicated English gentleman. According to Bruce, 'She was anxious that I should not go to Eton where both her husband and son were set on the road to modest intellectual prowess. Rather illogically, and I think unfairly, she attributed the plethora of wives, four in all, that my father collected to the influence of that seat of learning.' Apparently, Grandma Shand liked to say that 'it wasn't for nothing' that J. M. Barrie had made Captain Hook an Old Etonian. (It was her one joke.)

P. Morton's second wife went the way of his first – and almost as swiftly. By 1926 – the year of the General Strike and of the birth of Princess Elizabeth – he had moved on from Alys, and, by way of an assortment of other French girls, had settled in Lyons with the new love of his life: one Georgette Avril, the daughter of a local mill owner. He was divorced by Alys; he married Georgette; he acquired some shares in the family mill along the way.

These years – the late 1920s – were the years of P. Morton Shand's initial celebrity as a popular (yet, he hoped, profound) writer on food and drink – especially, of course, the food and drink of France. 1931 was the year of his celebrity as a serial divorcee. He had promised Georgette that his philandering days were over. He failed to keep his promise. Supported and encouraged by her family, driven to 'distraction' by his 'intolerable behaviour', she sued him for divorce on both sides of the Channel. In France, the magistrate hearing his wife's case against him, advised 'Monsieur Shand' to make his future *'outre-mer'*. In England, the judge hearing the petition against him concluded, 'There is, of course, no statutory means of preventing a man like the respondent from playing the havoc apparently he is capable of playing', but considered that 'a little wholesome publicity' might at least help advertise the man's character and so act as a warning to others. The *Daily Mail* (never much of a friend to the Shand family, it seems) rose to the judge's challenge and published a full account of P. Morton's marital misdemeanours. The publicity was extensive and embarrassing, but apparently did little to hamper the rogue adulterer's style. Within days of leaving the divorce court, P. Morton Shand was on his way once more to the register office.

His fourth wife, Sybil Slee (née Sissons), was English, the former wife of a naval commander, a Home Counties girl, already the mother of one daughter (Mary), and soon to be the mother of P. Morton's second daughter, Elspeth. He brought both girls up as his own – and, after his fashion, and given his track record, appears to have brought them up well. The older took up her stepfather's interest in architecture and eventually married an award-winning architect of note, Sir James Stirling. The younger showed an interest in architecture, too, but, when it came to matrimony, disregarded her father's advice. 'It does not matter who you marry,' said P. Morton Shand, 'so long as he isn't a politician, a lawyer or a Welshman.'[60] In the event, Elspeth (now, in her own right, Baroness Howe of Idlicote) married someone who was all three: Geoffrey Howe, QC, MP, sometime Chancellor of the Exchequer and Foreign Secretary, and now Baron Howe of Aberavon.

P. Morton Shand was evidently an easy man to love (or at least fall for) but a difficult man to live with. By the time he married Sybil, he was forty-three. He had not mellowed – he was, apparently, more irascible than ever – but his wandering eye had dimmed a bit and, to the surprise of many (and to the credit of Sybil), he made this marriage stick. He lived by his wits (which were considerable – and necessary, given that he had forfeited an income from his father) and died, aged seventy-two (a reasonable age, given his capacity for food and drink), in Lyons in 1960. He was certainly a 'character', but he was no 'role model'. It is probably fortunate for Camilla that her father did not follow her grandfather's example in life.

Indeed, Bruce Shand's career could not be more unlike that of P. Morton. During the First World War, P. Morton's service in the Royal Field Artillery was reckoned 'brief and undistinguished'; during the

---

[60] His maxims were many and various. Best remembered (and probably most typical) is his line: 'A woman who cannot make soup should not be allowed to marry.' He meant it. He called on the nation's 'patient, badly fed men' to take action. 'Let them rise up,' he said, 'and refuse to take to wife one who cannot assure for them, by competent direction or personal preparation, the happiness of a well-tended and varied table. An apron, Madame, can be as becoming as a ball-dress, a robe all too common in these days to inspire either envy or respect. A single cordon bleu is worth a whole generation of blue stockings.'

Second World War, P. Morton, too old for active service, became a pen-pusher for the Admiralty in Bath. His son Bruce, by contrast, was a war hero – a proper one.

Edwardian Daughter, Camilla's mother's mother's memoir of her early years, is a lovely book, witty, wonderfully evocative, yet essentially discreet. Sonia Keppel brings both her mother and 'Kingy' vividly to life, but she does not tell you they were lovers. Camilla's father's military memoir, *Previous Engagements*, is wonderfully evocative too, in its way quite as compelling as Sonia's, and just as discreet. Shand tells you there's a war on, but he does not mention that in it he won the Military Cross – twice. He's that kind of chap. According to his grandson, Ben Elliot (Camilla's younger sister's son), 'Major Bruce Shand is a magnificent, graceful, elegant man. He must be one of the few people left on this earth who really does say "What?" at the end of all his sentences; he is also the sort of fellow who refers to young women as "fillies".'

When I met him I found him to be exactly what you would expect: bluff, breezy, good-hearted, good-humoured, decent, discreet, almost a caricature of his kind – Denis Thatcher meets Osbert Lancaster, with just a pinch of Captain Mainwaring. When he graduated from Sandhurst in 1937, he joined a cavalry regiment, the 12th Royal Lancers, not because of its military record (going back to a notably heroic charge at the Battle of Waterloo), but because he 'fancied there'd be a chance of some good riding'. Horses, hunting, the army, the wine trade and service to Queen and country: these have been his life.

The war was tough, but exhilarating, too. 'We did our bit, I suppose,' is how Major Shand puts it. 'It was challenging, but worthwhile. It's wrong to single out any one individual. We were a regiment and we saw a bit of action.' They saw plenty of action, and right from the start. On 16 October 1939, the 12th, equipped with armoured cars, landed in France. On 10 May 1940, the 12th was the first regiment to cross the Belgian frontier. During the retreat that followed, they covered the withdrawal of the British Expeditionary Force, at one time holding a front of forty miles between Ypres and Nieuport. In his despatches, John Gort, commanding the army in France, concluded: 'Without the Twelfth Lancers only a small part of the Army would have reached Dunkirk.'

In September 1941, the 12th sailed for Africa with the 1st Armoured Division, leaving behind a detachment (not including Shand) sent to act as a mobile guard for the Royal Family and members of the cabinet. 'Yes,' chuckles the major, 'I might have spent the war at Windsor, hiding in the shrubbery.' Instead, he spent a year of it in North Africa and the balance in Germany, in the prisoner-of-war camp at Spangenberg Castle. The 12th served with the 8th Army throughout the Desert and North African campaigns. It was in the Libyan desert, shortly before the decisive battle of El Alamein, that the major had one of his most enjoyable wartime encounters. Winston Churchill, the prime minister, appeared, unexpectedly, to rally the troops. This is how the major – making a rare reference to his MC and bar – recollects the moment:

> My hand was being vigorously shaken.
> 'You're a very young man. How old are you?'
> 'Twenty-five, sir.'
> 'Well, well – and a major and you've got two of them.' He prodded vigorously at my medal ribbon. 'How splendid. But you look so thin.'

His next most memorable wartime encounter came not long after, at El Alamein, on 3 November 1942, as Montgomery's troops finally broke through Rommel's front line. It was less enjoyable. 'Rather a dreary performance,' says the major. 'I ran into a group of German vehicles. The only distinction was that it was said to be Rommel's HQ.'

It was night. There was rain: a sudden downpour. Young Major Shand, in an armoured vehicle, was leading his squadron forward when the unexpected encounter with a group of enemy vehicles occurred. 'Before I knew what had happened,' the major recalls, 'my own car was being heavily engaged.' He was hit in the face. He bears the scar under his eye to this day.

> Something like whiplash stung my cheek, and Sergeant Francis beside me slumped to the bottom of the car with a large hole in his chest, killed instantly. I could hear all the other cars firing away hard. My mouth was full of blood but I managed to tell Corporal Plant, my imperturbable driver, to turn the car around. I also tried to talk on the wireless but it had become dislocated.
> The car started to move but something hit it a tremendous blow, and I saw poor Plant subside over his wheel. A second later the car began to burn. Crawling forward I found that Plant was dead and I

prepared to leave the vehicle. I got through the top, jumped down, and sheltered under the leeward side. Firing was still going on around me.

I think I must have had a few minutes' blackout as I next remember Edward's car approaching, with him shouting 'Jump on.' I managed to clamber on and hung rather precariously on to his hand as we began to move. It was then that I was hit in the knee, and in the sudden shock I let go, although he tried to hold me. I do not remember hitting the ground. A buzz of German voices greeted my return to consciousness.

Major Shand survived the Second World War. Sergeant Francis and Corporal Plant did not. 'I suffered appalling remorse,' says the major. He remembers his comrades with respect, affection and regret. In Britain, on 15 November 1942, to mark the victory of El Alamein, bells were rung in churches the length and breadth of the land. It was the first time they had been sounded since the threat of German invasion in 1940. Half a century later, they rang again, over Westminster Abbey, on the day of a special service of thanksgiving and commemoration marking the fiftieth anniversary of the battle. The congregation included old soldiers and their families, and the Prince of Wales and his wife, Diana.

Major Shand's regiment is properly called The 12th Royal Lancers (Prince of Wales's). Major Shand, naturally, was invited to the service. Because his wife was ill – she was then seventy-one and ailing: she suffered from osteoporosis and died eighteen months later – he came accompanied by his eldest daughter. The major, seventy-five, looked remarkably fit and well, dressed in his morning suit (black tail coat, pinstripe trousers, black waistcoat with gold watch chain), sporting his medals on his left breast and, on his long, weather-worn face his wartime scar. Camilla, forty-five, looking pale and nervous, wore a cream blouse, frilly at the neck, with a long-skirted blue-black suit, with matching hat and boots. The Prince of Wales came accompanied by Diana because they were still married and this was an important national event. The princess, thirty-one, looked dazzling in a new Catherine Walker creation: white skirt, grey jacket, broad-brimmed hat and gloves.

The service was a significant occasion. It commemorated a key turning point in the Second World War and in our island history. The *Sun*, then, as now, the world's best-selling English language news-

paper,[61] reported it with the banner headline: 'MEMORIAL DAY
WRECKED BY CAMILLA'. The heroes and victims of El Alamein
were all but forgotten as the *Sun* gave its readers what they sensed was
the real story of the day:

A rare public show of togetherness by Charles and Diana was
wrecked yesterday – by the unexpected appearance of the prince's
ex-girlfriend.

The troubled pair had to walk right past Camilla Parker Bowles as
she sat in Westminster Abbey for a memorial service.

Charles politely acknowledged her with a knowing nod and a
smile as he walked past. But his unforgiving wife looked the other
way. Throughout the service of thanksgiving the two women did not
exchange glances.

They are known to loathe each other. And the princess even
stayed behind after the memorial to avoid walking past Camilla
again.

The *Daily Mail*'s report at least gave glancing recognition to the fact
that the service had something to do with military endeavour:

They were like the twin faces of war – the dullness of defeat and the
radiance of victory. As a piece of theatre it was compelling. The
Princess of Wales, her eyes wide, bright, and open, wearing a jacket
of shimmering silvery grey and tight-fitting white skirt. Camilla
Parker Bowles, a funereal figure, pale, thin, and hair flecked with
grey, in shapeless, sombre blue.

Major Shand was appalled by the press coverage and especially
distressed that inadvertently – 'unthinkingly' he now admits – he was
responsible for placing his daughter in the tabloids' firing line. 'It was .
very good of her to accompany me to the service and she couldn't have

[61] In 2002 the *Sun* had a circulation averaging 3,541,002 copies daily, followed by the
Daily Mail with 2,342,982, the *Daily Mirror* with 2,148,058, and *The Times of India* with
2,144,842. The Duke of Edinburgh told me that, in his view, the media's hostility really
set in around the year 1987: 'After [Rupert] Murdoch bought the *Today* newspaper
from Eddie Shah. Day after day there was a derogatory story about one member of the
family or another.' Prince Charles and his father do not see eye to eye on everything,
but they are as one on this. 'Those bloody people' is the phrase the Prince of Wales uses
habitually to describe members of the press.

been better company,' he said at the time. Why did she look so wan? 'I think she found it off-putting to be confronted by thirty-odd photographers outside Westminster Abbey.' Mrs Shand was unwell. Was Mrs Parker Bowles ill, too? 'As far as I am concerned, she is very well and remains in good spirits. The constant press scrutiny does not seem to have taken its toll on her.'

According to everyone to whom I have spoken about her, and from what I have seen of her at close range, she remains 'in pretty good spirits' most of the time. Her equable temperament is the secret of her survival. It has been her father's too. 'Mustn't grumble,' he says. 'I've been jolly lucky, what? Can't complain. "Steady as she goes" is not a bad motto.'

Those who know them both well say that all Camilla's strengths – her lack of guile, her resilience under pressure, her self-deprecating good humour, her uncomplicated sense of fun, her easy way with people, her modesty, her stoicism, her courage – are exactly those of her father. 'She's a good 'un,' says the major, proudly. 'All my children are.'

Camilla certainly inherited her father's love of riding and hunting – and his ability to ride hard, and well, and boldly. 'She can take fences with the best of them,' says the major. 'She doesn't flinch.' As with many an upper-class English countrywoman of her generation, Camilla's 'look' when walking the dogs is comfortable rather than chic. But when she goes hunting her turnout is impeccable. Indeed, it is worth studying the photographs. Until quite recently, when Camilla was caught on camera, you felt there was something not quite right about her grooming. But when hunting she has always looked immaculate. In every way, she is her father's daughter. For twenty years he was the Joint or Acting Master of the Southdown Fox Hounds. 'We can't have people turning up as if they've been wearing the same pyjamas for a month' is the firm line he has always taken.[62]

Diana (who, whether in town or country, managed somehow always to look both comfortable and chic) had an essentially metropolitan spirit. Camilla – and Charles – have always been most at ease in the

---

[62] As I write, I happen to be looking at a charming picture of the new Duchess of Cornwall, Countess of Rothesay, on her way to Craithie Church at Balmoral on the first day of her honeymoon. She is looking very smart in a nicely cut plum-red coat trimmed in Rothesay tartan with matching scarf. It reminds me of a line in one of Osbert Sitwell's volumes of family memoirs: 'We attended stables, as we attended church, in our best clothes, thereby no doubt showing the degree of respect due to horses, no less than to the deity.'

country. And very comfortable on horseback. A mutual interest in hunting – a shared love of the chase – was, in part, what brought them together in the first place – and then brought them together once more. Unless you know hunting people (or, for that matter, polo players), you cannot realise how the passion for their sport sustains them, informs them, underpins every aspect of their lives.

Released from Spangenberg, returned to England, based at the Bovington army camp in Dorset, on 2 January 1946, at St Paul's Church, Knightsbridge, Major Bruce Middleton Hope Shand MC, aged twenty-eight, married the Hon. Rosalind Maud Cubitt, aged twenty-four. It was a relatively low-key affair: a Wednesday wedding, albeit in a fashionable church. Bruce Shand had no close family in attendance, because he had no close family to speak of. He and Rosalind, however, created a family of their own and, as he puts it, in 'fairly short order'. Their three children, Camilla, Annabel and Mark, were born in 1947, 1949 and 1951. Thanks to the children, in the mid-1950s Bruce Shand met up again with his own father. He had seen him briefly in January 1936, at his grandfather's funeral, but not since. He admits, 'I don't think I'd have seen him again at all if my wife hadn't said that the children should meet their grandfather.' When they did meet, how did they get on? 'Not too badly.' Bruce Shand gets on well with most people. So does Camilla. It is an inherited characteristic.

Rosalind, of course, brought Cubitt money to the marriage. Bruce, thanks to his grandfather, had 'a bob or two' himself. They were comfortably off, by the standards of post-war austerity Britain, but they weren't 'what you'd call rich'. According to the major, London life in the 1940s 'could be quite gay – in the proper sense of the word', but it did not come cheap, especially if you were a young man about town who, as the major admits, enjoyed 'frequent and expensive dinners at the Mirabelle, nights at the Four Hundred, and considerable sociable drinking at the Ritz Bar'. Bruce in his twenties was very much at home in Mayfair, Piccadilly and St James's. He was one of the youngest and liveliest members of Boodle's, the eighteenth-century gentlemen's club once known as the 'Savoir Vivre'. The young major certainly knew how to live – to the extent that, before he was married, his finances became 'a bit of a jumble' and he had to be bailed out by a 'committee' of generous friends. (The friends were essential. His grandfather was dead, and his father was in debt himself.) Post-marriage, the major took his financial responsibilities more seriously. He had a bedrock of family funding, but it was not quite sufficient for everything: London life (a house in South Kensington), country life (a rented house in East Sussex, the Old Manor at Westdean), wining, dining, hunting, and then, of course, the school fees. Bruce Shand retired from the army in 1947, aged thirty, and sought gainful employment.

His easy manner and unselfconscious gregariousness combined with his handsome military bearing and distinguished war record suggested he might be a natural salesman, if he could find the right niche. His first job was 'fine but not ideal': he became a representative for a company marketing educational films to schools and colleges. It was not his natural milieu. Happily, he soon found the place that was. English society is an odd phenomenon. Just as, in England, rugby players (for no particular reason) seem to be drawn towards careers as estate agents, so, over several generations, gentlemen of the major's class and kind seem to have gravitated, in disproportionate numbers, towards careers in land management, the art market and the wine trade. At the start of the 1950s Major Bruce Shand became a wine merchant – and a connoisseur. He took a partnership in the long-established firm of Block, Grey & Block of 26 South Audley Street and set about the business of 'knowing' wines.[63] He started to read his absentee father's writings on the subject and was impressed. 'In those days,' he says, 'nobody had written about wine. Now we see five books published about it every day, don't we? But then he was rather a voice crying in the wilderness.'

Bruce Shand sustained a successful career in the West End wine trade and combined it with the life he really loved, that of a traditional English country gentleman. With Major Shand you really do get the complete package: MC and MFH. He epitomises the best of his kind. Self-deprecating from first to last, with distinction and 'a lot of fun along the way', he has done what a chap should do, serving his country, his county (he was Deputy-Lieutenant and Vice-Lieutenant of East Sussex over many years) and his Queen. Yes, the major is yet another of the very many of Camilla's forebears who have made it their business to give personal service to the sovereign – in

---

[63] Major Shand stayed in the wine trade throughout his career, in 1970 becoming chairman of Ellis Son & Vidler Ltd, wine merchants of London and Hastings. The name of Block, Grey & Block is still, occasionally, to be seen in houses where fine vintages are served: I was recently offered a (small) glass of Glen Grant 1902 whisky, bottled by Block, Grey & Block, and sold at auction for £1,550. 26 South Audley Street is now the home of Harry's Bar, a private club with a comfortable bar, a good Italian restaurant, and members who are smooth, well-heeled and not always English.

Bruce Shand's case, intriguingly, as one of Her Majesty's 'bodyguards'.

The only two bodies correctly described as 'bodyguards' to the monarch are the Yeomen of the Guard (not to be confused with the Yeomen Warders of the Tower of London) and the Gentlemen at Arms (formerly known as Gentlemen Pensioners). For sixteen years Major Shand served as an officer of the Queen's Bodyguard of the Yeomen of the Guard in a variety of capacities, as 'exon', 'ensign', 'adjutant' and 'clerk of the cheque'. The titles are archaic because the institution is ancient. Originally the 'Yeomen of the Guard of (the body of) our Lord the King' (or, in fifteenth-century Latin, '*Valecti garde (corporis) domini Regis*'), their role, since the reign of Henry VII, has been as a permanent military corps in attendance on the sovereign of England. They are the oldest existing body of the kind, having an unbroken record from 1485, as well as the oldest military body in England.[64]

The major is proud to have served the Queen as one of her body-guard, but does not pretend that his duties were more than ceremonial or in any sense onerous. He likes to tell the story of the time when, in attendance on Her Majesty for the State Opening of Parliament, 'dressed for the Battle of Waterloo',[65] his duty was to carry the royal

[64] The first official recorded appearance of the King's Bodyguard of the Yeomen of the Guard was at the coronation of its founder, Henry VII, at Westminster Abbey in October 1485, when it numbered fifty members. Henry VIII raised the strength of the Guard to six hundred when he took it to visit Francis I of France at the Field of Cloth of Gold. In Queen Elizabeth I's reign it numbered two hundred. The corps was originally officered by a captain (a post long associated with that of vice-chamberlain of the royal household), an ensign (or standard-bearer), a clerk of the cheque (or chequer roll, his duty being to keep the roll of everyone connected with the household), besides petty officers, captains, sergeants or ushers. In 1669, Camilla's forebear Charles II reorganised the Guard and gave it a fixed establishment of one hundred yeomen, officered by a captain, a lieutenant, an ensign, a clerk of the cheque and four corporals, which is the present organisation and strength. The only variation is that the captaincy is now a ministerial appointment filled by 'a nobleman of distinction' under the Lord Chamberlain, and that the old rank of corporals has been changed to exon, a title derived from 'exempt', i.e. exempted from regular regimental duty for employment on the staff.

[65] The major was an *officer* of the Guard. The dress worn by the *men* of the Yeomen of the Guard is essentially the same as it was in Tudor times. It has consisted from the first of a royal red tunic with purple facings and stripes and gold lace ornaments, red knee-breeches and red stockings (white in Georgian period only), flat hat, and black shoes with red, white and blue rosettes are worn. Elizabeth I added the ruff. The Stuarts replaced the ruff and round hats with fancy lace and plumed hats. Queen Anne discarded both the ruff and the lace. The Georges reintroduced the ruff. To the major

standard and lower it slowly once the Queen had passed from the royal gallery into the chamber of the House of Lords. The gallery was crowded with visiting dignitaries and members of the diplomatic corps and, in consequence, the gallant major, attempting to perform his simple duty with dignity in difficult circumstances, contrived to hook the handbag of a French visitor on to the end of his flagstaff. 'That was dramatic, what? The Queen was very amused by the whole thing.'

The Queen, of course, was very much less amused by the major's daughter's affair with her son. The Queen likes Major Shand. With his military background, his passion for riding, his unforced natural courtesy and straightforward sense of humour, he is very much Her Majesty's kind of man. The Queen is equally happy – in fact, even more so – in the company of the major's ex-son-in-law, Brigadier Parker Bowles.

The Queen has known and liked Andrew Parker Bowles over many years. Her mother, Queen Elizabeth, and the brigadier's parents, Derek and Dame Ann (DCVO, CBE, Chief Commissioner of the Girl Guides, 1966–75), were good friends and regular racegoing companions. The Parker Bowles lived in a fine house, Forty Hill, on the Highclere estate at Newbury in Berkshire – the estate belonging to the Queen's best friend and racing manager, 'Porchey', the 7th Earl of Carnarvon, who died on 11 September 2001. Horse racing is and was at the heart of the life of Andrew Parker Bowles and his parents, just as it is and was at the heart of the life of the Queen and her mother. The Queen and the

the most interesting feature connected with the dress is that the gold-embroidered emblems on the back and front of the coats tell the history of the consolidation of the kingdoms of Great Britain and Ireland. From 1485 till 1603, the emblems were the Tudor crown with the Lancastrian rose, and the initials of the reigning sovereign. When the Stuarts succeeded the Tudors in 1603, they substituted the St Edward's crown for the Tudor, and added under it and the initials the motto 'Dieu et mon Droit', which is still worn. Queen Anne restored the Tudor crown, and added the thistle to the rose on the union with Scotland in 1709. The Georges reverted to the St Edward's crown, and on the union with Ireland in 1801 George III added the shamrock to the rose and thistle. No change was made during Queen Victoria's reign, but Edward VII ordered the Tudor crown to be substituted for the St Edward's, and now the coats of the Guard are as they were in 1485, with the additions of the motto 'Dieu et mon Droit' and the shamrock and the thistle. Up until 1830 the officers of the Guard wore the same Tudor dress as the non-commissioned officers and men, but when William IV ordered that in future no civilian should be appointed to the Guard, and that the purchase and sale of officers' commissions should cease, the old Tudor dress was discontinued, and the officers were given the dress of a field officer of the Peninsular period.

brigadier get on famously. She is always happy to see him and it shows. (I have watched them chatting together at a party. Each is easy with the other, and it is not easy being easy with the Queen. She is the Queen, after all. At comparable close quarters, I have watched the Queen in conversation with the Prince of Wales. They did not seem so comfortable.) The Queen and Andrew Parker Bowles always have plenty to talk about – animals in general (the brigadier's last military posting was as head of the Royal Veterinary Corps), racing in particular – and there is never any awkwardness between them. There are certain matters, of course, they do not discuss – ever – and would not, for a moment, dream of doing so. The brigadier knows the rules and plays by them, always. He is a natural charmer.[66]

Porchey's son, Geordie, one of the Queen's godchildren and now 8th Earl of Carnarvon, told me, 'The Queen is more comfortable around men . . . She is easy with them, more chatty.' She is easy with Major Shand and Brigadier Parker Bowles. With Camilla, she is not the same. It is more difficult. I have seen the two of them together and you sense the strain. All her adult life, off and on, Camilla has known the Queen, yet in her presence, to this day, even though she is now married to her son, she is nervous and, try as she does, it shows. Those who have heard them talking together say that there is still something awkward, something uncomfortable, in their relationship. As the Queen said once to one of her ladies-in-waiting, 'It's nothing personal. It's the situation. It isn't easy.' The Queen, of course, wishes her son and his new wife every future happiness. That said, as she told her lady-in-waiting, 'One could wish things had been otherwise.'

Intriguingly, Major Shand, fiercely proud as he is of his daughter, and honoured, delighted and 'pretty amazed, what?' to find himself the father-in-law of the Prince of Wales, shares some of the Queen's regret. Bruce Shand and the Duke of Edinburgh are of an age, one born in 1917, the other in 1921. The major and the Queen have a broadly similar outlook on life. They know you can't turn back the clock, but they are not sure that all the changes they have seen in their lifetimes have been for the better. The major says what the Queen thinks, but

---

[66] In *Enemies of Promise*, Cyril Connolly wrote: 'All charming people have something to conceal, usually their total dependence on the appreciation of others.' I used to agree, until I spent time studying the likes of Major Shand and Brigadier Parker Bowles. These military charmers (interestingly, Captain James Hewitt, whom I know, and of whom more anon, is another) do not seem to be wanting appreciation so much as offering it. Their charm lies in the way they appear to be interested not in themselves, but in *you*.

might not put so bluntly. 'There's been a tremendous deterioration of conduct and respect,' he says, and who can deny it? Manners have gone by the board and promiscuity is rife. The so-called permissive society has taken its toll. Says the major, unambiguously, 'It's a pity that the ties of marriage have been so destroyed by it.' 'Divorce,' according to Bruce Shand, 'is a devil of a business.'

The major and his wife made their marriage stick: they were together for forty-eight years, from January 1946 up until Rosalind's death in July 1994. By the standards of both their families, they were exceptional. The truth is that Camilla's family history, on both sides – on all sides – is riddled with adultery, desertion and divorce. Her paternal grandfather, P. Morton Shand, of course, was a notorious divorcee. Her maternal grandfather, Rolie, 3rd Baron Ashcombe, was more circumspect, but his marriage still ended on the rocks. He and Sonia were divorced in 1947. He married again, a year later. He married for a third time in 1959. (His third wife was one Jean Garland, herself a serial divorcee: Rolie was her fourth husband.) Rolie's younger brother, Archibald Cubitt, Camilla's great-uncle Archie, was married first in 1926 and divorced first in 1933. He married again in 1934 and was divorced again in 1949. (His son, Robin, was divorced, too, in 1984.) Rolie's elder son, Harry Cubitt, 4th Baron Ashcombe since 1962, was first married in 1955; divorced in 1968; married again, in 1973 (to Camilla's flatmate at the time, Virginia Carington, twenty-two years his junior, the daughter of Peter Carington, 6th Baron and Conservative Foreign Secretary); divorced once more in 1979; he married, for the third time, almost immediately. His nickname was 'Mad Harry'. I do not know if his younger brother, Jeremy Cubitt, Camilla's uncle, Rolie and Sonia's second son, had a nickname, but I do know that he, too, was divorced, after just five years of marriage, in 1957.

The truth is: among the Shands, the Cubitts and the Keppels, divorce was commonplace. The point is: these people were ahead of their time. Nowadays, we take divorce for granted. If current trends continue, soon half of all marriages will end in breakdown. It was not ever thus. Figures from the Office of National Statistics show that in the United Kingdom, between 1960 and 2000, the number of divorces rose by 502 per cent. In 1960, in Britain, a divorce took place roughly every twenty minutes. Since 1980, a divorce has been occurring every three minutes. More people cohabit, fewer people get married, and still the divorce rate grows. Compared with the 1950s, there are 25 per cent fewer marriages but five times as many divorces every year.

Of course, divorce was easier for the Shands, the Cubitts and the Keppels: they had more money than most – and perhaps, too, a sense that they were above (or beyond) the rules that governed the rest of conventional society. 'Middle-class morality' was not for them. Until the advent of the 1969 Divorce Reform Act, when, in essence, blame was taken out of the equation and 'breakdown of marriage' became the sole ground for divorce in Britain, securing a divorce was a costly, complicated and messy business. It was also, in the main, socially unacceptable.

When I was a little boy, being brought up in middle-class London in the 1950s, living in mansion flats in Lower Sloane Street and on Gloucester Road, divorce was a word rarely spoken in anything other than a whisper. It was like cancer: something you did not talk about. And something, when it did occur, that was regarded not simply as sad, but as positively scandalous. This was the era before the publication of *Lady Chatterley's Lover* (1960), before the advent of the oral contraceptive pill (1960), before the first topless dress (1964), before the 1967 Abortion Act. It was a different world: people went to church, homosexuality was outlawed, marriage was for life (whether you were happy within it or not) and illegitimacy, 'having a child out of wedlock', was wholly beyond the pale. (A Gallup poll conducted in 1954 showed that 98 per cent of the population 'disapproved of single mothers'. A comparable survey conducted by Gallup in 2004 found only 38 per cent of those polled feeling that way.)

Half a century ago, whatever the Shands, the Cubitts and the Keppels might get up to, at court the position was clear: divorce was unacceptable. The sovereign was the Supreme Governor of the Church of England and the Church of England did not recognise divorce. Divorcees were not presented at court, were not invited to royal garden parties, were not expected in the royal enclosure at Royal Ascot.[67] The teaching of the Church of England was clear and the writ ran north of the border, too. When a divorced Scottish nobleman pleaded to be allowed access to a royal garden party in Edinburgh on the grounds that he had been able to remarry in church, Sir Thomas Innes of Learney, advocate, heraldic lawyer and Lyon, King of Arms – and so responsible

[67] In 1953, the 16th Duke of Norfolk, hereditary Earl Marshal and Chief Butler of England, responsible for organising the Queen's coronation, was asked by an anxious peer if his divorce would prejudice his invitation. Norfolk replied, 'Good God, man, this is a Coronation, not Royal Ascot.' At the next coronation, of course, if Charles outlives his mother, the principal participant will be a divorcee.

Daughters and Sons

for vetting the royal guest list – was implacable: 'That may well admit him to the Kingdom of Heaven but it will noo get him through the gates of the Palace of Holyroodhouse.'

In October 1949, Princess Elizabeth, aged twenty-three, married to the Duke of Edinburgh for two years, and with Prince Charles just eleven months old, made her first and, so far as I can tell, only public pronouncement on the issue of divorce. She addressed a massed meeting of the Mothers' Union in Central Hall, Westminster, and, in her familiar, thin, high-pitched voice, deplored the 'current age of growing self-indulgence, of hardening materialism, of falling moral standards' and laid the blame where she was quite clear it belonged. 'We can have no doubt,' she said, 'that divorce and separation are responsible for some of the darkest evils in our society today.' The words may have been drafted for her, but the sentiments will have come from her heart.

The Queen learnt of the evil consequences of divorce at her mother's knee. The Queen's father, George VI, died of cancer, aged fifty-six, in February 1952. His widow, Queen Elizabeth, was only fifty-one. 'He was so young to die,' she wrote to her friend Osbert Sitwell,[68] 'and was becoming so wise in kingship. He was so kind too, and had a sort of natural nobility of thought & life which sometimes made me ashamed of my narrower & more feminine point of view. Such sorrow is a very strange experience . . .' George VI had his weaknesses – he smoked excessively, he drank more than was good for him, he was liable to sudden bursts of temper (his notorious 'gnashes' that only his wife had the patience and skill to soothe) – but he was a good husband, a devoted father and, some would say, a great king. As a national leader he was put to the test during the Second World War and not found wanting. René Massigli, the French ambassador to London at the time of his death, wrote in a report to the French foreign minister: 'If the "greatness" of a king can be measured by the extent to which his qualities corresponded to the needs of a nation at a given moment in

[68] Sir Osbert Sitwell, Bart, CH, CBE (1892–1969) was a kind of literary jester to the court of Queen Elizabeth – much as Stephen Fry is to the court of Charles and Camilla. Sitwell was, as Fry is, scholarly, witty, a little dangerous (in a fundamentally safe way), admiring. Queen Elizabeth's favourite Sitwell anecdote was the one he told about his father, Sir George (also, of course, the father of Dame Edith and Sacheverell Sitwell). When challenged on something he had said, Sir George would omnisciently reply, with an air of final and absolute authority, and without deeming it necessary to offer proof or divulge the source of such, no doubt, mystical awareness, 'We happen to know.'

history, then George VI was a great king, and perhaps a very great king.'
According to Sir Alexander Hardinge, his private secretary, the strain
killed him. 'As a result of the stress he was under,' said Hardinge, 'the
King used to stay up too late and smoked too many cigarettes – he
literally died for England.' He died for England because he was King. He
was King because his older brother, Edward VIII, had put love before
duty and given up the throne to marry a divorced woman.

Until the abdication, George VI and Queen Elizabeth were Bertie
and Elizabeth, Duke and Duchess of York, and more than content to be
so. They had the privileges and perquisites of royalty, without the
burdens of sovereignty. When David (as Edward VIII was known to his
family) decided, finally, that he had 'found it impossible to carry the
heaven burden of responsibility and to discharge my duties as king as I
would wish without the help and support of the woman I love', Bertie
and Elizabeth stepped into the breech. They did their duty, but they
would rather David had been man enough to do his. When, some time
after the abdication, someone commented on how well David was
looking, Queen Elizabeth responded, 'Yes. And who has got the lines
now?'

There was no love lost between Queen Elizabeth and her brother-
and sister-in-law, the Duke and Duchess of Windsor. Queen
Elizabeth's niece, Margaret Rhodes, who was also her lady-in-waiting
and friend, told me, in the week the Queen Mother died, that 'Not
once in all the years I was with her – not once – did I ever hear her say
anything remotely unpleasant about the Windsors. I know she liked
David and, I promise you, I never heard her say anything uncharitable
about the Duchess.' Others tell a different story, claiming that Queen
Elizabeth blamed David for her Bertie's premature death much as
Queen Victoria blamed her son Bertie for the premature death of her
beloved Albert.

On 9 April 2005, the third anniversary of Queen Elizabeth's funeral
and the day on which Charles and Camilla were married, in his speech
at the wedding reception in Windsor Castle, the Prince of Wales, his
eyes pricked with tears, spoke of his 'beloved grandmother' and said, 'I
so wish she could have been here today.' Someone else who was at the
wedding, and who knew Queen Elizabeth well, told me, emphatically,
'If she had been, it would have killed her. She loved Charles dearly and
she liked Camilla, but she would not have wanted to see them as man
and wife. Not for a moment. And, in fact, had she still been alive, it
would not have happened.' Hugo Vickers, the historian and best-

informed of the biographers of Queen Elizabeth, agrees. 'He would not have dared put his friendship with his grandmother at risk. There came a time when she no longer mentioned Camilla's name.'

As Prince Charles and the new Duchess of Cornwall emerged alone from St George's Chapel after the blessing of their marriage, there was – before the rest of their families joined them on the steps – a fleeting echo of David and Wallis, the sometime King and the new Duchess of Windsor, standing alone on the steps of the Château de Candé, at Monts, near Tours, in France, just after they were married on 3 June 1937.

It is easy, of course, to draw parallels between the present Prince of Wales and the love of his life and the last Prince of Wales and the love of his – easy, but not necessarily useful. Camilla Parker Bowles and Wallis Warfield Simpson are comparable, but only superficially. Wallis, unlike Camilla, was a true outsider: an American as well as a double divorcee. She was introduced to David, then a dashing and popular Prince of Wales, in the winter of 1930, when he was thirty-six and she was thirty-four. The woman who introduced them was another of David's lovers, another American, Thelma Furness. Lady Furness (she married the 1st Viscount Furness in 1926 and divorced him in 1933) later described Wallis at that time as 'not beautiful . . . not even pretty': 'But she had a distinct charm and a sharp sense of humour . . . Her eyes, alert and eloquent, were her best feature. She was not as thin as in her later years – not that she could be called fat even then; she was merely less angular. Her hands were large; they did not move gracefully, and I thought she used them too much when she attempted to emphasise a point.' Chips Channon, meeting her soon after she and David had become an item, described her as 'jolly, plain, intelligent, quiet, unpretentious and unprepossessing', adding: 'She has already the air of a personage who walks into a room as though she almost expected to be curtsied to. At least she wouldn't be too surprised. She has complete power over the Prince of Wales . . .'

For several years before they were married, Mrs Simpson acted as hostess for the Prince of Wales at Fort Belvedere, his much-loved country house on the edge of Windsor Great Park – just as for several years Mrs Parker Bowles acted as hostess for Prince Charles at his beloved Highgrove. Both ladies were treated by staff and guests almost like royalty – but, in fairness to Wallis and Camilla, this was not what they demanded or expected: it is what happens when you become attached to a Prince of Wales and those around the Prince of

Wales know that is how he would like to see his mistress treated. In January 1935, Chips Channon wrote of Wallis in his diary: 'I think she is surprised and rather conscience-stricken by her present position and the limelight which consequently falls upon her.' Some sixty years later, in January 1993, at the time of the publication of the so-called 'Camillagate' tape, Mrs Parker Bowles felt much the same way.

Ultimately, whatever their past reservations, the British Royal Family and the British Establishment have behaved decently towards Camilla, in a way they could never bring themselves to do with Wallis. The Duchess of Windsor was never granted the dignity of becoming a Royal Highness; she and the Duke were obliged to live in exile and – as they saw it – in straitened circumstances. When George VI died, the £10,000 annual allowance that the Duke of Windsor had been granted by his brother abruptly ceased. The Duke came to London for his father's funeral and, from Marlborough House, on 22 February 1952, wrote to Wallis, who, tactfully, had remained in New York, to report briefly on how he had been received:

My own darling Sweetheart,
    Your letters and cables and our telephone talks have been my only props on this difficult, painful and discouraging trip. I'm making notes of all incidents and conversations for when we meet so won't sit up too late writing them for you now.
    Cookie [the Windsors' nickname for Queen Elizabeth] was sugar as I've told you and M [Dickie Mountbatten] and other relations and the Court officials correct and friendly on the surface. But gee the crust is hard & only granite below.
    George Allen [the Windsors' solicitor] has some sensible and con-vincing arguments over the £10,000 if only they'll play at Clarence House [the residence of the new Queen, Elizabeth II and the Duke of Edinburgh]. But I'm afraid they've got the fine excuse of national economy if they want to use it. We shall see & anyway we won't know anything for sure until the new Civil List. It's hell to be even this much dependent on these ice-veined bitches, important for WE as it is. . . .

WE – Wallis and Edward – were on their own. If, by 'the ice-veined bitches' he meant Elizabeth II and her mother, they maintained their *froideur*. The Windsors hoped to attend the new Queen's Coronation.

The new Queen's private secretary, Sir Alan Lascelles, declared that their presence would be 'condemned . . . as a shocking breach of taste'. When George Allen protested on the Windsors' behalf, pointing out, reasonably enough, that it was now more than sixteen years since the abdication, Lascelles offered a chilling rebuke. He and George Allen had served in the Great War: some things could never be forgiven or forgotten. 'Have you or I, for example, forgotten the Somme?'

The Windsors were rejected by the House of Windsor. They felt so alienated that, in 1957, the Duke drafted a statement to be published by his executors on his death:

> I wish to set down in clear, unequivocal terms my wishes with regard to my burial and which I wish to be observed . . .
>
> At the time of my Abdication, I stated publicly that I was quitting public affairs and that it might be some time before I returned to my native land. I must confess that at that time I had it in mind that circumstances might permit the permanent return of the Duchess and myself to live in England; but I hope I will not give offence to anyone when I say that such a state of affairs was not encouraged by members of my family.
>
> That being the case and because since my marriage I have enjoyed such happiness as can have been vouchsafed to few men, I have come to the conclusion that I would like to be buried in America, the country of my wife, and she in the fullness of time likewise. Accordingly we have made provision to be buried in Green Mount Cemetery, Baltimore. . . .

In the event, as the years went by, and the duke and duchess grew old and frail, there was a gentle thawing on the part of the Windsors at home towards the Windsors in exile. In 1964, the Duke had open-heart surgery in Texas and the Queen sent him flowers. In 1965, the Duke underwent an eye operation at the London Clinic and the Queen called to see him – and met the duchess for the first time since 1936, when the Queen, of course, had only been ten. In 1967, a plaque in memory of the Duke's mother, Queen Mary, was unveiled outside Marlborough House and the duke and the duchess were invited to sit in the front row – alongside the Queen, the Duke of Edinburgh and Queen Elizabeth The Queen Mother – at the dedication ceremony.

In October 1971, a few weeks before his twenty-third birthday, Prince Charles was in Paris and arranged to call on the Duke and

Duchess of Windsor at their villa in the Bois de Boulogne.[69] The visit was memorable, as the young prince noted in his diary at the time:

> . . . Upon entering the house I found footmen and pages wearing identical scarlet and black uniforms to the ones ours wear at home. It was rather pathetic seeing that. The eye then wandered to a table in the hall on which lay a red box with 'The King' on it . . . The whole house reeked of some particularly strong joss sticks and from out of the walls came the muffled sound of scratchy piped music. The Duchess appeared from among a host of the most dreadful American guests I have ever seen. The look of incredulity on their faces was a study and most of them were thoroughly tight . . .

Charles found an opportunity to have a private word with his great-uncle:

> He seemed in very good form, although rather bent and using a stick. One eye was closed most of the time, as a result of his cataract operation, but apart from that he was in very talkative form and used wide, expansive gestures the whole time, while clutching an enormous cigar . . . We got onto the subject of his relationship with his father [George V] and he said he had had a very difficult time

[69] The house is described – and illustrated – in fascinating detail in *The Private World of the Duke and Duchess of Windsor* by Hugo Vickers and others, 1995. When the Duchess of Windsor died in 1986, the lease of the property, and its contents, had to be disposed of – and along came Mohamed Al Fayed, the Egyptian-born owner of Harrods, 'the international businessman and philanthropist' who had already acquired and refurbished the Paris Ritz. Fayed, by his own account, poured $50 million into restoring the Windsors' Paris home and his efforts in the Bois de Boulogne and at the Paris Ritz earned him a Légion d'honneur from the French government. From the United Kingdom he received no recognition. He complained, 'Not one single official said, "Mohammed, thank you. We are grateful." Not one single letter.' In the summer of 1997, Fayed decided to clear out the contents of the Windsors' former villa, saying he needed 'more space for his family' – leading some to suggest he intended the house as a future home for his son, Dodi, and Diana, Princess of Wales. The sale went ahead after Dodi's and Diana's death. 'This is the biggest auction we've ever held in the United States,' said the man from Sotheby's. 'One has to go back to the 17th century to find anything comparable — the sale of the possessions of Charles I.' Among the 40,000 lots was the table on which the Duke, as Edward VIII, signed his abdication in 1936, and, from 1937, a three-inch-square piece of the Windsors' wedding cake which sold for $26,000 (£17,300), against a pre-sale estimate of $1,000 (£660).

with him and that Gan-Gan [Queen Mary] was a hard woman and he had been brought up extremely strictly.

Charles, of course, had similar reservations about his own upbringing. Though he later acknowledged that 'Uncle David' had become 'so remote that none of us really knew him', at their meeting he felt a real sympathy for him. He felt less generously inclined towards poor Wallis:

> While we were talking the Duchess kept flitting to and fro like a strange bat. She looks incredible for her age and obviously has her face lifted every day. Consequently she can't really speak except by clenching her teeth all the time and not moving any facial muscles. She struck me as a hard woman – totally unsympathetic and somewhat superficial. Very little warmth of the true kind; only that brilliant hostess type of charm but without feeling.

Charles has a vivid memory of his brief encounter with the Windsors in exile in the Bois de Boulogne: 'The whole thing seemed so tragic – the existence, the people and the atmosphere . . .' He was able to see, at first-hand, aged twenty-three, the price his predecessor as Prince of Wales had paid for putting love before duty and, against the wishes of his family and without the support of his people, marrying a divorcee.

Following the meeting, Charles and his great-uncle enjoyed a brief and friendly correspondence. It did not last long because the Duke's health was failing. He died in Paris on 28 May 1972, aged seventy-seven. Tens days before, the Queen and the Duke of Edinburgh, on a state visit to France, had taken Prince Charles with them for a final visit to the former King. The Duke of Windsor, though clearly dying and attached to a drip, insisted on being dressed to meet Her Majesty and, when she entered his room, 'with an effort of will that was remarkable' (according to his doctor), 'rose slowly to his feet and gave the traditional bow from the neck'. (These things matter very much to royalty. Indeed, if not to them, to whom?)[70] On 5 June 1972, his

[70] When I attended an investiture at Buckingham Palace not long ago, one of the Gentlemen at Arms told me that, in half a century of the ceremonial, 'there's really only been one noticeable change. At the beginning of her reign, as Her Majesty passed, everybody would have bowed or curtsied. Now nobody does.' It was interesting to note at Charles and Camilla's wedding that the members of the Royal Family all bowed and curtsied to the Queen on cue, but most of the rest of the congregation appeared unsure as to what to do, when to do it and how.

body was laid to rest, not in Baltimore, Maryland (he had changed his mind about the Green Mount Cemetery), but in the royal burial ground at Frogmore, by Windsor. Fourteen years later, on 24 April 1986, the Duchess of Windsor died, aged ninety. The last years of her life were lonely and blighted by dementia. At her death, she, too, was flown from Paris and buried, alongside her last husband, at Frogmore – the least honoured person there: the only woman ever married to the son and brother of a King to be denied the rank of Royal Highness.

When Prince Charles first visited him in Paris, 'Uncle David' talked about 'how difficult my family had made it for him for the past 33 years'. At her end, the Duchess of Windsor was given a funeral in St George's Chapel, Windsor, and Elizabeth II was there to see her out. By contrast, after a different 'difficult' thirty-three-year relationship, on 9 April 2005 the Duchess of Cornwall was given a blessing at St George's Chapel, Windsor, and Elizabeth II was there to see her in. Camilla is a Royal Highness, a rank in the gift – and only in the gift – of the Queen. One day, I imagine (and for many, until recently, this was quite unimaginable), she will even join that tiny and select band of women truly honoured by the sovereign: the Lady Companions of the Order of the Garter.

Why has Camilla, albeit after long years (years when the Queen was careful to see as little of her as she once saw of the Duchess of Windsor), at last been accepted by Her Majesty, and those around her, in a way that Wallis never was? It is partly because the circumstances were different. Edward VIII was King. Prince Charles is a king-in-waiting. It is partly because times have changed. Divorce was unacceptable in 1936 in a way it isn't in 2005: we live in a more forgiving and a more tolerant age. And the Queen, who was once quite rigid in her views,[71] has mellowed over time. It is partly, also, because Wallis Warfield (she reclaimed her maiden name by deed poll shortly before her marriage to the Duke of Windsor) was a double divorcee, and she and both her former husbands (Captain Earl Winfield Spencer Jr and Ernest Aldrich Simpson) were American, and conspicuously so. Camilla Shand (and Andrew Parker Bowles), by contrast, have always been essentially what the English upper classes used to term PLU: 'People Like Us'.

[71] A former private secretary to the Queen once quoted to me, approvingly, the celebrated dictum of Lord Shawcross, formulated in 'swinging' 1963: 'The so-called new morality is too often the old immorality condoned.'

Wallis was American and metropolitan. She was seen as ambitious and grasping. She wanted to be a Royal Highness – *so much*. Camilla is English and a countrywoman. 'Her only ambition,' according to one member of her family, 'is to make Charles happy.' He asked her to marry him. According to one of her oldest friends, 'She never put any pressure on him over being married – none at all, I promise you. She didn't ask for anything. She was thrilled about the wedding, but not bothered about titles or rank or anything like that.' Now she will get it all – in part because she asked for none of it. She has accepted the bad times and the good 'with grace', says her father. 'She is brave and tough,' according to her friend and Gloucestershire neighbour, the writer Jilly Cooper, 'but not in a nasty way. People who hunt have courage and a certain toughness. She churns inside and she hurts, but she never moans. She never complains and she never asks for anything. It has been a crucifixion for the Prince of Wales to hear her slagged off.'

I do not believe we will hear her being 'slagged off' in future in the way she has been in the past – and in the way the Duchess of Windsor was from the mid-1930s until her dying day – but she will still have her critics. Mark Bolland, who, as the Prince of Wales's deputy private secretary, was responsible for setting up the first Charles-and-Camilla 'photo opportunities', is not as unqualified in his praise of Camilla as some of her close family and friends. According to Bolland, 'Camilla is nervy and lacks stamina; she has never worked in her life and is terrified of being on public display.' Says one of her Gloucestershire friends, 'She is getting used to being on show. It doesn't really faze her. She's incredibly laid-back.' Says Mark Bolland, 'I love Camilla dearly, but she is monumentally lazy . . . a member of her family described her to me as "the laziest woman to have been born in England in the twentieth century".'

From what I have seen of Camilla, she is far from lazy. Since her wedding, hardly a day has passed without her undertaking a 'duty' of some kind, but if she is 'incredibly laid-back', as Bolland suggests, is that such a bad thing? Prince Charles says, plaintively, 'All the time I feel I must justify my existence.' Camilla does not feel that way at all. Happily for her, she has never been infected with what Queen Elizabeth The Queen Mother's friend Osbert Sitwell called 'the terrible, newly-imported American doctrine that everyone ought to do something'. At her wedding to Prince Charles, Camilla's father, Bruce Shand, said to a fellow guest, 'She seems to be coping. Take it as it comes. That's how we brought her up.'

Chapter Four

Parents and Children

'I am convinced that, except in a few extraordinary cases, one form or another of an unhappy childhood is essential to the formation of exceptional gifts.'

Thornton Wilder (1897–1975)

Oscar Wilde – whose wife, you will recall, was briefly engaged to Camilla's great-grandfather, Alexander Shand – maintained he 'could not be bothered' with people 'who went back to their childhoods for their tragedies'. On that basis, Wilde would have found the present Prince of Wales a little tiresome. Charles still bleats about the trials and tribulations of his youth. He talks about it less often, and less plaintively, than once he did, but, aged fifty-seven, he remains unhappy about many aspects of his upbringing. Camilla, by contrast, has no complaints to make about hers. Her childhood, she says, was 'perfect in every way'.

Camilla was brought up at The Laines, Plumpton, near Lewes, East Sussex (Telephone: Plumpton 890248). The house is a five-bedroomed former rectory, conveniently situated opposite Plumpton racecourse,[72] wide-spread, a little shambling, with ivy-clad stone and brick walls around the garden, wooden gates, well-tended flowerbeds, spacious lawns (one ideal for croquet), a scrunchy gravel drive and geraniums in pots by the back door. (Inside the back door, in Camilla's day, were a line-up of gumboots and a row of pegs on which to hang hacking jackets, dog leads and riding crops.) Because it was the 1950s – when children really could play safely in country lanes and brooks and

[72] I recommend an outing. Plumpton, with a two-hundred-year history, is one of the country's most successful smaller jump racecourses, staging sixteen National Hunt fixtures between September and May each year. It's 'a little gem', according to Major Shand, 'and only an hour from town by train'.

streams and bluebell woods were quite easy for all to find – and because she had dogs and ponies as part and parcel of her life (and a cat, of course, that snoozed for hours in the sunshine on top of the garden wall), Camilla is often described as having had an 'Enid Blyton sort of childhood'. In fact, it was much grander than that. Camilla, as a little girl, may have had some of the personality traits of George, the tomboy girl among the Famous Five, but Enid Blyton's children were essentially middle-class children and the Shands, without question, belonged to the upper class. The Shands had position and they had help – help in the house, help in the garden, help with the children. They were gentry. They opened their garden for the local Conservative Party Association summer fête. Enough said.[73]

When she was five and pretty as a picture – at least, in the one picture I have seen of her aged five she looks adorable: heart-shaped face; button nose; wide, knowing, eyes; arched, enquiring, eyebrows; truly golden curls – Camilla was sent to her first school. Dumbrells, at Ditchling, a village three miles from Plumpton, was a traditional preparatory and pre-preparatory school, named after its founders, the Misses Dumbrell, Victorian sisters from a respected East Sussex family. The school was established in the mid-1880s and, by every account, in 1952, when Camilla arrived, the values of the place – and the facilities – remained true to their Victorian origins. Stuffed animals in glass cases were a feature of the décor. As you came into the school, you would greeted by a huge, framed bat, a hundred years dead, its wings spread wide.

I have not been able to unearth any of the children who were at Dumbrells with Camilla, but Christopher Wilson, in *The Windsor Knot*, quotes a former pupil from the period as saying, 'A school inspector came and was dumbstruck. He never knew such a place could exist. The school was so harsh I used to say that a child who could cope with Dumbrells could cope with anything.' I wonder, in fact, if the school's regime was unusually grim, or was it, in reality, reasonably typical of its type and time? Private schools in England, after the Second World War

---

[73] I am sensitive to this, not only because it is how, as a schoolboy, I came to meet Camilla's grandmother in her lovely garden at Hall Place in Hampshire, but also because it reminds me of how inadequate I felt – and was made to feel – when I was the Conservative MP for the City of Chester and failed to provide my activists with a proper house and garden in which to hold fundraising events. The Duke of Westminster kindly allowed us to hold a ball in his stable block, but what my supporters really wanted was a member of parliament with, as one of them put it to me, 'proper grounds for entertaining'.

and throughout the 1950s, were Spartan places: there was no central heating, there was no double glazing, the cold stone floors were covered, if at all, with cold linoleum. At Dumbrells, on Wednesday afternoons, after games – hockey in winter, 'stoolball' in the summer (a Sussex variation of cricket and rounders) – you were expected to rinse off under a cold shower, under the stern eye of Miss Clarke, the long-serving headmistress, a former Dumbrells' girl herself. Miss Clarke was a disciplinarian. She believed it was never too soon to teach a child the meaning of the word 'No'. She believed in order and calm and learning by rote. 'A tidy girl will have a tidy mind' was one of her maxims. Apparently, to Miss Clarke, orderliness was everything. According to one former pupil, the headmistress decreed that any possession found not in its proper place was to be worn by the culprit for a whole day, including mealtimes: 'One of the older girls came to lunch wearing three hats; a younger one was sadly hampered by a large sewing basket tied to her waist.' Unruly children were punished by having to sit still and in silence underneath the headmistress's chair. Those guilty of serious misdemeanours received physical chastisement: a smack on the bare bottom with a wooden ruler.

Camilla, it seems, thrived in this environment. She was a robust child. In winter, her mother drove her to school. In summer, she was content to walk the three miles between Plumpton and Ditchling with the family nanny. By all accounts, without exception, she was a healthy, happy, lively, chatty, jolly little girl. School was fine and home was fun. She was not short of playmates: children from school and one or two from the village; her easy-going younger sister, Annabel (then, as now, her best friend); her mischievous baby brother, Mark; and, best of all, from the age of five onwards, a series of (I quote her) 'adorable ponies'. Horses were at the heart of Camilla's childhood – and they are standing her in good stead now. (Making small talk with the Queen is not easy, unless you understand horses and dogs. Camilla is totally at home with both.[74]) The Shands and the Cubitts have long been serious hunting families: Camilla's great-uncle Charles Cubitt was, for many years, the Master of the Crawley and Horsham Hounds; her father, Bruce, aged

[74] Just before Easter 2005, Camilla and Charles had dinner with the Queen and, according to one report, it was a very happy evening: 'yak yak yak' – and mostly about horses. It is the way to get Her Majesty going. Someone who was there told me that when the Queen first met Ronald Reagan, the US President, the conversation was quite stilted until Reagan chanced to remark, 'There is nothing better for the inside of a man than the outside of a horse.' From then on, they were firm friends.

only thirty-nine, was appointed Joint Master of the celebrated Southdown Hunt, next door.[75] Camilla learnt to ride with the Pony Club; she went on Pony Club camps: she loved it. She learnt to hunt with the Southdown: the terrain is strongly-fenced vale, wooded weald and open downland. A fellow huntswoman told me, 'It takes courage and a clear head to take those jumps. Camilla has both.'

The focus of the Shands' family life in the 1950s and early 1960s was The Laines. They were horsey people, county people (the major became a Deputy-Lieutenant of East Sussex in 1962), country people, and they were all – especially the major and Camilla – keen and knowledgeable gardeners. However, they also had a London home that was more than a mere base. It was a handsome, three-storey Victorian house in South Kensington. Every weekday, when not hunting, the major would take the 79 bus from South Ken to South Audley Street to go to work. The Shands had a London life – and London friends – as well as their country life in Plumpton – just fifty-five minutes from Victoria by train. (It takes a little longer nowadays, of course.) In 1957, when Camilla was ten, they decided that their daughter should continue her education in town. It was partly a matter of school fees (one of the family told me they were 'comfortable not flush': Bruce wasn't a wine merchant simply for the fun of it), but more the fact that Camilla was eager to be at a day school and was regarded as an 'absolute natural' for the one around the corner, at 133 Queen's Gate, London SW7.

I do not know any girls who went to Dumbrells at Ditchling, but I am familiar with more than my fair share of girls from Queen's Gate School. Indeed, for a while I went out with a girl who was in Camilla's class and I am a friend of one of the senior girls from Camilla's era at Queen's Gate. The girl I went out with shall remain nameless;[76] the senior girl is

---

[75] The Southdown, merged with the Eridge since 1981, is to the east of the Crawley and Horsham, and is celebrated because one of Major Shand's predecessors as Master was Norman Loder, MFH 1911–13, commemorated in Siegfried Sassoon's *Memoirs of a Fox Hunting Man*.

[76] I have got to hold something back for the autobiography. I will tell you she was very beautiful, but her parents were quite frightening. The family (there were just the three of them) lived in an elegant third-floor flat in a mansion block near the Natural History Museum. When, for the first time, I called at the flat to take the daughter to the theatre, I suffered a double dose of humiliation. First, I was offered sherry in the drawing room and managed to spill most of it on the cream-white carpet. Next, I let slip that I proposed taking my date into the West End by underground. Her father, meaning well no doubt, took me aside, pressed a ten shilling note into my hand and murmured, 'A cab, I think, don't you?'

the actress Lynn Redgrave. I will let Lynn make the case for the prosecution: 'I remember the place with nothing but disdain. I was the only girl who had a working mother. My mother was an actress [Rachel Kempson]. The idea was for us to leave as marriageable young ladies. The girls didn't think they had to learn much because all they had in mind was going to parties. Being a debutante and landing a rich husband was top of the agenda. There would be endless classes teaching us to be good wives and mothers. I was the odd one out because I wanted to have a career – and a career on the stage at that. My dreams were made fun of. Camilla, on the other hand, revelled in the whole concept of the school. She wanted to have fun, but she also wanted to marry well because that would be the best fun in her mind.'

The case for the defence is that, as I recall, the girls were all beautiful, had lovely skin (not to be taken for granted among teenagers), lovely manners (those were the days!), and a lot of fun. They were not overly academic (Camilla secured just one O level; she did not stay on for A levels: that was never the plan), but they did not strike me as being either vacuous or stupid. They were simply of their class and generation. Queen's Gate did its best to prepare young women for the real world – not our real world, perhaps, but a world that still existed nonetheless.

According to the novelist Penelope Fitzgerald, who taught French at the school, Queen's Gate was beginning to change at about the time Camilla arrived there in the late 1950s. 'Once upon a time,' she said, 'it was very much a school where the girls were taught how to write cheques, play bridge and recognise a well-laid table. Gradually, it was beginning to bring itself into the twentieth century. The traditional skills of the hostess, housewife and mother were still important, but the academic side – languages, history, science even – was really starting to make its mark.' Did Camilla – or 'Milla' as she was known at school – make her mark, too? According to Miss Fitzgerald, 'She was bright, lively, and rather sporty, as I recall. I think she did fencing. She was rather good at fencing.'

According to another school contemporary – another Lynn, another Queen's Gate girl with aspirations to become a performer, Lynn Ripley, also known as the 1960s pop singer Twinkle – Milla was 'looked up to' by the other girls. 'She had an inner strength. There was no question that she might do badly, with or without A levels. That didn't matter. She would live the life she wanted – that's what she exuded.' Green-eyed Lynn Ripley was a beautiful teenager (I still have the sleeve of the

EP of her 1965 recording of 'A Lonely Singing Doll' to prove it[77]); Milla
was not so obviously pretty. 'She wasn't a beautiful girl,' according to
Lynn, 'but she had a certain aura. What she lacked in looks, she made
up for in confidence. She had the same hairstyle then as she does today.'
The future Duchess of Cornwall was an essentially conventional child.
The future Twinkle was not. Lynn Ripley remembers Camilla as 'a
hoity-toity little madam':

> I used to wear way-out clothes, but Milla was always in twinsets,
> tweed suits and pearls. We didn't get on very well because she was
> into hunting and shooting. We used to have mammoth rows about
> that because I was totally against it. But she has a magnetism and
> confidence I envied like anything.
>
> She was one of those people who know what they want and know
> that they will be a success in life. She was only fifteen-and-a-half
> years old, but I knew even then that the world was going to hear a
> lot more of Milla Shand.

The world, of course, heard a great deal about Camilla's future
husband, Prince Charles, from the very moment of his birth. He was
world famous from day one. But as a child, unlike Camilla, he was not
one of those people 'who know what they want and know they will be
a success in life'. He was uncertain and unhappy. He felt lonely and
insecure. Where Camilla, at school, was admired by her peers, Charles,
at school, was teased or shunned by his. At fifteen and a half, Camilla
Shand was bright and breezy, awash with energy and confidence, full of
bounce and fun, at ease with herself and her surroundings, comfortable
with her family, her friends and her place in the world. Charles, at the
same age, was none of these things.

If Wordsworth is right and 'the child is father of the man', then this
chapter probably holds the key to the characters of our hero and
heroine, explains why they are as they are, and begins to let us see what

---

[77] Decca DFE8621. Twinkle's first hit was a controversial song she wrote herself,
'Terry', a record in the 'death genre' about a boy who is killed in a motorcycle accident
during a French lesson. 'Terry' climbed to Number 4 in the charts, possibly helped in
its ascent by being banned by the BBC. Her next success was 'Golden Lights', which
reached Number 21. Then Twinkle lost her sparkle. In the 1970s she enjoyed a brief
renaissance as part of Bill & Coo ('Coo', incredibly, was her father, Sidney Ripley,
leader of the Conservative group on the Greater London Council) and in 1982 she
surfaced once more with a remake of the Monkees' hit 'I'm A Believer'.

each wanted from – or could offer to – the other, when, first, they came to meet, and, ultimately, they came to marry. In her speech in the Waterloo Chamber at Windsor Castle on 9 April 2005, the Queen told her guests, 'My son is home and dry with the woman he loves.' One of the Royal Family said to me afterwards, 'Charles doesn't realise it, but the Queen understands him completely. She always has. She's nobody's fool.'

Charles, as we have seen (and will see again!), believes he had an unhappy childhood. He does not blame his position. He blames his parents. He acknowledges, at least, that his position is 'unusual'. In truth, it is, and always has been, extraordinary. When Charles was born – in the Buhl Room at Buckingham Palace just after 11.00 p.m. on Sunday 14 November 1948 – there was *dancing in the streets*! A crowd, three-thousand strong, had gathered by the Palace railings to await the news of the expected birth and, when it came, the dancing and the singing began. 'For he's a jolly good fellow,' the jubilant people chorused – not once, but more than forty times. At a quarter past midnight, a police car equipped with a loudspeaker appeared. The message was repeated over and over again: 'Ladies and gentlemen, it is requested from the Palace that we have a little quietness, if you please.' But the message was drowned by the noise of the singing. According to Dermot Morrah, *The Times* correspondent, Arundel Herald Extraordinary and Fellow of All Souls College, Oxford, it was not until 2.00 a.m. that all was quiet:

At last the chilly air and the extinguishing of lights inside the building achieved what the police had not managed. The parked cars that stretched far down the Mall were climbed into, started up and driven away. Enthusiasts who had long missed their last buses and Tube trains began to make their way home on foot.

Dermot Morrah (1896–1974) is the author of *To Be a King*, 'a privileged account of the early life and education of HRH The Prince of Wales written with the approval of HM The Queen'. It is elegantly written and well informed – not surprisingly. Morrah was a friend at court, and with good reason. He was the author of the speech that Princess Elizabeth broadcast from Cape Town on the occasion of her twenty-first birthday on 21 April 1947 – the speech that both marked her coming of age and defined her, the speech that until her '*annus horribilis*' address forty-five years later was, rightly, regarded as her most memorable and significant. The young princess, in South Africa with her parents, on her first overseas tour, addressed the Empire and Commonwealth, especially 'the youth of the British family of nations', and her words moved all who heard them:

There is a motto which has been borne by many of my ancestors – a noble motto, 'I serve'. Those words were an inspiration to many bygone heirs to the throne when they made their knightly dedication as they came to manhood. I cannot do quite as they did, but through the inventions of science I can do what was not possible for any of them. I can make my solemn act of dedication with a whole Empire listening. I should like to make that dedication now. It is very simple.

I declare before you all that my whole life, whether it be long or short, shall be devoted to your service and the service of our great Imperial family to which we all belong, but I shall not have the strength to carry out this resolution alone unless you join in with me, as I now invite you to do. I know your support will be unfailingly given. God help me to make good my vow and God bless all of you who are willing to share in it.

What she said, she meant. The words may have been drafted by Morrah, but the sentiments were her own.[78] Prince Charles does not quibble with his mother's commitment. Indeed, in his way, he shares it. He is the Prince of Wales, after all. His motto is '*Ich dien*': 'I serve'. Charles accepts – and admires – his mother's devotion to duty. What

[78] I am indebted to Morrah's daughter, Brigid, who, via her son, Tom Utley, the *Daily Telegraph* columnist, has given me the background to this story. In February 1947, Morrah sent his proposed draft of the speech to Sir Alan Lascelles, the King's private secretary, who was travelling through southern Africa with the royal party on board the White Train. At first, the draft went missing. According to Lascelles, who wrote to Morrah from the train on 10 March, 'The steward in the Protea diner had put it in the bar, among his bottles, little knowing that it was itself of premier cru.' Lascelles saluted Morrah's achievement: 'I have been reading drafts for many years now, but I cannot recall one that has so completely satisfied me and left me feeling that no single word should be altered. Moreover, dusty cynic though I am, it moved me greatly. It has the trumpet-ring of the other Elizabeth's Tilbury speech, combined with the immortal simplicity of Victoria's "I will be good."' Lascelles told Morrah how much it had pleased Princess Elizabeth and her mother: 'The ladies concerned, you will be glad to hear, feel just as I do. The speaker herself told me that it had made her cry. Good, said I, for if it makes you cry now, it will make 200 million other people cry when they hear you deliver it, and that is what we want.'

he regrets is what he regards as her 'emotional reserve', what the playwright Terence Rattigan called 'the English disease: the inability to express emotion'.

Charles's memories of his childhood are not happy ones. His grievances go back a long way. Nearly sixty years on, he can still recall his first pram, 'lying in its vastness, overshadowed by its high sides'. As he was growing up, he claims he felt 'emotionally estranged' from both his parents. He says he craved 'affection and appreciation' from them that they were either 'unable or unwilling' to offer.

How fair is this? Are the Prince's criticisms of his parents justified? According to the Duchess of Grafton, Mistress of the Robes and one of the Queen's oldest and closest friends, not at all. 'The Queen is a very warm person,' the duchess told me. 'We had our first babies at about the same time and I can tell you the Queen was a devoted mother, very loving, very involved.' Patricia Mountbatten, Lord Mountbatten's daughter and one of Prince Charles's godparents, agrees. 'The Queen and Prince Philip were first-rate parents,' she told me, 'utterly devoted to their children, and, by the standards of the time, incredibly hands-on.' Another of the royal couple's close friends and contemporaries is Gina Wernher, now Lady Kennard (one of Prince Andrew's godparents). She told me, 'I remember we stayed with them in Scotland when Charles must have been about one. The three of them were so happy together, easy and relaxed. Philip has been marvellous with his grandchildren, too. He's just good with the little ones.'

When I spoke with Margaret Rhodes, however, the Queen's cousin and childhood playmate struck a slightly dissenting note: 'I've seen Philip being absolutely sweet with his children's children,' she agreed. 'But with their own children,' she said to me with a sigh, 'it hasn't been easy. There's no use denying it. Things have gone slightly awry with Prince Charles . . . It's a fractured family. Terribly sad.'

When I pressed Mrs Rhodes to tell me why she felt this was, what she believed was the root cause, she said, 'Philip can't bring himself to be close with Charles. Perhaps you don't learn to give love if you haven't had love.'

Prince Philip's parents split up before he was ten. At the beginning of the 1930s, Prince Philip's father, the exiled Prince Andrew of Greece, moved to the South of France. Until his death in 1944, aged sixty-two, he lived, variously, sometimes on his own, sometimes with a lady friend, in a small flat in Monte Carlo, in modest hotel rooms, and on board a friend's small yacht in the harbour at Cannes. From the age of ten, Philip saw his father hardly at all. At the same time, at the beginning of the 1930s, Philip's mother, Princess Alice (Dickie Mountbatten's eldest sister), suffered a nervous breakdown and was incarcerated in a sanatorium in Switzerland. She was diagnosed as a 'schizophrenic paranoid', suffering from what one of her doctors called a 'neurotic pre-psychotic libidinous condition': sex and religion preyed on her mind. (Today she would more likely have been diagnosed as suffering from bipolar disorder, or manic-depression.) She remained a patient at the Bellevue Clinic at Kreuzlingen for two and a half years. When she was released, allowed 'freedom under surveillance', she spent the next five years leading a solitary, self-imposed nomadic life, travelling between Italy, Switzerland and Germany, living quietly in small hotels and in rented rooms. For two years Philip did not hear from his mother at all – not a birthday card, not a Christmas card, nothing. For five years – the years of his adolescence – he did not see his mother once.

Philip's four sisters – all older than him – were each married (to assorted German princelings) within the space of eight months, between December 1930 and August 1931. Philip, between the end of the 1920s, when his parents split up, and 1947, when he married Princess Elizabeth, had no settled home. He travelled between different boarding schools and the homes of different relations: his sisters and their husbands in Germany; his mother's mother, Princess Victoria, the Dowager Marchioness of Milford Haven, at Kensington Palace (where she had a grace and favour apartment); and his English uncle Georgie (Alice and Dickie's brother) in Berkshire. He did see his parents together one final time, in late November 1937, as a consequence of a family tragedy. A cousin was getting married in London and one of Philip's sisters, Cécile, and her husband (Georg Donatus, Hereditary Grand Duke of Hesse) and two of their children (their young sons, aged six and four), were all killed when the aeroplane in which they were travelling to the wedding crashed in heavy fog. Philip's parents gathered with the rest of the family for the funeral. Philip's childhood friend Gina Kennard told me, 'He loved his sisters very much and when Cécile was killed in that air crash, in 1937, it affected him deeply. He was very quiet. He didn't talk about it much, but he showed me a little bit of wood from the aeroplane. It was just a small piece, but it meant a lot to him.'

Prince Philip's parents were absent throughout his adolescence. His favourite sister, and her husband, and their sons – who had been a second family to him – were wiped out in 1937. (Their surviving baby daughter also died within two years.) His favourite English uncle, Georgie Milford Haven, who was also his guardian and provided him with his principal English home, died of cancer, aged forty-six, in the spring of 1938, as Philip was coming up to seventeen. It does not require a master's degree in psychology to see that Prince Philip suffered deprivation, loss and rejection during his childhood. That might explain why, as an adult, he has been wary of giving love too liberally – might it not?

But what about the Queen? I put the question to Margaret Rhodes. Her mother and Queen Elizabeth The Queen Mother were sisters. Margaret Rhodes and the Queen played together as children. I said to Mrs Rhodes, 'The Queen's childhood was very loving, wasn't it?' She pondered for a moment. 'The Queen was always reserved,' she told me, 'even as a child. And when she became Queen that did add to her reserve, very definitely. But you're right. The King adored both his daughters. And Queen Elizabeth was brimming with love.' At this point, Mrs Rhodes flung her arms wide open to illustrate to me the breadth and warmth of the late Queen Mother's embrace. 'Perhaps,' she concluded, 'having married someone who is like Philip, it is difficult to go on expressing emotion to an unemotional person. You find, in time, you can't express love any more.'

Margaret Rhodes, for several years, was lady-in-waiting to her aunt, Queen Elizabeth. She was with her when she died on Easter Saturday in 2002. Mrs Rhodes lives in Windsor Great Park, opposite Smith's Lawn, the polo field where Charles and Camilla had their famous first (or near-first) encounter. Mrs Rhodes and Queen Elizabeth, both widows, were friends and companions. It is quite possible that what she feels about Prince Philip, the late Queen Mother felt too. Queen Elizabeth always had reservations about her son-in-law. Her younger brother, David Bowes-Lyon (another of Charles's godparents), encouraged her. 'David Bowes-Lyon was a vicious little fellow,' according to Gina Kennard. 'He had it in for Philip right from the start. He was completely against him.' David Bowes-Lyon was the youngest son of a Scottish earl: his sister was married to the British King. Who was Prince Philip of Greece? Where were his parents? Weren't his sisters all married to Germans?[79]

---

[79] They were. Margarita (1905–81) married Prince Gottfried of Hohenlohe-Lagenburg; Theodora (1906–69) married Bertold, Margrave of Baden; Cécile (1911–37) married Georg Donatus, Hereditary Grand Duke of Hesse; and Sophie (1914–2001) married,

David Bowes-Lyon called Philip 'the Hun'. Occasionally, Queen Elizabeth did too – but 'only in fun', one of her friends assured me. I am not sure Prince Philip always got the joke. Indeed, one of his women friends told me that the coolness between Prince Philip and Prince Charles is, in part, a by-product of the long-standing tension between Philip and his late mother-in-law. 'He knew she called him "The Hun",' she told me. 'He didn't like it. He definitely felt the Queen Mother made difficulties between him and Charles.'

Once, talking with the Duke of Edinburgh about the difficulties in his relationship with Prince Charles, I began to say that I found it strange because, to me, father and son seemed to be so similar in so many ways: similar in mannerisms, similar in interests. The Duke interrupted me. 'Yes,' he said, 'but with one great difference. He's a romantic – and I'm a pragmatist. That means we do see things differently.' The Duke paused and shrugged, and said, with a slightly despairing laugh, 'And because I don't see things as a romantic would, I'm unfeeling.'

In my experience, Prince Philip is pragmatic and unsentimental, but not unfeeling. He certainly felt the deprivations of his childhood. 'As a

first, Prince Christopher of Hesse, and, later, Prince George of Hanover. At the family funeral following the aeroplane accident in 1937, both Kaiser Wilhelm (Queen Victoria's grandson, who lived until 1941) and the Nazi Third Reich were represented. Hermann Goering came in person. Because they were married to Germans, none of Philip's surviving sisters was invited to his wedding to Princess Elizabeth. At the time of the wedding, in November 1947, only two years after the end of the Second World War, Philip's youngest sister, Sophie, had three brothers-in-law awaiting denazification, one of them still interned. Philip's mother spent the war years living in Athens and when the Nazi threat to the Jews of Athens was at its height, she offered refuge to a family of Cohens. When neighbours enquired, she said that Mrs Cohen was a former Swiss governess to her children. When the Gestapo questioned her, she simply exaggerated her deafness and looked uncomprehending. In the late 1980s, some years after her death in 1969, surviving members of the Cohen family sought to honour the memory of Princess Alice. They secured for her a 'Certificate of Honour' as one 'Righteous among the Nations': she 'risked her life to save persecuted Jews'. In October 1994, Prince Philip and his surviving sister, Sophie, went to Jerusalem, to the Holocaust Memorial at Yad Vashem, to accept the posthumous award on their mother's behalf. In his speech on the day, Prince Philip said of his mother: 'As far as we know she had never mentioned to anyone that she had given refuge to the Cohen family at the time when Jews throughout Greece were in danger of being arrested and transported to the death camps. I suspect that she never thought of it as something special. She was a person with deep religious faith and she would have considered it to be a totally natural human action to fellow human beings in distress.'

little boy, he was very happy,' Gina Kennard told me. 'Very jolly, very lively.' They played together as children: they met when Gina was eight and Philip was six. 'As he grew older, he became more thoughtful, more introspective. He never saw his parents . . . And he minded that. He told me so. He was perfectly happy at boarding school, but he said to me – I remember this clearly – "Everybody has a family to go back to. I don't." ' When I went to meet Patricia Mountbatten and her husband, Lord Brabourne, they told me that the first – and most heartfelt – letter they received following the IRA bomb which, in August 1979, killed Earl Mountbatten of Burma, aged seventy-nine, and their son, Nicholas, aged fourteen, was from Prince Philip.[80] 'He feels things deeply,' said Lady Mountbatten. 'You can discuss matters of the heart with him,' said Lord Brabourne. They showed me their first visitors' book – from 1946, the year the Brabournes were married – and there, marking a visit over the weekend of 20–22 December, was Philip's signature. Next to it, in the address column, he had written: 'No fixed abode!'

Prince Philip is not overgiven to introspection. 'I'm not sure how useful it is,' he says. And, even at eighty-four, he does his best to look forward rather than look back. Certainly he has always made a point of not complaining about any aspect of his childhood. When, once, I raised the issue with him, and asked how he felt being shipped between schools and relations throughout his formative years, he was typically dismissive. 'It's simply what happened,' he said. 'The family broke up. My mother was ill, my sisters were married, my father was in the South of France. I just had to get on with it. You do. One does.' His loyalty to the memory of both his parents is impressive. He is not a gossip and, as a rule, especially for somebody with a reputation for irascibility, he is remarkably positive in his judgements of people. Occasionally, I have heard him make withering comments about members of his own family

---

[80] On 27 August 1979, Earl Mountbatten and his family, on holiday in County Sligo, set out for a day's fishing on their thirty-foot boat, *Shadow V*. The boat had barely left the harbour mouth when a fifty-pound bomb, planted on board, was detonated by remote control. Mountbatten, his grandson and a seventeen-year-old boatman were killed instantly. Others in the family were severely injured: John Brabourne's mother, Patricia Mountbatten, and Nicholas's twin brother, Timothy, were in a 'critical condition'. Lord Brabourne told me, 'Because we were in hospital – Patricia was in intensive-care – we couldn't attend Nicholas's funeral. Philip attended the funeral and he sent us the most wonderful letter describing it, full of detail – the colour of the sky, the sheep bleating in the field below the churchyard . . . it meant everything to us.'

– principally, Prince Charles, of course – but about his parents – who, in effect, left him without a settled home and family from the age of ten – I have only heard Prince Philip speak with sympathy, respect and affection. Fine portraits of them both hang in his study. To this day he wears his father's signet ring.

Prince Philip is not unfeeling. Nor, of course, is Prince Charles. Friends, and members of his family, have many stories to tell of Charles's thoughtfulness and sensitivity. In 2005, his godmother, Countess Mountbatten – 'Charles calls her his "favourite godmother",' Lord Brabourne says proudly – told me, 'Charles has always been very sensitive, very thoughtful, very kind. When Charles was a little boy, if he was given a sweet he'd offer it to you – straight away. He was always generous. And gentle. He loved animals. We asked him to be godfather to our twins [Nicholas, who was killed by the IRA bomb, and Timothy, now forty-one]. He was only sixteen. It was the first time he'd been a godfather. He took it very seriously. And, to this day, he's wonderful with Tim. Recently, he's been helping him with a scheme Tim has developed setting up bursaries at the Dragon School [in Oxford, the twins' prep school]. He went down and unveiled a plaque in Nicky's name. He's so good like that – really, really good. There is something very . . .' The countess paused, searching for the word. She found it. 'There is something very touching about him. He's a very touching person. He's still very vulnerable, you know. His father is, too, of course, but Philip tries to hide it in a way that Charles doesn't.'

Father and son – in much the same way – are quick to send hand-written letters of condolence, or commiseration, or congratulation, as required. The tone of voice – the turn of phrase – may differ, but the generous impulse is the same. And the reason for the differences in tone and phrase – Philip's style is more matter-of-fact; Charles's style is more florid – is that the Duke of Edinburgh is correct in his diagnosis of the essential difference between the two men: the father is a pragmatist and the son is a romantic.

The father is not introspective, but the son is. When I was visiting Highgrove, Prince Charles allowed me to inspect the small, circular mock-Gothic pavilion in the garden that he sometimes uses as his 'quiet place': somewhere to sit in peace, light a candle and reflect. It is a romantic's hideaway. I think Prince Philip would regard it as a piece of self-indulgent whim-wham. The father does not look back over his past life – the son does, sometimes wistfully, occasionally in anger, more often with regret. If Prince Philip has complaints to make about his parents or his upbringing, he has kept them to himself. When Prince Charles had complaints to make about his childhood, he shared them with the world.

In the early 1990s, Charles cooperated with the broadcaster Jonathan Dimbleby in producing a television film and biography that made plain that Charles was profoundly unhappy about many aspects of his upbringing. In his forties, going grey and with a pained expression, the Prince of Wales became the prince of wails. His mother was distant and ungiving. His father was brusque to the point of bullying. Charles's sad stories of small slights that left their scars were many and similar. When, as a little boy, Charles forgot to call his detective 'Mr' and simply used his surname, as he heard his parents do all the time, he was made to apologise. When he left a door open and a footman went to close it, Philip stopped the footman, barking, 'Leave it alone, man. The boy's got hands.' When, one winter on the Sandringham estate, young Charles was throwing snowballs at a police officer, Philip called to the policeman, 'Don't just stand there, throw some back!' When, again at Sandringham, Charles came back from playing in the grounds one afternoon, having lost a dog lead, his mother sent him straight out again, instructing him not to return until he had found what he had lost, reminding him, 'Dog leads cost money.' When, this time in London, young Charles was seen sticking his tongue out at the crowd watching him drive down the Mall, his father gave him a spanking. As a little boy at Buckingham Palace, he passed his mother's study one day and asked her to come and play with him. Gently closing the door against him, she said, 'If only I could.' When his parents returned from their post-coronation tour and Charles, aged five, was taken in *Britannia* to the port of Tobruk to greet them, the little boy attempted to join the line of dignitaries waiting to shake Her Majesty by the hand. 'No, not you, dear' were the mother's first words to her son after five months of separation.

Talking to Jonathan Dimbleby, Charles lamented his parents' emotional reserve in general and his father's harshness in particular. Charles was shy, nervous and sickly (as a boy he was frequently subject to colds, sore throats and bouts of influenza) – and his father made matters worse. According to the Prince's approved biographer, 'Without that gentleness of nature and subtlety of mind which might have helped coax the Prince out of his debilitating reticence, the Duke tempered his own affection with brusqueness, a disposition which served only to make his son withdraw even further from that open communication which would have benefited both of them.'

That Prince Charles should voluntarily talk to a broadcaster and journalist about family matters – and let the journalist have access to his diaries and private correspondence – seemed, to his parents, sheer foolishness. His mother's verdict (conveyed to me by another member of the family) was that Charles had been 'incredibly naive'. His father thought him 'bloody stupid'. The Queen and the Duke – instinctively wary of journalists and broadcasters, and with good reason – were simply appalled by the Dimbleby book. They could not see how their son's indiscretions – or special pleading on his own behalf – could serve his cause, or that of the Royal Family, in any way. They were also hurt by what their son had to say about them as parents. They might not have been perfect, but they had meant well. As the Duke of Edinburgh put it to me, 'We did our best.'

And their recollection of Charles's childhood was rather different from his own. Read Dimbleby (Prince Charles's authorised version) and you get the sense that the Queen, as a mother, was never there. According to Prince Charles, only in the nursery could he be assured of a cuddle: Mabel Anderson, his young Scottish nanny, was, in his words, 'a haven of security, the great haven', the one to whom he turned first for comfort and support. Read Dermot Morrah (the Queen's version) and you get a picture of Princess Elizabeth as a devoted young mum 'romping with the children on the nursery floor, bathing them and finally tucking them up in bed'. The Queen recalls that her routine was organised so as to ensure that she could spend time with her children – 'quality time' – every morning and every evening without fail: 'If she could snatch other moments during the day to be with them she did so, but nothing was ever allowed to encroach on these morning and evening playtimes so long as she was in London.' Prince Philip recalls taking Charles and Anne, regularly, during the summer holidays, cruising in his twelve-metre yacht *Bloodhound* and remembers these as 'good times, happy days'.

There are two sides to every story. The Duchess of Grafton, the Queen's Mistress of the Robes and friend, who, nearly sixty years ago, as Fortune Euston, was bringing up her young children at the same time as Princess Elizabeth, said to me, 'The Queen was a devoted mother and amazingly involved, considering all her responsibilities.' Countess Mountbatten, Philip's first cousin and one of Charles's godparents, said to me, 'You can see it from both sides, can't you? A resilient character such as Prince Philip, toughened by the slings and arrows of life, who

sees being tough as a necessity for survival, wants to toughen up his son
– and his son is very sensitive. It hasn't been easy for either of them.'
Patricia Mountbatten added, with a dry laugh, 'Anne, of course, as a
natural tomboy, presented no problems.'

Prince Charles Philip Arthur George was born at Buckingham
Palace in November 1948. Princess Anne Elizabeth Alice Louise was
born at Clarence House at 11.50 a.m. on Tuesday 15 August 1950.
Princess Elizabeth reported to a friend: 'Both Philip and I are very
thrilled about the new baby and we only hope that Charles will take
kindly to it. He has only seen Fortune Euston's baby at close quarters
and he then tried to pull her toes off and poke her eyes out, all of which
she took very kindly, having a brother of 2 who presumably did the
same.'

Mabel Anderson, who was a devoted nanny to both Prince Charles
and Princess Anne understood Charles's special vulnerability. Looking
back on them both, she acknowledged that Charles was 'never as
boisterous and noisy' as Anne: 'She had a much stronger, more
extrovert personality. She didn't exactly push him aside, but she was
certainly a more forceful child.'

Anne is like her father in many ways. Father and daughter have
always got on well. They undertake their public duties in the same
brisk, no-nonsense fashion; they compete with one another as to which
can fulfil the more engagements in the year; they vie with one another
as to which has the more efficient private office. They have an easy,
good-humoured, comfortable relationship. They don't brood about life:
they just get on with it. Philip was separated from his mother
throughout his adolescence, but refuses to use that as an excuse for
anything. He will not find fault with his mother, however hard you press
him. Anne will not find fault with hers, either – whatever Charles may
say. The idea that, as a mother, the Queen was remote and uncaring is
flatly rejected by the Princess Royal. 'I'm not going to speak for anyone
else,' she says, 'but I simply don't believe that there is any evidence
whatsoever to suggest that she wasn't caring. It just beggars belief. We
as children may have not been too demanding, in the sense that we
understood what the limitations were in time and the responsibilities
placed on her as monarch in the things she had to do and the travels
she had to make, but I don't believe that any of us, for a second, thought
she didn't care for us in exactly the same way as any other mother did.
I just think it's extraordinary that anybody could construe that that
might not be true.'

Prince Charles on his way to his first boarding school, Cheam, 1958

Annabel, Camilla and Mark Shand with their mother, Rosalind, in East Sussex, 1953

Prince Charles and Princess Anne, with their great-uncle and great-aunt, Dickie and Edwina Mountbatten, in Malta, 1954

Rite of passage: Camilla and her mother at Camilla's coming-out party at Searcy's, 1965

Rite of passage: Charles and his mother at his investiture as Prince of Wales, Caernarvon, 1969

After polo: Charles and Camilla, after a game, 1972

Camilla, aged 26, in 1974

Camilla, aged 31,
in 1979

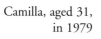

Prince Charles, aged
22, with Andrew
Parker Bowles, aged
31, in Kenya in 1971

A night at the opera:
Prince Charles and Princess
Alexandra, with Camilla Parker
Bowles in the background, 1975

A night at the theatre: Prince Charles with Andrew and Camilla Parker Bowles, 1976

Anne says she found her father demanding in a way that was encouraging and her mother tolerant in a way that allowed her children to find their own feet. 'If she'd been a disciplinarian,' says Anne, with a wry smile, 'and said "No" to everybody, we'd have all been psycho-analysed out of existence on the basis that we had too controlling a mother. We've all been allowed to find our own way and we were always encouraged to discuss problems, to talk them through. People have to make their own mistakes and I think she's always accepted that.'

'We are a family,' Prince Philip said to me, somewhat exasperated when I tried to probe him about the tensions within the House of Windsor. 'What do you expect?' The truth is: you expect ups and downs, good times and bad, some relationships that are better than others. Don't we all know that? Princess Anne adds, 'Judging by some families, I think we are all on pretty good speaking terms after all this time, and that's no mean achievement for quite a lot of families. I think we all enjoy each other's company.'

Today, I understand, Prince Charles, now settled with Camilla, has his misgivings about the Dimbleby book. At the time, he thought, taken in the round, it presented a fair account of his childhood. The book spoke of 'moments of misery at home', but mentioned 'much happiness' too. The book described a harsh father who 'hectored' his son, 'belittling' him, reducing him to tears in front of others, treating him in a 'rough way' that was 'very bullying', and lamented a mother who failed to 'intervene by protective word or gesture', but also acknowledged some of Charles's good times with his father – Philip patiently teaching his son the craft of model-making, Philip reading Longfellow's *Hiawatha* to him out loud – and recognised that both parents had 'a deep if inarticulate love' for their son, a love that was 'reciprocated'. The Dimbleby book was written at a difficult time in Charles's life: his marriage to Diana was in free fall, the 'war of the Waleses', as it became known, was at its height and the Dimbleby book and television programme were weapons in that war. Eleven years on, this book is being written at a good time in Charles's life: his marriage to Camilla has been happily achieved; he is, relatively, at peace with himself and the world; at his wedding reception, when, wrily, he said, 'Down with the press!' everybody cheered. He is not disowning the Dimbleby book (Dimbleby was a guest at the wedding); he is not wanting to rewrite history; he does not remember his childhood differently now from how he remembered it then; but he would like his parents – especially his mother – to know that he regrets, sincerely, any hurt needlessly caused.

In the autumn of 1948, before Charles was born, Princess Elizabeth declared, 'I'm going to be the child's mother, not the nurses.' Indeed, she was – but, inevitably, because she was a princess as well as a mother, because she was the heiress presumptive to a king who, though only fifty-three, was in failing health, and because it was the way of her class and her time, much of the day-to-day grind involved in childcare (to say nothing of the broken nights) was left to the nurses: Mrs Lightbody and Miss Anderson.[81] Helen Lightbody arrived on the recommendation of the King's sister-in-law, the Duchess of Gloucester, whose sons she had looked after, and departed, in due course, after what Prince Charles describes as a 'to-do' involving his father. The Duke of Edinburgh detected that Mrs Lightbody favoured his son over his daughter, indulging Charles's 'softness' while crushing Anne's 'spirit'. However, Mabel Anderson, a young Scotswoman, whose policeman father had been killed in the war during the German Blitz on Liverpool, stayed the course. She had no previous royal experience. Seeking employment, she simply placed an advertisement in a nursing journal and, to her amazement, shortly afterwards found herself being interviewed at Buckingham Palace by the heir to the throne. She gave the rest of her working life to the royal children, caring for Charles and Anne, and later for Prince Andrew and Prince Edward, and, finally, for Princess Anne's children, Peter and Zara Phillips.

When Charles was a little boy, Mabel was his nurse and nanny. When he was at home, she gave him comfort and cuddles; when he was despatched to boarding school she sent him Vosene for his dandruff and cheer-up messages for his morale. When he was an adult, she became his confidante and friend. He could pour his heart out to her, knowing she would listen to his troubles, but never betray him. She offered kindness, sympathy and common sense – and asked for nothing in return. When, eventually, she retired from royal service, she was given an apartment at Windsor, furnished and decorated to her taste at Charles's insistence and expense. One of his immediate family told me (in a sympathetic, not a sneering way): 'Charles has always needed a comforter. What he gets from Camilla is what he used to get from his nurse. He never got it from Diana.'

All his life, Charles has sought refuge from life's storms in 'the safe

[81] Both nurses were maiden ladies, but because Helen Lightbody was the more senior, she was given the courtesy title of 'Mrs'.

haven' provided by comforting, older women. His mistress, his grand-mother and his nurse are the prime examples, but there have been others. Dame Miriam Rothschild, the self-taught naturalist, was one. Kathleen Raine, the poet, was another. Rothschild and Raine were women of the same vintage, a little younger than Queen Elizabeth The Queen Mother. Both were born in 1908: Raine died in 2003, aged ninety-five; Rothschild died at the beginning of 2005, aged ninety-six. Each offered Charles friendship, understanding, encouragement and what he once called 'intellectual sympathy'. Dame Miriam was doubtless the cleverer of the two and, marginally, the more eccentric. A world authority on fleas, on butterflies, on pyrazines and chemical communication, she was nicknamed 'The Queen Bee' and, though she had little formal education and, she claimed, little academic ambition, she was so expert in so many fields that she gathered eight honorary doctorates, from Oxford in 1968 to Cambridge in 1999, and a fellow-ship of the Royal Society in between. On what would have been the eve of his wedding to Camilla, and turned out to be the eve of the funeral of Pope John Paul the Great, Charles made a point of attending the memorial gathering in her honour. The Prince and the naturalist had become friends in 1982 when she came to Highgrove to advise him on one of her specialities: how to plant and foster endangered wild flowers. Introduced by Lady Salisbury (another of the Prince's gardening gurus, another older woman of sense and sensibility), Charles and Miriam Rothschild remained friends and regular correspondents ever after.[82] 'She was an inspiration,' Charles said of her at the time of her death, 'and she seemed to understand instinctively what I was about.'

Charles felt closer still to Kathleen Raine. When she died, the *Guardian* described her as a 'singular poet who stood as a witness to spiritual values in an age that rejected them . . . a poet who believed in the sacred nature of all life, all true art and wisdom, and her own calling'. Charles was much taken with her philosophy and much comforted by her embrace. They met when Charles was still in his twenties. Raine said she thought at once, 'That poor young man – anything I can do for him, I will do, because he is very lonely.' In time,

[82] There is a striking photograph of her seated in the garden at Highgrove in *Highgrove: Portrait of an Estate* by HRH The Prince of Wales and Charles Clover. The authors remind us that it is Dame Miriam who discovered that the acceleration of a flea when jumping is twenty times that of a moon rocket re-entering the earth's atmosphere: 'The flea jumps off its knees, she explains, for if it jumped off its feet they would be shattered by the force.'

Charles repaid Raine for her devotion by giving his patronage (and practical assistance) to the Temenos Academy of Integral Studies, which she founded in London in 1990, as 'a university of wisdom'.[83] When Raine died in 2003, Charles spoke at her memorial service and his heartfelt eulogy was both personal and poignant to the point of self-parody:

> She was always there for me because above all she understood what I was about. That was of profound comfort in an age of growing misunderstanding and almost deliberate ignorance. . . She confessed she had never given the subject of the position I happen to occupy any thought until I came into her life. But her thought was not 'how wonderful to be royal' but 'that poor young man, he has the most difficult task in England'. . . She would remind me that 'you have a hard and wonderful part to play'. . . Her advice would come thick and fast: 'Dear, dear Prince, don't give that riff-raff an inch of ground, not a hair's breadth, stand firm on the holy ground of the heart. The only way to deal with the evil forces of their world is from a higher level, not to meet them on their own.' This was advice I concurred with wholeheartedly and still do . . . Letters would come winging their way after I had put my head above the parapet and, yet again the shells and bullets had been exploding all around me. 'Your chariot of fire between two armies,' she would write, 'is already guided by the divine charioteer. I cannot tell you how my heart rejoices that you have mounted that chariot. This is the great battle and where would you, our Prince, rather be than in that chariot? This is the great cosmic battle in which we are here to bear our parts.' You can perhaps imagine how re-moralising it was to receive such missives when, all around, the world seemed to become periodically

[83] 'Temenos' is the Greek word for the sacred area around a temple. Prince Charles's father is also interested in the relationship between nature, art and the spiritual. Unlike Charles, however, he makes a point of not talking too freely on such matters in public. When once I asked the Duke to talk on the record about things spiritual, he declined: 'If I start talking about religion, the press will say I'm barking.' We all know what happened when Charles admitted he sometimes communed with nature, talking to the flowers . . . However, Charles is unabashed. He remains patron of the Temenos Academy. On 28 April 2005, on its behalf, he hosted a reception and attended a concert given by Sir John Taverner. (It was a day when he gave time, too, to two of his other, controversial, causes: The Prince's Foundation for the Built Environment and The Prince of Wales's Foundation for Integrated Health. He also found time to meet up with a group of GPs recently returned from a teaching trip to India.)

madder and the powers of darkness – as Kathleen described them – closed in. She did her best to reawaken an Albion sunk in deadly sleep.

Kathleen Raine was a remarkable woman who led an interesting and complex life. When I met her, she was in her eighties and she rather surprised me by talking about sex and the undervalued power of what she called 'the erotic impulse'. She acknowledged that her own romantic life had been troubled (and troublesome)[84] and confessed, without embarrassment, that it was thrilling to have an intimate – though, of course, innocent – friendship and correspondence with a true prince. 'I'm an old woman,' she said, 'and he's a young man, and I just feel . . . what shall I say . . . protective?'

What Kathleen Raine felt about Charles when he was fifty-five, Catherine Peebles felt about him when he was five. Miss Peebles – known as 'Miss P' or 'Mispy' within the Royal Family – was Charles's governess.

At the outset of his education, Charles was instructed as his mother had been: privately, at home, by an intelligent young Scotswoman. The Queen's governess was Marion Crawford, known as 'Crawfie', who, having trained as a teacher in Edinburgh, joined the royal household in 1932 and stayed for sixteen years, supplying Princess Elizabeth – known within the family as 'Lilibet' – and her young sister, Margaret Rose, with their entire education, almost single-handed. Crawfie's self-created syllabus included Bible Study, History, Grammar, Arithmetic, Geography, Literature, Poetry, Writing and Composition (in the mornings), with Music, Drawing or Dancing after lunch, supplemented, over time, by lessons in constitutional history (for Lilibet) and, for both girls, by special classes in French, provided by a Mrs Montaudon-Smith (known as Monty), and, later still, in French Literature and European history, provided by a Belgian aristocrat, the Vicomtesse de Bellaigue (known as 'Toni': her Christian name was Antoinette). Lilibet's personal tutor in constitutional history was Sir Henry Marten, who was not given a diminutive because he was a man, in his sixties, and the

[84] Her first marriage, to Hugh Sykes Davies, failed; she then eloped with the founder of Mass Observation, Charles Madge; finally, she met the love of her life, the naturalist and author of *Ring of Bright Water*, Gavin Maxwell. He was homosexual. In one of her volumes of autobiography, *The Lion's Mouth* (1977), she describes how once, at his suggestion, they took off all their clothes and slept together, without sexual contact. 'Every night of my life since then,' she wrote, 'I have slept alone.'

vice-provost of Eton College. Marten described his royal pupil as 'a somewhat shy girl', who, when asked a question, 'would look for confidence and support to her beloved governess, Miss Crawford'.

A generation later, Charles could equally well be described as a somewhat shy boy who looked to his beloved governess for confidence and support. Mispy was Glasgow-born and experienced in the ways of young royals: her first charges had been Prince Michael and Princess Alexandra, the children of George VI's younger brother, the Duke of Kent. Charles, she found, was less robust than the Kents. She taught him reading and writing, a little history and geography, and a smattering of French, and she encouraged his early interest in drawing and music. She handled him with care, not so much because he was the heir apparent as because she recognised his fragility. 'He was very responsive to kindness,' she said, 'but if you raised your voice to him he would draw back into his shell and for a time you would be able to do nothing with him.'

His parents were understandably concerned to bring the little prince out of his shell. To that end, after three years of home tutoring, they determined to send him to school. 'The Queen and I,' said the boy's father at the time, 'want Charles to go to school with other boys of his generation and learn to live with other children, and to absorb from childhood the discipline imposed by education with others.' Charles was broken in, relatively gently, at a small London day school, whose motto, taken from Plutarch, will have appealed to the Duke of Edinburgh: 'A boy's mind is not a vessel to be filled, but a fire to be kindled.' Hill House, located in Hans Place, Knightsbridge, just behind Harrods and only a four-minute drive from Buckingham Palace, was a young school, with a bracing philosophy. Its founder, Colonel Henry Townend, an Oxford Blue at Association Football, president of the university athletic club, a gold medallist member of the British Empire team and winner of another gold medal for ski-running in Switzerland, was a firm believer in the competitive spirit:

> A sense of rivalry has to be encouraged and a boy must be led to discover something in which he can excel. He must be trained to react quickly in an emergency, have a good sense of balance and control, have the strength and ability to extract himself from a dangerous situation, and the urge to win.

When I met the Colonel (in the 1980s, looking for a school for my own son) I was impressed. Evidently, the Queen and the Duke of Edinburgh, meeting him thirty years earlier, were, too. The Duke, apparently, was particularly taken with the Colonel's no-nonsense approach, his commitment to team games and his belief in internationalism. The Colonel's visionary aim was to create a school where half the places would go to non-English children and, in time, one of the unique features of Hill House would be its double campus: one located behind Harrods, the other up a mountain in Switzerland.

For all his personal physical prowess, singleness of purpose and military background, Colonel Townend was, by most accounts, a kindly man, and the heir to the throne – the first ever to be educated at school – was given a friendly welcome by headmaster, staff and fellow pupils alike. From the moment of the Queen's accession in 1952, Charles had become Duke of Cornwall, Duke of Rothesay, Earl of Chester and of Carrick, Baron of Renfrew, Lord of the Isle, and Prince and Great Steward of Scotland. However, it was agreed that, at Hill House, the other boys should call him Charles and staff would address him as Prince Charles.[85] Each morning he was driven to school in a Palace Zephyr by a Palace chauffeur – accompanied by Mispy on his first day, but not thereafter. The headmaster's wife was always on parade to welcome him at the school's front door. But in every other respect the young Duke of Cornwall appears to have been treated as your average Hill House pupil – and he appears to have performed as one, too.

In 1968, with the Queen's blessing, Dermot Morrah revealed that Her Majesty 'judges her son to have been a slow developer'. Colonel Townend reported that Charles, aged eight, was good at writing, very good at reading, below form average at arithmetic ('Careful but slow – not very keen'), showed promise in French, had made a good start at Latin, showed a keen interest in Scripture and 'simply loves drawing and painting'. The headmaster also reported that the young prince had perfect manners, never asserted his rank and was never cheeky to staff. According to Morrah, Prince Charles's own memory is that he scarcely

[85] Discussing this issue of what to call the heir to the throne during his education, Dermot Morrah recalled the story told of Sir Herbert Warren, president of Magdalen College, Oxford, in conversation with the Japanese ambassador about the arrangements for the admission of the young son of the Mikado to the college. 'What is he called in his own country?' asked Warren. 'At home, it is etiquette to address him as the son of God,' explained the ambassador. 'That will cause no difficulty,' replied Warren. 'We are accustomed to the sons of important personages at Magdalen.'

realised he had any rank to assert: 'As to not being cheeky to the staff, he had before this been pretty heavily dropped on by his father for occasional thoughtless rudeness to Palace servants, and the lesson had no doubt sunk in.'

The Duchess of Cornwall only has fond and grateful memories of her father. 'He was wonderful when we were children,' she says. 'He's always been fantastic, a great support through everything.' Prince Charles, on the other hand, recalls being 'pretty heavily dropped on' by the Duke of Edinburgh on numerous occasions. At mealtimes, in front of guests, his father's banter regularly reduced the young Duke of Cornwall to silence and incipient tears. On one occasion, at the Braemar Highland Games, in front of a crowd of thousands, father publicly rebuked son for fidgeting. But there were good times, too . . .

In August 1957, while Camilla was in East Sussex, carrying off rosettes at a local Pony Club gymkhana, Charles joined his father on the Isle of Wight for the Cowes Yachting Week. As they returned from their first race on board the *Bluebottle*, Philip invited Charles to take the helm. Charles remembers the moment as 'exciting, satisfying'. He also remembers his first sensation of seasickness: 'Not at all pleasant.' But Cowes was good. And sailing up the coast to Balmoral was good, too. And Balmoral itself was 'wonderful'.[86] That summer, while Camilla was acquiring her first bra,[87] Charles was being kitted out in a new kilt – in the Rothesay tartan: large squares of hunting pink with smaller lime-green check and intervening lines of lime-green and white. (It was the tartan that trimmed the outfit and furnished the scarf for Camilla on her first public outings in Scotland in April 2005. Camilla loves the look of it. Apparently, it never appealed to Diana.)

For Charles, the summer of 1957 was a happy one. The autumn, however, was 'sheer hell'. Having survived a year as a day boy at Hill House – albeit with quite a few days away from school with colds,

---

[86] Balmoral has been a favourite royal retreat for 150 years. The estate – which was purchased by Prince Albert for Queen Victoria in 1851 – is owned and funded by the Queen personally (rather than as sovereign) and, between Balmoral, Birkhall and Glen Doll, comprises 18,659 hectares. The Queen and the Duke of Edinburgh honeymooned there, as did the Prince of Wales and the Duchess of Cornwall. If you would like to, you could, too. Her Majesty lets out a number of holiday cottages: for details see www.balmoralcastle.com.

[87] How do I know? A school friend of Camilla told me. She also told me that Camilla's 'first period was a doddle'.

coughs, influenza and tonsillitis[88] – Charles's parents decided that the boy was now ready to cope with the rigours of an English boarding school. The Queen, educated exclusively at home, and, though Head of State herself, brought up traditionally to accept the father as the natural head of the family, was content to be led by her husband in the matter of her own children's education. In September 1957, two months before his ninth birthday, Charles was despatched to his father's old prep school, Cheam – England's oldest preparatory school, founded in 1645 'for the sons of noblemen and gentry'.

The school had changed its location (from Surrey to Hampshire) since Philip had been a pupil a quarter of a century earlier, but the school's spirit remained the same. It was neatly encapsulated by the Duke of Edinburgh in his introduction to the official history of the school:

> Children may be indulged at home, but school is expected to be a spartan and disciplined experience in the process of developing into self-controlled, considerate and independent adults. The system may have eccentricities, but there can be little doubt that these are far outweighed by its values.

The eccentricities included the tradition, established by one of the nineteenth-century headmasters, of differentiating between the ranks of pupils by appellation. A boy who happened to be a peer of the realm was to be addressed by staff as 'my darling child'; the son of a peer was called 'my dear child'; a commoner was merely 'my child'. At Cheam, in 1957, however, the Duke of Cornwall, by command of the Queen, was to be addressed by the teachers as Prince Charles and by the other boys as Charles.

Her Majesty also wished it to be known that she expected the heir apparent to be treated 'in exactly the same way as other boys'. It was not easy when Charles's arrival at Cheam was front-page news; when the boy turned up, in a chauffeur-driven car, accompanied by the Head of State and her consort; when it was known that he was to have his personal detective on hand at all times, living in the school grounds. It was not easy, either, when the boy in question was so obviously different

---

[88] His tonsils were removed at the beginning of the summer term in an operation conducted at Buckingham Palace in the Buhl Room, the room where he was born. For a while, Charles kept the tonsils in a special jar and took them, as treasure, wherever he went.

from the other boys – not merely because of his position, but also because of his temperament. He was painfully shy. There were around a hundred other boys at the school, aged between eight and fourteen. He was nearly nine, but young for his age and quite unused to the hurly-burly of the playground. 'It was not easy to make large numbers of friends,' he recalled, many years later. 'I'm not a gregarious person so I've always had a horror of gangs . . . I have always preferred my own company or just a one to one.'

Charles remembers his first weeks at Cheam as the loneliest period of his life. 'He felt family separation very deeply,' said his nanny, Mabel Anderson. 'He dreaded going away to school.' His mother recalls that when the time came to leave Balmoral and set off for Cheam, 'he shuddered with apprehension'. He admits himself that for the first few weeks of term, at night he buried his head in his pillow and cried himself to sleep.

Cheam was not a cushy billet, but nor was it Dotheboys Hall. In Charles's day it was much as it had been in his father's, thirty years before: a traditional English prep school, complete with draughty corridors, austere dormitories, metal bedsteads, cold showers, wet runs, compulsory Latin, compulsory chapel, corporal punishment and compulsory games. Prince Philip appears to have thrived in this environment. Prince Charles struggled to survive. He did not enjoy the rugby. He was positioned in the second row of the scrum. 'There's nowhere worse,' he said. More than once, when the scrum collapsed, he had to endure the other boys' cries of 'Get off, fatty!'

He *was* a tad overweight – he was comfort eating – but when he was teased (or 'ragged' in prep school parlance) he did not cower or slink away: he hit back. As a result of these schoolboy tussles, he sometimes found himself in trouble. He was punished, as the other boys were, either by being confined in a classroom during 'free time' or sent into the grounds to do 'outdoor work'. On two occasions the headmaster felt obliged to administer 'six of the best'. According to Prince Charles, 'I am one of those people for whom corporal punishment actually worked . . . I didn't do it again.'

Inevitably, during five years at Cheam, the sun occasionally burst through the clouds. There was an English teacher he still remembers with affection, an inspiring pipe-smoking ex-Indian Army colonel. He was taught to memorise poetry and passages from Shakespeare – 'which in moments of stress or danger or misery . . . give enormous comfort and encouragement when you are older'. He took part in the school plays and found it easier to appear confident as someone else than as himself. There were consolations, too: as each week passed, there was one fewer week to go; he was allowed to bring his teddy bear to school as a comforter; and his great-uncle, Earl Mountbatten of Burma, arranged for him to have a subscription to the most popular adventure comic of the era, the *Eagle*. 'I like *Eagle* very much,' he told Lord Mountbatten. 'It's got such exciting stories.'[89]

Over time, at Cheam, Charles hit his stride. Eventually, he was made head boy. Overall, however, his recollection of his prep school is of an unsympathetic environment in which he felt mostly bleak and occasionally despairing. At the school itself, he tried to put on a brave face. At home, he left the women in his life – his mother, his grandmother, his nanny, his governess – in no doubt at all as to how unhappy he was. Even the Queen, the most circumspect of people, acknowledged to Dermot Morrah that her son's 'first few years at Cheam had been a misery to him'. And Her Majesty told Sir Martin Charteris (who told me) that she knew that of all the bad times Charles endured at his prep school, 'the worst moment' was one for which she was 'personally and entirely responsible'. It happened like this . . .

[89] Charles remained a devotee of the *Eagle* until he was fifteen. Before he became absorbed in the adventures of Dan Dare and the Green Mekon, his list of illustrated fictional heroes was headed by Babar the Elephant and Rupert Bear. In 1985, when Alfred Bestall, not the original but the most celebrated of the artists who drew Rupert, achieved his ninety-third birthday and was awarded the MBE, Charles sent him a charming message of congratulation – and thanks. 'As a child,' he said, 'I well remember your marvellous illustrations of Rupert Bear.'

Chapter Five

Two Worlds and Their Ways

'Time misspent in youth is sometimes all the freedom one ever has.'
Anita Brookner (b. 1938)

On Saturday 26 July 1958 Queen Elizabeth II had planned to perform the closing ceremony of the British Empire and Commonwealth Games in Cardiff, the capital city of Wales.[90] Due to an emergency sinus operation, Her Majesty was unable to attend and the Duke of Edinburgh, since 1957 a Prince of the United Kingdom,[91] deputised on her behalf.

---

[90] The story of the Games charts the decline of the British Empire. The concept originated with a clergyman, the Reverend Astley Cooper, who, in 1891, proposed a 'Pan-Britannic-Pan-Anglican Contest and Festival every four years'. The coronation of George V in 1911 prompted the Festival of Empire, which included a sporting element, but the first British Empire Games proper were held in Canada in 1930. From then until 1950, the parade of nations at the opening ceremony of the Games was led by a single flag-bearer carrying the Union Jack. In 1954, the Games were renamed the British Empire and Commonwealth Games. In 1970 they became the British Commonwealth Games, becoming the Commonwealth Games in 1978. The Royal Family have always been active supporters of the Games. Since 1958, there has been a relay of athletes carrying a baton bearing the Queen's Message of Greeting to the opening ceremony. The Games have been held once in Wales, and twice in England and Scotland. In 2006 they return to Australia for the fourth time. In 2010 they will be held in India for the first time and, according to the *New Delhi Times*, Charles and Camilla will be welcomed, 'possibly as King and Queen'.

[91] In 1947, the year of his marriage, Prince Philip of Greece became a British subject, taking his surname, Mountbatten, from his mother's side of the family. On his marriage, he was created a Royal Highness, made Duke of Edinburgh, Earl of Merioneth and Baron Greenwich of Greenwich. He had to wait ten years, however, before the Queen announced – at the end of an extensive Commonwealth tour undertaken by the Duke and in the wake of rumours about a 'rift' in their marriage – that, henceforward, her husband would 'carry the style and dignity of a prince of the United Kingdom'.

The occasion was broadcast live on television and, alerted by a telephone call from Martin Charteris, then assistant private secretary to the Queen, the headmaster of Cheam School invited a small band of boys, including Prince Charles, into his study to watch it on his television set. The head sat in his armchair; the boys, aged nine, ten and eleven, sat on the floor at his feet, or perched on the edge of the sofa. The small screen flickered into life. There was the stadium at Cardiff Arms Park, packed with a crowd of 36,000 spectators. There, on a podium, at the microphone, was Charles's father, making an announcement. The Queen, he explained, very much regretted that she could not be in Wales that day as she had an important message to relay to the people of Wales. However, said the Duke, Her Majesty had been able to record her message and it would be played over the loudspeakers now. In both the headmaster's study at Cheam and in the packed stadium in Cardiff, there was an expectant hush. The Queen's voice was high-pitched but unmistakable and crystal-clear. 'I want to take the opportunity of speaking to all Welsh people,' she said, 'not only in this arena, but wherever they may be. The British Empire and Commonwealth Games in the capital, together with all the festivities of the Festival of Wales, have made this a memorable year for the principality. I have therefore decided to mark it further by an act which will, I hope, give as much pleasure to all Welshmen as it does to me.'

What was coming next? The crowd sensed it was going to be something rather special. It was. The Queen continued: 'I intend to create my son Charles Prince of Wales today.' The stadium erupted. The cheering was long and loud and wildly enthusiastic – and then transformed into a heartfelt chorus of 'God bless the Prince of Wales'. The clamour was such that the Queen's voice was drowned. The tape was stopped. When the singing came to a finish, the tape was restarted and the Queen concluded her message: 'When he is grown up, I will present him to you at Caernarfon.' The cheering in the stadium started all over again.

In the headmaster's study at Cheam, there was cheering too – and applause. And a shout of 'Hip-hip-hooray!'. 'Congratulations,' said the headmaster. Charles said nothing. He sat there, cross-legged on the floor, face burning, mouth parched. He was appalled; bewildered; embarrassed – 'acutely embarrassed', he said later. 'All the others turned and looked at me in amazement,' he recalled – and he had no idea how to respond: what to do: what to say. He was nine and a half years old.

The Queen now regrets the sudden – and remote – way in which she broke the good news to her young son. It was good news as far as she was concerned. The Queen believes in what she does and values the customs and traditions of the British monarchy. Since the beginning of the fourteenth century English sovereigns have been granting to their eldest sons the title Prince of Wales. The title is not automatically assumed by the heir to the throne at birth and not every British monarch has been a Prince of Wales. It is entirely in the gift of the sovereign: Queen Victoria made her son Prince of Wales only a month after his birth. Elizabeth II waited until Charles was rising ten.

The title came to the English Crown in the old-fashioned way, by right of conquest, more than seven hundred years ago, when Edward Longshanks, Edward I,[92] crushed the forces led by Llywelyn ap Gruffydd, the only native-born prince to bear undisputedly the title Prince of Wales. The legend has it that, with Llywelyn defeated (and dismembered: his head then displayed on the sharp end of a pole), the victorious English King summoned the broken Welsh barons to meet him at Caernarfon Castle and there lifted their spirits and restored their morale by promising them a new Prince of Wales – one born in Wales who could speak no English. As the Welsh barons cheered, Edward produced his infant son, Edward of Caernarfon, who had been born in Wales and, indeed, spoke not a word of English – nor of any other language.[93] It is only a story. Edward of Caernarfon was already seventeen when his father created him Prince of Wales in 1301, some years after the defeat of the Welsh. Since Edward of Caernarfon, there have been twenty Princes of Wales and, in different ways at different times, every one of them has proved something of a trial to his parents.[94]

[92] Edward I, known as Longshanks (1239–1307), vanquisher of the Welsh and 'Hammer of the Scots' was a formidable fighter and a remarkable king who believed in the rule of law and established the beginnings of parliament as we know it. It was said that his son was his one great failure.

[93] Edward II (1284–1327) was an unfortunate man, affable but incompetent, who came to an unpleasant end – murdered at Berkeley Castle (by means of a red-hot poker) shortly after his enforced abdication. He had four children by his child-bride, Isabella of France, but preferred the company of his homosexual lover, Piers Gaveston, who also came to a sticky end – run through with swords and decapitated. Edward gave Gaveston many of the jewels Isabella had brought to England as part of her dowry, and, intriguingly (given the title by which the present Princess of Wales is known), ennobled his lover as the Earl of Cornwall.

[94] For a concise and entertaining account of their lives I recommend *The Princes of Wales* by Wynford Vaughan-Thomas. Vaughan-Thomas, a celebrated Welshman and

On 26 July 1958, Prince Charles, Duke of Cornwall, became Prince of Wales. He also became a Knight Companion of the Most Noble Order of the Garter, the most senior and the oldest British order of chivalry, founded by Edward III in 1348, of which the sovereign and the Prince of Wales are the only *ex officio* members.[95] Charles said later (in 1969, aged twenty, in his first-ever radio interview,[96] in the run-up to his one term at the University College of Wales at Aberystwyth and his investiture as Prince of Wales at Caernarfon), 'I think for a little boy of nine it was bewildering . . . And it perhaps didn't mean all that much then; only later on, as I grew older, did it become apparent what it meant.' Some years later still, at the beginning of the 1990s, he told a member of his family (who told me) that it really was from the day of the Queen's recorded announcement at Cardiff Arms Park that he sensed his childhood was ending and

distinguished war correspondent, told me when I met him that nothing in his career rivalled the start of it. In 1936, 'the year of the three kings', he joined the BBC and was sent to interview the former prime minister David Lloyd George. 'I found him in his hotel room, in his pyjamas, sitting in bed between two topless tarts. That's how I interviewed him. My next big assignment was the coronation of George VI. Those were the days.'

[95] Tradition has it that the Order's emblem and motto were inspired by an incident that occurred when young Edward III, fresh from his triumph against the French at Crécy and celebrating the capture of Calais, danced at court with Joan, Countess of Salisbury. The lady's garter fell to the floor: the King retrieved it and tied it to his own leg. Courtiers watching the scene laughed, only to be admonished by the monarch with the words, '*Honi soit qui mal y pense*' – 'Shame on him who thinks evil of this'. (Historians, however, reckon the Order's emblem was inspired by the strap used to attach pieces of armour, and that the motto referred to critics of Edward's claim to the throne of France.)

Legend gives Edward III's son, Edward of Woodstock, later known as the Black Prince, credit for acquiring the Prince of Wales's crest and motto at the Battle of Crécy. The blind King of Bohemia had insisted on being taken on to the field of battle and, not surprisingly, was swiftly slain. The Black Prince picked up the three ostrich feathers that had adorned the late King's helmet and appropriated them, along with his motto, '*Ich dien*': 'I serve'. Unfortunately, contemporary accounts of the battle make no mention of this incident and it is now thought that the motto originated with the family of his mother, Philippa of Hainault, in Flanders.

[96] It was given to Jack de Manio, a great broadcaster and delightful companion, famous for his rich voice, avuncular manner and inability to read the time correctly when presenting the BBC's *Today* programme. His work was done by 9.00 a.m. which is when he started drinking. I know because I went to several pubs near Broadcasting House with him in the early 1970s – pubs which, officially closed until 11.00 a.m., admitted the great broadcaster whenever he turned up.

what he called 'the awful truth' about his destiny began to dawn on him.

Charles's adolescence was not easy. Camilla's, by contrast, was what one of her contemporaries calls 'a doddle'. 'She must have had the usual ups and downs, teenage mood swings and what-have-you, but if she did, they didn't show. She really was very easy-going, very happy go-lucky, didn't seem fazed or troubled by anything.' Her pop-singing classmate, Lynn Ripley, said, 'I always thought she was the coolest girl in the school.' 'Cool', 'laid-back', 'easy-going', 'comfortable', 'confident' – these are words that never crop up when discussing Charles's childhood with his family or friends. In the case of young Camilla, those who remember her, and are willing to talk, talk of her only in these terms. Her childhood friend Broderick Munro Wilson (who has an engagingly fruity voice to match his name) attributes Camilla's youthful confidence and equanimity to her experience of horses and the quality of her parenting. 'There is a certain boldness required to riding, hunting and jumping,' he says, 'and that shone through with Camilla.' Munro Wilson, who recalls happy days with the local hunt being welcomed at The Laines, is a particular admirer of Camilla's father, Major Shand, 'a classic cavalryman, slim and imperial', and reports the major's verdict on how his children fared in adolescence: 'I don't think we had any more problems than anyone else. They've always been quite chatty. There haven't been any inhibitions in their upbringing that I know of.'

Charles was riddled with inhibitions. He was infinitely courteous, precociously so. He was carefully groomed, as a boy devoted to his nanny might be. (Look at the pictures of him as a youngster: the immaculate socks, the polished sandals, the crease-free shorts: the heart weeps.) He was painfully shy: he was the put-upon son of a hectoring father. He was awkwardly self-conscious; he was world-famous; he had his own detective; his mother was the Queen; but he did not feel special in any way at all. He felt, he says, 'embarrassed, quite often, by myself, by my position'. And by his appearance. He was not at all happy with his sticking-out ears.

During his adolescence, Charles's ears became an issue. (To an extent they still are: cartoonists take one or two features in the face of a public figure and exaggerate them. That's the way they work; in Charles's case they take his ears.) He had his tonsils out, and his appendix removed: should he have his ears pinned back? His great-uncle, Lord Mountbatten, felt he should. 'If you've got a problem and you can fix it, fix it,' was his pragmatic attitude. '"Pin back yer lugholes",' said Uncle Dickie, quoting one of the catchphrases of an entertainer of the day, Cyril Fletcher. 'You can't possibly be King with ears like that.' In 2005, Mountbatten's daughter Patricia told me, 'My father kept telling the Queen she should get Charles's ears fixed. They do look a lot better now. I don't know if anything was done. Perhaps it was. I must ask.' (I have. Nothing was done. As Charles grew older his ears simply appeared less protuberant. He is ready to laugh about them now. As a child, his self-consciousness over them frequently reduced him to tears.)

As a boy, Charles, though shy, was adept at making polite conversation with adults. He did not find joshing with his contemporaries so easy. He was not one for joining 'gangs' at school: he never liked bantering with groups. He was more than comfortable, however, in the company of his younger, tomboy, sister, Anne. It is clear from his letters home that he adored her. He admired her spirit, energy, sense of fun and courage.[97] He envied her easy way with their parents. He also 'simply adored' (his phrase) his baby brothers when they came along.

On the day Prince Andrew was born (19 February 1960) Charles was at Cheam, appearing in the school play, a Plantagenet drama written by one of the masters. Charles played Richard Crookback, Duke of Gloucester, and coped well with the sniggering that greeted the line, 'And soon may I ascend the throne . . .'[98] He was less happy at the end of the performance when the headmaster came on stage to announce to one and all that the Queen had given birth and that the Prince of Wales (that night's Duke of Gloucester) now had a younger brother (destined to be the Duke of York). As soon as Charles saw his baby brother, he was smitten. Like his father, Charles is very good with

[97] His admiration reached its apogee in March 1974, four months after Anne's marriage to Captain Mark Phillips when the princess and her husband were being driven along the Mall on their way back to Buckingham Palace after a charity film show. An armed man yanked open their car door and attempted to abduct the princess. Shots were fired. The assailant pulled Anne frantically by one arm while she held tight to her husband with the other. Eventually, police arrived in sufficient numbers to subdue the attacker. 'Her bravery and superb obstinacy were unbelievable,' Prince Charles recorded in his diary when he heard about the incident. 'My admiration for such a sister knows no bounds!' Today, brother and sister are still good friends, but the relationship is not as easy and intimate as once it was. I believe she has criticised Charles for 'self-indulgence' over the years, and he has been hurt by what he has called 'her lack of sympathy'.
[98] 'Prince Charles played the traditional Gloucester with confidence and depth: he has a good voice and excellent elocution, and very well conveyed the ambition and bitterness of the twisted hunchback.' *Cheam School Chronicle*, 1960.

babies. When Prince Edward arrived (10 March 1964) he was delighted
by him, too. Indeed, in the school holidays, by his own account, Charles
spent 'hours and hours' in the royal nursery playing with his younger
brothers. It was for them, in the summer of 1969, when he was twenty
and they were nine and five, that he wrote his children's story, *The Old
Man of Lochnagar*.[99]

As a schoolboy, Charles's relationship with his younger siblings was
affectionate and uncomplicated. His relationship with his contemporaries at school was less easy, not only because of Charles's diffidence,
but also because the other boys treated him differently. Some 'sucked
up'; others kept their distance; no one was entirely normal in their
behaviour towards him. And outside his family, of course, his relationship with members of the opposite sex was virtually non-existent.

Again, it was all very different in the adolescent world of Camilla
Shand. Camilla had younger siblings, too: a sister, Annabel, born in
1949, and a brother, Mark, born in 1951. The trio were close to one
another and fond of one another, and have remained so. 'None of us
has ever broken ranks,' said their mother, when invited to comment on
her elder daughter's alleged relationship with the Prince of Wales. As a
clan, the Shands are close and loyal. Annabel was marginally more
academic than Camilla, less bouncy as a child, more grounded as an
adult. Her one marriage, in 1972, aged twenty-three, to a Dorset
landowner, Simon Elliott, the son of an air marshal, has been sustained
and successful. She has been wife, mother (two daughters, one son: all
still on speaking terms), businesswoman (running her own antiques
emporium) and, from start to finish, through thick and thin, Camilla's
best friend. She joined the Duchess of Cornwall and her new husband
on their honeymoon: as we shall see, she was a pivotal figure at several

---

[99] Published in 1980, with charming illustrations by Sir Hugh Casson. According to
Jonathan Dimbleby, when, in the 1970s, encouraged by Laurens van der Post, Charles
began to study the writings of Carl Jung, recording his own dreams, he 'explored the
belief that dreams bring to the surface "the archaic knowledge" that a child carries into
the world with him, and which is inherited from his ancestors. He discovered the idea
of the "collective unconscious", that pool of ideas and images which humanity inherits
from other minds remote in time and culture. Contemplating the notion of the "Wise
Old Man", an archetypal figure representing that "superior insight" which Jung
discovered within himself, the Prince was encouraged by van der Post to believe that
this "guru" was, in his case, represented by the Old Man of Lochnagar – the mythical
figure created by the Prince who inhabited the mountains at Balmoral . . .' It was this
sort of 'mumbo-jumbo' (her phrase, not mine) that made Anne begin to feel that she
and her older brother were no longer on the same wavelength as once they had been.

of the key moments of the 'war of the Waleses' and its aftermath. Mark Shand – man about town turned travel writer and conservationist (of whose adventures, more anon) – 'absolutely adores' both his sisters, 'always did', though he admits, when he was eight, he wanted to murder one of them: 'She was everybody's favourite. She could do no wrong – and, when she did, I was blamed.' He says he 'loathed her with an obsessive passion' and recalls the night he determined to do her in: 'At midnight I wobbled naked along the moonlit passage to my sister's room and slowly pushed open the door. She was lying in her bed like a giant blancmange, mouth wide open.' Which sister was it? He won't say, of course. It is the code of the Shands: 'None of us has ever broken ranks.'

In Charles's young life, there were not many opportunities to meet girls and, because his movements were circumscribed and his circle was limited, even had he wished to, creating opportunities would not have been easy. For Camilla, it was different: there were boys in East Sussex: there were boys in South Kensington: and, as she was not heir to the throne, no invisible moat around her keeping potential admirers – or, even, straightforward friends – at bay. According to one of her Queen's Gate contemporaries, Carolyn Benson, who is still a friend: 'Camilla was funny and bright; boys loved her. Even when she was too young for them to have a sexual interest in her, Camilla always had lots of boy friends. She could talk to boys about things which interested them. She was never a girl's girl. She was always a boy's girl.' (Yes, this is what chaps like in a girl: someone who talks to them about them and their interests, their worries, their wonderful achievements, their exhausting day . . .) According to Carolyn Benson, Camilla wasn't particularly clothes-conscious, 'but she always exuded a sexy confidence over men. She was quite a flirt, she liked men . . . Camilla was always the one who made friends with boys first . . .'

Young Camilla made friends and impressed the boys. 'She was into boys much quicker than other girls of her age,' according to Broderick Munro Wilson. 'There was this daredevil element in her. She would make the running.' By every account, Camilla relished her adolescent years. Charles, meanwhile, struggled through his. He certainly did not relish Gordonstoun.

After five years following in his father's footsteps at Cheam, Charles, aged thirteen, continued along the same rocky path when he moved on to the next of his father's *alma maters*, the most celebrated: Gordonstoun School, on the Moray Firth, in Scotland. The school had been founded, in 1934, by a remarkable man: Kurt Hahn, a pioneering educationist and a refugee from Nazi Germany.[100] Hahn – not only Jewish, but also an outspoken critic of Hitler – had been arrested by the Nazis in March 1933. Later released, he fled to Britain, ending up in Morayshire, where he founded his famous school, at Gordonstoun House, in a location close to the sea and mountains, where the wind and weather were appropriate to his challenging educational philosophy. Hahn believed that young people were 'surrounded by a sick civilisation . . . in danger of being affected by a fivefold decay: the decay of fitness, the decay of initiative and enterprise, the decay of care and skill, the decay of self-discipline, the decay of compassion'. At Gordonstoun – where Prince Philip arrived in the autumn of 1934 and Charles followed him in the summer of 1962 – the regime was designed to tackle this decay.

It did so with vigour. The four hundred boys, regardless of size, age or weather conditions, wore shorts at all times. Each day began with a brisk run in the grounds followed by hot and cold showers and ended in 'pale-green dormitories' with 'crude wooden beds' where the windows were 'kept open throughout the night, which meant that those closest to them were likely to wake up with blankets rain-soaked or, in winter, covered with a light sprinkling of snow'. For Charles, the nights were always the worst part. In his sixth term, aged fifteen, he wrote home:

> I don't get any sleep practically at all nowadays . . . The people in my dormitory are foul. Goodness they are horrid. I don't know how anybody could be so foul. They throw slippers all night long or hit me with pillows or rush across the room and hit me as hard as they can, then beetle back again as fast as they can, waking everyone else in the dormitory at the same time. Last night was hell, literal hell . . . I still wish I could come home. It's such a HOLE this place!

Prince Philip had loved Gordonstoun. Prince Charles hated it. Philip, of course, though a prince, was only a Greek one. He was less

---

[100] Hahn (1886–1974) had been secretary and friend to Prince Max of Baden, former Chancellor of the German Empire, whose son Berthold had married Prince Philip's sister, Theodora, in 1931. In the 1920s Hahn and Max of Baden had founded a pioneering school together, based at the Baden family home, Schloss Salem, on the shores of Lake Constance, and designed as much to build the characters of its students as to educate them. Prince Max said of the school: 'I am proud of the fact that there is nothing original here. We have cribbed from everywhere, from the public schools, from Goethe, from Plato, from the Boy Scouts.'

conspicuous than Charles: he was not heir to the throne. As a teenager, Philip was also tall, outstandingly good-looking, remarkably self-assured and noticeably fit. Charles was none of these things. Indeed, it was on the rugger field that he suffered the worst of the bullying. In the scrum, his peers bashed him as hard as they could; and on the wing, when he got hold of the ball, they felled him, laying into him with boots and knees, elbows and fists. William Boyd, the novelist, and a school contemporary of Charles's, recalled hearing the triumphant cry: 'We did him over. We just punched the future King of England.'

Boyd's account of Gordonstoun in the 1960s, written with 'retro-spective revulsion' in 1985, makes grim reading. It depicts a 'reign of terror', with gangs of older boys 'beating up smaller boys', 'extorting food and money' from them. Ross Benson, another of Charles's contemporaries who also became a writer, as well as recalling the open dormitory windows that let in the rain and snow at night remembered how new boys were welcomed to the school. Some were trussed up in 'wicker laundry baskets and left under the cold shower, sometimes for hours'; others had a pair of pliers taken to their arms and twisted 'until the flesh tore open'. Charles, apparently, was spared these particular initiation rituals. He was, however, alternately, physically chastised and completely ignored – with those who did try to befriend him being accused of 'sucking up' to royalty and derided with loud, mocking slurping sounds. According to Benson, Charles was bullied 'maliciously, cruelly and without respite'. Gordonstoun was an unkind place: 'He was crushingly lonely for most of his time there.'

In 2005, I raised all this with Peter Paice who was 'Guardian' (the Gordonstoun equivalent of head boy) in 1962, the year that Charles arrived, and was detailed to keep a special eye on the young prince. Paice – whom I know well and trust[101] – says that the Boyd and Benson accounts do not tally with his own recollection of the school. 'I was a very sensitive boy when I arrived at Gordonstoun,' he says. 'I came from a prep school where there had been bullying. I didn't find it at Gordonstoun. I really didn't. In fact, the school's ethos was actively anti-bullying. I absolutely loved the school. I know Charles didn't. He told me so again the other day when I happened to meet him. I remember he was a bit shy, and perhaps a bit of a loner, but I never saw him being bullied. To be honest, I frequently saw him looking quite

---

[101] I have known him since I was a baby and he was a toddler. His father was my godfather.

happy. He enjoyed a lot that the school had to offer – the sailing, the music, the drama. I think he got into art and pottery at the school. I know he loved the countryside, the setting. Yes, there were runs and hot and cold showers, but it wasn't that bad. And we did keep a look-out for him. You had to. I remember the day we found two photographers up a tree trying to take pictures of him on the morning run. I worked alongside Donald Green, his detective, who lived in Windmill Lodge [Charles's school house]. He was 6′ 4″ like me, but powerful, well-built. He knew what he was doing. He was a great guy, assimilated himself into school life, got on well with everybody, loved the cricket, and did his best for Charles, I know.'

Donald Green was involved in the most notorious incident of Charles's school career – the 'cherry brandy' affair. In retrospect, it seems wholly ludicrous. At the time, says Charles, 'I thought it was the end of the world.' Here is Jonathan Dimbleby's authorised account of exactly what occurred:

> In his second year, [Charles] became a member of the crew of the *Pinta*, one of Gordonstoun's two ketches. On his first expedition in June 1963, he sailed into Stornoway Harbour on the Isle of Lewis. He and four other boys were given shore leave, to have supper and then see a film. His private detective, Donald Green, was with them.
>
> As they walked towards the Crown Hotel, they attracted a small crowd. By the time they were in the lounge, the onlookers had gathered round the window. Cameras began to flash. Hopelessly self-conscious and embarrassed by the attention, the Prince retreated 'desperately trying to look for somewhere else to go'. Followed by Donald Green, he walked straight into the public bar. 'I thought "My God! What do I do?" I looked around and everybody was looking at me. And I thought, "I must have a drink – that's what you are supposed to do in a bar." I went and sat down at the bar and the barman said, "What do you want to drink?" I thought that you had to have alcohol in a bar, so I said, "Cherry brandy". At that moment a journalist walked in . . .'

The journalist – 'that dreadful woman' as Charles later termed her – could not resist the story. Nor could the *Daily Mirror*. It was front-page news. Soon it was news around the world. At first, Buckingham Palace denied the story. Then they admitted it. Finally, Donald Green lost his job. The Metropolitan Police suspended him from royal duties. 'I have never been able to forgive them for doing that,' the Prince said later, 'because he defended me in the most marvellous way and he was the most wonderful, loyal, splendid man.' Charles was punished too – also with a demotion. He was deprived of his membership of the school's 'Junior Training Plan'. He said he would rather have been beaten.

He was accustomed to being beaten, of course – not by the masters, but by the boys. Whenever he could he retreated to the sick bay. 'I've been in bed for the last week,' he wrote home, 'suffering from a cold or 'flu, I'm not sure, but I came out on Thursday morning worst luck! It was much nicer in bed. I hardly get any sleep at the House [Windmill Lodge] because I snore and get hit on the head the whole time. It's absolute hell.'

'It's near Balmoral,' his father told him. 'There's always the Factor there [the estate manager]. You can go and stay with him. And your grandmother goes up there to fish. You can go and see her.' And he did, whenever he could. Queen Elizabeth The Queen Mother was a loving grandmother who always gave her favourite grandson an understanding shoulder to cry on and a warm bosom to embrace. She also told him stories of his grandfather and great-grandfather, George VI and George V, and of life at court before the war. She encouraged his interest in 'the beautiful things of life' (her phrase), in painting and sculpture, in music especially. She kindled in him his yearning for Italy. Charles adored his grandmother. His distress at her death, in 2002, was pitiful to behold. He was bereft. 'She was quite simply the most magical grandmother you could possibly have and I was utterly devoted to her,' he said. 'For me, she meant everything, and I have dreaded, dreaded this moment.'

Forty years earlier, what he dreaded most in life was having to go back to school. He complained in one letter home, 'Papa rushed me so much on Monday when I had to go, that I hardly had time to say goodbye to Mabel and June properly.' He wanted to be back with Mabel Anderson, his old nanny, and her assistant, June Waller, cocooned in the nursery, playing with little Prince Andrew. He missed his governess, too. 'It's a pity I can't have lessons at home again with Miss P,' he wrote. 'Oh dear! It's Monday tomorrow. However one Monday more means one less, there are only six and a half weeks now. I hope it goes quickly . . .'

When asked how Prince Charles was getting on at Gordonstoun, Prince Philip replied, 'Well, at least he hasn't run away yet.' In fact, he stayed the course and did rather well. Peter Paice is right: Charles enjoyed the setting, the sailing, the art, the music, the drama. And he valued the encouragement he was given by a number of his teachers. To this day, Charles acknowledges his debt to Robert Waddell, the Gordonstoun art master, who introduced him to the craft of pottery, and Eric Anderson, a young English teacher, who was at Gordonstoun for just two years and whose speciality was directing the school plays.[102] In 1964, Anderson cast Charles as Exeter in *Henry V*. The following year, he went for broke and cast the Prince of Wales as the thane who would be King of Scotland.

Macbeth, of course, is set, in part, at Glamis Castle, the ancestral home of Charles's beloved grandmother's paternal family, the Strathmores. One of the play's opening lines is, 'All hail, Macbeth, that shalt be King hereafter!'. The line got a titter, inevitably, but Charles's own performance was well received in every quarter – bar one.

Beforehand he was nervous, understandably. 'Tomorrow is the first performance,' he wrote at the time, 'and Mummy and Papa are coming to see the third one on Saturday night . . . I shall see them on Saturday and Sunday which is marvellous. I do hope they'll enjoy it . . . I shall be quaking in my boots before I go on stage tomorrow at 8 o'clock.'

To this day, Charles recalls the evening when his father came to Gordonstoun to see his son play the title role in *Macbeth* – and laughed. Charles recollects the mortifying moment vividly: 'I had to lie on a huge, fur rug and have a nightmare. My parents came and watched, along with other parents. I lay there and thrashed about and all I could hear was my father and "ha, ha, ha." I went up to him afterwards and said, "Why did you laugh?" and he said, "It sounds like The Goons."'

In due course, Charles pleased his father, and surprised both his parents, by being chosen as the school 'Guardian' – as Philip had

[102] At Fettes College, where he also taught, Anderson (b. 1936) cast the future prime minister, Tony Blair, as Mark Antony in *Julius Caesar*. He went on to become headmaster of Eton – where Princes William and Harry would go to school – and rector of Lincoln College, Oxford. He remains a friend and adviser to Prince Charles and, in the early 1990s, was instrumental in triggering The Prince of Wales Shakespeare School, a summer school for English and drama teachers, formed as part of Charles's campaign to guarantee Shakespeare's place in the national curriculum.

been before him and Prince Edward would be in his day.[103] And, academically, Charles did not do too badly either, achieving five GCE O levels (in French, History, Latin, English Language and English Literature: Maths and Physics were the two that got away), followed by two A levels (Grade B in History, Grade C in French), and becoming the first heir to the throne in British history to secure a university place on the strength of academic credentials alone.

Charles claims not to have enjoyed his five years at Gordonstoun, but they were formative years, nonetheless. He follows a hot bath with a cold shower to this day; he says the school helped develop his 'will-power'; he acknowledges that it also fostered self-discipline, 'not in the sense of making you bath in cold water, but in the Latin sense, of giving shape and form to your life'. The philosophy of Kurt Hahn that helped form Prince Philip helped form Prince Charles, too. The values that inspired Prince Philip's pet causes, such the Duke of Edinburgh Award Scheme and the Outward Bound Trust – self-reliance, fitness, forti-tude, skill, enterprise, endeavour – are not dissimilar from those that underpin the work of the Prince's Trust.

Sex, apparently, did not play a large part in the lives of the boys at Gordonstoun. As one of Charles's contemporaries put it, 'Sex wasn't so much frowned upon as sweated out of you.' It was Kurt Hahn's policy 'to kindle on the threshold of puberty non-poisonous passions which act as guardians during the dangerous years'. According to Adam Arnold-Brown, author of *Unfolding Character: The Impact of Gordonstoun* (1962), who was at the school when Prince Philip was Guardian, 'The tone of the school was manly and clean . . . we were forbidden to smoke; dirty talk and actions were taboo.' According to Peter Paice, when Charles arrived, the 'tone' had not much changed. According to William Boyd, however, Gordonstoun in the 1960s was awash with foul language 'of the vilest and coarsest sort' and local girls and the school kitchen maids were subjected to the indignities of 'male lust at its most dog-like and contemptuous'. Pornography and cigarettes were officially banned, but readily

---

[103] Prince Andrew, who also attended the school, missed out on the top job. Because Gordonstoun was not yet coeducational, Princess Anne was sent to Benenden, the girls' public school in Kent, where she was made captain of her house. In the fullness of time, she sent both her children to Gordonstoun. The Brabournes sent all of their children – five sons and two daughters – to the school. 'I'm not sure they enjoyed it all that much,' Lord Brabourne told me, 'but I'd been miserable at Eton. I didn't like the way Eton turned out what you might call "superior" boys.'

available. Prince Charles, by every account, did not take advantage of either.

While the adolescent Milla Shand was 'beginning to score' – 'only kissing', according to a Queen's Gate classmate, 'but quite serious kissing' – and regularly clambering on to the school roof for 'an illicit lunchtime fag', Charles was thinking about God rather than girls and deploring the smutty talk enjoyed by too many of his contemporaries. 'The language people use is horrid,' he complained. 'I think it is probably because they're too lazy to use anything else.' Aged sixteen, he was confirmed: he was serious about his Christian commitment.[104] Aged eighteen, in his last term at Gordonstoun, he was filled 'with horror' by the prospect of having to organise the school dance: 'The idea is so awful as thirty girls are being transported from an Aberdeen school to provide material . . .' In the event, the night passed off without untoward incident. 'Nothing ghastly happened,' Charles reported, 'and I wasn't head-hunted!'

When Camilla left Queen's Gate, in the summer of 1964, she was sent abroad, as 'gels' of her class and generation often were, to be given 'a bit of polish' at a finishing school in Switzerland. Camilla recalls having 'a lot of fun' at the nicely named Mon Fertile, where quality 'finish' was available in abundance. On the banks of Lake Geneva, Camilla and the other girls (mostly English, some American) were instructed in the virtues of good posture and a well-considered table-plan. (Mock not: how you come into a room, and how you stand, affects how you feel about yourself and how others feel about you; and I am told by those who know that the success of a dinner party depends as much on the quality of the *placements* as the texture of the soufflé.) There were classes, also, in French conversation, wine-tasting, needle-work, first aid, child care and domestic accounting. Mon Fertile prepared its young charges thoroughly for the adult lives they had in

---

[104] The confirmation took place in the royal chapel at Windsor and was conducted by the Archbishop of Canterbury. It was a significant moment for Charles and for his mother, Supreme Governor of the Church of England, whose faith is the foundation of her life. The Duke of Edinburgh attended, but disconcerted the Archbishop by quietly reading a book (that did not appear to be the Book of Common Prayer) throughout the service. As those who were at St George's Chapel, Windsor, on 9 April 2005, forty-one years after Charles's confirmation, can testify, Prince Philip has the knack, when he chooses, of being 'present' and 'absent' at the same time. The Duke was thoroughly genial on Prince Charles's second wedding day – as he had been on his first – but, on each occasion, nobody quite knew what he was thinking.

prospect – as hostesses, wives and mothers. These were well-heeled girls and expected to remain so: they were taught how to find their way around a menu and (in the winter term) how to negotiate the ski slopes at Gstaad.

When Camilla's younger sister, Annabel, left school, she followed the example of her notorious great-aunt, Violet Trefusis, and her celebrated great-grandmother, Alice Keppel, and travelled to Florence to learn about fine art. When Camilla had completed her course at Mon Fertile, she followed in the footsteps of her reprobate grandfather, P. Morton Shand, and went to Paris for a term. According to the Clarence House website, Her Royal Highness 'studied at the Institut Britannique in Paris'. According to Camilla, she had 'a great time', but her recollection of precisely what she studied is hazy. One of her contemporaries told me, 'She wasn't academic. She was a fun girl having a fun time. Growing up fast – but not too fast. We were all virgins.'

Today, according to health department statistics in the United Kingdom and the USA, most young people begin having sex in their mid-to-late teens, about eight years before they marry. Nowadays, more than 80 per cent of young people will have had sex before they leave their teens; and more than half of all seventeen-year-old girls have lost their virginity. Forty years ago, it was a different world. In the mid-1960s, wholesome girls might risk what was called 'heavy petting', but, as a rule, drew the line at intercourse. In 1964, when a sixth-form boy at my school published an article in a student magazine posing the question 'Is chastity outmoded?', the kerfuffle went on for weeks. Virginity was still a prized commodity – especially for girls. Even as late as 1969, Camilla's school friend, the pop singer Twinkle, could write a song lamenting the loss of a boyfriend who abandoned her because she would not have sex with him unless they were married: 'It was a woman that he wanted, not a lady.'[105]

[105] It was 'Darby and Joan', the B side of Twinkle's last notable single, 'Micky'. By 1969, pop songs were beginning to reflect the changing mores of the time. Rolf Harris could still make it to Number 1 with a squeaky-clean Christmas hit like 'Two Little Boys', but the coming morality was perhaps better represented by 'The Ballad Of John And Yoko', the Rolling Stones' 'Honky Tonk Women', and Jane Birkin and Serge Gainsbourg's heavy-breathing classic, 'Je t'aime . . . moi non plus', Number 1 in October 1969, denounced by the Vatican and banned by the BBC. 'Where will it end?' asked Mary Whitehouse of the National Viewers' and Listeners' Association. Thirty-five years later, we can tell her. In 2003, in a survey undertaken in the UK, the USA and Australia, 83 per cent of the episodes of the top twenty television programmes viewed

When she returned from her year in Switzerland and France, Camilla was still a lady – just. 'She had fun,' says one contemporary. 'She liked boys and they liked her.' Her looks had improved, too. As a young teenager, there had been something of the tomboy in her manner and appearance. By the time she had reached her eighteenth year, she had lost the puppy fat in her face to reveal quite striking cheekbones. She dressed well – not as a child of the sixties in the Twinkle mode (no kaftans, thank you), but as a Kensington girl whose mother had accounts at Harrods, Peter Jones and Harvey Nichols. She had an English look that was pleasing, not spectacular: mousey light brown hair, bright eyes, teeth unimproved by orthodontics, smiley face, good figure. The *Sunday Telegraph* columnist Rebecca Tyrrel, in her lively portrait of the young Camilla, says 'she was a posh and horsey girl with big breasts and thank goodness for them'. Tyrrel then quotes Camilla's childhood friend (and sometime dance partner) Broderick Munro Wilson: 'All our generation are breast men. I can't go out with a flat-chested girl.'

In 1993, at the time of the publication of the so-called 'Camillagate' tape, I was a member of parliament and I recall sitting in the Members tea-room at the House of Commons discussing Charles and Camilla's sex life with a small group of government ministers. One of them, giving the distinct impression he had got it from the horse's mouth, volunteered that the Prince of Wales likes 'a girl with something you can nuzzle up to'. When we pressed the minister to tell us more, he began to bluster, 'Come on, men, who here doesn't like a girl with healthy knockers?' Thus do members of Her Majesty's government idle away their coffee break . . .

Back in 1967, when Charles left Gordonstoun (where, you will recall, he complained 'The language people use is horrid'), he, too, was despatched abroad. On 20 December 1967, five weeks after his nineteenth birthday, he was sent to Melbourne to represent the Queen at the funeral of the Australian prime minister, Harold Holt.[106] He felt

by teenagers had sexual content, including 20 per cent with sexual intercourse; 42 per cent of the songs on the top CDs had sexual content, 19 per cent including direct descriptions of sexual intercourse; and, on average, music videos contained ninety-three sexual situations per hour, including eleven scenes depicting behaviour such as intercourse and oral sex.

[106] Holt (1908–67) disappeared at sea. Rumour was rife. Did he commit suicide? Was he a spy for the Chinese whisked away from Australian waters by submarine? Or, taking an early morning dip off the coast at Cheviot Beach, Victoria, had he simply underestimated the force of the waves and the strength of the current? To this day, despite enquiries official and unofficial, nobody knows.

the mission went well, reporting to his godmother, Patricia Brabourne, on his return: 'I am so glad to be able to do something like that for mummy. The Australians seemed very pleased that someone from the family had come out to show we still care.' In 2005, Patricia Brabourne told me, 'Charles was a serious young man. From a young age, he took his responsibilities very seriously indeed. He has a strong sense of duty. It's deeply instilled.'

While Camilla was accepting her destiny – as a fun-loving, horse-riding, upper-crust wife-mother-and-hostess-to-be – Charles was coming to terms with the realities of his – as Prince of Wales. On 31 October 1967, Camilla attended a Hallowe'en party in Knightsbridge, and Charles, for the first time, attended the State Opening of Parliament. The obligations of his position were falling on him thick and fast. On his eighteenth birthday he had been made Counsellor of State, eligible to succeed to the throne in his own right. In June 1968, still only nineteen, he had been installed as a Knight of the Garter. A month later, he endured his first mass trial by small talk: his debut appearance at a Buckingham Palace garden party.

As a child, Charles had very few foreign holidays. As a little boy, in 1954, he had been to Malta, Tobruk and Gibraltar, staying with the Mountbattens in Malta (where great-uncle Dickie was stationed as Commander-in-Chief of the Mediterranean Fleet) and welcoming his parents back from their post-coronation Commonwealth tour. In 1962, as an Easter break, he went with his father to visit his German cousins. He went to Germany again a couple of years later and, throughout his teens, enjoyed an annual skiing trip to Switzerland or Liechtenstein or Sweden, usually as the guest of fellow descendants of Queen Victoria, such as Prince Ludwig of Hesse or Crown Prince Carl Gustav of Sweden.

Charles had – and retains – a special fondness for Malta, where his father had first been stationed in 1949, on his appointment as first lieutenant and second in command of HMS *Chequers*, the Leader of the 1st Destroyer Flotilla in the Mediterranean Fleet. The time that Philip and Elizabeth – serving officer and naval wife – spent together in Malta in the early years of their marriage is reckoned by those who have known them longest to be certainly the 'most normal' and probably 'the happiest' time of their life. Charles first went to Malta on his own, in 1968, officially, as the guest of the governor general, Sir Maurice Dorman. He went again the following year, less officially, at the invitation of the governor's delightful daughter, Sibella. (Sibella kindly invited me, too.[107]) For Charles, the chief attraction of the island (other than Sibella, a fun girl, whose figure, I recall, was not dissimilar to Camilla's at the time) was the polo.

Polo has been one of the abiding passions of Charles's life. He says, quite simply, 'I love the game, I love the ponies, I love the exercise. It's the one team game I can play.' (And being the Prince of Wales, with a substantial income from the Duchy of Cornwall, happily it's a game he can afford to play.) 1968 marked the centenary of the All Malta Polo Club (president: Earl Mountbatten of Burma) and Charles, 'very dust-begrimed', was 'eternally grateful' to his great-uncle for 'arranging the games' and 'extremely proud' to have led the team that carried off the centenary trophy, the Prince Louis Cup. Mountbatten was assuming an increasingly important role in his life, as honorary grandfather, counsellor and friend.

Inevitably, as well as pleasure there was duty to be done in Malta: a garden party at San Anton Palace, the governor's residence, with around four hundred sweaty hands to be shaken. (This is why, on duty, the Queen and Princess Anne wear gloves in all seasons. Diana didn't; Camilla doesn't – yet.) Charles was becoming accustomed – if not wholly acclimatised – to life as a public figure. A girl who knew him well at the time told me, 'He was still quite shy. He did everything that was asked of him and tried really hard, but I don't think he found it easy. He was very sweet, very caring, a little naive in some of his views. He called himself a romantic and he could be quite sentimental – a bit soppy, really, and a bit over-serious when he tried to hold your hand or whatever.'

'A bit soppy' and 'over-serious' are not phrases that feature in any of the reports of Camilla in her late teens and early twenties, but Camilla's life was not challenging in the way that Charles's was. The young Camilla was – by every account – 'fun', 'easy', 'down-to-earth', 'dependable', 'sensible', 'good-hearted', 'strong'. She says, 'If people think I am strong, then it is all down to my family. I had so much love and security growing up, I never doubted my family would be there for me in times of crisis. Whatever happened, I knew I was wanted and loved. To give that to a child is the greatest gift of all.' The Duchess of Cornwall believes that 'the solid foundation' she was given by her

---

[107] I did not go, which I do now see was a mistake. I went instead to Moscow, which seemed a more exciting prospect at the time. I became friends with Sibella, who went to Badminton Girls' School, in the summer of 1966, when we both attended an arts festival organised by 'The Conference of Internationally-Minded Schools'.

childhood has provided her with 'the stability to face any upset'.

The crises and upsets would come later. The adolescent Camilla was not put to the test. Charles, as a young man, was put to the test time and again. Almost everything he did – or was encouraged or obliged to do – was, in part, a preparation for the bizarre role in life that destiny has thrown his way. Aged seventeen, in 1966, he was despatched to Australia for two terms to Timbertop, the outback campus of the Geelong Church of England Grammar School in Victoria. It was an invigorating experience, better than he dared hope, but, inevitably, it involved Commonwealth 'duties' and running the gauntlet of the Australian media. Three hundred and twenty correspondents were in attendance to cover his arrival Down Under.

Aged eighteen, in 1967, he arrived at Trinity College, Cambridge, to read Archaeology and Anthropology at the start of three years as a 'normal undergraduate'. Again, it was a rewarding experience – he studied conscientiously, he enjoyed the music and the drama (he appeared in assorted ludicrous outfits in a university revue, *Revulution*[108]), he secured a half-blue representing Cambridge at polo – but he was always aware that he was constantly under surveillance: a plainclothes police officer was in twenty-four-hour attendance; fellow undergraduates viewed him as a phenomenon; strangers in the streets gawped; the media sat in judgement. He later recalled, 'I tried using disguise once at Cambridge because I wanted to go along and see what was happening in a demonstration. I borrowed an overcoat, put up the collar and pulled down a hat over my eyes. I just looked like me trying not to look like me. And everybody kept looking. It's the same if you put on dark glasses: everyone wonders what on earth you're doing wearing dark glasses, particularly when the sun's not out!' When, by dint of effort, he passed his Part One examinations at the end of his first year, he was surprised to find his success accurately reported in the press. 'I am so pleased the papers have given the exam results a fair deal,' he wrote at the time. 'I have achieved my desire anyway, and shown them, in some small way at least, that I am not totally ignorant or incompetent!'

Aged nineteen, in 1968, he started to learn to fly. Again, it was an exhilarating experience – 'a mixture between fear and supreme enjoyment' is how he described his first solo flight – but it was a

---

[108] The best sketch was the simplest – written by Prince Charles himself. He came on to the stage carrying an umbrella and said, 'I lead a sheltered life'.

challenge undertaken, not for itself, but because, as heir apparent, he was committed, willy-nilly, to hands-on involvement in the armed services.

Aged twenty, in 1969, however, he faced what many might regard as the most daunting test of all: three months in Wales – meeting the people, learning the language, studying at the University College of Wales at Aberystwyth. Eleven years before, in her recorded message broadcast at Cardiff Arms Park, the Queen had created Charles Prince of Wales and had promised the Welsh people, 'When he is grown up I will present him to you at Caernarfon.' The date for Charles's investiture as Prince of Wales was set for 1 July 1969 and, in the run-up to it, Charles – wholly English and Scottish by upbringing – was to be given an immersion course in all things Welsh. It was neither a comfortable nor a happy experience. At the end of nine weeks as a student at Aberystwyth – missing his family and the sense of camaraderie he had begun to find at Cambridge – he gave his first television interview and failed to disguise his misery. He was questioned by Cliff Michelmore and Brian Connell (a respectful and avuncular double act) who probed him, gently, about reports that he had felt somewhat isolated at his Welsh university. Falteringly, but all too frankly, the young prince stumbled through his answer as best he could. 'You see,' he said, 'the trouble is that one has to remember that I'm in a slightly different position from several other people . . . I think out of certain necessity I have perhaps been more lonely, if they like it. I mean I haven't made a lot of friends, if that's what they mean . . . essentially it is, I suppose, compared with other people's lives, more lonely, and in this sense I've had a lonely time.'

Charles shows his vulnerability. 'And what good does that do?' asks his father. 'It shows he's human,' says his godmother, Countess Mountbatten. When I was researching my book about the Queen and the Duke of Edinburgh, two of the Duke's contemporaries – one male, one female – described the young Prince Philip to me as 'a cold fish'. While writing this book, several people – and not only of the Duke's generation – have described Prince Charles to me as 'a wet fish'. An ex-girlfriend told me she was not sorry when her friendship with Charles cooled because, 'He was a bit wet – quite self-absorbed and sorry for himself. Bit of a wimp, really.' In the French coverage of his 2005 wedding, the commentator repeatedly referred to the Prince's reputation as '*un mauviette*' – a wimp.

To those who admire and love the Prince of Wales, these slurs are as unfair as they are uncharitable. He did not find his time at Aberystwyth easy, but he soldiered on: he did his duty. And if he was unhappy, he had some cause. There was no general welcome in the hillside. There were some friendly faces to be sure (especially, if press reports of the time are to be believed, among women of riper years and teenage girls), but, in several quarters, there was open hostility. The Welsh Nationalist Party published protests. The so-called 'Free Wales Army' threatened 'military action'. In the week of Charles's arrival in his principality, a stick of gelignite exploded outside the police head-quarters in Cardiff and a force of more than one hundred officers was deployed around the Aberystwyth campus in what one newspaper described as 'the most elaborate security operation Wales has ever known'. In the event, Charles survived the protests and rode the storm. On 31 May, he addressed a gathering of six thousand of his Welsh subjects, at the Urdd National Eisteddfod, Wales's annual youth festival of poetry, music and drama. He spoke in Welsh and, instead of having 'bardic harps and druidic oaths' hurled at him as he feared, he was rewarded with a few moments of barracking followed by a friendly and sustained ovation. A month later, at Caernarfon Castle, in front of 3,500 invited guests, and a worldwide television audience estimated at five hundred million, he was formally invested as Prince of Wales. The investiture was a curious affair; yet, against the odds, in its own bizarre way, it worked.

July 1969 was a notable month in the modern world – Neil Armstrong stepped on to the moon; the Rolling Stones conquered Hyde Park – but, at the beginning of it, in a remote corner of North Wales, Queen Elizabeth II – encouraged by her 'progressive' Labour prime minister, Harold Wilson,[108] and his Secretary of State for Wales, George Thomas – turned the clock back some seven hundred years. The English had captured Caernarfon Castle from the Welsh in 1282. It was here that Edward I had declared his son – Edward II, born at Caernarfon in 1284 – the first English Prince of Wales. Seven centuries later, Edward's direct descendant, Elizabeth II, came to the same spot to 'crown' her son, Charles, the twenty-first Prince of Wales.

[109] Wilson (prime minister from 1966 to 1970 and 1974–6) prided himself on his 'modernity' and on his close relationship with the Queen. His successor, James Callaghan, who as a Welshman, Cardiff MP and Home Secretary, was on parade at Caernarfon, told me, 'Every prime minister likes to think that their relationship with the Queen is closer than that of any of their predecessors. It is one of our little vanities. The truth is what the royal family offer you is friendliness not friendship.'

It was a quasi-coronation – at the climax of the ceremony the Queen placed a coronet on her son's head – but it had no constitutional significance and precious little precedent. Apart from the original Edward of Caernarfon, only two of the twenty-one Princes of Wales had been 'presented' to the Welsh people in this way: Charles and his immediate predecessor, his unfortunate great-uncle David, later Edward VIII and Duke of Windsor. In 1911, George V's coronation year, David Lloyd George, Chancellor of the Exchequer and self-proclaimed 'Welsh wizard',[110] persuaded the new King that a 'mini-coronation' for his son at Caernarfon would be a powerful aid to Anglo-Welsh amity and a fitting finale to His Majesty's own coronation tour. The King agreed and the modern 'investiture' was born. The 1911 ceremony was an elaborate affair, remembered as 'militaristic, pompous and essentially alien', according to George Thomas (a devout Methodist as well as Welsh Secretary), who wanted to see something much simpler and more authentically Welsh in 1969.

The planning for Prince Charles's investiture began more than two years prior to the great day, in the spring of 1967. The Investiture Committee was chaired by the Duke of Norfolk, hereditary Earl Marshal and Chief Butler of England, but included a genuine Welshman in the slight, but dashing, figure of the Earl of Snowdon, son of Ronald Owen Lloyd Armstrong-Jones QC (of Plas Dinas, Caernarfon) and recently appointed Constable of Caernarfon Castle. Tony Armstrong-Jones, photographer of note and co-designer of the Snowdon Aviary at London Zoo, had married the Queen's sister, Princess Margaret, in 1960. 'You know about art,' the Duke of Norfolk said to him, 'you get on with it.' He did.

With his friend, the theatre designer Carl Toms, and John Pound from the Ministry of Works (who each received the CBE for their

[110] Prime minister, 1916–22. 'How can I convey to the reader who does not know him any just impression of this extraordinary figure of our time, this syren, this goat-footed bard, this half-human visitor to our age from the hag-ridden magic and enchanted woods of Celtic antiquity?' John Maynard Keynes asked the question in 1919. A. J. P. Taylor called him 'the greatest ruler of England since Oliver Cromwell'. Father of the Old Age Pensions Act and the National Insurance Act, war leader, orator, philanderer, when he was in his prime, in Wales they sang this song about him: 'Lloyd George, no doubt, / When his life ebbs out, / Will ride on a flaming chariot / Seated in state / on red-hot plate / 'Twixt Satan and Judas Iscariot. / Ananias that day to the Devil will say, / "My claim for precedence fails. / So move me up higher away from the fire, / And make way for the liar – from Wales!"'

efforts), Snowdon (who received the GCVO for his[111]) designed the whole shebang – and did so with some style. Central to their 'setting' in the castle courtyard were three thrones made of Welsh slate, positioned – in case of rain – beneath a huge Perspex canopy, emblazoned with the Prince of Wales feathers, supported on steel pikestaffs – 'just as Henry V would have done it if he'd had Perspex'.

In 2005, when I went to see Lord Snowdon to talk about the investiture, we sat in his study, side by side, on two of the chairs he designed for the event. 'The Ministry of Works were such snobs,' he told me. 'They wanted the VIPs to have grand chairs and the riffraff, as they called them, to sit on planks on the scaffolding. We weren't having it. So we made 4,000 chairs like this and they were sold at the end of the day, for £12 each. I bought six.'

I asked Snowdon if he had found the investiture fun. 'It was important,' he said. 'I was proud to do it. It was hilarious too. We had to go to pompous meetings at St James's Palace, to get our plans approved by the Garter King of Arms. You had to call him "Garter". His actual name was Sir Anthony Wagner, so you can imagine our nickname for him. There was a frightful row about the dragons we wanted to put on the banners. Carl said, "The dragons must have a knot in their tails: all dragons have knots in their tails." Garter wouldn't have it. Garter stood his ground. Eventually I said to him, "Oh, come on, Garter darling, can't you be a bit more elastic?" '

Snowdon designed a very natty uniform for himself to wear as Constable. 'It was dark green,' he told me, 'Welsh green, with a high collar, like an Indian collar. I know people mocked it at the time, calling me Buttons. In fact, it didn't have any buttons on it at all: it did up with a zip.' In 1911, the then Prince of Wales had been embarrassed by the

---

[111] 'The sovereign is the fount of all honour. Inevitably, those closest to the fount get splashed the most.' Lord Snowdon was made a Knight Grand Cross of the Royal Victorian Order, the order founded by Queen Victoria to reward outstanding personal service to the sovereign. After his divorce from Princess Margaret in 1978, Snowdon remained on cordial terms with the Royal Family. The Queen is especially fond of his children: some say she is more at ease with them than she is with her own. In recent years, the Queen and the Duke of Edinburgh have seen less of Snowdon, partly through circumstance, but also because of his roller-coaster of a private life: his second marriage foundered when, aged sixty-seven, he fathered a child by a young mistress who, it turned out, was one of several unconventional and ultimately unhappy alliances. Along the way one girl committed suicide. He is a legendary charmer and still Constable of Caernarfon. 'What are your duties?' I asked him. 'Lunch with you,' he said, without missing a beat.

costume he was obliged to wear, describing it as a 'preposterous rig'. Prince Charles was relatively comfortable in his. 'Charles was shit-scared. Of course he was – he was only nineteen. But he carried it off brilliantly. It was partly because he looked so young and vulnerable that it was so moving. And when he spoke in Welsh, it was clear how hard he'd worked to get it right. You couldn't fault him. Journalists asked me afterwards, "What went wrong?" The answer is, "Nothing went wrong."'

Snowdon is right. The day went well. The sun shone, the Welsh Nationalists stayed away, and a huge police presence kept would-be terrorists at bay. In the early hours of 1 July, a bomb exploded in Abergele, thirty miles from Caernarfon, killing the two men who were attempting to plant it by a government building. Later in the day, driving to the ceremony with George Thomas, Prince Charles thought he heard a second explosion. 'What was that?' he asked. 'Oh, a royal salute, sir,' replied Thomas, airily. 'Peculiar sort of royal salute,' said Charles, somewhat anxious. 'Peculiar sort of people up here,' said Thomas, MP for West Cardiff.

With or without Lord Snowdon as Buttons, the event did have a touch of the pantomime about it. It was a royal confection, artificial, contrived, a theatrical pageant designed for the television age (hence the need for the see-through Perspex awning), not – like a proper coronation – a religious ceremony rooted in history. While no decision will be taken until it has to be, I understand that, when the time comes for Prince William to become Prince of Wales, his father is not minded to put his son through a comparable charade.

Back in July 1969, Charles, relieved that it was over, drained by the event but content at its outcome, noted in his diary: 'For me, by far the most moving and meaningful moment came when I put my hands between Mummy's and swore to be her liege man of life and limb and to live and die against all manner of folks – such magnificent mediaeval, appropriate words . . .' The young Prince of Wales was moved, too, by the 'warming reception' of the crowds, not only on the day itself, when his mother, as promised, 'presented' him to the people assembled outside the castle gates (adjacent, he noted, to the public conveniences, police and TV vans), but over the next several days, when he went on an extended tour of the principality. 'I met so many people,' he said, 'and waved so much that I woke up in the middle of the night waving my hand.'

'The boy done well,' said George Thomas. And he knew it. On

7 July, he received this letter from his 'honorary grandfather', great-uncle Dickie, Earl Mountbatten of Burma – the man who, over the next ten years, would probably have a greater influence on him than any other:

My Dear Charles

Confidential reports on Naval officers are summarised by numbers . . . pretty poor 2 or 3, very good 7 or 8. Once in a way an officer achieves 9 – your father did it . . . your performance since you went with Fleet coverage to Wales rates you a 9 in my opinion . . . I'm sure you'll keep your head. Realise how fickle public support can be – it has to be earned over again every year. Your Uncle David had such popularity that he thought he could flout the Government and the Church and make a twice-divorced woman Queen. His popularity disappeared overnight. I am sure yours never will provided you keep your feet firmly on the ground. Well done, and keep it up,

Your affectionate and admiring Uncle.

The media, having seen Lord Snowdon as Buttons, now depicted Charles as Prince Charming – just as in time they would cast Diana as the fairy-tale princess and Camilla as one of the ugly sisters. For Charles, rising twenty, the investiture was also a rite of passage. 'Here comes the future,' he said to a friend that summer. 'No escape now.'

Chapter Six

Youth and Its Season

'The wine of youth does not always clear with advancing years; sometimes it grows turbid.'

Carl Jung (1875–1961)

For Charles, rising twenty, the investiture at Caernarfon was a unique rite of passage. For Camilla, rising eighteen, the debutante season of 1965 was a rite of passage, also: one she shared with 310 other like-minded girls.

The anthropologist Arnold Van Gennup – who coined the phrase – does not feature the London debutante season in *The Rites of Passage* (1908), his ground-breaking ethnographic study of the rituals of transition in a variety of indigenous cultures around the world, but he might have done. The season is an English phenomenon: a four-month period, running from March to July each year, during which young ladies of quality 'come out' into society for the first time. Buffed and coiffed, plucked and polished, for sixteen tumultuous weeks, wearing a range of lovely frocks, and strings of pearls, they go to parties and dances – and to the Henley Regatta and to Royal Ascot – and to more dances and more parties. They go to see and be seen: they go to meet and be met. When it all started, of course, they went in search of a mate.

The debutante season, as Camilla knew it in the mid-1960s, had its roots in the eighteenth century. In 1780 King George III held a ball in honour of his wife, Queen Charlotte. The ball – designed to mark Her Majesty's birthday and to raise funds for the pioneering maternity hospital to which she gave her name – established the tradition whereby young ladies of breeding were presented at court. The tradition survived for almost two centuries and involved a ritual as enthralling as any observed by Arnold Van Gennup on his travels. At the moment of 'presentation', the doors of the Throne Room at Buckingham Palace opened wide and in processed a fairy-tale phalanx of debutantes, each one a seventeen-year-old virgin (supposedly), each in full court dress, with train (of prescribed length), each with three tall ostrich feathers (no more) held precariously in her hair. As they entered the royal presence, the debutantes dropped a deep curtsy and then began a delicate and complex piece of choreography: a pains-takingly rehearsed backwards walk – requiring you to look steadfastly ahead while nonchalantly manoeuvring the train of your dress behind you – culminating in a second curtsy.

The last debutantes' presentation at court took place on 18 March 1958. The Queen brought the tradition to a close on the grounds that it was elitist and antiquated. Her husband, Prince Philip, considered the ritual 'bloody daft'. Her sister, Princess Margaret, said, 'We had to put a stop to it. Every tart in London was getting in.' Seven years later, when Camilla Shand had her 'season', Queen Charlotte's Ball was still a key event, but it was held at the Grosvenor House Hotel, not Buckingham Palace, and the young ladies curtsied, not to Queen Elizabeth in person, but to a six-foot-tall birthday cake, symbolising Queen Charlotte.

The annual Queen Charlotte's Ball came to the end of its long run in 1994. There is still a 'season' of sorts – rich folk gives dances for their daughters; there's a debutantes' fashion show at the Dorchester Hotel, and a youngsters' charity ball at the Savoy – but it isn't what it was, not simply because society isn't what it was, but, principally, because young women do not need to meet young men in the way that once they did. In Camilla's mother's day, you were expected to be a virgin when you married and, in your eighteenth year, you expected to 'come out' and, through your season, meet a range of eligible young men (all 'PLU'), one of whom you might very well end up marrying. That's how it had been for generations. In 1965, that's how it still was for Camilla and her kind. You were a 'deb' and the young men were known as 'debs' delights'. As a deb, you only had one season: as a deb's delight, you could be on the circuit for several. As ever in life, good men were in short supply.[112]

We know that Camilla was one of 311 debutantes in her year

[112] My season as a deb's delight was a brief one. I did not cut the mustard. My most vivid memory is of a ghastly night in 1966 that began with a cocktail party in Knightsbridge and ended with a ball at Hurlingham. To get from one to the other, we young people were ferried in mini-buses generously supplied by the parents of the deb whose

because a man called Peter Townend was on hand to keep count of the numbers and ensure that only the right sort of girl entered the lists. Townend was the social editor of *Tatler* magazine and, after debutantes ceased to be presented at court in 1958, it was, essentially, his remarkable memory and genealogical knowledge that kept the 'deb season' going for the next forty years. He knew who was who – and, more important, who came from where – and acted as the self-appointed gatekeeper to the garden of delights that was 'the season'.[113]

We know that Camilla's year was launched with a coming-out party on Thursday 25 March 1965 because a woman called Betty Kenward was on hand and, in her column, 'Jennifer's Diary', in the magazine *Queen*, she reported the occasion in the peculiar style that was her trademark:[114]

The Honourable Mrs Shand's cocktail party for her attractive debutante daughter, Camilla, was another successful party. This was one of the very first of the debutante cocktail parties and might have been a bit sticky as, at the beginning of any season, the young people

particular night this was. Aged eighteen, in my shiny dinner jacket, I sat at the back of the bus, squeezed up against an alarmingly sophisticated seventeen-year-old girl who, as she lit her cigarette, asked, 'Have you ever seen a match burn twice?' 'No,' I replied naively. She waved the lighted match towards me. 'Now it's burning once,' she said. She stubbed the match out on the back of my hand. 'Now it's burning twice!' I can hear her shrill laughter even now.

[113] Townend died, aged eighty, in 2001. Towards the end, he was obliged to let his genealogical standards slip and cast his net quite wide to recruit girls to his debutantes' list. He even wrote to my wife to enquire whether our daughters might be interested in 'the season'. They weren't, but we marvelled at how he had discovered our address and the dates when the girls turned seventeen.

[114] The look that was her trademark featured a large bow at the back of her bouffant hair. Born in 1904 to a good family ('I am a true Cockney,' she said, 'I was born in Cadogan Gardens'), married in 1932, divorced in 1942, with a son to bring up alone, she joined *Tatler* during the war and her column was called 'Jennifer's Diary' because the editor said she 'looked like a Jennifer'. For almost forty years her column – in *Tatler*, then in *Queen*, then *Harpers & Queen* – was essential reading for all who cared about 'society'. She denied she was a snob: she claimed she simply 'had standards'. In 1960, Tony Armstrong-Jones, taking photographs for *Queen*, made the mistake of approaching her, only to be told, 'My photographers never speak to me at parties.' A year later, when the news came that Armstrong-Jones was to marry Princess Margaret, Mrs Kenward is said to have spent the afternoon in her office, kicking her wastepaper basket disconsolately and intoning: 'What a turn up this is.'

have not yet got to know each other, but both the hostess and Camilla did plenty of introducing and it went with a swing.

Mrs Kenward wrote in a special code well understood by her regular readers. For example, if a debutante was described as 'pretty' you could assume she was passably fair, but if the poor girl was described as 'spirited' you could take it she was as plain as they come. The Kenward report on the Shand bash for Camilla tells us all we need to know: Camilla was a nice-looking girl (not a beauty) and she and her mother worked like billy-o to get a slow-starting party moving – and succeeded.

The party was held at Searcy's, 30 Pavilion Road, Knightsbridge, SW1, a fine Georgian house, traditionally appointed, conveniently located at the back of Harrods, and hired out by families whose own London homes were not large enough to accommodate the necessary numbers. Camilla had 150 guests: her parents remained in attendance throughout, but the other older guests, such as Mrs Kenward, departed by nine o'clock, leaving the young ones to enjoy themselves. In her book about Camilla, the journalist Caroline Graham quotes a partygoer saying, 'It was a fairly raucous affair. Most of the coming-out cocktail parties were rather stiff and dull. But Camilla's was fun. She wore a lovely white dress and was the life and soul of the party. Everyone had such fun, the cocktails stretched on until eleven at night. Everyone got tipsy and Camilla was at the centre of it, throwing her head back telling bawdy jokes. She must have danced and flirted with every man in the room.'

That is not quite as the Duchess of Cornwall remembers it. For a start, though a virgin, she did not wear white. Turn to the section between pages 000 and 000 and look at the photograph of Camilla and her mother taken at the beginning of that evening. They look quite apprehensive and their appearance – apart from Camilla's fringe and her favourite chandelier earrings – has a distinctly sedate, 1950s feel to it. Another partygoer – to whom I was directed by someone close to the Duchess – told me, 'It was a fun evening, I'm sure, but I don't recall excessive tipsiness or bawdy jokes or anything like that. Camilla is very jolly and a great mixer, but I think all this stuff about her being a serial flirt is much exaggerated.' The Duchess's friends are concerned that there is a myth developing that, in her late teens and twenties, Camilla, not-so-pretty-but-oh-so-sexy, was the proverbial good time had by all – and they want to scotch it. That said, they are not denying that, within forty-eight hours of her coming-out party, on the night of Saturday 27 March 1965, Camilla lost her virginity.

It is at this point that Sir Michael Peat, private secretary to the Prince of Wales, is throwing up his hands in despair and reflecting on how right he was to scoff at my promise to write this book 'in a sympathetic, rounded, balanced and accurate way!'. (The exclamation mark is his.) What on earth has Camilla's virginity got to do with the life and work of the Prince of Wales? The answer, of course, if unfortunately, is everything.

When Camilla lost her virginity, in the spring of 1965 (in the month, incidentally, when Goldie, the golden eagle, also spread his wings and found freedom, escaping from his cage at London Zoo), it was a defining moment. It was the moment that, as it turned out, sealed her fate. It was the moment that transformed her – overnight – from 'unsullied creature' into 'used goods'. It was the moment that settled her destiny. She might become a royal mistress. She could not expect to become a royal bride. It is absurd, I know, but it is true, nonetheless. As Countess Mountbatten, Charles's godmother and cousin, put it to me, forty years on, in the spring of 2005, 'With hindsight, you can say that Charles should have married Camilla when he first had the chance. They were ideally suited, we know that now. But it wasn't possible. Camilla had "history" and the Prince of Wales couldn't marry a girl with "history". He really couldn't. It just wasn't on.'

Bob Dylan was in Britain in the spring of 1965, singing 'The times they are a-changin''. And they were – for many, but not for all. 'It isn't the place of the royal family to initiate change, is it?' Countess Mountbatten asks, rhetorically. 'The Queen,' she reminds me, 'is a traditionalist. She is also Supreme Governor of the Church of England. She takes her role seriously.' And, in 1965, the teaching of the Church of England was clear: no sex before marriage. In 1965, too, the Church of England was still a force to reckon with. In September 1965, a Gallup poll survey suggested that, in England, only 2 per cent of the population said they were atheists, while 94 per cent claimed to belong to a church of some kind and 66 per cent said it was the Church of England.

1965 was also the year in which Mrs Mary Whitehouse set up her National Viewers' and Listeners' Association to 'tackle BBC bad taste and irresponsibility'. Mrs Whitehouse believed the 'amount of sex on television' was 'undermining the moral fabric of the nation'. She was a Christian, a housewife and a mother, and her views – while mocked in the media – were shared by millions of her generation. She had a very down-to-earth way with her. She said, uncompromisingly, 'Sex before marriage is wrong. It is morally wrong. It's also a mistake. And I'll tell you why. Do it once and you'll do it again. Do it twice and you'll do it a third time. And promiscuity only leads to unhappiness and ruined lives.' Betty Kenward agreed – and with reason. In her memoirs, published in 1992, she told the story of her unhappy childhood and revealed that her mother had had a number of affairs, both before and after her marriage, the social consequences of which had been made brutally apparent to Betty during her third term at finishing school. She had become friends with a girl called Bunty, with whom she hoped to share a room the following term; but when Bunty arrived back 'she told me very sweetly that her aunt would not let her share a room with me as my mother was living with a man who was not her husband'. Young Betty was 'shattered, but it made me realise early on what a lot high standards mean in life'.

According to Nigel Dempster, doyen of London gossip columnists from the 1960s to the 1990s, the young man who claimed Camilla's virginity was a Burke – not from the peerage, but nevertheless from 'a relatively top drawer'. Kevin Burke, nineteen in 1965, was a good-looking boy, just out of Eton. Camilla's mother, née Rosalind Cubitt, was the daughter of a baron. Kevin's mother, née Rosalind Norman, was the daughter of a baronet. Camilla's father, Major Bruce Shand, was a wine merchant, huntsman and Vice-Lord-Lieutenant, with property in Kensington and East Sussex. Kevin's father, Sir Aubrey Burke, was vice-chairman of Hawker Siddeley, the aircraft manufacturers, High Sheriff of Hertfordshire, a shooting, fishing, sailing man, with properties in Bovingdon, Chiddingfold and Cap d'Antibes. Camilla and Kevin were a good match.

I cannot confirm that Camilla and Kevin first slept together on the night of 27 March 1965, because I am too much of a coward to ask the Duchess directly and Mr Burke is too much of gentleman to tell. What he will say, however, is that they went out together for the best part of a year and that Camilla was 'terrific fun, enormously popular', 'attractive and sexy'. 'She was never tongue-tied or shy and she always had something amusing to say.' Kevin Burke was a debs' delight who definitely cut the mustard: 'Every night we went to two or three cocktail parties and then a dance. All you needed was enough petrol for the car and to pay for your cleaning and the rest was provided. It was the best time and I had the best partner you could wish for. Camilla was always at the centre of things. She was never bad-tempered. She knew how to have fun . . . I remained with Camilla all that year. I suppose we were in love. Then she ditched me.'

Camilla knew how to have fun and the fun she had with Kevin – and, as we shall see, shortly thereafter, with other young bucks about town – made it possible for Prince Charles to sleep with her when they came to meet, but impossible for him to marry her when they came to fall in love.

It is different today,[115] but until very recently, in the matter of matters hymenal, there was one rule for princes and quite another for potential princesses. Princes were expected to have played the field, but the young women chosen for them as brides were required to be virgo intacta. Princes, of course, were not alone in maintaining this double standard. Men in general hoped for virgin brides (and insisted that their daughters remain chaste until matrimony), while somehow taking it for granted that other men (lesser men?) would provide their wives and daughters for pre- and extra-marital relations. From where we view it, this scheme of things, reeking of hypocrisy and inequity, seems absurd, and wrong, but until the rise of the women's movement in the 1960s, though technically frowned on by the Church, it was the way of the world, and not seriously questioned by anybody.

Edward VII, as Prince of Wales, stationed with his regiment in Ireland, lost his virginity, aged nineteen to the actress Nellie Clifton. George V, as a young prince in the 1880s, shared a girl with his older brother, Prince Eddy. They kept her for their pleasure in a small house in St John's Wood. (Eddy's chief interests were polo and sex; however, the former gave him a bad back, and the latter venereal disease. He, not George, would have become Prince of Wales and King had he not died in January 1892, the day before his twenty-eighth birthday.) George V's two oldest sons, David and Bertie (destined to become Edward VIII and George VI respectively) also enjoyed lively pre-marital sex lives. David, as a young Prince of Wales, had a host of relationships before the onset of his long-lasting infatuation with Wallis Simpson. His first sustained love affair, begun in 1918 when he was twenty-three, was with Freda Dudley Ward (the liberal wife of a Liberal MP) and it is from David's

[115] I happen to be writing this on the very day that Zara Phillips, the twenty-four-year-old daughter of the Princess Royal, has moved in with her boyfriend, England rugby international, Mike Tindall. The couple have moved into a four-bedroomed love-nest, known as The Bothy, on the Princess Royal's Gatcombe Park estate, and not an eyebrow has been raised. ('What once were vices are now manners.' Seneca.)

frank (and fruity) letters to Freda[116] that we learn that it was in Paris, towards the end of the First World War, that Bertie lost his virginity. As David put it, that is where 'the deed was done'. David, revelling in his relationship with Freda, encouraged young Bertie, eighteen months his junior, to find himself a married mistress too. Bertie took up with Sheila Chisholm, known as 'Sheilie', a lively young Australian woman (who had married Lord Loughborough, known as 'Loughie', in Cairo in 1915),[117] and David and Freda and Bertie and Sheilie called themselves 'The Four Dos' – and did. 'What marvellous fun we 4 do have, don't we Angel?' wrote the Prince of Wales to his paramour, '& f— the rest of the world.' Ignoring at least three of the Ten Commandments, the two future Supreme Governors of the Church of England were co-conspirators in the happy game of youthful adultery. 'After tea,' David reported to Freda in a late-night letter in June 1919, 'I managed to lure Loughie away on the pretext of wanting to play a few more holes of golf on the local course, so as to give Sheilie a chance of being alone with Bertie; they said they were tired & we left them . . . I'm sure Loughie doesn't suspect Bertie at all!'

Prince Charles emerged from the 'swinging sixties' much as his great-uncles had rolled into the 'roaring twenties': ready to sow his wild oats. He was encouraged to do so – quite specifically – by another of his great-uncles, Dickie Mountbatten. As Mountbatten's daughter, Patricia, explained to me, 'My father was always fond of Charles, but when Charles was in his late teens and early twenties they became

---

[116] He sent her more than two thousand and a selection, covering the period from March 1918 to January 1921, was published in *Letters from a Prince*, edited by Rupert Godfrey, in 1998. The letters addressed to 'my vewy vewy own precious darling beloved' are littered with bad language and baby-talk, but give a clear, if unflattering, flavour of the prince, his attitudes and way of life. (Also of his sense of humour: 'Q. What is the difference between looking into a woman's eyes & into a horse's eyes? A. You have to get off the horse!!!!')

[117] They had a son, Tony, born in 1917 and were divorced in 1926. In 1928, she married Sir John Milbanke, known as 'the boxing baronet', and, after his death, Prince Dimitri Obolensky. Lord Loughborough, who drank and gambled, committed suicide jumping off a building in 1929. Sheilie's youngest brother, Roy Chisholm, married another lively Australian girl, Mollee Little, whose claim to fame is that she enjoyed a brief romance with the Prince of Wales when he visited Australia in 1920. Mollee's son, brought up as Tony Chisholm, was born nine months after his mother's fling with the prince and, in later life, nicknamed 'The Duke', was said to bear an uncanny resemblance to the Duke of Windsor. In 1996, Barbara Chisholm, Tony's own illegitimate daughter (by an Aboriginal servant), volunteered to take a DNA test to prove her royal connection. What lives these people lead!

especially close. That's when the relationship really blossomed. The great thing about my father is that you could talk to him about absolutely anything. There was nothing you couldn't say to him. He was totally open and completely frank. There were no taboos. Charles and Philip have always had a rather strained relationship and I don't believe I've ever seen Charles have what you would call an "intimate conversation" with the Queen. The Queen is wonderful – quite wonderful – but she and Charles couldn't really talk about what you might call "matters of the heart". Actually, it's not unusual for children to find it easier to talk to their grandparents than their parents. My father was like a grandfather to Charles and, yes, he certainly encouraged him to sow his wild oats.'

On Valentine's Day 1974, Earl Mountbatten of Burma, aged seventy-three, wrote to the Prince of Wales, just turned twenty-five, with this advice:

> I believe, in a case like yours, the man should sow his wild oats and have as many affairs as he can before settling down but for a wife he should choose a suitable, attractive and sweet-charactered girl *before* she met anyone she might fall for. After all Mummy never seriously thought of anyone else after the Dartmouth encounter when she was 13! I think it is disturbing for women to have experiences if they have to remain on a pedestal after marriage.

Mountbatten had been on parade at the Royal Naval College, Dartmouth, on the weekend of 22–23 July 1939, when the young Princess Elizabeth, by her own admission, had first thought that her cousin, Prince Philip of Greece, then eighteen, might be the love of her life. Mountbatten had been on parade, too, at the beginning of the 1920s when David and Bertie were sowing their wild oats. He has sown a few himself, in his time. He was clear that Charles, until he 'settled', should play the field. Indeed, he was ready to provide the field in which the playing might take place. Broadlands, the Mountbatten country house in Hampshire, was made available to Charles as a trysting-ground whenever he required it. Countess Mountbatten puts it rather more decorously: 'My grandfather was very happy for Charles to entertain friends at Broadlands as often as it suited him.' It was at Broadlands that Charles and Camilla first slept together on a regular basis.

It was not Mountbatten, however, but another old boy of similar vintage, R. A. Butler, who introduced young Charles to the girl with whom he lost his virginity, and through whom he met Camilla.

When, in 1967, it was settled that Charles should complete his academic education at Cambridge University, the heads of a number of colleges competed for the honour of having the heir apparent as a member of their college. 'Rab' Butler, a deeply experienced politician,[118] and Master of Trinity since 1965, lobbied Mountbatten, among others, and won the day. Charles went to Cambridge to read Archaeology and Anthropology and, through dogged endeavour, and because he's no fool, secured a 2:1 in his end-of-first-year exams. He then told Butler that he would like to change subjects, switching to History, with an emphasis on the British constitution. 'But why?' asked the Master of Trinity. 'Because I'm probably going to be king,' replied the Prince of Wales.

Charles denies this story – which was one of Lord Butler's favourites. Indeed, Charles is irritated by quite a bit of what he regards as Butler's *post hoc* 'myth-making' about his time as an undergraduate at Trinity. Butler, at the time and after, was written up in the media as Charles's Cambridge mentor – a kind of thinking man's Mountbatten – and played up to the part the press assigned to him with gusto, giving chatty, avuncular, interviews about the Prince to all and sundry. For example, in 1974, Butler told Ann Leslie of the *Daily Mail* that, 'rather regrettably', at Cambridge Charles's 'cronies tended to be conventional huntin' and shootin' Army types from public schools'. Charles's reaction to this was unequivocal: 'Most of what Rab Butler says is preposterous and a reflection of some curious desire to be seen as my constitutional and philosophical tutor without whom I would still be a semi-moron.'

Still more infuriating to Charles was the interview Lord Butler gave four years later to another journalist, Anthony Holden, in which the Master of Trinity suddenly set out his stall as a latter-day Lord Pandarus. Just as Pandarus secured Cressida for Troilus at the height of the Trojan war, so, Butler revealed, he had secured the lovely Lucia Santa Cruz for the lonely Prince of Wales in the chill winter of 1967.

Butler, as deputy prime minister and then Foreign Secretary in the

[118] Wartime education minister; post-war Chancellor of the Exchequer, Home Secretary and Foreign Secretary, often described as 'the best prime minister we never had', he claimed to lack the 'killer instinct' necessary to take you to the top. In 1966, he said, 'A prime minister has to be a butcher and know the joints. That is perhaps where I have not been quite competent, in knowing all the ways you can cut up a carcass.'

early 1960s, had become friends with Victor Santa Cruz, Chilean ambassador to the Court of St James from 1959 to 1970. Santa Cruz was an Anglophile (educated at Stonyhurst), a gentleman (a member of White's, the Turf Club and the Beefsteak), and a friend at court (the Queen awarded him an honorary GCVO in 1965). He and his wife, Doña Adriana, had two sons and two daughters, including Lucia, 'a most charming and accomplished girl' (according to Lady Butler), who was working for the Master of Trinity as a research assistant on his memoirs. The Butlers thought the young people would get on famously and arranged a dinner party at the Master's Lodge for them to meet. It worked a treat. And shortly after, according to Lord Butler, at Charles's request, the old pander 'slipped' a key to the Master's Lodge to his young researcher. (His book was called *The Art of the Possible.*) 'Charles,' claimed Lord Butler, 'asked if she might stay for privacy.' Lucia, according to Lady Butler, was just the girl for Charles at that particular stage in his development: a 'happy example of someone on whom he could safely cut his teeth, if I may put it thus'.

Had he been alive I doubt that Lord Butler would have been invited to the Prince of Wales's second wedding in April 2005. Lucia Santa Cruz was there, however. She and Charles were close at Cambridge, not simply because of a mutual attraction, but because she seemed to understand him – and the world from which he came – in a way that most of his fellow undergraduates did not. They remain close because Lucia is the soul of discretion and the only true friends a prince can have are the ones who do not blab.

Lord Butler said far too much, and most of what he had to say Charles considered not simply 'preposterous', but patronising and impertinent too. According to Butler, Charles 'grew' under his guidance: 'When he arrived he was boyish, rather immature, and perhaps too susceptible to the influence of his family.' According to a fellow undergraduate, 'He did seem young for his age and he stuck out like a sore thumb because he was such an oddity. He was very prim and proper, incredibly strait-laced, very serious. And he seemed to come from another age. When we were wearing jeans and t-shirts, he was still wearing tweed jackets and ties, cavalry twill trousers and highly-polished brogues. He wasn't one of us. We knew it. He knew it.' He felt it, too. He referred to his Cambridge contemporaries as 'hairy, unwashed student bodies' and admitted that, on the whole, he pre-ferred his own company – and that of the 'hills and trees' – to theirs.

Charles was at Cambridge at the end of the 1960s, but he was hardly

Just good friends:
Charles and Camilla
in 1975

Nicholas Soames and
Camilla Parker Bowles
in 1976

On the town: Charles and Camilla in 1976

In the country: Charles and Camilla in 1979

Andrew and Camilla Parker Bowles at the *Horse and Hound* Ball, 1977

Lady Diana Spencer, aged 19, waiting to watch Prince Charles play polo, 1981

Every picture tells a story: two future Princesses of Wales, Lady Diana Spencer, aged 19, and Camilla Parker Bowles, aged 33, on their way to watch Prince Charles ride in the Amateur Riders Handicap Steeplechase at Ludlow in October, 1980. The prince finished second.

Four weddings and two funerals: Wallis Simpson and the Duke of Windsor on their wedding day, 3 June 1937, at the Chateau de Condé, nears Tours, France

Camilla with her father, Major Bruce Shand MC, and her husband, Andrew Parker Bowles, on her wedding day, 4 July 1973, at the Guards' Chapel, Wellington Barracks, London

Princess Diana and Prince Charles on the balcony of Buckingham Palace on their wedding day, 29 July 1981

The Prince of Wales and the Duchess of Cornwall on the steps of St George's Chapel, Windsor, on their wedding day, 9 April 2005

Prince William, Prince Harry and Prince Charles on the day of Diana's funeral, 6 September 1997

Prince William, Prince Charles and Prince Harry at the funeral of Queen Elizabeth the Queen Mother, 9 April 2002

a child of his time. This, after all, was the era of student marches and peace demos, of flower power and psychedelia, of sex, drugs and rock and roll. Courtesy of Lord Butler, and the lovely Lucia, Charles got his portion of free love, but the rest of the excitements on offer at the dawning of the age of Aquarius were not to His Royal Highness's taste. As Diana said some years later, 'Charles was an "old fogey" before the term was invented.'

Academically, Charles did well at Cambridge, perhaps not by the standards of Lord Butler (who, naturally, had secured a Double First in his day), but certainly by his own lights. Charles achieved a lower Second. It was, he said, 'a great relief'. His Cambridge years had not been altogether easy for him, because he had not found it easy to be at ease with his contemporaries and they had not found it easy to be at ease with him. He was self-conscious and felt awkward making friends with strangers; and they were self-conscious because he was the Prince of Wales. There were no clear rules of engagement.

In this respect, the next six years were much easier for Charles: he joined the armed services where everyone knows where they are. The dress code is uniform and the ranks are pre-ordained. There is what T. S. Eliot called 'the security of known relationships'. And in case of any misunderstanding, Buckingham Palace set out the protocol: to senior officers and those of equal rank, Charles would be known as 'Prince Charles', while junior ranks would call him 'Sir'. Off duty, as he was now of age, he would be treated with the customary courtesies due to the heir to the throne: everyone would either bow or curtsy on meeting him, addressing him first as 'Your Royal Highness' and afterwards as 'Sir' or 'Prince Charles'. As Mountbatten reflected, 'The great thing about the services is: give an order and it's usually obeyed.'

Charles kicked off his service career in March 1971 with a six-month stint as a flight lieutenant in the Royal Air Force. At the RAF training college at Cranwell, he felt immediately at home. He was among people whose style and stamp he understood and trusted. Their approach to the world, to their work, and to him, was something with which he was familiar. He was accustomed to men in uniform. Inside and outside the palaces and castles he called 'home' there they always were; he had been surrounded by them, and comfortable with them, since childhood. His parents' equerries – ever on call – were (and are) youngish officers seconded to royal duty from one of the armed services. Charles's own first equerry – whom he had got to know when he had accompanied the young prince on his first trip to Australia as a schoolboy – was a squadron leader, David Checketts, formerly an equerry to the Duke of Edinburgh. Charles's father, his grandfathers (George VI and Prince Andrew of Greece), his great-grandfathers (George V, Lord Strathmore, George I of Greece and Louis Battenberg, 1st Marquess of Milford Haven) all served in the armed services – several with distinction. His great-uncle, 'honorary grandfather' and mentor, Earl Mountbatten of Burma, had only retired as Chief of the Defence Staff in 1965. This was his world.

While there were those who argued that the heir to the throne should be given a grounding in all three armed services, on the basis that he would be spending much of his life in the uniforms of each, Mountbatten took the view that he must have a 'mother service', one, as he put it to his great-nephew, 'that you really belong to and where you can have a reasonable career'. Charles was content to be persuaded and, after his six months at RAF Cranwell (where he showed that he shared his father's enthusiasm and aptitude for flying), he followed in the family tradition and moved on to the Royal Naval College, Dartmouth, to embark on a five-year career as a naval officer. It was to prove a not unchallenging experience – he had to contend with seasickness and the trigonometric trials of ocean navigation – but he was doing it, as he put it, 'For Mummy and Country!', and for the first time in his life away from home, the upside outweighed the down. He served in a series of warships: *Norfolk*, *Minerva*, *Jupiter* and *Hermes*. He took – and passed – all the requisite exams. With the Fleet Air Arm, he learnt to fly helicopters. (He logged more than five hundred hours at the controls of a Wessex 5 double-engined helicopter.) Ultimately, as he put it, 'the great and terrifying day had arrived': on 9 February 1976 he took command of the coastal mine hunter HMS *Bronington* at Rosyth. He did well. His men liked him and, by every account, respected his modesty, seriousness and determination. His end-of-career report from the senior officer of his squadron was all that he could wish: 'In spite of enormous outside pressure Prince Charles has attained an excellent level of professional competence as a Commanding Officer. He has a natural flair and ability for shiphandling and consequently his manoeuvres have been a pleasure to witness.'

A few years later, at the time of the Falklands conflict in 1982, Charles expressed regret that during his own service career he had not been 'tested in action' as his younger brother, Andrew, had been while serving with the Fleet Air Arm in the South Atlantic. However, a retired Fleet Air Arm senior commander wrote to me recently to say that it is 'quite wrong' for anyone – least of Charles – to suggest that 'the DoY had a far more authentic service career than his elder brother'. 'Not so. Prince Charles did the normal courses and flying training and served in 845/846 Naval Air Squadrons in the Commando support role. He pitched in like anyone else, was shown no favouritism, was an excellent poler (pilot) and was immensely popular. HRHTPoW has an excellent rapport with the military and, in particular, the Royal Navy.' That is the general verdict. 'Yes, he was first-rate as a naval officer,' a member of his family said to me. 'He doesn't lack physical courage. Far from it. He's brave. He's tough. And he's proved that he has real leadership qualities. That's what makes the fact that he's such a wimp in other areas so odd.'

On Friday 5 November 1971, as Sub-Lieutenant Prince Charles RN, nine days off his twenty-third birthday, was flying from Brize Norton in a crowded RAF Britannia to Gibraltar to take up his first posting on the destroyer HMS *Norfolk*, Camilla Shand, eight months off her twenty-fifth birthday, was on her way to a Bonfire Night party in East Sussex. In 2005, I asked a friend of the family to tell me what she was like at the time. 'Happy-go-lucky,' he said. 'Her mother was still alive. She was single and fancy-free. I don't think she had a care in the world.'

Camilla belonged to that dwindling breed of young women who had a small amount of private means, a little bit of the right sort of education and almost no worldly ambition to speak of. She did work – she did a bit of temping; she had a series of secretarial jobs in the West End; she spent a year amid the chintz and swags of the upmarket interior designers Colefax & Fowler (very much her milieu: understated English country-house style) – but she was not working to build a career. As a girlfriend of the time put it, 'Nine-to-five wasn't important. Evenings, weekends, horses, hunting, people, parties, that's what counted for Camilla. She moved with a lively crowd.'

She shared a flat in Belgravia with another girlfriend, Virginia Carington, who was just a year older than her and, as mentioned earlier, the daughter of Peter Carington, Defence Secretary in Edward Heath's cabinet at the time. Virginia was smart (well, she was an Hon.), but the flat wasn't: it was at the wrong end of Belgravia, in an ugly post-war block (Stack House) in Cundy Street, off Ebury Square, at the back of Victoria Coach Station. One witness described the interior as 'typical Camilla':

Her bedroom looked like a bomb had hit it. Virginia was fairly tidy and organised and Camilla drove her nuts, in the nicest possible way. Virginia once told me, 'You know, Camilla has this inability to hang anything up on a hanger. And she has an aversion to cleaning fluids of any description. You should see the state of the bathroom when she's been in it.' But she was so sweet, it was impossible to be angry with her.

That winter, when Charles was on board HMS *Norfolk*, taking part in a NATO exercise in seas 'so violent', he said, 'that I honestly felt on occasions that the ship was never going to right herself', Camilla was unwinding in the Caribbean sun. Her winter break in Barbados came courtesy of her Cubitt uncle, her mother's younger brother, known formally as Henry, 4th Baron Ashcombe, known to family and friends as 'Mad Harry' – and with good reason. He lived life in the fast lane. Generously, he invited Camilla to bring a friend to join his house party: Camilla brought Virginia and – instantly – Mad Harry was smitten. He was forty-seven and not long divorced. Virginia was twenty-five and ready to be bowled over. Under the palms and over the rum punches, love blossomed. To the dismay of Virginia's parents, and the surprise of Mad Harry's friends, the affair turned into more than a holiday romance. On 1 January 1973, the Hon. Virginia Carington became the second Lady Ashcombe. Camilla's flatmate was transmogrified into her step-aunt. It did not last.[119]

Lord Ashcombe's Barbados house party was memorable in more ways than one. His guests of honour were Jacqueline Onassis, wife of the Greek shipping magnate and supertanker pioneer Aristotle Socrates Onassis, and widow of the assassinated American President, John Fitzgerald Kennedy, and Jackie's younger sister, Princess Lee Radziwill. Lee, like her sister, was married to an older man (a Polish prince, Stanislaus Radziwill, nineteen years her senior), and, following their divorce in 1974, she married another older man (the film director Herbert Ross: that didn't last either), but along the way – so the rumour went – Princess Lee's conquests included Camilla's younger brother, Mark Shand.

Mark is four years Camilla's junior and a loose-limbed, languid gentleman charmer in the tradition of Major Bruce Shand – but without the military manner. The major went to Rugby and Sandhurst.

[119] Virginia and Mad Harry were divorced in 1979, when Lord Carrington became Foreign Secretary in Margaret Thatcher's cabinet and Lord Ashcombe married a lady rejoicing in the name of Mary Elizabeth Chipps.

Mark went to Milton Abbey (where they are good with dyslexics) and to Sotheby's in Bond Street where he took a fine arts course before setting himself up as a freelance art dealer. (Princess Lee Radziwill was an interior decorator; Mark specialised for a time in art deco. They had plenty in common.) Now in his fifties, Mark Shand is a distinguished travel writer, conservationist and champion of the cause of the endangered elephant,[120] but in the 1970s he was a famously tousle-headed, fast-living lad about town. He is good-looking still, but in his twenties he was – in our mutual friend the actress Joanna Lumley's phrase – 'an absolute dreamboat'. The model Marie Helvin said he was 'heaven'. Bianca Jagger, apparently, was driven to distraction by the sight of his 'snake tattoo'. 'Is this the sexiest man in London?' the London *Evening News* asked in 1979, before going on to describe 'his shaggy locks, Nureyev hips and casual, bored manner'. Whatever he had, it worked – and for women of all ages. Through Lee Radziwill (twenty years his senior), he met her niece, Caroline Kennedy, the late President's teenage daughter. When she was eighteen, encouraged by Mark, Caroline came to London to take the same fine arts course at Sotheby's as he had taken. She enjoyed it. She had fun with Mark, too.

'The Shands have got the shag gene,' a friend of the family said to me recently. 'No question. Big time.' I think it was meant as a compliment. When I repeated the remark to a member of the Royal Family, he laughed and said, 'That's the problem in a nutshell. They never said that about Queen Elizabeth [The Queen Mother], did they? About the Duchess of Windsor perhaps.'[121]

---

[120] His book *Travels with My Elephant* was his award-winning account of a life-changing experience: a trek across India by elephant. In 1990, he decided to settle down and married actress Clio Goldsmith, daughter of Teddy Goldsmith, founder of *The Ecologist* magazine. (Clio still features on assorted websites that offer 'nudie pix' of starlets of the 1980s.) Mark maintained that in the cause of wildlife conservation he had found a proper purpose in life. 'I've taken all my life,' he said. 'Now it's time to put something back.'

[121] Wallis Simpson had two marriages and sundry liaisons before her affair with the then Prince of Wales. According to Christopher Wilson in *Dancing with the Devil* (2001), she also had a four-year post-marital affair with a wealthy American playboy, Jimmy Donahue, a homosexual, twenty years her junior. The playwright Noël Coward (a good friend of Queen Elizabeth's) knew the Windsors without warming to them. Coward's lover and companion Graham Payn told me Coward told him that, in the 1930s, the stories about 'Mrs Simpson's sexual prowess were legion. Apparently, she could do the most extraordinary things with her private parts. "Wonderful in a houri," said Coward, "not so essential in a Queen."'

This is totally unfair, say friends of the new Duchess of Cornwall. In the run-up to her wedding to Prince Charles, when the *Daily Mail* was publishing extracts from Christopher Wilson's book *The Windsor Knot*, a friend of Camilla's told me that the bride-to-be was 'in despair'. 'She's being vilified. They're dragging up her past and making it sound so lurid. They're making it sound as if she was sleeping around like some tart. It's monstrous. She had a couple of boyfriends. And then she met Andrew [Parker Bowles]. And then Charles, of course. And that's it.'

In fairness to Christopher Wilson, if you read him carefully, while he quotes a friend of the Shands from Sussex saying 'Camilla had been fooling around from an early age', and paints a lively picture of the London scene in the 'swinging sixties', he does not accuse the young Duchess of promiscuity. He is less sympathetic towards Andrew Parker Bowles and what he calls 'the army officer's helter-skelter love life'. When Camilla and Andrew first met she was nineteen and he was twenty-seven. According to Wilson, the 'complexity and variety' of Andrew's sex-life meant the couple would be 'lovers – on and off – for seven years before they finally married':

> While Camilla wore white for the wedding at the Guards Chapel, followed by a reception at St James's Palace, she has participated in a love imbroglio worthy of a French farce or a cheap sex novel, depending on the reader's tolerance of those times. For it truly was the era of free love; and while its more vocal advocates tended to come in kaftans and long moustaches, it was not their province alone. . . Andrew Parker Bowles, no hippie he, breathed the scented air of the sixties with relish. Possessed of a dazzling charm, outstanding looks, a brave athleticism, and private means, he found that few women could resist him.

Parker Bowles was certainly no hippie. He was a Guards officer, a lieutenant in the Blues and Royals, a Catholic, educated at Ampleforth and then at Sandhurst, whose parents had all the right connections. His father, Derek, a sire of the family of the Earls of Macclesfield, with income from property in north London, and a fine house by Newbury racecourse (and a London *pied-à-terre* by Kensington Palace), was a friend of Queen Elizabeth The Queen Mother. Andrew was one of her godchildren and a page at Elizabeth

II's coronation.[122] His mother, Ann, was Chief Commissioner of the Girl Guides and shared the family enthusiasm for the turf. She was the daughter of Sir Humphrey de Trafford (late of the Coldstream Guards) and the Hon. Cynthia Cadogan (daughter of Viscount Chelsea). Sir Humphrey had owned the 1959 Epsom Derby winner, Parthia. Andrew was brought up around horses: he was a fearless amateur jockey and an efficient polo player.

Camilla met Andrew through his younger brother, Simon, who was working for Bruce Shand at the major's wine merchants in South Audley Street. All the witnesses (Camilla included) agree: she was instantly smitten. He was older, smoother, funnier, more dashing than any man she had encountered before. He had seen the world (he was just back from New Zealand where he had been serving as ADC to the governor general): he was willing to introduce Camilla to some of its delights:

> His greatest gift to women was the knowledge that sexuality was healthy – something to be explored. That openness about sex was his gift to Camilla. She was very innocent when they met, but they spent many, many nights together. He schooled her in the ways of the world.

This accolade comes from an unnamed lady quoted by the former *Daily Mail* diarist Nigel Dempster in *Behind Palace Doors*. The book provides a gripping, if largely hostile, account of Andrew Parker Bowles's way with women at the time:

> In London, Andrew lived in a small bachelor apartment in Portobello Road in Notting Hill, and it was there that he and Camilla began what friends remember as 'a very hot affair indeed'.

[122] Not a page to Her Majesty, but to the Lord Chancellor – which was appropriate as it was Andrew's forebear, Sir Thomas Parker, who had become Baron of Macclesfield (later Earl) on his appointment as Lord Chancellor in the reign of George I. The 6th Earl's son, Algernon, married Emma, daughter of the 4th Baron Kenyon, lord-in-waiting to Queen Victoria, Edward VII and George V. Their son, Eustace Parker, married Wilma, daughter of Henry Ferryman Bowles, 1st baronet and sometime MP for Enfield, and with their son, Derek, Andrew's father, introduced the surname Parker Bowles. Through his assorted forebears Andrew Parker Bowles is linked, variously, with William the Conqueror and with me. (My great-great-uncle was a Kenyon, from the offshoot of the Kenyon family that founded Kenyon's, the funeral directors – over several generations undertakers to the Royal Family.)

Andrew was already an accomplished lover and quickly proved himself to be an unfaithful one, too. He had a penchant for beautiful titled women, including Lady Caroline Percy, who was already the steady girlfriend of a baronet . . .

According to Dempster, Parker Bowles used Camilla as his plaything, dropping her and picking her up at will as he pleased. He quotes Lady Caroline Percy: 'Andrew behaved abominably to Camilla, but she was desperate to marry him. When I was with him I discovered he was also having an affair with a married woman.' According to the Dempster/Percy account, Camilla responded to Andrew's wanton behaviour with some wantonness of her own: she 'bedded' Rupert Hambro, an old Etonian debs' delight (just four years her senior) who, having trained as an accountant with Peat Marwick, had recently joined the family banking business. Says Nigel Dempster: 'Rupert knew that their affair was futile because of Camilla's obsession with Andrew, but he liked her and knew they would always be friends. He still remembers the masochistic glee she took in telling him about tricky situations Andrew's unfaithfulness sometimes caused. But she often saw the funny side of things afterward: her girls' talk always had the funniest lines and the best anecdotes.'

In one of these anecdotes, Camilla turns up unexpectedly at Andrew's Portobello Road pad at breakfast time only to discover the dashing lieutenant in his underpants with a leggy young lady in dishabille skulking in the bathroom. Camilla sees the girl, turns to Andrew and gets given the line, 'Rather plain, old man. Couldn't you do better than that? What's wrong with you? Happy to have someone else's shop-soiled goods are you?'

Inside Clarence House, they tell me they are not familiar with *Behind Palace Doors*. And when I attempt to repeat some of the best anecdotes and funniest lines, a friend of the Prince and the Duchess – who has known them for more than thirty years – interrupts and says, 'Utter claptrap, absolute hogwash. Camilla does not talk like that, never has. We're talking about people in their twenties, back in the sixties and seventies. Nobody can honestly remember who said what to whom and when or where. But that's not the point. The point is that Camilla and Andrew weren't engaged at the time. They were free to see whoever they pleased. Camilla had two or three boyfriends at most. Andrew may have had a few more, but he was older and a chap and all that. The point is they were just doing what young people were doing at the time.

It's nothing to make a song and dance about.' 'Rather like Tom Parker Bowles and the cocaine?' I suggested, helpfully. 'Exactly,' said the old friend of the royal couple, 'Precisely. Tom was never seriously into cocaine. It was just what was happening at the time.'[123]

Camilla Shand and Andrew Parker Bowles dated, off and on, for almost seven years before, officially, they became engaged in the spring of 1973. Nobody (even at Clarence House) seems to dispute that Camilla, at the time, was more focused on Andrew than he appears to have been on her. Even his best friends (and he has many) acknowledge his roving eye. In 1970, apparently, on leave from a stint with his regiment in Germany, Andrew, aged thirty, took a shine to Princess Anne, aged nineteen. Their flirtatious friendship is said to have blossomed into a full-blown affair during the week of Royal Ascot. (You can assume an equine presence at all the key turning points in this story.) Some say it was to the future Brigadier Parker Bowles, head of the Royal Veterinary Corps, that the future Princess Royal, Lady of the Garter, yielded her virginity – but how do they know? Others say that the relationship was a serious one and there was talk even of Andrew marrying Anne – but given her comparative youth at the time and the fact that he was a Catholic, that seems to me an improbable suggestion. Many say that it was Camilla's jealousy of Andrew's relationship with Anne that drove her to pursue Prince Charles – but, say Charles and Camilla, that simply is not true.

The legend has grown up that Camilla, stung by her lover's infatuation with the Queen's daughter, determined to seek her revenge by outclassing him at his own game and seducing the Queen's son. She had the motive – and she found the opportunity, on the polo ground at Smith's Lawn in Windsor Great Park. There, by the woods where Edward the Confessor went hunting a thousand years before, in the

[123] Tom Parker Bowles was born in 1974 and educated at Eton and Oxford. At university he was cautioned for possession of two drugs: Ecstasy and cannabis. In May 1999, at the Cannes Film Festival, a *News of the World* reporter fingered him for 'supplying' cocaine. 'I was totally set up,' he later explained. 'I mean, a very pretty lady at the beach asked me out for a drink and I thought great, you know, then she asked me if I could get her some coke. I said, "Well, I wouldn't really know where to get it." But the thing is, it's so easy. So, I did. I got caught. I was much younger.' Although subsequently seen taking cocaine at a party, and advised for a while to steer clear of his godfather Charles's sons, William and Harry, so as not to appear as a bad influence, Tom is now older, wiser, married, and following in the footsteps of his great-grandfather, P. Morton Shand, as a successful food writer. The closest he gets to drugs these days is at the kitchen chopping board. 'Chillies,' he says, 'are a sort of culinary cocaine.'

park first laid out by her forebear Charles II, Camilla, the great-granddaughter of Edward VII's last mistress, inspired by Alice Keppel's example, approached the heir to the throne and propositioned him.

That is almost certainly how the story will be told when the movie comes to be made. However, the Prince of Wales and the Duchess of Cornwall would prefer you to know the truth. I am told I can tell you, 'It wasn't like that at all.' Yes, in the early 1970s, Camilla was a frequent spectator at polo matches played at Smith's Lawn, but she did not go there in hot pursuit of Charles, or indeed of Andrew, both of whom played there quite regularly. She went, initially, because she had a girlfriend, Carolyn, whose father, Colonel Gerard Leigh, happened to be the chairman of the Guards Polo Club[124] and, knowing her interest in horses, invited her along. Yes, she had a number of polo playing men friends, but it was not at Smith's Lawn that she first met Prince Charles, and, if she had, she would certainly not have introduced herself out of the blue. She would have waited to be presented.

Charles and Camilla, once they had become friends, did indeed often meet up in the margins of polo matches at Smith's Lawn, but that is not where they first met. Charles insists that he was introduced to Camilla for the first time by a mutual friend: Lord Butler's research assistant on *The Art of the Possible*, the glamorous daughter of the Chilean ambassador, his girlfriend from his Cambridge days, the lovely Lucia Santa Cruz. According to Charles, Lucia called and said she had found 'just the girl' for him – 'and she had'.

Charles says now what he said then: he fell for Camilla almost at once. He liked everything about her. He says, 'You couldn't not.' He liked her look: her hair, her smile, her unaffected dress sense. He liked her unaffected manners: instinctively courteous, but always natural. There was nothing forced or awkwardly formal about her – and yet she never overstepped the mark. She wasn't brittle or 'pseudo-sophisticated' (his phrase). She was down-to-earth, uncomplicated and fun. And funny, too. He loved her laugh. They shared a sense of humour: he still found the comedy of *The Goons* hilarious: she said she did, too. She was easy to be with; she was undemanding; she was

---

[124] He is now a vice-president. The president, since the club was formed in 1955, has been the Duke of Edinburgh. Originally called the Household Brigade Polo Club, it changed its name in 1959 and is now the largest polo club in Europe, with around 160 playing members (including Charles and both his sons) and a thousand non-playing members – of whom you could be one. (The joining fee is currently £150 and the subscription £225 per year.)

understanding. She lived in a ground-floor flat in Victoria (she was unpretentious: he loved that about her), but she was a country girl at heart (and he loved that, too). She had been brought up in the world of hunting and horses. She was a soldier's daughter. Her father was a Vice-Lord-Lieutenant and a Yeoman of the Guard. Her forebears included courtiers and admirals and eccentrics – and, of course, a king's mistress or two. The attraction between Charles and Camilla was immediate and mutual, and passionate.

Chapter Seven

Men and Wives

> What infinite heart's ease
> Must kings neglect that private men enjoy!
> And what have kings that privates have not too,
> Save ceremony, save general ceremony?
>   William Shakespeare (1564–1616), *Henry V*

Why did Charles not propose to Camilla when first he had the chance? He says today that he first knew for sure that he wanted to marry her in December 1972. He says that even before that, in the summer of 1972, he knew that he loved her, 'completely'. Why did he not seize the moment then, when they were both young and free?

'Because he's incapable of making up his mind,' says Rosa Monckton. 'It's his besetting sin.' Rosa – the granddaughter of Walter Monckton, friend and adviser to Edward VIII at the time of the abdication[125] – was Diana's closest girlfriend at the time of her death in 1997. In 2005, Rosa told me that she and Diana had discussed the possibility of Charles marrying Camilla, but Diana was convinced it would never happen, because, as Diana said, 'Charles can't make a decision.'

---

[125] 1st Viscount Monckton (1891–1965), barrister, MP, influential Minister of Labour in Churchill's post-war government, he became a friend of the Prince of Wales at Oxford and drafted his abdication speech of 1936. 'He wrote King Farouk's, too,' his granddaughter told me, 'an interesting double.' Rosa Monckton worked for Asprey and Tiffany before creating her own 'Rosa Monckton' jewellery and fashion brand. She was introduced to Diana at the beginning of the 1990s by a mutual friend, Lucia Flecha da Lima, wife of the Brazilian ambassador. 'Lucia called me and said, "I've got somebody who really seems to need some help. I think she needs to talk to someone who isn't part of the establishment, someone discreet." We met first, not at all discreetly, in Harry's Bar' in South Audley Street – once, of course, the address of Major Shand's wine merchants, Block, Grey & Block.

This is a charge regularly made against the Prince of Wales. The same people say that he only proposed to Diana when he did because his father forced his hand and that he only divorced Diana when he did because his mother told him he had to. Unsurprisingly, it is a charge that Charles's friends reject. One of his closest friends told me, 'Charles was on the brink of proposing to Camilla in 1972, at the time of his twenty-fourth birthday [on 14 November], but he didn't because he felt he was too young for marriage – that his parents wouldn't wear it. He felt he wouldn't really be able to settle down until he left the navy. Also, he wasn't certain how his proposal would be received.'

I think – given what we know of Camilla's heritage, of her character, of her enthusiasm for the story of her great-grandmother's attachment to Edward VII – we can safely guess (can't we?) that, had the Prince of Wales proposed to her at the end of 1972, he would have received the same answer then as he received when eventually he did ask her thirty-two years later. Camilla, apparently, professes not to recall exactly how she felt at the time. One of her friends told me, 'She loved going out with Charles, of course she did, but she didn't think it was "going anywhere". He was away for weeks on end and when he was away she was still seeing Andrew [Parker Bowles]. I think she was torn. And Andrew, on the face of it, was a much more realistic bet than Charles.' Another old friend takes a less ambivalent line: 'If Charles had popped the question, she'd have leapt at it. I don't know why he didn't. There was an incredible electricity between them, right from the start. They clicked. They were on the same wavelength. You should have seen the way they looked at one another. There was something very special going on. It was instant attraction.'

It was an 'instant attraction' that began in the summer of 1971 and developed and deepened over the next eighteen months. The couple met at polo matches at Smith's Lawn; they had supper together; they went to Annabel's nightclub in Berkeley Square; they went back to Camilla's flat in Victoria; they met for long weekends – and snatched nights – at Broadlands, the Hampshire home of Lord Mountbatten. It seems to be agreed by all concerned that, when they were apart, it was Charles who made most of the running, sending Camilla elaborately worded love notes and initiating lengthy, intimate, late-night telephone conversations, the nature and tone of which would eventually become notorious. It seems to be agreed, also, that Mountbatten was a key player, the only 'adult' in Charles's world to know about Camilla at the time.

'You don't talk about affairs of the heart to your parents, really, do you?' Mountbatten's daughter, Patricia, said to me when I went to see her and her husband, John Brabourne, in the early summer of 2005. 'Charles was very close to the Queen Mother, of course, and to Mabel Anderson, but I don't think he would have discussed Camilla with them – certainly, not then. But he could discuss anything with my father, *anything*. And when he joined the navy and was stationed at Portsmouth, it wasn't far from Broadlands so it was easy for him to drive over. He loved going there.'

And Mountbatten loved having him. In January 1972, Charles was serving as a sub-lieutenant in HMS *Norfolk* in dry dock at Portsmouth and got over to Broadlands as frequently as he could. 'It's lovely having him here,' his great-uncle wrote in his diary, 'we've had so many cosy talks. What a really charming young man he is.' In the summer of 1972, Charles was transferred to HMS *Dryad*, the Royal Navy shore station at Portsmouth, for a series of training courses. Again, he visited Broadlands whenever possible. 'As you know only too well, to me it has become a second home in so many ways,' Charles wrote to Mountbatten, 'and no one could ever have had such a splendid honorary grandpapa in the history of avuncular relationships.' When Charles was at sea, his 'honorary grandpapa' – a widower since 1960 – missed him greatly and, in his letters, told him so: 'I've been thinking of you – far more than I had expected to think of a young man – but then I've got to know you so well, I really miss you very much.'

There was a deep mutual affection between the old man – Mountbatten was now in his seventies – and the young prince. Patricia Mountbatten told me, 'My father was a wonderful communicator, right to the end of his life, and I know he talked to Charles about everything – the navy, the problems of royalty, his position, history, love. He respected my father and I think, so long as he was there, he followed his advice.' About a year before his great-uncle's murder, Charles sent him one of many thank-you letters (written in that slightly over-the-top style that is Charles's hallmark – and was that of Mountbatten and of Queen Elizabeth, too – but is not at all how either the Queen or Prince Philip write): 'I was deeply grateful for our conversation yesterday morning and being able to pick your brains on the subjects was an *immense* help. As I said to you yesterday, I have no idea what we shall do without you when you finally decide to depart. It doesn't bear thinking about, but I only hope I shall have learnt *something* from you in order to carry it on in some way or another.'

Charles was also close to Mountbatten's favourite daughter, Patricia, and her husband, John Brabourne, and, through his twenties, spent several holidays with them in their beach house on the island of Eleuthera in the Bahamas. Lady Mountbatten told me, 'I think they were some of his happiest days. He came on his own – literally. There was just his detective, that was all. And the local policeman. No entourage, nothing. He slept in the maid's room. He got up very early in the morning, about six, and walked along the beach, went for a skinny-dip, and watched the birds. He loved listening to the wind in the trees. He loved the breeze – the stronger the breeze, the more he loved it.' Charles said, 'I've never experienced life more closely resembling paradise on earth.' (I have stayed there, too: he is right.) 'Charles was always happy on Eleuthera,' said Lady Mountbatten, 'because it was just us, just family, mucking in together.' Charles helped with the cooking: scrambled eggs and bread-and-butter pudding were his signature dishes. He helped with the washing-up, too. 'It was there that I realised,' Lady Mountbatten told me, 'that what he most wanted in the world was a normal family life. He wanted what we've got – John and I – that's all.[126] That's all he's ever wanted – a straightforward, uncomplicated, family-centred life.'

The Brabournes have been married for nearly sixty years. To see them together is touching because they are so obviously a mutually necessary double act: they complete one another's sentences; they pay each other little compliments; they sit side by side in identical arm chairs, a contented king and queen in their domestic kingdom. That said, when I was last with them, inadvertently I provoked a disagreement between them. When Lady Mountbatten repeated her line that all Charles had ever wanted was a normal family life with a like-minded partner, I suggested to her that if he had married Camilla when he had first had the chance that is what he might have achieved. 'No,' she said at once, with quite a sigh. 'It wouldn't have been possible, not then.

[126] Lady Mountbatten's turn of phrase prompts me to share with you the origin of the Queen's celebrated turn of phrase, 'My husband and I . . .' The Queen used the formula so frequently that eventually it became a joke and she was forced to drop it. It originated at the beginning of her reign, when the Queen and Prince Philip were staying with the Brabournes for a shooting weekend in late November. Her Majesty had brought the draft of her Christmas broadcast with her and tried it out on her hosts, who enjoyed it, but suggested that the phrase 'I and my husband' – used several times in the speech – did not feel quite right. Patricia Brabourne suggested that 'My husband and I' might sound better.

Camilla had "a history" – and you didn't want a past that hung about. And she was a subject. And nobody marries a subject.'[127]

Patricia Mountbatten reads the *Guardian* (and the *Independent on Sunday*), but she is also the great-great-grandchild of Queen Victoria and Prince Albert – which Lord Brabourne is not.[128] While his wife was still speaking, he interrupted her and said firmly, 'Charles misjudged it. He didn't pursue her.' Lady Mountbatten turned to him, 'But Charles was at sea for months on end – how could he?' Lord Brabourne shrugged. Clearly, in his view, if a man wants a girl enough he stays the course and he lets her know how he feels. 'He misjudged it,' he repeated. 'He wouldn't have got anywhere anyway,' said Lady Mountbatten with finality.

What we might term Charles and Camilla's 'first affair' came to an end just before Christmas 1972. ('Puppy Love', appropriately, was one of the hits of the year.) The heir to the throne was not yet halfway through his naval training. He was appointed to the frigate HMS *Minerva* and destined to spend eight months at sea. He joined his new ship, docked at Portsmouth, at the beginning of December. Over the weekend of 9–10 December, he stayed with his great-uncle at Broadlands. Camilla was invited, too. The Prince took them both – honorary grandpapa and established girlfriend – on a guided tour of the ship, followed by lunch. The following weekend, 16–17 December, the Prince was back at Broadlands – and so was Camilla. It was, the Prince wrote bleakly to Mountbatten, 'the last time I shall see her for eight months'. It turned out to be the last time they would meet as single people.

That weekend, as I understand it, Charles declared his love, but not his hand. He whispered sweet nothings, but said nothing of substance. He made no commitment, and he asked for none. Sometimes the actions we do not take are indeed more significant than those we do. This was the weekend when the likes of Lord Brabourne reckon Charles

---

[127] Oscar Wilde, when giving a lecture, invited questions from his audience. He said he would be happy to talk on any subject. A gentleman at the hall asked him for his opinion of Queen Victoria. Wilde replied immediately, 'Her Majesty is not a subject.'

[128] He has an interesting heritage nonetheless. He is the 7th Baron (and 16th baronet), the son of the 5th Baron Brabourne GCSI, GCIE, MC, JP, MP, sometime Viceroy and acting Governor General of India who married the daughter of the 6th Marquess of Sligo. John succeeded to the family titles in 1943, when his elder brother was shot after escaping from a train in Italy and being recaptured. He was awarded a CBE in 1993 for his contribution to film and television.

'had his chance' – and missed it. 'This was looked for at your hand, and this was balked.'[129]

Charles went to sea and Camilla went back to Andrew Parker Bowles. Charles was twenty-four, naturally reticent, reluctant to commit himself (except inside his own head), and, given his age, and position, perhaps understandably, unready to settle down. Andrew was thirty-three, and (in one of Princess Margaret's favourite turns of phrase) 'a different gether altothing'. He might not be the most reliable suitor, but, when focused, he had fire in his heart and brimstone in his liver. His style of wooing would have met with Sir Toby Belch's approval. He saw off his royal rival with ease and despatch: he 'banged the youth into numbness'. On 15 March 1973, Andrew Parker Bowles and Camilla Shand announced their engagement. Charles was on board his ship in the West Indies when he heard the news. He was bereft, bewildered, he confessed to his great-uncle, that 'such a blissful, peaceful and mutually happy relationship' should come to a close like this. Now, he told Mountbatten, wanly, he would have 'no one' to go back to in England. 'I suppose the feeling of emptiness will pass eventually,' he said.

According to Carolyn Gerard Leigh, 'There was never any question then of Charles marrying Camilla. He was much younger, simply a nice boy . . . Camilla was conscious of her select status but she never wanted to be queen.' Camilla wanted to be Mrs Parker Bowles. According to another friend, an older man, 'Andrew and Camilla were definitely in

---

[129] Sir Toby Belch reproving Sir Andrew Aguecheek for his 'dormouse valour' in *Twelfth Night*, one of Charles's favourite plays. As a lover Sir Andrew fails to seize the moment and see off his rival for the hand of the Countess Olivia: 'You should then have accosted her,' says Sir Toby, 'and with some excellent jests, fire-new from the mint, you should have banged the youth into dumbness. This was looked for at your hand, and this was balked: the double gilt of this opportunity you let time wash off, and you are now sailed into the north of my lady's opinion; where you will hang like an icicle on a Dutchman's beard, unless you do redeem it by some laudable attempt either of valour or policy.' 'An't be any way,' responds Sir Andrew, 'it must be with valour; for policy I hate.' Charles – who, in the early 1990s campaigned effectively to ensure a continuing place for Shakespeare in the national curriculum – turns regularly to the national poet for solace and for guidance. He can quote by heart Henry V's soliloquy on the burdens of kingship: 'What infinite heart's ease / Must kings neglect that private men enjoy! And what have kings that privates have not too, / Save ceremony, save general ceremony?' Inevitably, the line of Sir Andrew Aguecheek's that is his favourite is the most wistful: 'I was adored once, too.' (At this point, you either smile in sympathy with the Prince – or, like his father at *Macbeth*, you laugh out loud.)

love when they married. They were a good match. I'm sure they both went into it wanting to make it work. But Camilla knew from the start what Andrew was like. She might have thought, even in the early days, that her friendship with Charles could continue after she was married. She was very aware – very, very aware – of her heritage. She talked a lot about Mrs Keppel and Edward VII.'

Having become engaged on the Ides of March (as Charles noticed), Camilla and Andrew were married on American Independence Day, 4 July 1973. The wedding, at the Guards Chapel, Wellington Barracks, a few hundred yards from Buckingham Palace, was a grand affair, with eight hundred guests (one hundred more than were invited to Camilla's second wedding in 2005), so many that some of the congregation in the Chapel were left standing. The bride looked lovely, in a shower of tulle – a ten-foot-long veil – and a £2,000 dress (pure white, with ruffled trim along the neckline and hem) designed by Belville Sassoon. The groom, in morning suit rather than military uniform, looked debonair – and remarkably fresh, given the riotous nature of his stag party at White's Club in St James's the night before. ('The party got slightly out of control,' confessed the groom's brother, Simon Parker Bowles. 'There was a lot of broken crockery and glass, and chairs . . . I've paid the damages bill.')

The reception was held across Green Park, a few minutes' walk away, at St James's Palace, headquarters of the Yeomen of the Guard, the Queen's Bodyguard, of which the father of the bride was then the proud 'Exon'. The royal guests included Queen Elizabeth The Queen Mother, her daughter, Princess Margaret (soon to end her marriage to Lord Snowdon) and Princess Anne (soon to begin her marriage to Captain Mark Phillips). Prince Charles was invited, but was obliged to decline on the grounds of 'duty': he was attending independence day celebrations elsewhere.

Other accounts of the wedding make much of Charles's absence. In her book about Camilla, Caroline Graham quotes one of the guests as saying: 'Everyone thought it rather odd he was not there. He sent a telegram and used the excuse he was aboard ship. But no one bought it. He is the Prince of Wales, for goodness' sakes; had he wanted to be there, it could easily have been arranged . . . But everyone knew the real reason. He simply could not face watching Camilla walk down the aisle.'

Prince Charles finds this kind of comment 'typical but intensely irritating'. If he could have been there, he would have been there. He was unavailable because he was due in Nassau at the time, as the Queen's representative at the official celebrations marking the independence – after three hundred years of British rule – of the seven hundred islands of the Bahamas. As he points out, the timetable for the Bahamian independence celebrations was agreed some time before Camilla and Andrew were even engaged. He is frustrated, too, because remarks like this – printed and repeated *ad nauseam* – remind him that so many people who should know better, simply do not understand how 'the system' works. So much of what he does as Prince of Wales is preordained, not in his gift. As a little boy, he says, he wanted to be 'the proverbial engine driver'; then, when he went on a yacht for the first time, he thought he might be a sailor; and then, a soldier, 'because I had been watching the Changing of the Guard'. Then what he calls 'the awful truth' began to dawn: 'When I started shooting I thought how marvellous it would be to be a big game-hunter . . . I went from one thing to another until I realised I was rather stuck.' Charles does what his 'duty' requires and he feels this sense of duty, he says, 'intensely'.

While Andrew and Camilla were setting off for what, at the time, they described as 'a brief but idyllic honeymoon' in the South of France, at Cap d'Ail, where the weather was apparently 'just right', Charles was three thousand miles away, in a stifling tropical heat working the crowds (there were 2,500 guests at one garden party – all of whom hoped to meet him), taking salutes, making speeches (five in all), unveiling plaques, laying foundation stones, touring schools, visiting hospitals and, ultimately, enduring the indignity of the moment when the union flag was lowered for the last time and the Bahamian Minister of Finance went 'berserk', according to the Prince, jumping up and down and shouting 'Hooray!' at the top of his voice, which made him look 'extraordinarily stupid and damned rude'.

As Charles pursued his 'duty' as heir to the throne and recently promoted lieutenant in the Royal Navy, Major and Mrs Andrew Parker Bowles began to build their domestic life together. They bought a handsome part thirteenth/mainly seventeenth-century manor house in Wiltshire – Bolehyde Manor, at Allington, near Chippenhan – and, while Andrew spent the inside of the week with his regiment in London, his young bride (now twenty-six), with knowledgeable input from her sister, Annabel, set about creating a properly comfortable English country-house home. Camilla's taste in decoration was more 'shabby grand' than Colefax & Fowler chic, more Queen Mother than Princess Michael of Kent. The garden was her special domain. It is – in large measure due to Camilla's hard graft – a beautiful garden, stone-walled, with small gazebos by the old gate, two Elizabethan pavilions, unexpected shrubs and climbers, traditional roses and herbaceous beds. There is a courtyard, too, with tender plants, a vegetable and fruit garden, and a greenhouse yard.[130] Camilla spent endless hours in the garden, in comfy trousers and a baggy jumper. 'She has always been happy to get her hands dirty,' says her friend the novelist Jilly Cooper, who understands the ways of the Aga-aristocracy. Says Jo Hansford, 'celebrity hair colourist', at whose salon Camilla, in recent years, has been getting her nails done: 'She likes to feel the soil.'

Bolehyde Manor was a good house for dogs and children and, soon, Camilla had both. On 18 December 1974, Tom Parker Bowles was born. Intriguingly, the official website for the Prince of Wales gives Tom's names as simply 'Thomas Henry', while, according to his baptismal certificate, Tom was christened 'Thomas Henry Charles'. The oversight may be deliberate, prompted by awareness at Clarence House that rumour has long had it that Tom is, in fact, not his official father Andrew's offspring, but the bastard son of the Prince of Wales.

In olden days, as we have seen, royal princes sired illegitimate offspring almost as a matter of routine. Camilla is descended from the Dukes of Richmond and the Earls of Albemarle as a direct consequence of Charles II's easy-going approach to paternity. There are those who remain convinced that Camilla's grandmother, Sonia Keppel, was the illegitimate daughter of Edward VII. George V, as Duke of York, was rumoured to have had three children before he married Princess Mary of Teck. Edward VIII, as Prince of Wales, is supposed to have fathered an Australian boy called Tony in his cabin on board the battle cruiser HMS *Renown* in 1920. The Duke of Edinburgh, I believe, is currently in correspondence with a late middle-aged German individual who claims to be his offspring and will not be gainsaid – despite the fact that Prince Philip was serving in the Royal Navy in the Far East at the time of the alleged conception, and to have fathered the child would have

[130] You can visit the garden and I recommend a visit. Call 01249 652105 for opening times. The house, sadly, is not open to the public, though, if you peer through the windows, you get a flavour of its charms and history. In the late thirteenth century, Thomas de Bolehude held the deeds to the property. In 1635 it was sold to John Gale, whose family lived in the house for around four hundred years. Legend has it that one of the Gales was the first man to fly. He made a pair of wings, took off successfully, but fell into the moat in the attempt.

necessitated his flying secretly to Berlin at the height of the Second World War.

What great ones do – or do not do – the less will prattle of. Why, the rumour-mongers say, if Charles is not the father of Tom Parker Bowles, should the Prince establish a trust fund to benefit Tom to the tune of £2 million? The answer is that Charles is a wealthy and generous man and the fund is to benefit both Tom and his sister, Laura Rose (born in 1974), because Charles loves their mother, is very fond of them and senses that something 'is due to them' for the turbulence caused to their lives as a consequence of his relationship with their mother during their formative years. Also, as a courtier put it to me, 'HRH knows his children and grandchildren will always be looked after financially. He can't put the Duchess's children on the same footing, of course, but he wants to do what he can in their interests.'

At the time of Tom Parker Bowles's conception – in March 1974 – Charles was on the other side of the world, serving on HMS *Jupiter* as communications officer, on the last leg of a Royal Navy tour to Commonwealth and other friendly nations that, in his journal, the Prince dubbed 'The Incredible Pacific Voyage, 1974'. The tour climaxed – in the very days of Tom's conception in Wiltshire – with *Jupiter* docking at San Diego, California, and Charles undertaking a high-profile series of goodwill engagements. Witnesses to his whereabouts at the time included the state governor, Ronald Reagan, and assorted local luminaries, among them Frank Sinatra, Ava Gardner, Charlton Heston and 'my only pin-up' (as he put it), Barbra Streisand.

Charles is adamant that his physical relationship with Camilla did not resume at this stage. She had ditched him (to use Kevin Burke's phrase) and he accepted his lot. They were no longer lovers, but they could still be friends. When Camilla asked him to be Tom's godfather he was, he said, 'honoured and delighted' to accept. The christening took place at the Guards Chapel and, this time, Charles was there: the ceremony was arranged with his diary in mind.

Shortly after he had received the news of Camilla's engagement to Andrew Parker Bowles, back in the late spring of 1973, Charles, at sea in the West Indies, had heard about a second engagement, in its own way as disconcerting as the first. The Duke of Edinburgh wrote to his eldest son with the 'good news' that his younger sister, Anne, was due to marry a cavalry officer (of The Queen's Dragoon Guards), her fellow equestrian (and three-day eventing Olympic champion), Lieutenant Mark Phillips. Charles received the news with, as he put it, 'a spasm of shock and amazement'. He was reduced, he acknowledges, to 'tears of impotence and regret'. It was not simply that he had reservations about his future brother-in-law (Charles is credited with giving Mark Phillips the nickname 'Fog'), it was quite as much the fact that he dreaded the idea of 'losing' his beloved sister. Until the time of her marriage, Anne had been one of Charles's linchpins – sister, friend and ally. When Camilla's younger sister, Annabel, married Simon Elliot in 1972, Camilla did not lose her: the sisters remained best friends. In her life, Camilla has been lucky in not losing her linchpins: her sister, her brother, her father, even her first husband, they are all her friends still. When her mother died in July 1994, Camilla was almost forty-seven. Charles, by contrast, not as easy or comfortable with his parents as Camilla was with hers, was less fortunate. As we shall see, from the spring of 1973 onwards, Charles began to feel that, one by one, he was losing the key linchpins of his life, the allies, the 'safe havens', the 'rocks against adversity', the people who 'understood'.

Princess Anne married Mark Phillips on 14 November 1973,[131] Prince Charles's twenty-fifth birthday, at Westminster Abbey, before a congregation of a thousand and a television audience of many millions. 'I shouldn't wonder if their children are four-legged,' the Queen is supposed to have remarked. When the first of the children arrived, in 1977, Andrew Parker Bowles was asked to be Peter Phillips's godfather and was, he said, 'honoured and delighted' to accept. At the time of Anne's engagement, in May 1973, two months after Camilla's engagement in March, Charles reflected: 'I can see I shall have to find myself a wife pretty rapidly, otherwise I shall get left behind and feel pretty miserable.'

In the event, from the spring of Camilla's and Anne's engagements, to the spring of his own, eight years passed, 'pretty desultory much of it', he said to a friend recently, 'though I suppose I had some fun'.

In the early 1990s, when he cooperated with Jonathan Dimbleby in making the book and television film about his life, Charles was happy to provide the broadcaster with a flavour of some of the 'fun' from his navy days:

[131] They separated in 1989; the marriage was dissolved in April 1992, and, on 12 December the same year, the Princess Royal married Commander Timothy Laurence, RN, at Crathie Church, near Balmoral. In July 2004, promoted Rear-Admiral, Laurence was appointed Assistant Chief of the Defence Staff, making him the armed services' highest-ranking member of the Royal Family since Lord Mountbatten was appointed Chief of the Defence Staff in 1959.

When he was with HMS *Norfolk*, curiosity had led him to follow his brother officers into Toulon's red light zone. With fellow officers from HMS *Minerva*, he had acquainted himself with the inside of a Colombian brothel, where – as an observer – he noted the lurid green lights and equally lurid *mesdames*; one of these painted ladies had momentarily placed a hand on his thigh, which had added 'yet another of life's essential experiences to my collection. Not literally, I hasten to add.' However, he was far from immune to the attractions of a romantic encounter. He succumbed to a commanding officer's daughter in the West Indies, and in Venezuela was much taken by the wife of a polo player. 'Never in my life,' he wrote of this encounter, 'have I had such dances as I had with this beautiful lady. She is unbelievable is all I can say and I danced with every conceivable part of her. I fell madly in love with her and danced wildly and passionately, finally doing a Russian dance at one stage which cleared the floor because I was wearing my mess boots . . .'

Dimbleby describes Charles at this time as 'an unworldly suitor', 'an innocent abroad', 'a tentative explorer blessed with an inconvenient conscience, whose sense of propriety invariably intervened to challenge his basic instincts'. This may well have been the case when it came to brief encounters with showgirls, *mesdames* and variously sized and equipped 'trophy hunters' in foreign parts, but at home, on leave, behind closed doors, I get the impression the heir apparent was less abashed and tongue-tied than Dimbleby's account suggests. A girlfriend of Charles's from the same period – who has never spoken about her relationship with the Prince before – told me that she did not think he was the least bit unworldly or tentative during their time together. 'He was lovely,' she said. 'A little shy, perhaps, but how fantastic to meet a man who isn't full of himself. He was really sweet, but he wasn't wishy-washy. He was a proper romantic gentleman. And sexy with it. He was a prince, too, of course. And you knew it. And he knew it. And that's pretty exciting.'

There are those among Charles's family and friends who feel that, as a would-be lover, the heir apparent rather exploited his princely status during what he now calls his 'footloose years'. I am told that he may even be among them. One of his cousins said to me, 'He got through quite a few girls in those years and I'm not sure how well he treated some of them. I think he's a bit ashamed of some of that now.' Dimbleby touches on this in his book, but, understandably, glosses over most of the detail, sparing the reader (and the Prince) the names and case histories of most of the young lovelies (and there were dozens) who caught the royal eye through the 1970s. An exhaustive list would be impossible – the Prince is quite proud of the fact that the names of several of those to whom he was closest at the time have never seen the light of day – but I hope he will forgive me for including a representative selection to help paint the picture.[132]

The first of his serious post-Camilla relationships was with Georgiana Russell, a young woman more obviously glamorous than Camilla (she worked for *Vogue* magazine), but the same age as her (that is to say, eighteen months older than Charles) and from a not wholly dissimilar background, though, possibly, as we used to say, 'a cut above'. Georgiana's father was neither a soldier, wine merchant nor a Yeoman of the Guard, but he was a diplomat, Her Majesty's ambassador to Spain and a GCVO. As the Shands were related to the Ashcombes and the Albemarles, so the Russells were allied to the Dukes of Bedford. As the Shands had places in Kensington and East Sussex, so the Russells had places in Chester Square and east Kent. Both Major Shand and Sir John Russell were Joint Masters of their respective local hunts. Georgiana had much to commend her and Charles was quickly smitten. He told her he loved her almost at once, but over time – the relationship lasted, off and on, for nine months – she came to the conclusion 'He had a funny way of showing it.' Eventually she decided her princely lover had 'long lost the art of unselfishness' and she ditched him in the course of what was supposed to be a romantic holiday at Balmoral. The problem, it seems, was that Charles did as he pleased – assuming, without asking, that what pleased him would please his girlfriend, too. Standing on the banks of the River Dee, Georgiana decided she had had enough. According to a witness, the late Stephen Barry, Prince Charles's valet

[132] He may not. The Prince of Wales devotes most of his waking hours to his duties and to a multiplicity of good causes, from the Prince's Trust to the British Forces Foundation, and yet most of the millions of words written about him are about his personality, his private life and his past. It was ever thus. Not long ago, I interviewed the Polish-born film director, Roman Polanski, justly celebrated for *Knife in the Water*, *Repulsion*, *Rosemary's Baby*, *Chinatown* and *The Piano*, but world-famous because his wife was brutally murdered in California in 1969 and forever notorious because, eight years later, he was forced to leave the United States having had sex with a thirteen-year-old girl. 'The media laid my silhouette in a morgue a long time ago,' he told me, with a wry smile the Prince of Wales would recognise. 'The picture is set. There is nothing I can do to change it. Whatever I say will make no difference. Every interview is the same. Always.'

at the time,[133] 'She was freezing cold and eating scraps because the prince was on one of his economy drives. I think she thought the week would be rather glamorous – a romantic interlude in the Highlands with her prince. Nothing of the kind. He was standing with his feet in icy water all day, while she was bored out of her mind. I thought then that she was not going to last the course and I was right.'

Next up was Lady Jane Wellesley, an exact contemporary of Charles, a childhood friend, and, better still, daughter of the 8th Duke of Wellington, the descendant of a true national hero and a good friend of Charles's mother. The media was convinced this one would last the course. Indeed, the press talked up the prospects to such an extent that, in 1975, Charles felt obliged to use a speech to the Parliamentary Press Gallery to make a rare public reference to his private life. 'I have read so many reports recently telling everyone whom I am going to marry,' he said, 'that when last year the Duke of Wellington's daughter was staying at Sandringham a crowd of 10,000 people turned up when we went to church. Such was the obvious conviction that what they had read was true that I almost felt I had better espouse myself at once so as not to disappoint so many people . . .'

Lady Jane liked Prince Charles (she still does: she was a guest at his wedding to Camilla), but she was not inclined to marry him. When cornered in the street and pressed on the subject by insolent hacks in the mid-1970s she made her position clear: 'I don't want another title.

---

[133] Author of *Royal Service*, one of many books written by former royal servants unable to resist the temptation to spill the beans. (The best of their kind are *The Little Princesses*, by Marion Crawford, the Queen's childhood governess, and *A Royal Duty*, by Paul Burrell, footman to the Queen and butler to the Prince and Princess of Wales. Both books are revelatory, well-written and essentially sympathetic – though still considered beyond the pale at Buckingham Palace and Clarence House.) Paul Burrell is bisexual and Stephen Barry was homosexual (he died of AIDS) and Diana, Princess of Wales, who was anything but homophobic (indeed, she rather enjoyed her status as a gay icon), used to make teasing remarks about the number of homosexuals among Prince Charles's retainers. She was meaning to be naughty, but she was also being unfair. For generations, royal service has attracted members of the gay community. As the wholly straight Lord Charteris, sometime private secretary to the Queen, put it to me, 'I think it's the guardsmen they're drawn to.' I recall visiting Buckingham Palace as far back as 1983 (when I was younger, prettier and enjoyed minor notoriety as a daytime television presenter) and, finding myself alone in one of the state rooms half an hour early for my appointment, was entertained by a foursome of fluttering footmen who – against all the rules, I'm sure – insisted on us taking photographs of one another in assorted regal poses. 'We're the Queen's queens,' chorused one of them.

I've already got one, thank you.' She passed on Charles,[134] and, inadvertently, passed him on as well, because his next sustained affair was with a then friend of Lady Jane's, introduced by her to him at a dinner party at her house in Fulham in the summer of 1975. Davina Sheffield was blonde and beautiful (a picture editor's dream), well-spoken, well-bred (PLU, but not an aristocrat), and a complete success when taken to Balmoral. She was serious-minded – during the affair, she took several months out to travel to Vietnam to work in a children's orphanage – and her life was touched by tragedy: her mother was brutally murdered by intruders at her family's Oxfordshire home. Many thought (some even in Charles's family) that, though 'a subject', Davina Sheffield was in with a chance. Then it transpired that the golden girl had a fatal flaw: 'history'. The press unearthed an ex-boyfriend, James Beard, an Old Harrovian (need more be said?), who confessed, when pressed, that he had lived with Davina in a cottage near Winchester where they had enjoyed 'a full sexual relationship'. For good measure, and no doubt meaning well, he added, 'I think Prince Charles is a very impressive man and I am sure they will be very happy.' Finally, Beard sealed his ex-girlfriend's fate with his parting shot: 'I think she will make an extremely good queen and a magnificent wife.' And that was that.

Wherever she happens to be – Balmoral, Sandringham, Windsor, Buckingham Palace – the Queen has six national daily newspapers laid out for her to scan at breakfast time each day: *The Times*, the *Daily Telegraph*, *Daily Mail*, *Express*, *Mirror* and *Racing Post*. By all accounts, she reaches for the last first, rarely, if ever, asks to see the *Sun* and, possibly (hopefully) does not even know of the existence the *Daily Star*. Nevertheless, Her Majesty knows what is going on, and, in the mid-1970s, she and the Duke of Edinburgh were perturbed by the number and nature of the newspaper stories featuring the heir to the throne and 'the women in his life'. At one point, in 1975, Prince Philip wrote to his son cautioning him against 'parading' his girlfriends in public. Charles accepted the warning, but resented it coming from his father in the form of a letter. 'I only wish other people who say these things would do it to one's face,' he complained to Uncle Dickie.

As we shall see in a moment, when Diana Spencer enters the fray,

[134] And everybody else. She remains unmarried to this day, although the press have hopes that, if he asks her, she might be ready to marry her current boyfriend, my friend Anthony Holden, serial biographer of the Prince of Wales, who, intriguingly, has grown less admiring of Charles the more he has written about him.

Charles had what Diana called 'a problem' with his father and his father's preferred method of communication. The Duke of Edinburgh is a pragmatist and a man of action. If he sees a problem, he wants it resolved. If he has an idea, he is ready to express it. He despatches letters and notes and memos to all and sundry. He types them himself. He uses them to send a message, make a point, raise a thought, quickly, concisely and, he trusts, with as little ambiguity as possible. Given his generation, and the fact that he is not a touchy-feely sort of man, he uses them, too, to say those things that, within a family, are sometimes more comfortably written down than spoken out loud. Thirty years on, I believe Prince Charles, now in his fifties (as Prince Philip was in 1975), and an assiduous correspondent himself, is more understanding of his father's approach, but, back then, it rankled.

Of course, by no means all of Charles's early romances involved 'a full sexual relationship'. Many of his girlfriends were just that: girls who were friends. And Charles's parents were relatively comfortable with these young women when they were daughters of friends of the family. There was no problem, for example, with Leonora or Jane Grosvenor, sisters of the Duke of Westminster; nor with Victoria and Caroline Percy, daughters of the Duke of Northumberland; nor yet with Charlotte Manners, daughter of the Duke of Rutland, or her cousin, Libby Manners. There was some sensitivity about Angela Nevill (her father, Lord Rupert Nevill, was the Duke of Edinburgh's private secretary at the time), but none whatsoever about Lady Henrietta FitzRoy, daughter of the Duke of Rutland (once thought of as a potential husband for the Queen, whose wife, of course, is Mistress of the Robes), nor with Lady Cecil Kerr, daughter of the 12th Marquess of Lothian (Lord Warden of the Stanneries and Keeper of the Privy Seal of the Duke of Cornwall). There was even another Camilla on the list: Lady Camilla Fane, daughter of the 15th Earl of Westmoreland, then a lord-in-waiting to the Queen, later Master of the Horse.

The aristo girls (my list is just a sampling) passed muster because, as a rule, they knew the rules. The problems tended to arise with those of less certain provenance, such as the exotic Colombian beauty Cristabel Barria-Borsage, who caught the Prince's eye in the summer of 1977, on one of his polo-playing days. His official companion for the day was another of his aristocratic girlfriends, Lady Sarah Spencer, the twenty-two-year-old eldest daughter of the 8th Earl Spencer, whose youngest daughter, Diana, was about to turn sixteen. Charles and Sarah were an item for a while, though Charles's post-polo behaviour that day did little to help their relationship, to say nothing of Sarah's morale and health. (She was recovering from anorexia nervosa at the time.) Having taken a fancy to Miss Barria-Borsage, the Prince bundled Lady Sarah into the back seat of his car with his detective, ensconced his new enthusiasm next to him, and drove the party back to London – where he abandoned Sarah, said goodnight to his detective and bedded the Colombian beauty. Apparently, the Prince of Wales has no recollection of any of this, but I like to think the story may be true because the lady herself gave an account of it that it would be difficult to believe anyone could make up. As the couple clambered into bed, Miss Barria-Borsage, uncertain of the appropriate court etiquette, asked her lover, 'What shall I call you, Charles or sir?' 'Call me Arthur' came the royal reply.

When Charles was still in his mid-twenties he made the mistake of saying, in public, 'The right age for marriage is around thirty. By this time you have seen a great deal of life, met a large number of girls, been able to see what types of girls there are, fallen in love every now and then, and you know what it's all about.' As the 1970s wore on and the Prince approached his thirtieth birthday, and 'the right age for marriage', the press's game of *cherchez la femme* went into overdrive. 'It's very hard on them,' Charles acknowledged. 'I have layers to protect me, but they are not used to it. It tends, sometimes, to put the really nice ones off. Poor Jane Wellesley; I am shielded, but how can she be protected?' (Indeed.)

Any girl with whom the Prince was spotted became a prospect. It was open season. As well as the improbable (the actress Susan George, star of Sam Peckinpah's lurid *Straw Dogs*) and the impossible (Lord Manton's daughter, Fiona, who did not simply have 'history': it turned out she had bared all in the pages of *Penthouse*), there were a couple of complete non-starters. In July 1977, the *Daily Express* scooped the world with the 'news' that Charles was about to marry Princess Marie-Astrid of Luxembourg, declaring 'the formal engagement will be announced on Monday'. There was nothing in it – and never could have been. As Charles said at the time, 'If I marry a Catholic, I'm dead. I've had it.' For the same reason, the idea of his espousing Princess Caroline of Monaco, the daughter of Prince Rainier and Grace Kelly, was equally far-fetched. The couple did meet. To the irritation of the Prince, the princess was late: she was a film star's daughter and, apparently, behaved like one. There was no magic in the air, but the press would have their story and so conjured some up from nowhere.

Charles set the record straight. 'Before I arrived the world had me married to Caroline,' he said. 'With our first meeting the world had us married, and now the marriage is in trouble.'

As the years passed, Charles became increasingly conscious that the time was coming when he *must* marry. He knew there was no alternative. Marrying is one of the duties that befall a Prince of Wales. To this day, in everything he does, he feels what he calls 'the weight of expectation'. It is a burden, he admits, that, at times, he has found 'very difficult to come to terms with'. As he approached his thirtieth birthday, the idea of finding a wife – the right wife – became positively oppressive. 'Obviously, there must be someone, somewhere for me,' he said. 'When you get to my extraordinary stage of decrepitude, you begin to think about things like that . . . You look at a girl and think, "I wonder if one could ever marry her?"'

He knew what he was looking for – at least in theory. With his mentor, Lord Mountbatten, though not with his parents, he had discussed the issue, time and again. His thinking on the subject was clear and, when he expressed it, the words were entirely his own, but the underlying philosophy was entirely that of his great-uncle:

Marriage is a much more important business than falling in love. I think one must concentrate on marriage being essentially a question of mutual love and respect for each other. Creating a secure family unit in which to bring up children, to give them a happy, secure upbringing – that's what marriage is all about, creating a home. Essentially, you must be good friends, and love, I'm sure, will grow out of that friendship. I have a particular responsibility to ensure that I make the right decision. The last thing I could possibly entertain is getting divorced . . . My marriage has to be for ever.

It's sad, in a way, that some people should feel that there is every opportunity to just break it off when you feel like it . . . And marriage isn't only for the two people who form the marriage; it's also for the children of that marriage . . . But if they were the children of people who simply dashed from one place to another with different people all the time, they'd turn into the most extraordinary individuals – as happens only too often. If you feel you can change it, change your mind and try anybody else at the drop of a hat, then that's sad. Marriage is something you ought to work at. I may easily be proved wrong, but I certainly intend to work at it when I get married.

I'd want to marry somebody who had interests which I understood and could share. Then look at it from the woman's point of view. A woman not only marries a man, she also marries into a way of life, into a job, into a life in which she's got a contribution to make. She's got to have some knowledge of it, some sense of it, or she wouldn't have a clue about whether she's going to like it. If she didn't have a clue, it would be too risky for her, wouldn't it?

If I'm deciding on whom I want to live with for the next fifty years – well that's the last decision in which I'd want my head to be ruled entirely by my heart. It's nothing to do with class; it's to do with compatibility. There are as many cases of marriages turning out unsatisfactorily because a man married above himself as there are when he married below. Marriage isn't an 'up' or 'down' issue anyway: it's a side-by-side one.

Mountbatten – whose thinking, whose generation, whose own experience of life and love are reflected in every phrase of what Charles had to say – was his great-nephew's great hero. 'I admire him, I think, almost more than anybody else,' said Charles in his mid-twenties. 'He's a very great person . . . People love him because he is incredibly honest, straightforward, and doesn't mind what he says at all, to anybody and never has done from the year dot. He is, I think, the centre of the family . . .'

The head of the family and her husband, the Queen and the Duke of Edinburgh, were admirers of Dickie's also; they were enormously fond of him, but I think they felt they had the measure of him, too. Mountbatten was a great achiever – and a great operator – but at times he had to be taken with a pinch of salt. He did rather feel he had the answer to everything.[135] And Prince Philip, though mostly amused, was occasionally irritated by Mountbatten's almost proprietorial interest in his eldest son. (There are many photographs of the three of them together: the body language is revealing. Mountbatten, almost invariably, has his right hand on Charles's right shoulder and Philip, almost always, is standing a little apart, with his arms crossed, as you can see from the photograph included in this book. Perhaps Philip, whose own paternal grandfather was assassinated before he was born,

[135] 'His vanity, though child-like, was monstrous,' wrote his official biographer, Philip Ziegler, 'his ambition unbridled.' Ziegler's *Mountbatten* and *Edwina Mountbatten* by Janet Morgan are probably the two books I have most enjoyed reading during my research for this one.

and whose father, in large part, disappeared from his life when he was ten, was subconsciously envious of the easy affection Mountbatten and Charles showed for one another. Who knows?

In his twenties, Charles said, 'I've fallen in love with all sorts of girls and I fully intend to go on doing so.' His great-uncle, as we have seen, encouraged him in this, giving him not only the opportunity (at Broadlands) but also, on occasion, even acting as facilitator. In March 1974, for example, just as Camilla, in Wiltshire, was conceiving Tom, Charles, in San Diego with HMS *Jupiter* on the goodwill mission to the US Pacific Fleet, was falling in love with a beautiful blonde named Laura Jo Watkins. Laura Jo, tall, intelligent, talkative, was the daughter of Admiral James Watkins, a friend of Lord Mountbatten's since the 1950s when Watkins had been stationed in Malta with the US Sixth Fleet. Charles was much taken with Laura Jo and hoped to see more of her. Great-uncle Dickie did what he could to assist, inviting her to London that summer, ostensibly to be a guest at the farewell party for the departing American ambassador, Walter Annenberg, in fact to spend more time with Prince Charles, on leave from HMS *Jupiter*. On 13 June 1974, Charles made his maiden speech in the House of Lords, the first royal speech of its kind for ninety years. His theme was the use of leisure time in the United Kingdom and the need to encourage community service among young people. As he spoke – fluently, with feeling and to a purpose – Laura Jo looked on admiringly from the visitors' gallery. Charles was pleased to have her there, though somewhat irked (as were his parents) that, in the press, her presence was given rather more coverage than the content of his speech. The media, briefly, became as enamoured of Laura Jo as the Prince (she was another picture editor's dream) and began writing her up as the 'Wallis Simpson of our time' – which, as Charles noted, was wholly ludicrous since Laura Jo was not simply younger and prettier than Mrs Simpson had been when she and the last Prince of Wales started courting: Laura Jo was unmarried. When, the weekend after his House of Lords debut, Charles turned up to play polo at Cowdray Park, the huge crowds, and the garrison of photographers, were in for a disappointment. 'You don't think I'm such a bloody fool as to bring her here today, do you?' said the Prince. And, once again, that was that.

Lord Mountbatten was a man of many parts. In Charles's life, he played Lord Pandarus, and Lord Polonius, too. Repeatedly, he encouraged his nephew to 'sow his wild oats', to have 'as many affairs' as he could, but equally, in time, he expected his princely protégé to settle down with 'a suitable and a sweet-charactered girl before she meets anyone else she might fall for'. Naturally, he had just such a girl in mind.

Mountbatten was, in Prince Philip's teasing phrase, 'dynastically aware'. Prince Charles said of his uncle, truthfully, 'He knows more about my immense family than anybody else. He has written relationship tables: he knows who everybody is related to as far back as . . . Charlemagne, on his side!' For Mountbatten, a descendant of Charlemagne and a great-grandson of Queen Victoria, it would have been a glorious thing to find himself grandfather to the next Queen of England.

Mountbatten's fond and fervent hope was that Charles might marry his granddaughter, Lady Amanda Patricia Victoria Knatchbull, the younger daughter of Mountbatten's older daughter, Patricia Brabourne. Charles had known Amanda, nine years his junior, almost since she was born. He had first registered her particular charms, however, in the spring of 1973, during his memorable holiday on the paradise island of Eleuthera, when he was twenty-four and Amanda was still fifteen. She was bright (one of the first girls to go to Gordonstoun), beautiful and blossoming. By Charles's own account, the weather was glorious, the sea was warm and everyone was permanently in their swimwear. 'I must say,' Charles reported to his great-uncle, 'Amanda really has grown up into a very good-looking girl – most disturbing.'

Almost a year later, on 14 February 1974 (coincidentally his daughter Patricia's fiftieth birthday), Mountbatten wrote to Charles, at length, about love in general, and Amanda in particular. Mountbatten said he had noticed 'how deeply' fond his now sixteen-year-old granddaughter had become of the Prince and he hoped – so hoped – that, over time, something permanent might come of it . . .

Thirty years earlier, in the mid-1940s, when Charles's father – then Prince Philip of Greece – had been exactly the age Charles was now, Mountbatten had been writing to him about his marriage prospects in similar, well-intentioned, pressing terms. Mountbatten hoped – so hoped – that, over time, his nephew and Princess Elizabeth might form an alliance. He was ready to do anything in his power to assist. On more than one occasion, Philip had to urge his uncle to moderate his enthusiasm. In September 1945 he wrote to him: 'Please, I beg you, not too much advice in an affair of the heart, or I shall be forced to do the wooing by proxy.' In January 1947, as the prospect of an engagement grew closer, Philip wrote to Mountbatten about the impact his uncle's attitude might have on his bride-to-be: 'I am not being rude, but it is apparent that you like the idea of being the General Manager of this little show and I am rather afraid that she might not take to the idea as docilely as I do. It is true that I know what is good for me, but don't forget that she has not had you as Uncle *loco parentis*, counsellor and friend as long as I have . . .'[136]

Charles, in his day, was more amenable to his great-uncle's interference than his father had been in his. Indeed, Charles did not regard it as interference. He saluted Mountbatten for his 'amazing ability for giving good advice', for his 'sound reason' and 'sensible and wise opinions about all things'. In his reply to his great-uncle, written from HMS *Jupiter*, far from dismissing Mountbatten's proposal, he welcomed it. Amanda, he agreed, was 'incredibly affectionate and loyal', with 'a glorious sense of fun and humour' – 'and she's a country girl as well which is even more important'. 'Perhaps being away,' Charles told his great-uncle, 'and being able to think about life and about the future (and her) has brought ideas of a marriage into a more serious aspect . . .' He concluded that the more he thought about the idea of marrying Amanda, 'the more ideal' the prospect seemed to be.

In due course, when Charles did eventually ask his cousin Amanda to marry him, she turned him down. 'Why?' I asked Lady Mountbatten. 'No spark,' she said simply.

Over five years, between 1974 and 1979, Charles and Amanda grew increasingly close. They met with increasing regularity – on Eleuthera, in London, at Broadlands, at Windsor and Balmoral – and Mountbatten was convinced they were 'moving slowly towards ultimate marriage'. Amanda's parents thought it might happen, too. It didn't, and when it didn't Charles was not entirely surprised. He confessed that he had been trying 'to put myself into her shoes in an effort to imagine what it would be like to be asked' and doubted that anyone would willingly take on the 'immense sacrifice' and 'great loss of freedom' involved in marrying the heir to the throne. Amanda, of course, was immensely fond of her cousin, admired him hugely, shared many of his interests (in the natural world, in the environment, in philosophy and psychology) and loved him for the way in which he so

[136] Mountbatten was an incorrigible matchmatcher, fascinated by genealogy and ever ambitious to improve the fortunes of his kith and kin. At the beginning of the 1930s, he prepared for his cousin David, then Prince of Wales, a list of eighteen unmarried European princesses, ranging from the thirty-three-year-old Alexandra of Hohenlohe-Langenburg to Princess Thyra of Mecklenburg-Schwerin, who was a mere fifteen.

clearly loved her parents and their family life and so adored her grandfather – but she couldn't marry him. Mountbatten had taught Charles that 'fondness and friendship and shared interests' were the ideal basis for marriage, that from 'mutual affection and respect' love would grow. For Amanda, that was not quite enough.[137]

Charles proposed to Amanda in August 1979, on board the royal yacht *Britannia*. When she said 'no' – with great sweetness, but leaving no room for hope – Charles accepted her answer 'immediately' and said he 'wasn't at all surprised'. There were no hard feelings. They are still friends. (Amanda was another 'ex' at the Windsor wedding in April 2005.) On 13 August, from *Britannia*, Charles wrote to his great-uncle Dickie, telling him of Amanda's visit and reporting to him that she had described, in glowing terms, the many charms of the Mountbattens' summer holiday home at Mullaghmore in County Sligo on the west coast of Ireland. 'I do wish I could come and see it,' Charles said, wishing his great-uncle a restful holiday, hoping to see him soon and telling him that he was off himself on a fishing holiday shortly, to Iceland.

Two weeks later, on 27 August 1979, Earl Mountbatten of Burma, aged seventy-nine, was murdered by the IRA. It was mid-morning when Mountbatten and half a dozen members of his family set out for a day's fishing in their thirty-foot boat, *Shadow V*. The boat had barely left the harbour at Mullaghmore when it was ripped apart by a fifty-pound bomb. Eyewitnesses described a 'roaring' explosion which threw the boat high into the air, smashing it into tiny pieces. Mountbatten, his grandson Nicholas, aged fourteen, and the young Irish boatman who was with them, Paul Maxwell, were killed instantly. Mountbatten's daughter Patricia, her husband John Brabourne, and another of their sons, Timothy (Nicholas's twin brother), were severely injured. Doreen, Lady Brabourne, survived the night, but died next morning.

Within hours, the news reached Charles in Iceland. He was devastated. 'A mixture of desperate emotions swept over me,' he recorded in his journal, '– Agony, disbelief, a kind of wretched numbness, closely followed by fierce and violent determination to see that something was done about the IRA . . .' He was angry, and bereft. 'I had always dreaded the day when he would die . . . In some

[137] In due course, when she was thirty, in October 1987, she married a different Charles, Charles Ellingworth.

extraordinary way he combined grand-father, great uncle, father, brother and friend . . . Life will *never* be the same now . . .'

In his grief, Charles sought consolation. He turned to Camilla Parker Bowles.

Chapter Eight

A Prince and His Passions

'So heavy is the chain of wedlock that it needs two to carry it, and sometimes three.'

Alexandre Dumas (1802–70)

One day in May 2005 – the very day, as it happens, that Her Royal Highness The Duchess of Cornwall undertook her first 'solo engagement' as a member of the Royal Family, opening the University of Southampton's Epidemiology Resource Centre – I received a telephone call from Countess Mountbatten of Burma.

Lady Mountbatten had been reflecting on a conversation we had had a few days earlier and had something she wanted to add. She said, 'You know you asked me whether my father would have approved of Charles's relationship with Mrs Parker Bowles – after she was married, that is – and I said, "No", and you asked me, "Are you sure?" and I said, "Yes", emphatically . . . Well, I've just remembered something. Years ago, when I was about to marry John, in 1946, I said to my father, "I'm very fond of John and I'm sure we'll be very happy, but he doesn't make me go weak at the knees, if you know what I mean." I asked my father what would happen, if down the road, after I was married, I happened to meet a man who did make me go weak at the knees, a man who could sweep me off my feet. What would I do then? "Nothing," he said, "Nothing at all. You would know your duty. Your duty will stop you doing anything stupid." He was very clear about that.'

Mountbatten encouraged Charles, while unattached, to sow his wild oats. He made it possible for him to see – and sleep with – Camilla when they were both young and single. He did it for a reason. When Mountbatten married Edwina Ashley in 1922, he was just twenty-two and sexually inexperienced. Twenty-seven years later, in 1949, in a confessional letter to his wife – written in the aftermath of one of the

204

couple's rows and headed, appropriately, 'At Sea' – he told Edwina, 'As a young man I had religious scruples about doing more than kiss a woman until one was married. I often wonder if you realise how little I knew about marriage before we married . . .' According to Janet Morgan, Edwina's official biographer: 'As a lover Dickie was unsatisfactory. He was enthusiastic but awkward, Edwina was tense. Unlike his father [Louis of Battenberg], who as a twenty-six-year-old bachelor had enjoyed a delightful affair with Mrs Lillie Langtry [the actress, a year his senior], Dickie had married with no previous practice of love-making.'

Mountbatten believed he had married too young and with too little experience. He did not want Charles – in so many ways the son he never had – to make the same mistake. He advised Charles to have 'as many affairs' as he could, not so much to 'get it out of his system' as to learn something of the arts of love. If Camilla Shand – a country girl and a fine horsewoman[138] (or, indeed, Susan George, the actress and star of *All Neat in Black Stockings*) – could assist in this, all to the good. Great-uncle Dickie was keenly aware that, if he had been a more accomplished lover himself, Edwina might have been less inclined to seek solace – and satisfaction – elsewhere.

Mountbatten once told a friend, 'Edwina and I spent all our married lives getting into other people's beds.' However, Philip Ziegler while accepting that Edwina was certainly 'a goer' – her affairs were many and some were splendid[139] – doubts that Mountbatten was promiscuous. Mountbatten, according to Ziegler, conducted two protracted love affairs outside his marriage, but, says Ziegler, 'though he liked to imagine himself a sexual athlete, he seems in fact only to have had slight enthusiasm for the sport'. Mountbatten's daughter, Patricia, told me she concurred with Ziegler's conclusion that her father 'loved the

---

[138] It was Lord Longford (of all people), in 1971, over lunch at the Garrick Club, on the day following his installation as a Knight of the Garter, who told me, 'The Queen enjoys sex, as I do. People who ride tend to. It's very healthy.' I had not before realised there was a correlation of any kind between horse-riding and sex, but apparently there is. Indeed, during my research for this book, almost every other person I interviewed told me (without being prompted) that polo players and those who ride to hounds are notorious for both their sexual appetite and their sexual prowess. (I once rode a donkey on Camber Sands.)

[139] Her celebrated relationship with Jawaharlal Nehru was probably more an *amitié amoureuse* than a full-blown affair, but, from quite early in her marriage, Edwina took lovers – and the reasons why she did so (to assert herself as much as from sexual frustration) are explored in Janet Morgan's gripping biography, *Edwina Mountbatten: A Life of Her Own*.

company of women, sought their affection and had an almost irresistible urge to use them as confidantes', but that his real energy – his colossal life-force – was channelled into his working life. Lady Mountbatten told me that, though her father was, on the whole, 'enormously understanding' of her mother, Edwina's sundry affairs did cause him hurt and did undermine their family life. She said to me: 'He would never have encouraged Charles in that direction.'

Indeed, as Charles approached his thirtieth birthday, Mountbatten became concerned about his great-nephew's behaviour, and told him so. Mountbatten was never afraid to speak his mind. Charles, he had noticed, was becoming increasingly self-centred, self-indulgent and spoilt. The Prince of Wales's selfish conduct was causing his great-uncle sleepless nights. It put him in mind of the last Prince of Wales, Charles's other great-uncle, the black sheep of the family. In April 1979, Mountbatten wrote to Charles: 'I thought you were beginning on the downward slope which wrecked your Uncle David's life and led to his disgraceful Abdication and his futile life ever after.' Charles flared up at this, but then calmed down and accepted Mountbatten's strictures – and the wisdom of them. Charles had no wish to continue on what Mountbatten called 'your Uncle David's sad course'. In a letter to a friend at the time, Charles confessed, 'I am becoming rather worried by all this talk about being self-centred and getting worse every year. I'm told that marriage is the only cure for me – and maybe it is!'

That was on 15 April. Eighteen weeks later, Lord Mountbatten was dead and Prince Charles turned to Camilla Parker Bowles. In truth, he had never turned away from her.

In the immediate aftermath of her marriage, while he was serving in the navy, frequently at sea for long stretches, and she was a new bride, establishing her new life in Wiltshire and having babies, Camilla and Charles had not seen as much of each other as they might have liked, but they had not lost touch. They were still friends. 'She is my best friend,' said Charles and, now that Mountbatten was dead, she was the only person on the planet in whom Charles felt he could confide completely. Mabel Anderson, his nanny, and Queen Elizabeth, his grandmother, were full of love and understanding, as ever, but they were elderly ladies nonetheless. There were certain matters that you could not discuss with them. To Camilla he could say anything. And he did – on the telephone, by letter, and, best of all, standing in the kitchen at Bolehyde Manor, leaning against the work surface, mug or glass in hand, sharing his woes – and his hopes – and his plans with his best friend, as she prepared lunch or dinner and listened to what he had to say. ('Diana never listened,' one of Charles's family told me. 'It was always about her, never about him.')

Andrew Parker Bowles appeared to go along with this because, at the time, he quite liked Charles; perhaps, too, he was flattered by the Prince of Wales's interest in his wife and family. Also, in his view, 'exes' can and should get on in a civilised manner. Just as Charles maintained his friendship with Camilla, so Andrew maintained his with Princess Anne. In 1981, when Princess Anne's daughter, Zara, was born, Andrew became one of her godparents. A little later in the 1980s, as Anne's marriage to Mark Phillips began to disintegrate, Andrew was on hand to offer consolation.[140]

To Charles, in the 1970s, one of the advantages of his close friendship with Mrs Parker Bowles was that, on the whole, it went largely unremarked. Close friends of the Parker Bowles's noticed, of course; and, apparently, there was gossip among some of the polo-playing fraternity; and, needless to say, there were family servants and royal protection branch police officers with suspicions. I was told by a friend of the family that Camilla's grandmother, Sonia Cubitt, in her mid-seventies in the mid-seventies (she died, aged eighty-six, in 1986), was concerned that Camilla, only recently married and with Tom not yet a toddler, was 'too close' to Charles and raised her worries with her daughter, Rosalind, although not with Camilla herself. The world was told, by a sometime member of Mrs Cubitt's staff, that, when Charles was in the navy and stationed at Portsmouth, he would rendezvous with Camilla at her grandmother's house, Hall Place, at West Meon in Hampshire. The servant's testimony – rich in evocative detail – is sure to feature in the TV mini-series when it comes to be made:[141]

---

[140] A courtier said to me, *apropos* Princess Margaret and her lively love life, 'Adultery, like talent, runs in families. Just as the Redgraves "do" acting, these people "do" adultery. At it like ferrets. It's in the genes. They can't help it.' In this instance, however, when I say 'consolation', I am not trying to imply anything more than friendship. Rumour had it that Princess Anne and Andrew Parker Bowles resumed their affair as Anne's first marriage collapsed, but I was not there. I do not know. Parker Bowles is not telling and, while I have had the opportunity, I have not had the courage to raise the matter with the Princess Royal.

[141] Various versions of the Charles and Camilla story are currently being prepared for the screen. The first due on air is a two-hour television film, *Whatever Love Means*, with a script by William Humble, whose previous work includes dramatisations of the comedian Tony Hancock's descent into suicide and the concert pianist John Ogden's struggle with schizophrenia. The director is David Blair, whose credits include *Malice Aforethought*.

I well remember the first time the prince came to Hall Place. He arrived at 6.00 pm and after a few minutes of talking to Mrs Cubitt he vanished into thin air with Camilla . . . [who] had been wandering round all day wearing a pair of jeans with no zip – the flies were held together with a safety pin. This sort of behaviour shocked Mrs Cubitt and she demanded to know whether Camilla was going to change into a frock before the prince's arrival. 'I can even see your drawers, Camilla,' I heard her bellow. Camilla's reply was, 'Oh, Charles won't mind about that.' The manner of her reply indicated that it didn't matter because he'd seen it all anyway.

The servant (a butler – of course) did not see them 'actually at it', but he had seen enough to know what was going on. When the Prince of Wales's policeman announced that he was going into the garden in search of the Prince, the butler intervened:

I persuaded him not to go looking. He'd have been very embarrassed if he had – they were up against a tree doing what Lady Chatterley enjoyed best. I saw it myself. As soon as they went into the garden they headed straight for the avenue of beech trees and into the shadows – they were oblivious to everything around them.

What the butler saw, he kept to himself – at the time. Between 1973 and 1980, if the Prince of Wales was having an affair with another man's wife, the press did not spot it. They were distracted elsewhere, searching out, not the mistress, but the potential wife-to-be. Charles was written up – week in, week out – as 'the world's most eligible bachelor'. If he was seen with a girl – whoever she was, however unlikely – she might be 'the one'. In the months following the murder of Lord Mountbatten, the assorted sightings included Jane Ward (who worked as assistant manager at the Guards Polo Club), Sabrina Guinness (who was taken to Balmoral and, reportedly, fell foul of both the Queen and Prince Philip)[142] and Anna Wallace, the daughter of a

[142] Sabrina had 'history'. Her previous escorts included Mick Jagger and Jack Nicholson. When she arrived at Balmoral, she remarked that the car that met her at the station look liked a Black Maria, to which the Duke of Edinburgh responded, 'You would know all about Black Marias.' The Duke does not recall the remark and says, if he said it, it was obviously intended as a joke. Apparently, when Sabrina made to sit down, the Queen snapped at her that she was about to sit 'in Queen Victoria's chair' and would she, please, not. The visit was not a success.

Scottish landowner, whom Charles met while hunting and who – for six months or more – was considered a real runner.

The one they missed was in many ways the most intriguing. Zoë Sallis was an Indian-born actress, ten years Charles's senior and the former mistress of the five-times-married Irish-born actor and director John Huston, in whose epic *The Bible . . . In the Beginning* she appeared and by whom she had a son, Danny Huston, at the age of seventeen in 1979. Miss Sallis was a Buddhist and felt that Prince Charles, in line to become Supreme Governor of the Church of England, needed to be one too. With impressive determination she telephoned Buckingham Palace day after day, until eventually – amazingly – she was granted an audience with the Prince of Wales.

Charles – hungry for spiritual comfort and enlightenment – was immediately intrigued and quickly captivated. Miss Sallis presented His Royal Highness with a copy of *The Path of the Masters*, a compelling guide to a range of the teachings of the gurus of the East. The book, first published in France in 1939, was the work of Julian Johnson, a Kentucky-born surgeon who abandoned his medical practice in California to travel to Beas in India to serve his personal guru, Sawan Singh. At the heart of *The Path of the Masters* is an account of the history and practice of what came to be called Surat Shabd Yoga, or Sant Mat (Santon-Ki-Shiska), which attempts to induce a consciously controlled 'near death experience'. Mastery of this practice, according to adepts of the tradition, enables one to experience regions of light and sound beyond the normal waking state, providing glimpses into higher realms of consciousness.

Charles was hooked. The potential of nirvana – the Buddhist beatitude that promises the extinction of individuality and absorption into the supreme spirit – and the charms of Zoë Sallis proved, briefly, irresistible. Under her guidance, he became a vegetarian, gave up shooting and pondered the possibilities of the transmigration of souls, wondering in which form his late lamented great-uncle might soon return to earth.

For Charles it was an exhilarating experience, but it came to an abrupt conclusion.[143] His newly appointed private secretary, Edward

[143] As did the life of Julian Johnson, who did not live to see the publication of his masterwork. In 1939, shortly before publication, he died – either killed in a tragic accident – tripping over during a heated argument with a fellow mystic and hitting his head against a rock – or murdered by an envious rival, depending on which rumour you choose to believe.

Adeane (the son of the Queen's former private secretary, Sir Michael Adeane, and the same age, incidentally, as Miss Sallis), said 'it's got to be stopped'. And it was. Adeane, apparently, indicated to the Prince that if Her Majesty learnt about the degree of His Royal Highness's devotion to his spiritual adviser, Her Majesty would be 'deeply concerned'. Adeane's warning was sufficient. The relationship ceased.

But Zoë Sallis left her mark. Jonathan Dimbleby, in his 1994 biography of Charles, did not mention Miss Sallis by name, but acknowledged Charles's debt to the insights he gleaned from *The Path of the Masters* – particularly the assertion that religious experience should be seen as 'an individual sensation, free of creed and dogma but compatible with all faiths' – and noted that what the Prince 'was soon to say about alternative medicine, architecture and the environment sprang from a spiritual feeling for the mystical in mankind; and his themes were given focus by a growing anxiety about the disintegration of communal identity in Britain – a condition he was prone to attribute to the fruits of scientific materialism'.

In 1979, the media's obsessive interest in Charles's amatory adventures was at its height. He did his best to accept it as philosophically as he could, but, as he put it at the time, 'It's a *bit* depressing sometimes when I try to get on with things.'

The 'things' he was getting on with by now were many. In the press, he was photographed either on the polo field or on the ski slopes or in the company of one of the bevy of beauties apparently jostling for consideration as a potential bride-to-be. In his head, however, he was becoming increasingly concerned with the range of good works that will come to be seen as his lasting achievement as Prince of Wales – notably the Prince's Trust, established in 1976 to find 'challenge and adventure,'[144] combined with an element of service, for young people', and the stewardship of the Duchy of Cornwall, in which he began to show a detailed, proactive interest from the beginning of the 1980s.[145]

---

[144] In his correspondence and memoranda, Prince Charles uses underlining for emphasis at every opportunity. Prince Philip uses double, and sometimes triple, exclamation marks for the same purpose. I am told that both the Queen and the Duchess of Cornwall are 'more measured' in their writing.

[145] The Duchy of Cornwall, one of the largest and oldest landed estates in Britain, was created in 1337 by Edward III for his son, Prince Edward, the Black Prince. A charter ruled that each future Duke of Cornwall would be the eldest surviving son of the monarch – and the heir to the throne. Since the fourteenth century the Duchy's main purpose has been to provide an income, independent of the monarch, for the heir

At the end of 1976, Charles, aged twenty-eight, had retired from active naval service. His final appointment had been in command of his own ship, HMS *Bronington*, a coastal minehunter, based at Rosyth. For ten months he had coped – and coped well – with the twin challenges of seasickness and being in command of thirty-three men, all very different from him. It was a satisfying, if occasionally daunting, experience, but by the time it was over he was ready for *terra firma* and different responsibilities. Initially, he was not certain what those responsibilities might be. He said at the time: 'My great problem in life is that I do not really know what my role in life is. At the moment I do not have one. But somehow I must find one.'

One thought was that he might become Governor General of Australia. Another, even more improbable, was that he might become British ambassador to France.[146] In the event, Charles did what his father had done when the Queen's accession had forced the end of his naval career upon him (and, to an extent, what his great-uncle David had done as Prince of Wales): he created a portfolio of useful activities that reflected his range of interests and enabled him, he hoped, to 'make a difference' to the lives of those he sought to serve. Already he had a range of involvements: with the Duchy of Cornwall, with the Prince's Trust, with the Prince of Wales Environment Committee, and as Mountbatten's successor as president of the United World Colleges, a movement to establish international schools founded on principles akin to those that inspired Kurt Hahn to found Gordonstoun. Already he was colonel-in-chief of five regiments, chancellor of the University of Wales and patron of both the Royal Anthropological Institute and the British Sub Aqua Club. To these involvements and appointments

apparent. When there is no male heir, the Duchy reverts to the monarch, and its income to the Exchequer. The Duchy's total area is about 141,072 acres (57,091 hectares), with more than half the estate not in Cornwall, but in Devon. There are nearly 250 let farms or smallholdings, and the estate owns residential properties, shops and offices, as well as a portfolio of stocks and shares. The holdings, in hectares, range from just sixteen in London and twenty in South Glamorgan to 644 in Gloucestershire and useful tracts of land in Cornwall (7,664 hectares), Somerset (5,973) and Herefordshire (5,437).

[146] This notion was conjured up, apparently, by Peter Carington, father of Camilla's sometime flatmate, Virginia, and Christopher Soames, Governor of Southern Rhodesia (1979–80) and formerly British ambassador in Paris (1968–72). Lord Soames's son, Nicholas, was already a close friend of Charles's (having been his equerry at the beginning of the 1970s) and his daughter, Charlotte, as we shall soon see, was about to become a close friend of Andrew Parker Bowles.

he began, gradually, to add more and more – deciding, from the start, however, that he would try not to take on anything unless he actually cared about it and felt he could make a proper contribution.

The working life he began to establish once he left the navy, combining his own growing portfolio of interests and activities with an increasing number of official duties on behalf of the Queen – for example, in 1977, visiting Ghana, the Ivory Coast, Canada, the USA and Canada; in 1978 visiting Brazil, Venezuela, Yugoslavia, and representing the United Kingdom at the funerals of Sir Robert Menzies in Australia and Jomo Kenyatta in Kenya – is essentially the working life he maintains to this day. You will find an overview of his achievements as Prince of Wales in Appendix A on pages 325–7. Listing his interests is relatively straightforward; defining what he does to further them is more complicated. Sometimes, it is a matter of simply being a morale-boosting figurehead; at others, it is a question of detailed, sustained, hands-on commitment, being not only the catalyst, but the individual who thinks and leads and follows through. (The former can be more taxing than the latter: meeting, greeting, glad-handing, joshing, cheering, sympathising, listening, can be extra-ordinarily draining. Developing a concept, drafting a paper, leading a meeting, while possibly more challenging, is also more rewarding.) One government minister who has received lengthy memoranda from Charles – 'over-written and confused' in the opinion of my source – described the Prince to me as 'a right royal pain in the backside'. Others – and of those I have spoken to, they are in the vast majority – describe him when on duty variously as 'wonderfully effective', 'infectiously enthusiastic', 'courteous', 'considerate', 'good-hearted' and 'kind'.[147]

The former prime minister Margaret Thatcher told me, 'Charles cares deeply about what he does and people respond to that.' The former Foreign Secretary, Douglas Hurd, describes him as 'a complete star'. And, having seen him in action at close range myself, in an assortment of very different situations, with a variety of very different types of people – from the young (through the Prince's Trust) to the old (at an Abbeyfield sheltered home for the elderly), from serving soldiers (through the British Forces Foundation) to eccentric clergymen

[147] 'Do emphasise his kindness,' said my friend, Richard, 7th Earl of Bradford, a contemporary of Charles's at Trinity College, Cambridge. 'A few years ago, we were inspecting some of the Duchy forests together and my back was playing up. He noticed and, at once, asked what he could do to help, offered to get me his car, and what have you. As a man, he is kind, generous and thoughtful.'

(fundraising for Chester Cathedral) – and having had the privilege of observing other 'magic people' at close quarters – Bill Clinton, Nelson Mandela and Desmond Tutu, for example – I would say there is certainly something special about the presence of the Prince of Wales, something that goes beyond the allure that is somehow attached automatically to senior royalty and the hugely famous. In my experience, in the presence of the Queen most people are awed; in the presence of the Duke of Edinburgh they are stimulated, challenged and entertained; in the presence of the Prince of Wales, they are impressed (and surprised to be so) and, often, oddly moved. This is how Joanna Lumley put it to me: 'You feel he really cares; you sense he is really listening; you feel better for his company.' What Charles 'does' is not easy to define, but, as Noël Coward said of Liberace, 'he does what he does very well'.

As Charles entered his fourth decade, he was developing a role. He had a mistress. Now he needed a home and a wife. He found the home rather more easily than he found the wife, but then, in the case of the home, he knew what he was looking for. Courtesy of the government, through the 1970s he had an 'official' country residence at Chevening House in Kent – but it was not a home, it was a mansion, with 150 rooms and a 3,500-acre estate, formerly the seat of the Earls Stanhope, bequeathed to the nation in 1967 and administered by a trust. It was huge, historic and not to the Prince's taste. In the spring of 1978, in a note to his private secretary, he wrote: 'It would be so much more fun if the Duchy would purchase a nice house with a small farm, having sold somewhere less useful in Cornwall, for instance. Where I could learn some practical farming for a start – as well as being my own master.' What he had in mind was 'somewhere decent and attractive to the West of London – ie in Gloucs. or Wilts or Somerset'. He found it.

Highgrove House, in the hamlet of Doughton, just outside Tetbury in Gloucestershire, had been the country home of Maurice Macmillan, MP, son of the Queen's third prime minister, Harold Macmillan.[148] It was an imposing building, with a neo-classical façade, but the size was

---

[148] Harold Macmillan was MP for Stockton-on-Tees and Bromley, but his homes were in London and Sussex. Maurice was MP for Farnham and his homes were in London and Gloucestershire. Those were the days before MPs had to pretend to live in their constituencies. (When I became MP for the City of Chester in 1992, and had homes in Chester and London, the most irritating and frequently put question to me was, 'Where's your *real* home?' 'Happiness,' a fellow MP said to me at the time, 'is the constituency in the rear-view mirror.')

manageable (four good reception rooms, just nine bedrooms), the garden had 'capabilities' and the price (around £800,000) was within the Duchy's budget.

I say the garden had 'capabilities', but, at the time Charles bought the property, you would need to have been Lancelot Brown or the Prince of Wales to have recognised them. There was parkland to the east of the house, and a home farm of around three hundred acres, but the garden, as a garden, was virtually non-existent. When, not long ago, I visited the now near-perfect garden at Highgrove (one of the treats of my garden-visiting life[149]), Charles told me that the house, when he first saw it, was 'a bit dishevelled' and the garden 'frankly, not up to much': a scruffy thorn bush or two, even scruffier shrubbery, a dreary lawn, divided by a long path, and 'a pretty dreadful square pond'. Why did he take it on, I asked him? 'Madness,' he said, laughing. 'Why on earth did I decide I wanted to live here? I don't know. In the early days, I sometimes wondered if I'd done the right thing. It felt very English and I loved that. There was a kitchen garden too and I liked that. But I think it was the cedar tree that persuaded me – two hundred years old, on the west side of the house. It's beautiful. I think it was the cedar that settled it.'

Everyone else, of course, thinks it was Camilla that settled it. Highgrove House is a twenty-minute drive from Bolehyde Manor. Mrs Parker Bowles, seven years into her marriage, helped the Prince of Wales, still a bachelor, decide that Highgrove was the home for him. She was a contentedly married woman, with two small children, but she was also Charles's counsellor and friend. Because she knew and understood him so well, she encouraged him both to become her neighbour and, for his own sake, to develop Highgrove as (in his phrase) 'the outward expression of my inner self'. Years later, when Diana complained that her marriage was a bit crowded because there were three in it, she might have said four, because Highgrove itself played such an important part in her husband's life. In 1991, ten years

[149] I have had the privilege of visiting many of England's loveliest gardens. (For two seasons, in the 1980s, I presented a TV series, *Discovering Gardens*.) While writing *Philip & Elizabeth: Portrait of a Marriage* I was a guest of Nigel Nicolson at Sissinghurst, where the garden created by his mother, Vita Sackville-West, is rightly regarded as one of the wonders of the gardening world. Even so, the gardens at Highgrove, combining the formal and the wild and natural, created by Charles, initially with the help of his friend the Marchioness of Salisbury, are, without doubt, the loveliest I know. If you get the chance to visit them, leap at it.

after her marriage, in one of the conversations she recorded for Andrew Morton's book, *Diana Her True Story*, the Princess of Wales reflected on what Highgrove meant to her:

> He said he wanted to be in the Duchy vicinity, but it's only eleven miles from her house. He chose the house and I came along afterwards. First went there after he bought it. He had painted all the walls white. He wanted me to do it up even though we were not engaged. I thought it was very improper but he liked my taste.

At around the same time, ten years into his unhappy marriage, Charles reflected on the impact of Highgrove on his life:

> I have put my heart and soul into Highgrove – and I will continue to do so while I can. I have also put my back into Highgrove and, as a result, have probably rendered myself prematurely decrepit in the process . . . All the things I have tried to do in this small corner of Gloucestershire have been the physical expression of a personal philosophy. When I was younger I recall the nascent stirrings of such a philosophy; I felt a strong attachment to the soil of those places I loved best – Balmoral, in Scotland, and Sandringham, in Norfolk. As far as I was concerned, every tree, every hedgerow, every wet place, every mountain and river had a special, almost sacred, character of its own.

Apparently, when a girlfriend of Diana's came across these remarks by Charles (in the introduction to Charles Clover's book about the Prince's development of the Highgrove estate), the girlfriend telephoned the princess and read out to her just one sentence: 'All the things I have tried to do in this small corner of Gloucestershire have been the physical expression of a personal philosophy.' She read out the line twice, then the two friends dissolved into peals of derisive laughter.

In due course, Diana did, in fact, help Charles decorate Highgrove. She chose an interior designer (Dudley Poplak) who was a friend of her mother's (and who had done up her mother's house) and, by her own admission, was given 'a free hand' by the Prince to organise the decoration as she pleased. Diana 'did up' Highgrove, but she never felt truly at home there. She did not like 'the Highgrove set' ('They were all oiling up,' she said, 'basically, kissing his feet'), she was not interested in hunting (Charles and Camilla's great shared enthusiasm), she felt no stirrings (nascent or otherwise) when it came to gardening. Camilla liked 'to feel the soil'. Diana did not.

Camilla helped Charles choose Highgrove. Bizarrely, Camilla also helped Charles choose Diana – or, at least, as we shall see in a moment, she gave Charles's uncertain choice her encouragement and blessing. Camilla was now, once again, at the heart of Charles's life. This period – from the aftermath of the murder of Mountbatten in the summer of 1979 to the eve of his marriage to Diana in the summer of 1981 – was the epoch of what they would term their 'second affair'. And – incredibly – they were conducting it virtually in public.

For example, in the summer of 1980, at the Windsor Castle ball to celebrate the eightieth birthday of Queen Elizabeth The Queen Mother, Charles spent the entire evening on the dance floor with Mrs Parker Bowles. Lieutenant Colonel Parker Bowles (as he now was) observed the scene with a tolerant eye (as well he might: he was rumoured to be much taken with Lord Soames's daughter, Charlotte) but Charles's official 'date' for the evening, the beautiful but fiery Anna Wallace (shortly to be nicknamed 'Whiplash Wallace') was not amused. 'Don't ever, ever ignore me like that again!' she raged. 'No one treats me like that – not even you.' The Prince took no heed. A few weeks later, at a polo ball at Stowell Park, the Gloucestershire home of the meat millionaire Lord Vestey, there was a repeat performance. Once again, Charles ignored Anna and spent the whole evening on the dance floor with Camilla. Enough was enough. Miss Wallace made her excuses and left.

The next polo ball of the season was the last: the Cirencester Polo Club Ball, hosted by the 8th Earl Bathurst (an enthusiastic timber grower: he and Charles talked trees) in the grounds of Cirencester Park. According to one witness, who knew Charles well, what happened that evening was 'quite astonishing'. Jane Ward, assistant manager of the Guards Polo Club, did not like what she saw, but gave a graphic report of it, nonetheless:

Charles and the Parker Bowleses shared the same table, and Charles spent the whole evening dancing with Camilla. They were kissing passionately as they danced – on and on they went, kissing each other, French kissing, dance after dance. Andrew wasn't quite sure how to react – he sat there smiling and saying to people: 'HRH is very fond of my wife. And she appears to be very fond of him.' He seemed not uncomfortable with what was going on, but other people were, especially the older ones. Some were embarrassed and shocked and upset that the whole thing was so blatant.

Among the older people who were concerned – not that night, but at around that time – were Camilla's parents. Major Shand, I am told, said little, but Mrs Shand became increasingly anxious. She liked Charles – and it was exciting to have the Prince of Wales coming to call – but she liked her son-in-law, too, and she loved her daughter and her grandchildren and she was fearful that 'things would get out of hand' and people – especially the children – would get hurt.

Camilla, however, was quite relaxed. She felt (in a friend's phrase) that 'she knew her Andrew'. She was a conscientious and loving mother, and she was also, she believed, secure in one of those marriages that work because husband and wife have an 'understanding'. Andrew was a charmer with a roving eye: in 1980, posted to Southern Rhodesia, as chief liaison officer in the run-up to independence, it was almost an inevitability that he should make a bee-line for the governor's daughter. Camilla was, famously, the great-granddaughter of Alice Keppel: it was, she felt, almost an inevitability that she should be the mistress of the Prince of Wales.

By the summer of 1980 (contracts were exchanged on Highgrove that July), Charles had a home and a mistress. Now all he wanted was a wife.

Charles first saw Diana Spencer when she was just a baby, in the summer of 1961, when he was twelve. He encountered her now and again, during her childhood, on the Sandringham estate. He met her properly for the first time in 1977, two years after her father, Edward John (known as Johnnie), Viscount Althorp, had succeeded as 8th Earl Spencer (so inheriting the family home, Althorp, in Northampton-shire)[150] and a year after he had married, as his second wife, the

[150] The family acquired the estate in 1506. It is magnificent, running to 1,500 acres with a house the size of a palace. In 1603, Sir Robert Spencer became Baron Spencer, one of the first of the peers created by James I. The earldom came the family's way in 1765, during the reign of George III. John Spencer, the 1st Earl Spencer, was the great-grandson of John Churchill, 1st Duke of Marlborough. The 2nd Earl Spencer was William Pitt's First Lord of the Admiralty and, later, Home Secretary. The 3rd Earl was Chancellor of the Exchequer and, before his translation to the House of Lords, Leader of the House of Commons responsible for carrying through the 1832 Reform Bill. The 5th Earl was Lord-Lieutenant of Ireland, Lord President of the Council and First Lord of the Admiralty. Diana's forebears included the various offspring of Charles II and

formidable Raine, Countess of Dartmouth.[151] Johnnie's father had been 'a good man', Lord-Lieutenant of Northamptonshire, a knowledgeable fine arts' enthusiast and, *inter alia*, secretary of the Society of Dilettanti. His mother, Cynthia, was the second daughter of the 3rd Duke of Abercorn and had been a Lady of the Bedchamber to Queen Elizabeth The Queen Mother since 1937. Johnnie was equerry to George VI for the last two years of his reign and to Elizabeth II for the first two years of hers. In 1954, when Johnnie, aged thirty, married Frances Ruth Burke Roche, aged eighteen, she was, according to the reports of what, inevitably, was described as 'the wedding of the year', 'the youngest bride to be married in Westminster Abbey this century'. Her parents were the 4th Baron Fermoy and Ruth Gill (younger daughter of a Scottish gentleman), a close friend of Queen Elizabeth The Queen Mother, and one of her ladies-in-waiting from 1956. At the wedding, the Queen and the Duke of Edinburgh were guests of honour. After the wedding, Johnnie and Frances moved into Park House on the Sandringham estate. The Queen and the Duke of Edinburgh were their next-door neighbours. As Diana said, years later, she had known the Queen since she was tiny – 'so it was no big deal'.

Johnnie and Frances had five children in quick succession: a son who did not survive, three daughters – Elizabeth Sarah Lavinia, born 1955; Cynthia Jane, born 1957; Diana Frances, born 1961 – and, at last, in 1964, an heir, Charles Edward Maurice, Viscount Althorp. This longed-for boy was named (by royal permission) after the Prince of Wales and the Queen (with no thought to what the future might hold) agreed to be one of his godparents.

The Spencer marriage was not a happy one. The Spencer divorce was acrimonious – spectacularly so. Frances turned out to be what used

---

Lucy Walter, Charles II and Barbara Villiers, Charles II and Louise de Kéroualle, and James II and Arabella Churchill – the Dukes of Grafton, Richmond, Bedford and Abercorn, and the Earls of Lucan, the Earls Waldegrave and the Earls of Albemarle among them.

[151] She was nicknamed 'Acid Raine' by the Spencer children. I met her through knowing her mother (Barbara Cartland, the novelist) and her son (William Lewisham, who was a contemporary at Oxford, and much envied because he had a refrigerator in his rooms at Christ Church). My last encounter with her was an unhappy one: seated next to her at a British Tourist Authority awards ceremony, she talked throughout the proceedings, so that as my name was announced as a recipient of an award, I missed the moment and failed to hear my accolade. When I registered that I should be on stage accepting my trophy, I made to move and whispered to Lady Dartmouth, 'Please excuse me a moment'. She looked at me crossly and said, 'Where are you going?'

to be called 'a bolter'. As Diana put it, one day, in 1967, 'Mummy decided to leg it.' Frances ran off with Peter Shand Kydd, whose money came from wallpaper but whose life was that of a Scottish sheep farmer. (He had a sheep station in New South Wales, as well.) Frances sued for divorce on the grounds of Johnnie's 'cruelty'. Johnnie countersued on the grounds of Frances's adultery. Friends on both sides took sides – Frances's mother siding, significantly, with her son-in-law, not her daughter. After much much-publicised blood-letting, the High Court decided in Johnnie's favour: he secured custody of his children.

Diana was six when Frances 'legged it' and eight at the time of the acrimonious custody battle. Diana had a difficult relationship with her mother. She adored her father. 'I was my father's favourite.' she said. 'There's no doubt about that.' She despised her stepmother. Eventually, in 1989, at her brother Charles's first wedding, she told Raine how she felt about her. 'I hate you so much,' she said. 'If only you knew how much we all hate you for what you've done, you've ruined the house, you spend Daddy's money and what for?'

In 2005, Rosa Monckton told me, 'The root of all her problems was her early life. It was so damaged. She talked a lot about that. She talked particularly about the feeling of being abandoned – abandoned by her mother when she was a little girl, abandoned by her father when he married Raine, and then abandoned by her husband when he went back to Camilla. She thought it was so odd that strangers professed love for her, but those who were supposed to be closest to her had abandoned her. She was very lonely. Because of all that happened to her, she suffered from chronic insecurity – it never left her, even after years of being Princess of Wales. She had a total lack of confidence and an enormous capacity for unhappiness. She found it easier to be unhappy than happy.'

In 1977, when Charles first registered Diana on a visit to Althorp to see her sister, Sarah, it was because Diana was 'jolly' and had a wonderful, girlish 'bounce' that he took to her. Her first reaction to him was, 'God, what a sad man.' She said, 'He came with his Labrador. My sister was all over him like a bad rash and I thought, "God, he must really hate that." I kept out of the way.' Diana was only sixteen. Charles was twenty-eight and her sister's boyfriend – though, as Diana later admitted, she did have crushes, 'serious crushes on all sorts of people, especially my sisters' boyfriends'.

Charles's dalliance with Sarah fizzled out. Some say she tried too hard. Others say she was the first to lose interest. In any event, early in

1978 she declared, 'I think of him as the big brother I never had', adding, rather less tactfully, 'I would not marry a man I did not love, whether it was a dustman or the King of England. If he asked me, I would turn him down.' Soon after, in April 1978, her young sister, Jane, aged twenty-one, married, for love, neither a dustman nor a king, but an amiable (if a little serious) older man, Robert Fellowes, aged thirty-seven, recently appointed assistant private secretary to the Queen and son of Sir William Albemarle Fellowes, agent to the Queen on the Sandringham estate. Diana was chief bridesmaid. Diana was a guest, too, at the Buckingham Palace ball, marking Charles's thirtieth birthday, in November 1978. That was the first time she saw him in Camilla's arms. Mrs Parker Bowles was a guest at the ball and, naturally, the Prince danced with her. Another guest at the ball told me, 'Even then you could tell there was something electric between them. They shared a secret.'

The same guest shared a secret of a different sort with me. He is a close friend of Charles and felt, from the outset, that the Prince's marriage with Diana Spencer was a mistake. 'What do you think Charles saw in her?' I asked him. 'She had fabulous bazookahs,' he said, with a grin, 'I think he liked that.'[152] That is not how Charles remembers it – or, at least, it is not how he tells it. According to Charles (and, in fact, to Diana, too) Charles was initially drawn to Diana, not by her physical attributes, but by her sympathy.

In the summer of 1980, just as Diana was turning nineteen, she found herself at a house party at New Grove, near Petworth in Sussex, the home of Robert de Pass (a naval officer turned sugar broker and exact contemporary of the Duke of Edinburgh) and his wife, Philippa (friend and lady-in-waiting to the Queen). The son of the house, Philip, just turned twenty-two, was a chum of Diana's and, bumping into her in London during the week, on the spur of the moment he invited her to join the party, explaining that Charles was to be the guest of honour, and adding, according to Diana, 'You're a young blood, you might amuse him.' She did better than that. She touched his heart.

[152] He added, when I raised an eyebrow, 'That's a compliment, for f—'s sake.' In my experience, Prince Charles does not use bad language and is squeamish about coarseness of any kind. Not so some of his friends. Indeed, my experience of the hunting set – including the women – is that they talk quite freely – and fruitily – about sex and are not shy when it comes to traditional Anglo-Saxon expletives. More than one witness has reported to me that Camilla, out hunting, on horseback, taking a fence, in full cry, can turn the air dark blue.

Charles and Diana had their first, proper conversation that Saturday night, at New Grove, seated side by side on a bale of hay, at a post-polo barbecue. (Years later, Diana said, 'If it wasn't for bloody polo, none of this would have happened. She wouldn't have met him and I wouldn't have married him.') As the sun began to set and the night grew cold, the couple fell to talking about Charles's great-uncle, Earl Mountbatten of Burma, murdered ten months before. Diana said to Charles, 'You looked so sad when you walked up the aisle at Lord Mountbatten's funeral. It was the most tragic thing I've ever seen. My heart bled for you when I watched. I thought, "It's wrong, you're lonely – you should be with somebody to look after you." '

'The next minute,' according to Diana, 'he leapt on me practically.' In her version of events, Charles was 'so obvious', not 'very cool', 'all over' her, right from the start. He simply recollects thinking 'how sweet' she was. He was taken by her innocence and 'greatly touched' by what she had said about his loneliness. She seemed, he said to a friend soon afterwards, in immediate sympathy with his predicament, both as a person and as Prince of Wales.[153] He seemed, said Diana, in the recordings she made, ten years later, for Andrew Morton's famous book, very pressing indeed – but she played hard to get: 'Frigid wasn't the word. Big F when it comes to that.' She was a virgin, and planned to remain so until her wedding night.

Charles and Diana saw one another, off and on, over the next few months. 'I came in and out, in and out,' she said, 'then I went to stay with my sister Jane at Balmoral . . . I was terrified – shitting bricks.' She had not stayed at Balmoral before. She was just nineteen, 'the youngest there by a long way'. 'I wanted to get it right,' she said. She need not have worried. She passed muster with the Queen. And with the Duke of Edinburgh. And, it seems, with Camilla, too. Camilla was at Balmoral. 'Mr and Mrs Parker Bowles were there at all my visits,' said Diana. There were three in this marriage right from the start.

Camilla was Charles's best friend. Camilla was Charles's mistress. Charles believed that Camilla understood him as no one else did. It was inevitable that, as Charles began to consider the possibility of marrying Diana, he discussed the pros and cons with his closest friend. Marcel Proust puts it rather well: 'Like everybody who is not in love, he imagined that one chose the person whom one loved after endless

[153] 'She loved me for the dangers I had passed, And I loved her that she did pity them.' *Othello*, Act I Scene 3.

deliberations and on the strength of various qualities and advantages.' Diana had a lot going for her. Camilla and Charles were agreed on that.

Later, Diana claimed that she realised quite quickly 'there was someone else around'. With Charles, she was invited to stay at Bolehyde Manor – time and again. Camilla was solicitous and friendly – and, of course, slightly nearer her mother's age than her own – but, according to Diana, there was something too knowing about her and, to Diana's way of thinking, too proprietorial when it came to Charles. 'I'd been staying at Bolehyde with the Parker Bowleses an awful lot,' she recalled, 'and I couldn't understand why she kept saying to me, "Don't push him into doing this, don't do that." She knew so much about what he was doing privately and about what we were doing privately . . . Eventually I worked it all out . . .'

Throughout their courtship, it seemed to Diana that whenever she saw Charles, Camilla was there, too. Diana went to stay at Balmoral: there was Camilla. Diana went to dine at Buckingham Palace: there was Camilla. Diana was invited to Broadlands: Camilla knew about it before she did. Diana went to support Charles at Ludlow races – in 'action man' mode the Prince was giving it a go as an amateur jockey – and, naturally enough, Camilla came, too. (With the benefit of hindsight, and as you can see from the photograph included in this book, the body language of Diana and Camilla, photographed side by side at Ludlow races, tells its own story.)

It began at Balmoral in the summer of 1980 and, in Diana's phrase, 'sort of built up from there'. Then, as she put it, 'the press seized upon it'. The sightings were sufficient in number and the young lady's credentials were impeccable. Evidently she had no 'history' and, self-evidently, though 'a subject', she came from quality stock: like Lady Elizabeth Bowes-Lyon, now Queen Elizabeth The Queen Mother, Lady Diana Spencer was the daughter of an earl and came from an established family with all the right royal connections. She was also as pretty as a picture. The media decided, in unison, that she was the one. They sought her here, they snapped her there: flick through the tabloid newspapers of the autumn of 1980 and you will find 'Lady Di' just about everywhere.[154] Indeed, you will even find her where she wasn't.

[154] It was a strong season for news: Ronald Reagan was elected President of the United States; Michael Foot was elected Leader of the Labour Party. Steve McQueen and Oswald Mosley died. John Lennon was shot dead in New York and, on TV, viewers of *Dallas* discovered who shot JR. The competition notwithstanding, Diana Spencer was

On 16 November 1980, the *Sunday Mirror* ran a story suggesting that, ten days before, Diana had been sighted, after dark, secretly joining the royal train, parked for the night in a siding at Staverton in Wiltshire. Charles was already on board the train: Diana, the paper alleged, had been closeted with him for several hours . . . What had they been up to?

'Nothing,' said Diana, fiercely, indignant that her virtue was being impugned. She was not on the royal train on the night in question – nor on any other night. She had witnesses (her flatmates) who would vouch that she was tucked up in bed, alone, in Earl's Court on the night the *Sunday Mirror* was suggesting she was bunked up with Charles in the Staverton siding. Charles was indignant, too. He deplored the modern media's 'general rush for sensationalism' and reminded the world that 'honesty and integrity are vital factors in reporting'. Indeed, they are. And accuracy is critical, too.

The *Sunday Mirror* story was inaccurate. The paper's source had certainly seen a fair-haired lady board the royal train on the night in question, but it was not Diana: it was Camilla. Swept along in the general rush of Di-mania, the *Mirror* had, as the editor later acknowledged, 'fingered the wrong filly'. When Charles told the Queen's press secretary that Diana had not boarded the royal train, he was telling the truth. When Michael Shea, the Queen's press secretary, denounced the report as 'total fabrication', he believed what he said. When Diana's mother wrote to *The Times* complaining about the 'lies and harassment' to which her teenage daughter was being subjected, she only knew the half of it.

Diana said the press attention was 'simply unbearable'. And it was not only Diana and her family who did not like it. The Queen and the Duke of Edinburgh were increasingly uncomfortable, too. According to Diana, 'The feeling was I wish Prince Charles would hurry up and get on with it.' According to Charles, he was 'in a confused and anxious state of mind', 'terrified of making a promise and then perhaps living to regret it'. According to Diana, 'The Queen was fed up', and the Duke of Edinburgh decided to take action.

pursued by the press relentlessly. The most reproduced image of her was a photograph taken at the Young England nursery in Pimlico where she was helping out part-time. She has a child on one hip and another by the hand. Her legs are seen in silhouette through her floral skirt. 'That's the last time I'm photographed without a petticoat,' she said.

Charles turned thirty-two on 14 November 1980. He was now two years beyond what he had once suggested (in the light of his great-uncle's experience) was the appropriate age for a man to marry. He now had before him the prospect of a bride who appeared to be exactly what Mountbatten had wished for him: 'a suitable, attractive and sweet-charactered girl'. She was innocent and eligible, ready and willing. Why did he hesitate? In his father's view, it was now time for Charles to put up or shut up, to marry the girl or leave her in peace. Prince Philip wrote to his son to say so. Charles should either propose to Diana, counselled his father, so 'pleasing his family and the country', or release her. He really must not let her go on dangling in the wind like this. It was not fair, or kind, or sensible.

The Prince of Wales did not welcome the Duke of Edinburgh's intervention. Indeed, so angry and resentful did he feel about his father's letter that, for quite a while afterwards, he carried it about in his pocket, producing it, without prompting, to show to family and friends. When I first went to meet her, Patricia Mountbatten, Charles's godmother, said to me, 'I take it you've seen the letter? It wasn't a bullying letter at all. It was very reasonable.' That is not how it seemed to Charles at the time. Charles said that his father's letter made him feel 'ill-used but impotent'. Faced with what he regarded as a parental 'ultimatum', he felt himself emasculated, cornered, compelled almost, to do what he did next. After weeks of indecision – 'It all seems so ridiculous because I do very much want to do the right thing for this Country and for my family,' he confided to his diary on 29 January 1981 – Charles telephoned Diana and suggested they meet. At a little after 5.00 p.m., on Friday 6 February, at Windsor Castle, the Prince of Wales, aged thirty-two, asked Lady Diana Spencer, aged nineteen, to marry him. According to her own account, she giggled nervously, and said, 'Yes, yes, of course, yes.' He then 'ran upstairs and rang his mother'.

Given all his reservations, why did Charles propose to Diana? Was he simply bounced into it by his overbearing papa? And given her doubts, why did Diana accept his offer of marriage without a moment's hesitation – 'bearing in mind,' as she put it herself, that she already knew 'there's somebody else around'? Christopher Wilson, author of *The Windsor Knot* and first biographer of 'the triangle' has no doubts. 'Charles and Diana both wanted to marry, for entirely their own reasons,' he says. 'Common to both was a barely veiled ambition – on her side, to become Princess of Wales and ultimately queen; on his to secure a wife acceptable to both himself and the populace, who would provide an heir.'

Friends of both Charles and Diana dispute this view. They say that neither of them was as calculating – or as cold – as Christopher Wilson suggests. Indeed, they are distressed that the Wilson analysis of Charles and Diana's motivations for marriage is rapidly becoming accepted as the orthodoxy. In 2005, Rosa Monckton reminded me, 'Diana was nineteen when Charles proposed – an uneducated nineteen, so naive. She'd not had a proper boyfriend. She had no idea. She felt she was in love with him. Of course, she did. But she knew nothing. Her idea of romance was a Barbara Cartland novel.'[155] (The first time I met Diana, in the early 1990s, the first thing we talked about was her teenage devotion to her step-grandmother's fiction.[156]) Paul Burrell, one-time footman to the Queen and, later, butler and confidant to Diana, told me, 'When they got married, Diana was completely in love with him – completely.' A member of her family told me, 'Camilla may have been obsessed with being the Prince of Wales's mistress – I don't know – but Diana was not obsessed with becoming Princess of Wales. She wasn't calculating like that at all. She was a young girl, truly in love for the first time – and hoping and expecting her love to last a lifetime.'

Charles's family and friends also deny that his approach to his first marriage was either calculating or cynical. Back in the 1980s, when cracks in the marriage were already on public show, the former King Constantine of Greece – who is charm and discretion personified, and keeps himself close to his royal English cousins – told me, 'Charles married with absolutely the best intentions. Of course, he loved her. I know he wanted to make it work, very much so.' In 2005, a friend of Charles's told me, 'The idea that he was just out to find a young wife who would produce the necessary heir-and-a-spare is wholly wrong. I

---

[155] Dame Barbara Cartland (1901–2000) was the author of at least 723 romantic novels. Her titles included *The Hidden Heart*, *The Dream Within*, *The Price of Love* and *A Princess in Distress*. Diana told me, 'In those stories was everyone I dreamed of, everything I hoped for.'

[156] The second thing we talked about was the knitwear designer George Hostler. Diana bought jumpers designed by George from a small shop off Kensington High Street. So did I. For a while in the 1970s and 1980s, appearing regularly on television, George's jumpers became my 'trademark'. I asked Diana to explain to me why it was that when she wore one of George's jumpers, everybody swooned, but when I did, everybody jeered. 'Maybe they look better on a girl,' she said, charitably. (Elton John was a customer of George's, too.)

think he really loved her, and when some of us expressed our reservations about her suitability, he didn't want to know.'

At the time, a number of Charles's friends had grave reservations about the match, 'not,' as one of them put it to me, 'because we had anything against Diana at the time – that came later – but because we realised they simply weren't going to be compatible.' Nicholas Soames blamed the Duke of Edinburgh for bouncing the Prince of Wales into the marriage. Patricia Mountbatten's son, Norton Romsey (who had inherited Broadlands on the death of his grandfather), and his wife Penny, separately and together, in no uncertain terms, raised their concerns with Charles. Penny Romsey's fear was that Diana had 'fallen in love with an idea not an individual' and that, apart from a largely unspecified mutual interest in 'the countryside', Charles and his intended bride appeared to have absolutely nothing in common.

Nevertheless, on Friday 6 February 1981, at Windsor Castle, Charles proposed to Diana. She said he said, 'I love you so much', and she said she believed him. On Tuesday 24 February, at Buckingham Palace, the engagement was formally announced and the happy couple faced the world together for the first time. With the television cameras rolling, they were asked if they were in love. Diana said, at once, 'Of course.' Charles added, *sotto voce*, 'Whatever "in love" means.' One of Charles's friends said to me recently, 'Do get the quotation right, for God's sake. It really annoys him that people think he said "Whatever love means". He didn't. It's always misquoted and I think he sees that as yet another example of the way he is generally misunderstood – and almost always misreported. To Charles, the idea of being "in love" is something from romantic fiction. What interests him is love itself. When he married Diana his hope was that their love would deepen and grow, that it would be a nurturing love, that together they would create a home and a family with love at its heart. That was what he wanted and what he set out to achieve. He understood completely about love. It was the "in love" nonsense that he had a problem with.'

Whatever it meant, and whatever Diana believed at the time, Charles was certainly not 'in love' with his young fiancée. Indeed, he had doubts about the engagement from the very moment he had committed himself to it. His godmother, Lady Mountbatten told me, 'He tried to get out of it. He really wasn't sure he wanted to go through with it.' He had made what he called '*la grande plonge*', but was not sure whether he was now waving or drowning. To some friends he said, 'I do believe I am very lucky that someone as special as Diana seems to love me so much'; to others he expressed a growing concern about his fiancée's relative youth, awesome naivety and disturbing physical and mental frailty.

On the eve of the announcement of the engagement, to protect her from the press, Diana moved from the Earl's Court flat she shared with three girlfriends to a suite at Clarence House where she felt very much alone. A few days later, she moved on to Buckingham Palace where a set of rooms on the nursery floor had been prepared for her. According to Carolyn Bartholomew, one of her flatmates, it was when she went to live at Buckingham Palace that 'the tears started': 'The little thing got so thin. I was worried about her. She wasn't happy, she was suddenly plunged into all this pressure and it was a nightmare for her.' She developed the eating disorder known as bulimia nervosa. She filled herself with food – a huge bowl of sugar-coated cornflakes covered with fruit and smothered with cream, for example – and then went to the bathroom and threw up. At her worst, she repeated this gorging-disgorging routine four or more times a day: her twenty-nine-inch waist shrank to twenty-three.

Charles was bemused and alarmed by his bride-to-be's condition. When, a few years earlier, Diana's sister, Sarah, had suffered from anorexia nervosa, Charles had taken a sympathetic interest in her condition. He was concerned for Diana, too, but alarmed, also, for himself, and uncertain how best to proceed. Elizabeth Longford, royal biographer and friend to the Queen, told me in the early 1990s, 'I think Prince Charles hoped it was just a severe case of pre-wedding nerves, but the Queen, I know, believed it was something more fundamental, a psychological condition brought on by problems during Diana's difficult childhood.' Diana herself, fifteen years later, after her separation (and therapy), was clear about the root cause of her bulimia, the 'secret disease' as she termed it: 'You inflict it upon yourself because your self-esteem is at a low ebb, and you don't think you are worthy or valuable. You fill your stomach up four or five times a day – some do it more – and it gives you a feeling of comfort. It's like having a pair of arms around you, but it's temporary, temporary. Then you're disgusted at the bloatedness of your stomach, and then you bring it all up again.'

Diana yearned to have 'a pair of arms' around her, but, as she said, 'Unfortunately they were around someone else.' As Diana saw it, Camilla was part of the picture from the start – and never left it. 'She was there,' she said, 'right from the beginning.' When Diana arrived at Clarence House on the eve of her engagement, there was no word of welcome from Charles, but there, waiting for her on her bed, was a handwritten note from Camilla: 'Such exciting news about the engagement. Do let's have lunch soon when the Prince of Wales goes to Australia and New Zealand. He's going to be away for three weeks. I'd love to see the ring. Lots of love, Camilla.'

Camilla says her letter to Diana was entirely well-intentioned; that Charles had encouraged her to be friends with his fiancée; that she believed at the time that the Prince's marriage to Diana would mean that her romantic relationship with him was at an end and that, therefore, she was anxious to establish a normal friendship with the girl who would one day be Queen.

In 2005, one of Camilla's friends told me, 'Camilla encouraged Charles to marry Diana. She genuinely wished them both well. She sincerely wanted to help. People say she was two-faced. She was anything but. She told Charles that he must make his marriage work – and that she was going to use this as an opportunity to make her marriage work again too. She was still very much in love with Andrew.'

In 1995, Diana's recollection of the situation was rather more jaundiced. According to Diana, 'They were still in love. They were never not in love.' When Charles went off on his official trip to Australia and New Zealand, Diana and Camilla did indeed have lunch and Camilla was certainly friendly – but Diana was suspicious. 'She asked me if I planned to go hunting when we were at Highgrove. I said I thought not. She seemed well pleased by that. She was already working out what was going to be her territory and what was going to be mine.' Camilla's friends say Diana's remark perfectly illustrates Diana's paranoia. If Camilla talked about hunting at that lunch – and it was a quarter of a century ago: understandably, she has no clear recollection of what anyone said – it was simply because she was trying to find out what Diana's interests were: she was hoping to get to know her better. 'That's all, please believe it.' She had no evil intent.

Diana did not believe it. 'I caught on to what they were up to pretty quickly,' she said. 'I just knew something was going on. You can tell, can't you?' Diana was disconcerted that Camilla always knew about the Prince's plans before she did. Diana was distressed when she found that Charles had sent Camilla flowers using the pet names that he and Camilla had for one another: 'To Gladys from Fred'. Diana was distraught when, two weeks before the wedding, she discovered a bracelet that Charles had had specially made as a present for Camilla: a gold chain with, attached to it, a blue enamel disc featuring the letters

F and G intertwined – 'Fred' and 'Gladys', as Diana read it, 'together forever'.

Charles is not going to dignify this with any kind of comment at this distance in time. As he sees it, no useful purpose is served by raking over the embers now. Whatever he had to say, he said at the beginning of the 1990s when he cooperated with Jonathan Dimbleby on his authorised biography of the Prince. According to Dimbleby, Charles understood Diana's concern about Camilla and sought to reassure her that while, yes, Camilla had indeed been 'one of his most intimate friends', now that he was engaged to be married 'there was, and there would be, no other woman in his life'. Emphatically, Dimbleby maintained that, from the moment of his engagement until the day of his marriage, the Prince of Wales saw Camilla 'on only one occasion and that was more than four months later to say farewell', concluding:

> His feelings for Camilla Parker Bowles had not changed [she was his 'touchstone', his 'sounding board'], but they had both accepted that their intimacy could no longer be maintained. Anxious not to seem dismissive, the Prince consulted one of his friends about the most graceful way to mark his gratitude for her understanding and support. Some days later, he asked Michael Colborne [a member of his office since 1975] to arrange the purchase of a bracelet with the letters GF stamped on it. As Colborne knew very well, GF stood for Girl Friday, the Prince's nickname for Mrs Parker Bowles, whose role in his life was thus neatly commemorated.
>
> In July, the bracelet was duly delivered to Colborne's office, where it joined a pile of cards and presents, a small sample of the scores of thousands which had begun to pour into Buckingham Palace in the weeks leading up to the wedding for Colborne to wrap. Somehow Diana Spencer discovered the bracelet and evidently concluded the worst.
>
> Later, she confronted Prince Charles. He explained the bracelet. She was not mollified. There was a heated discussion in which the Prince insisted that, as an act of courtesy, he felt obliged to give Camilla Parker Bowles the bracelet in person. A few days later, true to that word, he gave her the present and said goodbye for what both of them intended to be the last time.

Apparently, 'Bollocks to that!' was Diana's reaction when she was told what Dimbleby had written. Diana disputed the Dimbleby defence.

'Come to think of it,' she said, 'GF probably stood for "Great you-know-what"! If he'd really wanted to give her up he wouldn't have gone on seeing her and calling her. He told me it was over, but it wasn't. He lied. On my wedding day, I walked down the aisle not thinking about what was happening, but looking out for her. Can you imagine?'

Diana disputed it. Diana's friends disputed it – and still do. One of them said to me, 'Diana wanted to believe that Charles had given up Camilla, but everything that happened made it clear he hadn't. He just couldn't keep away from her. And the damage he did was irreparable. Diana's mother abandoned her for someone else when she was six. Her father abandoned her for the sake of the she-witch [Raine Spencer]. And then, poor girl, she discovered that Charles, her husband-to-be, was abandoning her before they were even married. Of course, she was an emotional wreck. What a way to treat any nineteen-year-old, never mind the woman you are going to marry.'

Stephen Barry, Charles's valet at the time, disputed it, too. Or perhaps he didn't entirely. Charles claimed that he saw Camilla only once between the announcement of his engagement and his wedding day. Perhaps he did – on the Monday night of his wedding week, at the Buckingham Palace ball to celebrate the royal marriage. After the ball was over, Diana was driven to Clarence House for the night. Charles remained at Buckingham Palace and, according to his valet, Camilla stayed too. Barry claimed his master took his mistress 'to bed in the very week of his wedding'. 'It seemed incredible,' he said. 'Certainly incredibly daring, if not incredibly stupid.'

Chapter Nine

Two Daughters and Their Destinies

'To marry is to domesticate the Recording Angel. Once you are married, there is nothing left for you, not even suicide, but to be good.'

Robert Louis Stevenson (1850–94)

In the run-up to his wedding to Diana, Charles had many qualms. He shared them with Camilla. He shared them with his parents. He shared them with his sister, Anne.

Camilla was in no doubt: Charles must go through with the marriage. Diana was an ideal bride. At the time, Camilla, reportedly, described the Prince of Wales's teenage fiancée as 'a mouse'. In retrospect, Diana said she felt she had been a 'sacrificial lamb'. Camilla's friends now say that if Camilla called Diana 'a mouse' it was only because Diana did seem young and shy and tentative, not because, at the time, Camilla felt in any way patronising or hostile towards her.

When Charles raised his misgivings about the marriage with his own family, he was given short shrift. I am told the Queen, privately, shared her son's concerns about Diana's 'apparent instability' and her 'rather rocky' family history, but said little to Charles by way of comfort or counsel. I understand that the Duke of Edinburgh, irritated by Charles's apparent shilly-shallying, shook his head wearily and made it clear that Charles, having made a commitment, must now see it through and stop whingeing: 'Nobody's interested.' Anne shared her father's pragmatic approach. 'Just close your eyes and think of England' she is said to have said.

Diana had her reservations, too. 'It wasn't just her,' she said fifteen years later (in conversation, Diana spoke of Camilla frequently, but did her best to avoid mentioning her name), 'it was Charles, too. Non-tactile. Wouldn't touch. Didn't seem to want to. Then all of a sudden, woosh. Mostly cold, mostly not there, not calling, nothing, then all of a sudden he's there again. Hot and cold. Hot and cold. I didn't understand what was going on. So immature, me. Little girl lost.' After the episode with the Fred and Gladys bracelet, Diana, by her own account, told her sisters, 'I can't marry him, I can't do this, this is absolutely unbelievable.' 'Well, bad luck' was their response. 'Your face is on the tea-towels so you're too late to chicken out.' Charles and Diana were married at St Paul's Cathedral in the summer of 1981 – on 29 July, the traditional feast day of Saint Martha, patron saint of housewives, whose iconographic attributes are a ladle and a broom.[157] Fifteen years later they were divorced. The decree nisi was granted on 15 July 1996, and the decree absolute on 28 August – the feast day of Saint Augustine of Hippo, the fourth-century divine noted for his maxim, 'Audi partem alteram': 'Hear the other side'.

There are certainly two sides to the sorry story of the marriage of Charles and Diana, and, having friends who are and were friends to each of them, I have heard both sides, in detail, time and again.

According to Diana's camp, Charles, from the outset, proved to be selfish, self-indulgent, thoughtless, unsympathetic, uncaring and cruel. In 2005, Rosa Monckton put it to me like this: 'Charles was self-absorbed without being self-aware – a pretty deadly combination.' Pestered by Diana, he did try to dress in a marginally less old-fogeyish manner, but he made no serious effort to share his young wife's interests and took no trouble to like her friends. He was older than her and more experienced: he had a duty of care which he neglected, almost from the start. Faced with her frailty – her post-natal depression, her mood swings – he was unable to cope. Faced with her cries for help – her bulimia, her attempts at self-injury – he turned away and sought solace in the arms of the one woman he had loved all along, Camilla Parker Bowles.[158] He was weak yet wilful, pathetic yet petulant. He behaved like a spoilt child. He lacked emotional intelligence and generosity of spirit. Above all, and increasingly, he

---

[157] Martha (sister of Lazarus) is also occasionally represented with a dragon . . . which she subdued. She sprinkled him with holy water, put her sash about his neck and then led him to the slaughter.

[158] At the beginning of the 1990s, in a conversation with Lord Charteris, the Queen's longest-serving courtier pointed me in the direction of this line from *The Unquiet Grave* by Cyril Connolly: 'The true index of a man's character is the health of his wife.' Charteris, I have no doubt, was inviting me to compare and contrast the Queen's robust and life-long good health with the frailty of the then Princess of Wales.

Lady Diana Spencer,
painted by Bryan Organ,
at the time of her engagement
to Prince Charles, 1981

Andrew Parker Bowles, being painted by Lucian Freud, after his divorce from Camilla, 2003-04

Prince William of Wales was christened William Arthur Philip Louis on 4 August 1982 in the Music Room at Buckingham Palace, by the Archbishop of Canterbury, Dr Robert Runcie. His godparents were, *l – r*, the Duchess of Westminster, Sir Laurens van der Post, Lady Susan Hussey, Lord Romsey, Princess Alexandra and, *seated r*, ex- King Constantine II of the Hellenes

William, Diana and Charles at Kensington Palace, Christmas 1982

Lt Col Andrew Parker Bowles, at Buckingham Palace in February 1984, having received his OBE, with Camilla and their children: Tom, aged 9, and Laura, 5

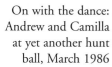

On with the dance: Andrew and Camilla at yet another hunt ball, March 1986

Summer and sunshine: Camilla Parker Bowles and the Prince of Wales on holiday in Turkey, 1989

Parting of the ways: Andrew
and Camilla Parker Bowles
in the summer of 1993

Alone at Middlewick House: Camilla in
the week of her divorce, January 1995

A'hunting she will go:
Camilla riding to hounds
with the Beaufort Hunt
in 1995 and 1997

What they must endure . . . the Prince of Wales with the author, at St James's Palace, October 1995

. . . photographers keeping vigil outside the Ritz Hotel in Piccadilly, before the first 'sanctioned' photograph, January 1999

Here they come . . .

. . . Here they are . . . That's it.

'The first kiss': Mrs Parker Bowles welcomes the Prince of Wales to the reception in honour of the fifteenth anniversary of the National Osteoporosis Society, June 2001

Another day, another kiss: Charles with Camilla's sister, Annabel Elliott, at the Integrated Health Centre in Poundbury, Dorset, Charles's model village, November 2004

Absent friend: Tom, Camilla and Laura Parker Bowles at the party for Tom's book – the party that Charles missed because he was at the funeral of Sheik Zayed, November 2004

Happy days: Charles and Camilla at the Mey Games in Scotland, August 2004

was jealous – pitifully jealous – of his young wife's popularity with the public.

Diana, according to Charles's friends, was a sad case, almost from the start, and quickly became a malevolent one. In 2005, a senior member of Charles's family said to me of Diana, 'I do genuinely think she was a very wicked person – yes, she was *wicked*.' She was in love with the position not the Prince. She never came close to understanding her man – or trying to. She never came close to understanding his role as Prince of Wales – or appeared to want to. She made to attempt to share his hopes and ambitions; she resented his range of interests: she demanded a cull of some of his closest friends. Whatever he liked or enjoyed, she was determined not to. When he said he loved Balmoral more than anywhere, she said she found it 'boring, boring, boring'. When he tried to interest her in the development of Highgrove and its garden and grounds, she said she wanted to move. She was perverse; she was prickly; she was (in the words of one of Charles's closest friends) 'an absolute pain – and potty with it'. She came from a dangerous background – a dysfunctional family with a history of marital and mental instability – and it showed. Diana was difficult, deceitful and manipulative. She made up stories, she told lies, she had affairs. She really was beyond the pale.

As their marriage unravelled, Diana and Charles took it in turns to tell their story from their own perspective. *Diana: Her True Story* by Andrew Morton and *The Prince of Wales: A Biography* by Jonathan Dimbleby still make for gripping reading. Through the special pleading, you can hear the pain and hurt and heartache on both sides. Read both books and you realise at once that Charles's friend Nicholas Soames was right when – shortly before the marriage – in a heated exchange with the Duke of Edinburgh's private secretary (Lord Rupert Nevill), Soames described the proposed union of Charles and Diana as 'a terrible mismatch' that was 'doomed, utterly doomed'.

Today, Charles says he has said all he will ever say about his first marriage. He does not resile from anything he told Jonathan Dimbleby at the beginning of the 1990s, though, with hindsight, he does now regret some of it. He spoke then simply because he felt he had been traduced and that at least, in his words, 'some of my side of the story' needed to be heard. Even though he still believes that his own behaviour during his first marriage has been sadly misunderstood by some – and wilfully misinterpreted by others ('Down with the press!') – he recognises that no useful purpose can now be served by saying anything about it on the record, 'anything at all, at all, at all'. The embers of his first marriage have gone cold. Others may choose to rake them over. He has no desire to assist.

We will not be hearing Camilla's side of the story either, at least not in her own words. Just as the new Duchess of Cornwall now chooses the shade of her frocks from the same colour palette as the late Queen Mother, so, like Charles's beloved granny (in Charles's view, the perfect role model for his wife), Camilla is determined never to give an interview.[159] 'What's to be gained?' she says – in private. She is taking a leaf out of the book of another exemplary consort, the late Sir Denis Thatcher, who declined all invitations to be interviewed, with the explanation: 'My father told me as a boy: whales don't get killed unless they spout.'[160]

When his wife was prime minister, Denis Thatcher said simply, 'So long as I keep the lowest possible profile and neither write nor say anything, I avoid getting into trouble.' The Duchess of Cornwall is content to accept a certain amount of 'profile' – she knows it goes with the territory – but because she is no fool, and is not interested in fame (she has had enough publicity to last several lifetimes), and, whatever her detractors say, is not ambitious for herself, she recognises that her own and her husband's – and the monarchy's – interests are best served if she turns up where required, when required, looking appropriate, with friendly small talk for those she meets but not a word of any sort for the press. Prince Charles came to regard his first wife as a rival. Camilla is to be what Queen Elizabeth was to George VI: a consort, an

[159] In the run-up to her wedding in 1923, Lady Elizabeth Bowes-Lyon made what seems to have been the only unforced error of her public life. An enterprising reporter from the *Star* newspaper turned up at her parents' Mayfair front door and asked Lady Elizabeth for an interview. He was granted one. George V was not amused. 'Those filthy rags of newspapers' was how the King regarded the press. Elizabeth never spoke on the record to a journalist again – and the coverage she received over the remaining eight decades of her life was extraordinary and, almost always, adulatory.

[160] Denis Thatcher was utterly convinced of the value of a vow of silence. When Sarah Ferguson was Duchess of York and complained to him about the 'awful press' she was getting, he replied, 'Yes, Ma'am. Has it occurred to you to keep your mouth shut?' At a dinner at the White House in honour of Margaret Thatcher, President George Bush Sr spoke in her praise. As expected, Mrs Thatcher responded. Then, unexpectedly, Barbara Bush rose to her feet and said a few words, after which all eyes turned towards Denis. Reluctantly, he stood up, and offered his audience just fifteen words: 'As Julius Caesar said upon entering Cleopatra's tent, "I have not come here to talk."' Then he sat down.

encourager, a good companion and best friend. To Charles, Diana was none of these things.

Charles married Diana in 1981, but his matrimonial mentor, if he had one, was his late great-uncle, Lord Louis Mountbatten, whose views on a wife's contribution to a successful marriage had been formed two or more generations before. When Mountbatten was married in 1922, he said, uncontroversially at the time, 'I think the greatest happiness is found when the husband works at his career and his wife looks after the home and children.' When asked whether his bride had ambitions for herself, Mountbatten responded, 'Career for Lady Louis? Why, she's going to be my wife, career enough!' Consciously or not, Charles was working to Mountbatten's agenda. He was looking for a wife in the comforting mould of his grandmother (Queen Elizabeth) or his godmother (Patricia Mountbatten): instead he found himself hitched to a complex and complicated young woman quite as interested in her own problems as in his. As Princess Margaret said, 'They were two very needy people.'

Off the record or on, however, to this day Charles is adamant that he went into his first marriage intending it to succeed. On the eve of the wedding, he sent Diana 'a very nice signet ring' and a note of praise and encouragement. 'I'm so proud of you,' he wrote, 'and when you come up I'll be there at the altar for you tomorrow. Just look 'em in the eye and knock 'em dead.' Diana was overjoyed: 'over the moon,' she said. Of the day itself she said, 'I remember being so in love with my husband that I couldn't take my eyes off him. I just absolutely thought I was the luckiest girl in the world.' She did take her eyes off him, of course. 'Walking down the aisle,' she recalled, 'I spotted Camilla, pale grey, veiled pillbox hat . . . her son Tom standing on a chair . . . vivid memory.'

By her own admission, Diana was 'obsessed by Camilla totally'. She had ensured that Mrs Parker Bowles's name was struck off the draft list of the 120 'friends and family' who were invited to the Buckingham Palace wedding breakfast, but there was no escaping her during the honeymoon. Cruising in the Mediterranean in the royal yacht *Britannia*, two photographs of Camilla fell out of Charles's personal diary. 'Can you believe it?' she said later. 'On our *honeymoon*! And he wore her effing cufflinks too.' The cufflinks, each bearing two intertwined Cs, were a parting gift from Camilla to Charles. 'She is simply a dear and valued friend,' the new groom protested to his young bride. Diana was unconvinced. 'I couldn't get the woman out of my head,' Diana said. 'I know she was in his mind all the time. Couldn't get her out of mine.'

By Jonathan Dimbleby's account, Charles rather enjoyed his first honeymoon:

When he was not sailing or bathing, he sat in the sun reading from a selection of books provided for him by [Laurens] van der Post,[161] including his own study of Carl Jung, *Jung and the Story of Our Time*. Otherwise he sat in the Duke of Edinburgh's cabin where he wrote copious letters of gratitude to those who had helped make such a success of the wedding. 'All I can say is that marriage is very jolly and it's also extremely nice being together in *Britannia*,' the Prince wrote on the second day of their cruise, adding indulgently, 'Diana dashes about chatting up all the sailors and the cooks in the galley etc. while I remain hermit-like on the verandah deck sunk with pure joy into one of Laurens van der Post's books . . .'

Diana's account of the same honeymoon is rather different. 'I remember crying my eyes out,' she recalled. 'I was so tired, for all the wrong reasons totally.' (They did have sex, but, according to Diana, infrequently, and – so she told a girlfriend who told me – 'when it happened, it wasn't up to much.'[162] Later, according to the same

[161] 1906–96, the South African writer and adventurer who had become one of Charles's most influential mentors since they first met in the early 1970s. There is a fascinating, if partial, account of their relationship in *Storyteller: The Many Lives of Laurens van der Post* by J. D. F. Jones. Jones says van der Post found in the Prince 'not only a gratifying disciple but a young friend he admired and loved'. Van der Post felt he understood Charles in a way his own family did not. 'He's been brought up in a terrible way,' he said. 'He's a natural Renaissance man. A man who believes in the wholeness and totality of life . . . Why should it be that if you try to contemplate your natural self you should be thought to be peculiar?'

[162] There are two sides to most stories. In March 1996, at the House of Commons, I happened to have dinner with Dame Barbara Cartland, Diana's favourite childhood author, long-standing friend of Lord Mountbatten, and mother of Raine, who had married Diana's father in 1976. Dame Barbara was full of concern for the plight of the Prince and Princess of Wales. 'It's so sad for them both,' she said. 'It's heartbreaking. Of course, you know where it all went wrong? She wouldn't do oral sex, she just wouldn't. It's as simple as that. Of *course* it all went wrong.' (Dame Barbara was full of intriguing insights to the intimate life of the Royal Family. That night she also told me that it was Lord Mountbatten – 'Darling Dickie, no one knew him as I did' – who had pioneered the zip fastener instead of fly buttons and had persuaded the then Prince of Wales to

girlfriend, Charles became 'much more demanding', but, apparently, from Diana's perspective, 'it was no more satisfactory'.)

After the cruise on *Britannia*, the newly-weds joined the Royal Family for a holiday at Balmoral. 'That's when the truth dawned,' said Diana. 'That's when the realisation set in.' Rosa Monckton told me, 'She had been so full of hope, so full of naive love. She was such a warm person, but she felt frozen out.' She felt uncomfortable with her in-laws and unsupported by her husband. The days were bad, but the nights, she said, were worse. 'My dreams were appalling. At night I dreamt of Camilla the whole time.'

In fairness to Charles, he did try to help – in his own way. He telephoned his guru, Laurens van der Post, then aged seventy-five, and asked him up to Balmoral to see Diana. In 2005, one of Charles's friends said to me, 'It's easy to scoff now, but what else could Charles do? He had a problem in his marriage, only eight weeks into it. He couldn't really talk about it with his mother or his grandmother. He didn't dare talk about it with his father. Mountbatten was dead, so he turned to the only other father figure he had. Now everybody says van der Post was a fruitcake and a phoney, but people respected him. Mrs T respected him.[163] Charles turned to him because he believed him to be a wise and caring man, and Charles was desperate. He wanted to get at the root of Diana's problem. He wanted her better. He wanted her happy. He really did.'

Diana said, 'Laurens didn't understand me.' Whether he did or did not, undoubtedly he cared. As he said, he would do anything for 'my prince'. And Charles was 'frantic' for Diana to get help. At van der Post's suggestion, Diana, now painfully thin because of her bulimia, agreed to undergo a series of twice-weekly sessions with a London-based psychotherapist, Dr Alan McGlashan, a close friend of van der Post. According to J. D. F. Jones, van der Post's biographer,

---

follow suit. 'But it all went wrong at a very smart supper party in Biarritz. The Prince went to the cloakroom, but, poor lamb, didn't dare emerge because the zip got stuck! He had to slip out by the back door. He was furious, had all the zips taken out of his trousers.'

[163] Many still respect him, even acknowledging his tendency to add colour to the stories of his already colourful life. He was introduced to Margaret Thatcher in the mid-1970s and drafted his own Conservative manifesto for her consideration. She was stimulated by his ideas and his company and, over a period of fifteen years, she took his advice on a wide range of issues, from the future of southern Africa to the loss of the will to work in British society.

McGlashan gave van der Post just one account of his 'progress' with his royal patient – or, rather, of his lack of it – 'writing that the Princess was surrounded by a bevy of frightened doctors who seemed to think that they were confronting not just a serious illness but also a dynastic crisis, and had been tackling it with all sorts of pills and anti-depressants and "Behaviourist" techniques.' This range of 'treatments', Jones notes, 'was the start of a rumour which, during and after the royal divorce, would be fanned by spin doctors in both palaces – that Diana was mentally unstable.' McGlashan, apparently, after his initial session with Diana, would have none of this. According to Jones, 'He assured Laurens that he found Diana to be a normal, though very unhappy, young woman, trying bravely to cope with her situation. He thought that he would be able to help her with her emotional problems so long as she realised that the analytic process took time.'

In the event, Diana saw McGlashan only seven or eight times before deciding to seek help elsewhere – almost anywhere and everywhere, as it turned out. Charles, however, continued to see Dr McGlashan over several years and they developed 'a special relationship' that the Prince greatly valued. (Previously, Charles had been consulting Ingaret van der Post, Laurens's second wife, who, while not a fully qualified psychotherapist, had a reputation as a gifted interpreter of dreams. When Ingaret died in 1997, Charles, unexpected and unannounced, turned up at her funeral. 'He is a very sweet and thoughtful man,' a former equerry said to me. 'Do make that clear in your book. He failed to make Diana happy, but it wasn't for want of trying.')

Charles's friends and family are agreed: he did his best, but it was not easy. His godmother, Lady Mountbatten, told me, 'He tried, he certainly tried. I remember, before they were married, they came to lunch and I asked to see the engagement ring, and Diana said it was in her bag in the sitting room. "Charles, go and fetch it," she said. And he did. He tried to please her, but she wouldn't be pleased. She hated the Bahamas. She hated Balmoral. Everything he liked, she hated. He was ready to sell Highgrove to please her. He cut off his friends to please her. I remember he took us around Kensington Palace and he showed us the attic rooms and he said, rather sadly, "I did think it would be nice to have the German cousins over to stay, but Diana doesn't want to . . ."'

Charles tried with Diana, but it was not easy – so he turned to

Camilla. A psychologist might say – would say, in fact[164] – that it is the classic behaviour of cheating husband: he undermines his wife, belittles her, even suggests she is in need of psychiatric help, in order to justify his own infidelity. Suzie Hayman, one of Britain's leading marriage guidance counsellors (and author of a number of 'Relate' guides to making first – and second – marriages work) says, 'When a man is being unfaithful he has to shift the blame so it's your fault, not his. He will say to himself, "She's not paying enough attention to me. We don't have sex often enough. I'm not getting what I need from this relationship." This way, he can absolve himself of all the guilt and blame of sleeping with someone else.'[165]

Charles, however, is adamant that, at the start of his marriage at least, he turned to Camilla simply for solace, not for sex. On his honeymoon, he telephoned her from *Britannia*. He wrote to her as well. He called her again from Balmoral. According to his valet, Stephen Barry (who served the Prince for twelve years), 'Camilla was a habit he could not break, an obsession he did not wish to conquer.' Barry claimed that, even in the immediate aftermath of his marriage, Charles would telephone Camilla from his office 'most days': 'If it was impossible to call, he would write a letter which would be smuggled out without the Princess's knowledge. It was extraordinary. The Prince simply had to be in constant contact with Camilla or he could not function properly. If he went without his daily phone call, he would become tetchy and ill-tempered.'

Although Diana maintained that, once, she clearly overheard Charles, on his telephone in the bathroom, telling Camilla, 'Whatever happens I will always love you,' the Prince's friends protest that Stephen Barry's account of Charles's behaviour is greatly exaggerated. They point out, too, that the former valet is conveniently dead so that his testimony cannot be tested.

What they concede – what Charles himself admits – is that the unhappy Prince, bemused and bewildered by his wife's bulimia, by her depressive state, by her inability or unwillingness to share his interests or work with the grain of his way of life, turned to Camilla, 'almost

---

[164] See *The Script: The 100% Absolutely Predictable Things Men Do When They Cheat* by Elizabeth Landers and Vicky Mainzer (2005). It is more profound than it sounds.

[165] It seems, in Charles's case, however, others must share some of the blame. According to Suzie Hayman: 'A man who is unconditionally loved by his parents will be less likely to have affairs when he is married because he is secure enough in himself to give all of himself to his wife.'

inevitably' – as one of them put it to me – for 'comradeship and understanding – which, let's face it, he wasn't getting much of at home'.

Camilla's strength was she did not ask for anything – and she offered everything, most especially a willingness to listen to his woes. She also, by contrast with the hapless Diana, seemed so healthy, so straight-forward, so *normal*. 'Camilla is thoroughly dependable,' says her friend Jilly Cooper. 'You can rely on her. She's completely down-to-earth and absolutely straight.' From the start of his marriage to Diana, Charles and Camilla shared telephone conversations and exchanged letters. Quite soon, they began to meet.

The first public sighting of Charles and Camilla, reunited, took place on Monday 2 November 1981, three months and four days after Charles and Diana's wedding. Charles decided to ride to hounds that day and joined the Vale of White Horse Hunt at Ewen, near Cirencester. Whether by chance or design, Mrs Parker Bowles went hunting with the VWH that day, too. Along with the hunt's pack of hounds came a pack of Fleet Street's finest. Charles was not amused. According to reports, he turned bright red and bellowed at them, 'When are you going to stop making my life a total misery?'

Charles and Camilla continued meeting on the hunting field, some-times with the VWH, sometimes with the Beaufort, occasionally further afield, in Leicestershire, with the Quorn or the Belvoir. 'What they got up to,' said Diana, 'God knows.' They say they 'got up to' nothing: they met as friends, that's all. They say, too, that, throughout, Camilla urged Charles to do everything he could to help his wife and to make his marriage work. The one thing they did not do – which Diana wanted and which, she maintained, she asked of Charles time and again – was not to see or speak to one another. Charles felt that was an 'unreasonable' thing to ask and unnecessary also, since there was nothing untoward in his relationship with Mrs Parker Bowles at the time.

Diana would have preferred Charles and Camilla to stay apart. Instead, they came closer together. The idea of moving away from Highgrove – to Belton House, near Grantham in Lincolnshire[166] – came to nothing. Charles and Diana stayed where they were. Instead,

---

[166] Then the home of the 7th Lord Brownlow (only son of Perry Brownlow, lord-in-waiting and good friend to the last Prince of Wales and Mrs Simpson), now a National Trust property – and well worth visiting. (For opening times call + 44 1476 566116.) The beautifully symmetrical Restoration house (featured as the home of Lady

in time, it was the Parker Bowles's who moved house, selling Bolehyde Manor and moving – as chance would have it – a little closer to Highgrove, to a beautiful eighteenth-century manor house in the charming village of Pickwick, near Corsham, in Wiltshire. Middlewick House, built in Cotswold and Bath stone, with a fine country garden and five hundred useful acres, is the epitome of an upper-crust English family's country home. It would not suit a footballer's wife, but for the gardening, hunting wife of a military man – granddaughter of a lord, best friend to the Prince of Wales – it was heaven. It was also a fifteen-minute drive to Highgrove.[167]

Through the 1980s, Charles and Camilla saw more and more of one another and Charles and Diana saw less and less. Charles spent an increasing amount of his free time at Highgrove, while Diana was more comfortable at Kensington Palace. Diana said of the Prince and Camilla, 'They had an interest in common: my husband.' The truth is that Charles and Camilla shared so much – and not only the secret of their enduring love. They were the same age and on the same wavelength. They had everything in common: a love of gardens and gardening, a feeling for the English countryside, a sense of history, a love of riding to hounds, an exhilaration at the thrill of the chase, an easiness with dogs, a familiarity with a certain aristocratic and hunting set, a love of music (opera, especially), an appreciation of fine art, a love of Italy . . . As one of Charles's siblings put it: 'They were made for each other.' Charles and Camilla had everything in common – including the conspiracy of their affair and a shared sense of guilt.[168] Diana and Charles had nothing in common – except their children.

Catherine de Bourgh in the BBC production of *Pride and Prejudice*) had much to commend it, but, after three visits, Charles decided it was simply too big, too far from Duchy of Cornwall territory and too expensive to run. Diana was disappointed.

[167] The rumour persists that Charles bought Middlewick House for Camilla. Not so. The Parker Bowles, while not wildly rich, had means of their own. Bolehyde Manor was sold for around £500,000 and, in 1986, on the death of her grandmother, Sonia Cubitt, Mrs Keppel's elder daughter, Camilla received a useful legacy.

[168] According to the seasoned marriage guidance counsellor I consulted on this question, the element of 'conspiracy' in an illicit affair is often part of the excitement that fuels it. 'The lovers become co-conspirators,' she explained. 'They feel "It's us and our 'secret' against the world."' She also said, 'Most decent people, especially those with children, feel guilty when they are having an affair, but they manage to live with the guilt by blaming others – usually their marriage partner – for making the marriage untenable and the affair somehow "inevitable". It is usually only when the affair is exposed – or grows stale – that guilt is transmuted into shame and, then, remorse.'

Interestingly, in the battle for the reputations of Charles and Diana, representatives of both camps – so pitilessly vituperative in their attacks on the integrity and character of their villain of choice – offer a guarded truce in the matter of the Wales's children. When it comes to Prince William (born 21 June 1982) and Prince Harry (born 15 September 1984), it seems to be agreed by both sides that both parents, in their different but equally loving ways, meant well and did their best. Nobody doubts that Diana was a devoted, conscientious and loving mother. Her children were the centre of her universe. They were also her anchor. As she said, 'They kept me on track, focused.'

While Charles and Diana might disagree on almost everything else – where to live, what to wear, where to go on holiday, what music to play in the car: you name it and they were contrary about it – when it came to the upbringing of their boys they were relatively, and commendably, as one. Diana disliked the 'old fogey' element she found in Charles, but she was not against tradition. Her brother and her father had both been educated at Eton and Diana was content for William and Harry to go there too. (Tom Parker Bowles, unlike his father and Camilla's father, also went to Eton, but he was seven years older than William: at school, the boys did not overlap.) It irked her that she was often accused of having tried to stop her husband enjoying the traditional country sports of fishing, shooting and hunting. 'That's total rubbish,' she said. Rosa Monckton told me, 'Diana positively encouraged the boys to develop that part of their heritage. She said "Balmoral isn't for me", but she fully accepted it as part of their heritage.'

Diana was irked by the fact that Charles had hoped that their second child would be a girl (and said as much, not just to her, but to the world), but conceded that, rather to her surprise, when the boys were babies, Charles turned out to be an involved and enthusiastic hands-on father. She felt he neglected her, but she never accused him of being negligent towards his children. 'He loved the nursery life,' she said, 'and couldn't wait to get back and do the bottle and everything. He was very good, he always came back and fed the baby.' As the boys grew older, and the parents grew further apart, Charles's devotion to his sons did not diminish, but he was less hands-on. Rosa Monckton told me, 'He was very absent as a father.'

In 1991, Charles was irritated by the repeated publication of a photograph depicting Diana with outstretched arms greeting her boys when they came out to join the royal couple on an official visit to Canada. What annoyed Charles was not so much the image of Diana as a doting mum, evidently thrilled to see her sons, but the implication that he, by contrast, was – as his parents had been – a stiffer, more formal, less overtly loving father. If that is what people thought, it was unfair. He might be ill-at-ease and 'non-tactile' with his wife (Diana's phrase), but with his sons he has always been comfortable and physically affectionate.

In 1997, at Diana's funeral, Charles (understandably dazed and troubled by the whole experience) was further hurt and confused by the passage in Charles Spencer's funeral oration that touched on William and Harry and the nature of their upbringing. In the course of his address, Diana's brother, referring to Diana's sons, spoke directly to Diana's spirit, and, on behalf of his mother and his sisters, with a catch in his throat, solemnly vowed 'that we, your blood family, will do all we can to continue the imaginative way in which you were steering these two exceptional young men so that their souls are not simply immersed by duty and tradition, but can sing openly as you planned'. Outside Westminster Abbey, the multitude of mourners, listening to the young earl's oration through loudspeakers, started to applaud. Quite slowly, the noise of applause filtered into the Abbey itself. The congregation began to clap. The applause rumbled down the nave. William and Harry, a little uncertainly, clapped, too. Prince Charles closed his eyes and tapped the side of his leg.

Five years later, in 2002, when I talked to Charles Spencer about his sister's funeral, he told me he had had no intention of upsetting Prince Charles – or any of the Royal Family – with his remarks. He had simply spoken as he had felt at the time, from the heart. I asked him how much hands-on involvement the 'blood family' had in fact had with his nephews in the years since his sister's death. He admitted, 'Not a lot', explaining that it had not proved necessary. He told me, 'Prince Charles is obviously a good father and the boys are doing really well. I think Diana would be very happy about the way they have grown up. She'd be very proud of them.' I asked Earl Spencer how he felt about Camilla. He said, 'It's none of my business. I wish Charles every happiness. He should do whatever he wants to do.'

In the course of writing this book, everyone to whom I have spoken has been full of praise for William and Harry. Rosa Monckton told me, 'William has inherited his mother's luminosity. He's got a huge sense of fun, but more than that, he can just walk into a room and it stops. He's got something very special.' Major General Andrew Ritchie, Commandant of the Royal Military Academy Sandhurst, where Harry enrolled in May 2005, told me, 'He's a good lad, first-class.' Mark Cann, who plays polo with Charles and William and Harry, told me, 'They are absolutely excellent together – great mates, great team players. No problems off the field or on. Quite the reverse.' The only person to express a reservation of any kind to me has been Paul Burrell, Diana's former butler and co-keeper of her flame. In the summer of 2004, he told me he was anxious that Charles was not as involved as he might be in his sons' everyday lives. 'The drugs thing is bad,' he said, 'worrying, frightening.' (Tom Parker Bowles's use of cocaine, when younger, has been widely reported. In 2002, St James's Palace confirmed Harry, then aged seventeen, had 'experimented with cannabis on several occasions'. These are children of their times, no more immune to the temptations of the modern world than any of their contemporaries – but vastly richer than most of them.)

In the 1980s Charles was a good father who took true delight in his children. At the same time, he was an unhappy husband who felt trapped in an increasingly loveless marriage. 'Did he ever consider breaking out of it?' I asked his godmother, Pamela Mountbatten. 'No, I'm sure not,' she said. 'I remember two or three lunches in Montpelier Walk [the Brabournes' London home at the time] when I tried to make an opening, but he didn't want to discuss it. He thought it was a life sentence.'

To Charles, at the time, his future looked entirely grey. To the public at large, it seemed quite golden. In 1984, for example, to mark Harry's birth, my wife, Michèle Brown, published a book that became a best-seller: *Prince Charles & Princess Diana: Portrait of a Family*. It was what the market wanted: an enthusiastic account of the young Royal Family in general, and, in particular, a glowing celebration of Diana as model modern mother and paragon among princesses. Whatever was happening to Diana in private – and the birth of her children had not cured her psychological ills or lessened her obsession with Camilla – in public the young Princess of Wales was hitting her stride. Her love affair with her husband – such as it had been – was over: her love affair with the world was now beginning.

'Quite mysteriously,' a watching courtier noted at the time, 'a visit by a young princess with beautiful blue eyes and a superb natural complexion brought gleams of radiant sunshine into the dingiest streets of the dreariest cities. Princes who do their duty are respected, beautiful Princesses have an in-built advantage over their male counterparts.'

That last paragraph is not, in fact, about Diana. The time was 1948;

the country was France, the visiting princess with beautiful blue eyes was the young Elizabeth; and the courtier was her private secretary, Jock Colville. 'In four hectic days,' he reported after the future Queen's first foreign tour with the Duke of Edinburgh, 'Princess Elizabeth had conquered Paris.' Yes, forty years before the phrase 'the Diana effect' became common currency, Colville watched Elizabeth going about her business and described what amounted to the same phenomenon.

Diana's popularity irked Charles. In the early years of his marriage, he felt torn: he was both proud of the impact Diana made on the public, and resentful. When he arrived at an event unaccompanied, with a lopsided smile, half-laughing, he would apologise: 'I'm afraid you've just got me today – sorry to disappoint you.' Later on, the coverage Diana received – and the way in which she courted it – drove him almost to despair.

It was not envy only. Yes, he was jealous of his wife's extraordinary popularity – shame-facedly, he half-admitted it to friends – but he was also troubled by it. And so were his family. The Queen and the Duke of Edinburgh – much more sympathetic to Diana than some of the press would have had you believe – were not perturbed by the fact that their daughter-in-law was popular with the public. What worried them – and Charles – was the sense that Diana allowed her popularity to go to her head. Philip recalled – and Charles knew – that Elizabeth was adored once, too – as much as Diana was. In the late 1940s and early 1950s, in Britain, in France, in countries around the world, thousands – tens of thousands, sometimes *hundreds* of thousands – turned out to cheer her. Once upon a time, Elizabeth and Philip were seen – and talked about – and written up – as characters from a fairy tale. The difference between them and Princess Diana, they felt, is that they did not take it personally. The Duke of Edinburgh said to me, 'You won't remember this, but in the first years of the Queen's reign, the level of adulation – you wouldn't believe it. You really wouldn't. It could have been corroding. It would have been very easy to play to the gallery, but I took a conscious decision not to do that. Safer not to be too popular. You can't fall too far.'

The Duke of Edinburgh has never had a problem playing second fiddle to the Queen. Whatever difficulties he faced in the early years, behind palace doors, dealing with snooty courtiers, whatever domestic tensions there may have been, on occasion, between him and his wife, since 1952, Prince Philip has accepted, without demur, that his principal *raison d'être* as Duke of Edinburgh is to support the Queen. He never upstages her. In public, he always defers to her. He accepts that she is – must be – the centre of attention. Indeed, he insists upon it. If a photographer gets too close to Her Majesty, the Duke doesn't hesitate to bark, 'Get out of the Queen's way, people want to see her.'

Charles had a problem with Diana, however: Diana wasn't the Queen: she was the consort. He was the heir apparent – and the one who exhausted himself, year in, year out, writing speeches, chairing meetings, launching initiatives. Charles was supposed to be the focus of attention. Diana was supposed to be the 'support act'. Instead, by public demand (or so it seemed), the roles were reversed: Charles became the sidekick, while Diana became the star.

Charles had another problem, too. Diana was beautiful. Her beauty was a delight for us (and a gift to picture editors) but a challenge for Charles, and, to an extent, for Diana, also. The eminent Irish psychiatrist Professor Anthony Clare told me, 'You can be too beautiful. Extremes are difficult for human beings to cope with. Great physical beauty does not lead to happiness. Marilyn Monroe wasn't very happy. Princess Diana wasn't very happy.' According to my tame marriage guidance counsellor, 'There are exceptions to every rule, but, as a generalisation, successful couples tend to be of a comparable age, educational ability and attractiveness.' On a scale of beauty from one to ten, a contented couple might expect to be within a point or two of one another. If you look at the photographs, you can see that, when they were young, Princess Elizabeth was beautiful (truly so) and Prince Philip was handsome (astonishingly so). With Charles and Diana it was different. On the scale of beauty, he hovered around five while on a good day (at least in the eyes of the average beholder) she veered between eight and ten.

Charles was made painfully aware of this particular element in their mismatch. For example, on tour together in Australia in 1985, they went on repeated walkabouts and when Charles climbed out of the official car he would hear the crowds giving off an involuntary groan of disappointment if they were on the side that he, rather than Diana, was set to 'work'. He listened to the crowds and heard their disappointment: 'Oh no, she's on the wrong side.' He gazed at bookstalls as they drove past, and his wife's face – not his – gazed back at him from the covers of, seemingly, every magazine. He leafed through the newspapers and saw photographs of Diana and her dazzling smile and contrasted them with the cartoons of himself that inevitably featured his protuberant ears. Diana was treated as an iconic beauty, a dream-princess come true. He was regarded, he felt, at best as bit of a letdown, at worst as a figure of fun. He was disconcerted, hurt and undermined by 'the fatuous remarks and insults . . . rude comments shouted out, gestures made, plastic masks waved about, woundingly unnecessary things written in the papers about me etc'.

With Camilla, of course, none of these problems will apply. Camilla is attractive, and her grooming and her wardrobe, especially since her engagement, have been faultless, but her looks don't dazzle.[169] On the marriage counsellor's beauty scales the Prince of Wales and the Duchess of Cornwall probably weigh in ideally, within a point or two of one another. And Camilla, while she wants to be liked by the public (she is only human) has no burning need to be loved by them. She hopes to please and she will do her best; but she has no desire to be anything but a consort. She will offer her husband support and encouragement. She will not be a star; she will not upstage him. That is not her talent; that is not in her temperament. A member of the Royal Family said to me, 'Using the title Duchess of Cornwall works in two ways. It is a reassuring signal to the world that she has no pretensions to be what the late Princess of Wales was. Equally important, it is a reassuring signal to her husband that she has no intention of being like the Princess of Wales. Also, of course, Charles has invested much more of himself in the Duchy than he has in the principality. He's more Cornwall than Wales.'

Diana was a star. She was also a diva. In Canada, for the opening of the Expo in Vancouver, the Princess, painfully thin, fainted from hunger and exhaustion. Charles was unsympathetic: he suspected she had done it for effect. In London, at the State Opening of Parliament, Diana appeared with her hair in a chignon and claimed the limelight from the Queen. An infuriated Princess Margaret complained to her sister, 'How dare she try to make a fool of you like that?' In Africa, in India, in South America – all over the world! – Diana embraced the

---

[169] It ill behoves me (bug-eyed, middle-aged, balding) to make personal remarks about anybody, but the cliché about Camilla is true: close to, especially when she is animated, she is much more attractive than she appears when frozen in a photograph. (She and her husband know this – hence the decision to use informal photographs of the couple for the stamps issued to mark their marriage.) Diana, by contrast (at least in my experience), was exciting to be with (she had the glamour of fame), and fabulous in photographs, but, face to face, not a *non-pareil* of beauty. Coming away from drinks with her in December 1992, I see I noted in my diary: 'Everyone said how wonderful she was looking. I thought (ungallantly) that her skin had rather gone to pot: a sort of light pebble-dash effect on her beaky nose.'

sick and hugged the young. Princess Anne, hands-on president of the Save the Children Fund since 1970, commented disdainfully, 'The very idea that all children want to be cuddled by a complete stranger I find utterly amazing.'

Charles and Diana's marriage, doomed from the outset by fundamental incompatibility, disintegrated with a heart-breaking, mind-numbing, soul-destroying inexorability. Charles admitted it had 'all the ingredients of a Greek tragedy'. Diana said it was 'misery', 'going nowhere', 'just hell'. Which of them was first unfaithful? (Does it matter?) Diana maintained that, in his heart, Charles had been an adulterer from the start. He denied it. He denies it still. He is sticking to the essentials of the story as he set them out to Jonathan Dimbleby at the beginning of the 1990s:

> Following his engagement to the Princess in February 1981, the Prince had made virtually no contact with Camilla Parker Bowles for over five years. Apart from the one occasion before the wedding, when he gave her the 'farewell' bracelet, he saw her only fleetingly at occasional social gatherings. Aside from a few telephone conversations during the four months of his engagement and only one after his marriage (when he rang to report that the Princess was pregnant with William), they had not talked to each other at all: like his other close friends she had been wholly excluded from his life. Until he reached the point of desperation, when, as he would later confine himself to saying in public, his marriage had 'irretrievably broken down', he had been loyal to his wife and faithful to his marriage vows.

Diana read this and scoffed. 'Who does he think he's fooling?' she asked a friend, who replied, 'Probably himself.' 'Yes,' said Diana. 'He probably believes it.' He did. He does. For five years, from 1981 to 1986, his 'intimacy' with Camilla was put on hold. Eventually, in desperation, he rekindled their 'earlier friendship', for fear that if he didn't he might go 'stark, staring mad':

> . . . He once again began to talk to her on the telephone and they started to see each other at Highgrove; she usually came with either her husband or some of the Prince's other close friends, and the opportunities to be alone with each other for any length of time were infrequent. That they loved each other was not in any doubt: in

Camilla Parker Bowles, the Prince found the warmth, the understanding and the steadiness for which he had always longed and had never been able to find with any other person.

This, then, was the start of their third affair: episode three of the mini-series.[170] What appears to have triggered – or at least, in the Prince's eyes, to have legitimised – the resumption of regular carnal contact with Camilla turned out to be a misapprehension. Diana became friendly with a handsome young merchant banker, Philip Dunne, son of the Lord-Lieutenant of Herefordshire, godson of Princess Alexandra. Charles began to wonder if Diana and Dunne might be having an affair. It seems they weren't, but they were seen to be happy together, playful and flirtatious, on holiday, skiing at Klosters (with Prince Charles in attendance), and at a weekend house party at Gatley Park, near Leominster, Dunne's parents' home (with neither Prince Charles nor the senior Dunnes in attendance when the princess stayed overnight). On 13 June 1987, at the party after the wedding of the Marquess of Worcester (son of the 11th Duke of Beaufort) to the actress (turned environmentalist) Tracy-Louise Ward (granddaughter of the Earl of Dudley), as Diana took the dance floor with Philip Dunne (and, according to a witness, 'danced like a dervish', only stopping occasionally to mop her brow with the hem of her dress), Charles took a more sedate turn on the dance floor with a former flame (Anna Wallace) and then settled down at a side table with Camilla Parker Bowles. As Diana and Philip danced the night away, Charles and Camilla simply slipped away. Nobody seemed to care what anybody saw – or thought – any more.

That summer, when Charles went away to Italy for a week to paint watercolours, Camilla was of the party. Diana was not. In September, when Charles went up to Balmoral, Camilla came, too. 'Amongst the hills, rivers, trees and animals that I love so much' he sought peace, consolation and the companionship of the one woman he felt 'understood' him completely. 'I just want to be with her all the time,' he

---

[170] When I used the phrase in front of Charles's father recently, he winced. The Queen and Prince Philip are grown-ups: they are not naive; they know the ways of the world. They accept that marriages break down and adultery happens. What dismays them is the way these sad and private occurrences are played out on television and in the tabloids for the amusement of the masses. When, in 1994, Charles's confession of adultery filled the front pages (and pages 2, 3, 5, 7 and 11), the Queen, reportedly, sighed, pursed her lips and murmured, 'So it's come to this.'

said. He stayed at Balmoral, without seeing his wife or children, for thirty-seven days and thirty-six nights. The press was counting. And watching. And mistaking what they saw. As a consequence of a paparazzi picture, the rumour went round that another old flame, Dale Tryon, wife of the 3rd Baron Tryon (banker and sometime page of honour to the Queen) was part of the Prince's house party and, by implication, once again 'part of the prince's life'.[171] 'The fact that she wasn't within six hundred miles of the place didn't seem to matter,' sighed the unhappy heir to the throne. The press were agin him. In private, he railed against the 'hurricane of self-righteous, pontificating, censorious claptrap in the newspapers' and admitted to friends that, confused and run-down, he could see no 'light at the end of a rather appalling tunnel'.

In the press, of course, Diana was portrayed as the wronged wife, left alone to go about her duties, in her saintly way, and to bring up her children, virtually on her own, while her hapless, hopeless, husband indulged himself, mooning about in the Kalahari desert in the company of his Jungian guru (van der Post took Charles on a four-day African retreat that spring), taking his ease in the Tuscan hills with his paintbrushes, holing up at Balmoral with old friends – and old flames.

'God, it was so unfair,' a friend of Charles and Camilla's told me, looking back eighteen years to the unhappy summer of 1987. 'Charles was in a black hole and couldn't see a way out. I think he fantasised about escaping to Italy, living in exile with Camilla, but it was only a fantasy. He knew there was no escape. He knew his duty. All this guff about him being selfish and self-absorbed is quite wrong. Grossly unfair, in fact. He's always been the first to think of others.[172] He cared about

[171] Dale Harper, who married Lord Tryon in 1973, was Australian and nicknamed 'Kanga' by Prince Charles who also once described her as 'the only person who understands me'. She had her problems: born with spina bifida, she survived cancer of the uterus, severe depression and a mysterious fall from a hospital window which left her confined to a wheelchair. She died of septicaemia, following an operation, in November 1997. During her last unhappy months, in the aftermath's of Diana's death and the collapse of her own marriage, she tried repeatedly to make contact with Charles, but, reportedly, he did not return her calls.
[172] There is touching evidence of this in Jonathan Dimbleby's biography of the Prince. That September, when Charles was at Balmoral and preoccupied with his own troubles, he took time to write a long and thoughtful letter to his friend Nicholas Soames, following the funeral of Soames's father, which the Prince had attended. 'Relationships with fathers can be such complex ones,' he wrote. 'I remember we often talked about

Diana, believe it or not. The marriage had broken down, but he worried about her and the boys. He hated the way the press pursued her.' I interrupted my witness to observe that the press, while pursuing Diana, nonetheless remained on her side. This prompted something of an explosion: 'Bloody right. She saw to that. Let's get this straight. Diana had a string of flirtations and affairs. Mannakee, Waterhouse, Hewitt, James Gilbey, Hoare, Carling, and God knows who else. She was not a saint. While Charles was torturing himself with guilt, Diana was playing the field.'

In fairness to Diana, and to the memory of Barry Mannakee (who had been her personal protection officer, until his alleged 'over-familiarity' with the princess had him transferred to other duties), they were friends, not lovers. Diana may have called him 'the love of my life' (it was a phrase she used of several people), and she was certainly distraught when Charles broke to her the news of his death in a motorcycle accident, but Mannakee – a father-figure and shoulder to cry on – is not to be tossed into the same bed as the rest of the list of Diana's alleged lovers. Her relationship with David Waterhouse (a young army major), while it irritated Charles, may have been, like her relationship with Philip Dunne, simply a fun, flirtatious friendship. The wife of the England rugby captain Will Carling was certainly unhappy about her husband's friendship with the princess, and the wife of the art dealer Oliver Hoare was alarmed to be on the receiving end of a series of apparently anonymous phone calls that turned out to come from Diana, but whether these relationships were more than *amitiés amoureuses* I cannot tell you. We know about Diana's affairs with James Gilbey, gentleman car salesman, and Captain James Hewitt, polo-playing Guards officer, because one was inadvertently revealed with the publication of what became known as the 'Squidgygate' tapes,[173] and the other Diana freely admitted to in her

---

our own relationships with our own respective fathers and how they've not been easy always. But that difficulty pales into insignificance when faced with the fact that a very important figure in one's life is no longer going to be there but is embarking on a mysterious journey into a new and more glorious dimension.' In Dimbleby's book, and in *Charles: Victim or Villain?* by Penny Junor, there are many examples of the Prince's thoughtfulness and generosity of spirit.

[173] So called because in the course of Diana's late-night conversation with Gilbey, recorded on New Year's eve in 1989 (and published by the *Sun* in August 1992), he called her 'Squidge' or 'Squidgy' fourteen times, as well as 'darling' fifty-three.

celebrated *Panorama* interview in 1995: 'Yes, I adored him, yes, I was in love with him.'[174]

In my conversation with Charles's friend and apologist, I pointed out to him that Diana's friendships and affairs happened over a period of years and only happened at all because there was an emotional vacuum in her life. 'And the point I'm trying to make,' Charles's friend countered, 'is that if Diana was complaining about Charles and Camilla – and she was, we know that – she was guilty of double standards.'

Diana, rightly or wrongly, did not see it that way. To her, Charles was the guilty party and Camilla was her enemy. Indeed, at the beginning of 1989, Diana chose to engage the enemy face to face. At a party, in honour of Camilla's sister Annabel's fortieth birthday, hosted by Sir James and Lady Goldsmith at their handsome house on Ham Common, Diana decided to confront her husband's mistress. According to her own account of it, she 'psyched' herself 'up something awful' and engineered a moment alone with Mrs Parker Bowles. She had decided she was 'going to make an impact'. I think we can assume she did. This is how Diana told the story:

> I said to Camilla: 'Would you like to sit down?' So we sat down and I was terrified and I said: 'Camilla, I would just like you to know that I know exactly what is going on between you and Charles, I wasn't born yesterday.' . . . It wasn't a fight – calm, deathly calm and I said to Camilla: 'I'm sorry I'm in the way, I obviously am in the way and it must be hell for both of you but I do know what is going on. Don't treat me like an idiot.'

That night, Diana said, she 'cried and cried and cried': 'I cried like I had never cried before – it was anger, it was seven years' pent-up anger coming out.' It was also, of course, the beginning of the end.

In her confrontation with Camilla in 1989, Diana claimed she knew what was going on between her husband and his mistress. We can claim it, too, of course, because rightly or wrongly, a conversation between

---

[174] I took James Hewitt to be a wholly preposterous figure until I read his book *Love and War* and met him. The book, which is as much about his military career (he commanded a tank squadron in the Gulf war and secured a mention in despatches) as his relationship with Diana, is self-deprecating and endearing. The man is a natural charmer, good-looking, funny and engaging. I can quite see why a vulnerable girl might fall for him.

Charles and Camilla from later that same year is now in the public domain.[175]

I have been pondering for some time whether or not my book should

[175] How come? When the existence of the so-called 'Camillagate' tape first surfaced, in January 1993, I was an MP and, for what it's worth, the general view at the House of Commons at the time was that this tape – and the 'Squidgygate' tapes recorded around the same time, and another tape, of a conversation between the Duke and Duchess of York when Prince Andrew was serving in HMS *Campbeltown* – indicated that the British security services were spying on members of the Royal Family. (The rumour went round that between twenty and thirty further tapes of intimate conversation between the Prince of Wales and Mrs Parker Bowles were in existence.) Old buffers in the Commons tea room, eager to appear 'in the know', insisted this sort of electronic surveillance was 'routine' – 'Security need to know everything about everybody – be grateful: it's in the national interest.' Others thought that the younger royals were being 'targeted' because rogue elements in intelligence wanted to expose their nefarious activities which they believed, were undermining the credibility of the monarchy. I happened to be friendly at the time with Geoffrey Dickens, the stout (and stout-hearted) MP for Littleborough and Saddleworth, who decided to investigate. He tried to table a parliamentary question demanding an enquiry into the matter, but was told by the Speaker that would not be possible. There is an established convention that undercover work by the security services is not to be openly scrutinised by parliament. Geoffrey pressed on, and, eventually, the prime minister, John Major, agreed to set up two separate enquiries looking into different aspects of the affair. Both came to the same conclusion: there was no evidence that MI5 or any other branch of the security services were 'bugging' members of the Royal Family and, indeed, there was no reason why they should consider or need to do so. Geoffrey was not impressed. He remained convinced that the only people with equipment of sufficient sophistication to make the recordings were members of an intelligence service – either our own or that of another country. His view was that the recordings were officially coordinated, as part of general security, by GCHQ (the Government Communication Headquarters) at Cheltenham (who, via satellite, would be able to track the Prince of Wales's cellular phone), but that the 'Camillagate' tape that was published was unofficially leaked by a mischief-maker at GCHQ anxious to expose the private behaviour of the heir to the throne.

In 2005, I raised the matter with Dame Stella Rimington, head of MI5 at the time. She told me: 'Geoffrey Dickens got it wrong. As far as I know, the recordings of the calls – all, I think, made on mobile phones – were made by one or more private individuals using a fairly standard piece of kit then, and probably still, quite freely available. Mobile phones are more secure now from casual eavesdropping. None of the British intelligence services routinely or in any other way spy on the Royal Family. It is nonsense to claim that this needs to be done in order to protect their security. The security of the Royal Family is the responsibility of the Metropolitan Police Royalty Protection Squad and of the forces in whatever area they are visiting. Any specific threat information that became available to the intelligence services would be passed on to them. The only consequence of those incidents was to better advise the Royal Family on telephone security.'

include a full transcript of the so-called 'Camillagate' tape. I have decided it should, not simply because it exists and so, inevitably, is part of the story, but principally because the content of the tape is so revealing. It shows us how passionately Charles and Camilla felt for one another; how intimate they were; and how desperate they felt about their situation. It also, I think, tells us much about the way in which their relationship worked – the balance between them – and it gives us a clear and immediate picture of their characters and their world. (That said, it is also a gross invasion of privacy and if, at this point, you choose to move swiftly on to the beginning of the next chapter, I salute you.)

If you are still here, read on – and read, perhaps, as you might read the script of a radio play. In your mind's eye, picture the scene. In your mind's ear, hear the voices. The date is Sunday 17 December 1989. It is late at night.

Charles is staying at Eaton Lodge, on the Duke of Westminster's estate, at Eccleston, on the outskirts of Chester. He has had a long and tiring week, starting in London, finishing in North Wales. His programme has included a reception at Kensington Palace for the Prince's Trust, a dinner for the Royal Opera House Trust, standing in for the Queen at Buckingham Palace to receive overseas diplomats who have come to court to present their credentials, and a range of quite complex meetings related to his wide range of interests. The week has culminated with a short tour of North Wales, supporting local enterprise and regional development in Wrexham and Mold. He has now come back over the Welsh border to North-West England, to Chester, to stay with his old friend, Anne, Duchess of Westminster. She is a splendid lady, seventy-four, doughty but great fun, known to her friends as Nancy.[176] The dowager duchess's principal claims to fame are that she was the fourth wife of the 2nd Duke of Westminster (known as Bendor, after his grandfather's chestnut Derby winner) and, in her own right, was the proud owner of Arkle, arguably the greatest

---

[176] She died in 2003, aged eighty-eight, having been fifty years a widow. (In 1947, when she married Bendor, famously the richest man in England, she was a woman of means herself and became eligible for a trust on marriage. The duke said, 'You don't think people will say I married her for her money?') When I was MP for Chester she entertained me at Eaton Lodge on a number of occasions. 'She's wonderful value,' I noted in my diary after lunch one Sunday in November 1993, 'a game old bird, with a deep, deep voice, a low-slung bosom and a big heart. She has no idea who I am, but so long as she's got a fag on the go and there's plenty of g in the g & t, she's the easiest company in the world.'

steeplechaser of all time. Racing and fishing are her life. Charles is a regular visitor to Lochmore, her house near Lairg in Sutherland, where fine fishing is to be had on the River Laxford. Nancy adores Charles (I know this because she told me so) and she is another of the warm and motherly older women in whose company he feels secure. That said, as you will see from his conversation with Camilla, he does not feel that he can confide in Nancy to the extent of asking her whether he and Camilla might share a bed under her roof. Nancy was also a good friend and racing companion to Queen Elizabeth The Queen Mother, and a chatterbox.

Camilla is at home, in Wiltshire, at Middlewick House. Her week has been less challenging. She has been following her favourite pursuit, hunting, riding to hounds with the Beaufort, one of England's oldest hunts, covering some of hunting's most rewarding terrain.[177] She has also been getting ready for Christmas, making preparations, putting up decorations, welcoming her children home from school. Laura is eleven; Tom will be fifteen tomorrow. Her husband, Andrew, is away. When she refers to him, she calls him 'A'. At one point, she also calls him 'it' – not, I think, listening to her, in an especially hostile way: more by way of depersonalising him, transforming him from a husband, which he was, into an obstacle, which he was also.

As you read the conversation, I think you will agree you could only be in England in 1989. There is a Middle England reference to BBC Radio Four's Monday morning programme *Start the Week*. There is an ambulance drivers' dispute that, helpfully, is keeping Andrew Parker Bowles away: the army is on stand-by to assist as necessary. There is a confused and convoluted exchange between the lovers about how best to get from one place to another (via the M25 and the M4, if not Royston and the M1) that seems to come straight from a script by Alan Ayckbourn or David Nobbs.

Naturally, proper nobs also feature in the dialogue. Camilla has been staying in York, at Garrowby, the home of the 3rd Earl of Halifax – another Charles, married, extraordinarily, to another Camilla Parker Bowles. (In 1976, Charles Irwin, as he then was, who had once been

---

[177] The Dukes of Beaufort have been hunting since the title was established in 1682 – and the hunt's dress is peculiar to its heritage: green coats for the huntsman and whippers-in and, for the members, a blue coat with buff facing, the Beaufort liveries. The hunt's territory lies in Gloucestershire and Wiltshire, stretching from Bath in the south to Malmesbury in the east, to just short of Cirencester in the north and Chipping Sodbury in the west.

touted as a potential husband for Princess Anne, married Camilla Younger, of the Younger brewing family, ex-wife of Rick Parker Bowles, younger brother of Andrew – who, of course, had also had a dalliance with Princess Anne. The point is not simply that this is a small circle: it is that Charles and Camilla – our Charles and Camilla – shared friends and interests in a way that Charles and Diana never could. Charles and Camilla went hunting from Garrowby with the Middleton.[178])

In their conversation, Camilla tells Charles she missed him 'so much' while she was at Garrowby. They discuss where their next tryst is to be. Camilla mentions that she has 'talked to David' about it. This, I reckon, is Leopold David Verney, known as David, 21st Baron Willoughby de Broke, who lives at Ditchford Farm at Moreton-in-Marsh, conveniently close to both Highgrove and Middlewick, and whose own marriage had recently hit the rocks. Unfortunately, David may not be able to accommodate the lovers because he has the children 'of one of those Crawley girls' staying with their nanny. The 'Crawley girls' I take to be the widows of Andrew and Randall Crawley, the sons of Aidan Crawley, MP turned television executive, who had been tragically killed in an aeroplane accident the year before.[179] The children, therefore, could be either Charles and Jessica – the offspring of Andrew Crawley and his wife, Sarah Lawrence, daughter of Murray Lawrence, the chairman of Lloyd's – or, more probably, Aidan, Cosima and Galen, the children of Randall who was married to Marita Phillips, daughter of 'Bunny' Phillips, sometime lover of Edwina Mountbatten, and Gina Wernher, childhood friend of Prince Philip. (Marita's sisters include Sacha, the Duchess of Abercorn, and Natalia, the present Duchess of Westminster, the arrangements for whose daughter's wedding eventually triggered the wedding of Charles and Camilla.)

When Camilla mentions ringing up 'Charlie' there is some confusion as to which Charlie she means. Charles assumes she is talking about the Charlie who lives nearby, at Bowood House, at Calne in Wiltshire:

[178] And, sixteen years later, they were back at Garrowby – in circumstances no one could have conceived as remotely possible in 1989. In June 2005, the Royal Ascot race meeting was held in York and the Queen stayed at Garrowby as the guest of Lord Halifax, with the Prince of Wales and the Duchess of Cornwall, as man and wife, in attendance.
[179] The Crawley family has been beset by tragedy. Aidan was later killed in a car crash. Having lost her father and both brothers in tragic accidents, on 26 December 2004 Harriet Crawley also lost her husband, who was killed in Sri Lanka by the Boxing Day tsunami.

Charles Maurice Petty-Fitzmaurice, Earl of Shelburne and, later, 9th Marquess of Lansdowne – a good man (president of the Wiltshire Playing Fields Association), not long married to his second wife. Camilla mentions Northmore, a stud near Newmarket, then owned by Hugh van Cutsem (son of the racehorse trainer Bernard van Cutsem, and, through his mother, great-grandson of the 4th Marquess of Northampton). Hugh and Emilie van Cutsem of Hillborough House in Thetford were then close friends of Charles and Camilla – as were (and are) Charlie and Patty Palmer-Tompkinson of Dummer Grange, near Basingstoke, in Hampshire, whose names also crop up in the course of the lovers' conversation. (Charlie Palmer-Tompkinson was a former member of the British Olympic skiing team. Patty was seriously injured at Klosters in 1988 in a skiing accident that killed a young royal equerry, Major Hugh Lindsay, and nearly claimed the life of the heir to the throne.)

All these people – the walk-on characters in this extraordinary royal drama – have much in common: breeding (their own, of course, and, in several cases, that of horses as well); familiarity with one another (this is a closed world); age (they are mostly the same age as Charles and Camilla or two to ten years older); interests (hunting, country sports, fine art); fierce loyalty to the Prince of Wales (they know Charles's secret and are ready to be co-conspirators); and, finally, the all-important fact that – in Charles's phrase – these are people he 'liked and Diana wanted ostracised'.

When the transcript of this conversation first saw the light of day – published, in January 1993, in an Australian women's weekly, *New Idea*, and then republished and pored over around the world – the focus and the comment concentrated almost exclusively on the elements within it of what we might call Charles and Camilla's 'sex-talk'. This was written up as being at best puerile, at worst uncomfortably crude. In fact, when you hear it, it sounds simply playful: ridiculous and rude – the Goons gone sexy – but not brutish or nasty. The truth is that there is a physical yearning between these two – aged forty-one and forty-two at the time – that many middle-aged couples would envy.

What is most revealing to me, however, is not the sex talk (almost every illicit affair is fuelled by sexual desire), but the way in which, time and again, through a conversation lasting no more than eleven minutes, Camilla, of her own initiative (not prompted by Charles), supports her man: boosts him, praises him, encourages him, does for him what he never felt his father or his mother or his wife would do; she tells him how wonderful he is. She asks to read his last speech; she tells him she'll be right behind him when he makes his next one; she reminds him he's 'a clever old thing' who has been working so hard and who needs to give that 'awfully good brain' of his a good night's rest. She tells him, 'I'm so proud of you' and he tells her, 'Your great achievement is to love me.'

Sadly, we do not have transcripts of any conversations, however brief, between Charles II and Louise de Kéroualle, or Edward VII and Mrs Keppel, but we do have this. It is remarkable, revealing, and, I find, oddly moving.

One final thing: as they speak, I sense that Charles – on his battery-driven cellular phone – is lying in bed, while Camilla is still up. I imagine she has come from her bathroom to her bedroom to take his call.

Charles: . . . he thought he might have gone a bit far.

Camilla: Ah, well.

Charles: Anyway, you know, that's the sort of thing one has to beware of. And sort of feel one's way along with, if you know what I mean.

Camilla: Hmm. You're awfully good at feeling your way along.

Charles: Oh, stop! I want to feel my way along you, all over you and up and down you and in and out.

Camilla: Oh.

Charles: . . . particularly in and out.

Camilla: Oh, that's just what I need at the moment.

Charles: Is it?

Camilla: I know it would revive me. I can't bear a Sunday night without you.

Charles: Oh, God.

Camilla: It's like that programme, *Start the Week*. I can't start the week without you.

Charles: I fill up your tank.

Camilla: Yes, you do.

Charles: Then you can cope.

Camilla: Then I'm all right.

Charles: What about me? The trouble is, I need you several times a week, all the time.

Camilla: Mmm. So do I. I need you all the week, all the time.

Charles: Oh God, I'll just live inside your trousers or something. It would be much easier.

Camilla (laughing): What are you going to turn into? A pair of knickers? (Both are laughing) Oh, you're going to come back as a pair of knickers.

Charles: Or, God forbid, a Tampax, just my luck. (He laughs)

Camilla: You are a complete idiot. (She laughs) Oh, what a wonderful idea.

Charles: My luck to be chucked down the lavatory and go on and on forever swirling round on the top, never going down.

Camilla (laughing): Oh, darling.

Charles: Until the next one comes through.

Camilla: Or perhaps you could just come back as a box.

Charles: What sort of box?

Camilla: A box of Tampax, so you could just keep going.

Charles: That's true.

Camilla: Repeating yourself. (Laughing) Oh darling, I just want you now.

Charles: Do you?

Camilla: Mmmm.

Charles: So do I.

Camilla: Desperately, desperately, desperately. Oh I thought of you so much at Garrowby.

Charles: Did you?

Camilla: Simply mean we couldn't be there together.

Charles: Desperate. If you could be here – I long to ask Nancy sometimes.

Camilla: Why don't you?

Charles: I daren't.

Camilla: Because I think she's so in love with you.

Charles: Mm.

Camilla: She'd do anything you asked.

Charles: She'd tell all sorts of people.

Camilla: No, she wouldn't, because she'd be much too frightened of what you might say to her. I think you've got – I'm afraid it's a terrible thing to say, but I think, you know, those sort of people feel very strongly about you. You've got such a great hold over her.

Charles: Really?

Camilla: And you're . . . I think, as usual you're underestimating yourself.

Charles: But she might be terribly jealous or something.

259

Camilla: Oh. (She laughs) Now that is a point. I wonder, she might be, I suppose.

Charles: You never know, do you?

Camilla: No, the little green-eyed monster may be lurking inside her. No, but I mean, the thing is you're so good when people are so flattered to be taken into your confidence. But I don't know they'd betray you. You know, real friends.

Charles: Really?

Camilla: I don't . . . (Pause) Gone to sleep?

Charles: No, I'm here.

Camilla: Darling, listen. I talked to David tonight again. It might not be any good.

Charles: Oh, no!

Camilla: I'll tell you why. He's got these children of one of those Crawley girls and their nanny staying. He's going, I'm going, to ring him again tomorrow. He's going to try to put them off till Friday. But I thought as an alternative perhaps I might ring up Charlie.

Charles: Yes.

Camilla: And see if we could do it there. I know he's back on Thursday.

Charles: It's quite a lot further away.

Camilla: Oh, is it?

Charles: Well, I'm trying to think. Coming from Newmarket.

Camilla: Coming from Newmarket to me at that time of night, you could probably do it in two and three quarters. It takes me three.

Charles: What, to go to, um, Bowood?

Camilla: Northmore.

Charles: To go to Bowood?

Camilla: To go to Bowood would be the same as me really, wouldn't it?

Charles: I mean to say, you would suggest going to Bowood, eh?

Camilla: No, not at all.

Charles: Which Charlie then?

Camilla: What Charlie did you think I was talking about?

Charles: I didn't know, because I thought you meant . . .

Camilla: I've got lots.

Charles: Somebody else.

Camilla: I've got lots of friends called Charlie.

Charles: The other one – Patty's.

Camilla. Oh, oh there. Oh, that is further away. They're not . . .

Charles: They've gone.

Camilla: I don't know, it's just, you know, just a thought I had if it fell through, the other place.

Charles: Oh right. What do you do, go on the M25, then down the M4, is it?

Camilla: Yes, you go, um, and sort of Royston or M1 at that time of night.

Charles: Yes, well, that'll be just after, it will be after shooting anyway.

Camilla: So it would be, um, you'd miss the worst of the traffic, because I'll, er, you see the problem is I've got to be in London tomorrow night.

Charles: Yes.

Camilla: And Tuesday night A's coming home.

Charles: No.

Camilla: Would you believe it? Because I don't know what he is doing, he's shooting down here or something. But, darling, you wouldn't be able to ring me anyway, would you?

Charles: I might just. I mean tomorrow night I could have done.

Camilla: Oh, darling, I can't bear it. How could you have done tomorrow night?

Charles: Because I'll be – (he yawns) – working on the next speech.

Camilla: Oh, no, what's the next one?

Charles: A Business in the Community one – rebuilding communities.

Camilla: Oh, no, when's that for?

Charles: A rather important one for Wednesday.

Camilla: Well, at least I'll be behind you.

Charles: I know.

Camilla: Can I have a copy of the one you've just done?

Charles: Yes.

Camilla: Can I? Um. I would like it.

Charles: Okay, I'll organise it.

Camilla: Darling . . .

Charles: But I, oh, God when am I going to speak to you?

Camilla: I can't bear it, um . . .

Charles: Wednesday night?

Camilla: Oh, certainly Wednesday night. I'll be all alone, um, Wednesday, you know, the evening. Or Tuesday. While you're rushing round doing things I'll be, you know, alone until it reappears. And early Wednesday morning, I mean, he'll be leaving at half past eight. He won't be here Thursday, pray God. Um, that ambulance strike, it's a terrible thing to say this, I suppose it won't have come to an end by Thursday?

Charles: It will have done.

Camilla: Well, I mean for everybody's sake it will have done, but I hope for our sakes it's still going on.

Charles: Why?

Camilla: Well, because if it stops he'll come down here on Thursday night.

Charles: Oh no.

Camilla: Yes, but I don't think it will stop, do you?

Charles: No, neither do I. Just our luck.

Camilla: It would be our luck, I know.

Charles: Then it's bound to.

Camilla: No, it won't. You mustn't think like that. You must think positive.

Charles: I'm not very good at that.

Camilla: Well, I'm going to. Because if I don't, I'll despair. (Pause) Hmm. Gone to sleep?

Charles: No. How maddening.

Camilla: I know. Anyway, I mean, he's doing his best to change it, David, but I just thought, you know, I might ask Charlie.

Charles: Did you say anything?

Camilla: No, I haven't talked to him.

Charles: You haven't?

Camilla: Well, I talked to him briefly, but you know, I just thought I – I just don't know whether he's got any children, that's the worry.

Charles: Right.

Camilla: Oh . . . darling, I think I'll –

Charles: Pray, just pray.

Camilla: It would be so wonderful to have just one night to set us on our way, wouldn't it?

Charles: Wouldn't it? To wish you happy Christmas.

Camilla: Happy . . . Oh, don't let's think about Christmas. I can't bear it. (Pause) Going to sleep? I think you'd better, don't you, darling?

Charles: (Sleepily) Yes, darling.

Camilla: I think you've exhausted yourself by all that hard work. You must go to sleep now, darling.

Charles (sleepily): Yes, darling.

Camilla: Will you ring me when you wake up?

Charles: Yes I will.

Camilla: Before I have those rampaging children around. It's Tom's birthday tomorrow. (Pause) You all right?

Charles: Mm. I'm all right.

Camilla: Can I talk to you, I hope, before those rampaging children . . .

Charles: What time do they come in?

Camilla: Well, usually Tom never wakes up at all, but as it's his birthday tomorrow he might just stagger out of bed. It won't be before half past eight. (Pause) Night-night, my darling.

Charles: Darling . . .

Camilla: I do love you.

Charles: Before –

Camilla: Before half past eight.

Charles: Try and ring?

Camilla: Yeah, if you can. Love you, darling.

Charles: Night, darling.

Camilla: I love you.

Charles: I love you too. I don't want to say goodbye.

Camilla: Well done for doing that. You're a clever old thing. An awfully good brain lurking there, isn't there? Oh, darling, I think you ought to give the brain a rest now. Night-night.

Charles: Night, darling, God bless.

Camilla: I do love you and I'm so proud of you.

Charles: Oh, I'm so proud of you.

Camilla: Don't be silly, I've never achieved anything.

Charles: Yes you have.

Camilla: No you haven't.

Charles: Your great achievement is to love me.

Camilla: Oh, darling, easier than falling off a chair.

Charles: You suffer all those indignities and tortures and calumnies.

Camilla: Oh, darling, don't be silly. I'd suffer anything for you. That's love. That's the strength of love. Night-night.

Charles: Night, darling. Sounds as though you're dragging an enormous piece of string behind you with hundreds of tin pots and cans attached to it. Must be your telephone. Night-night, before the battery goes. (He blows a kiss) Night.

Camilla: I love you.

Charles: I don't want to say goodbye.

Camilla: Neither do I, but you must get some sleep. Bye.

Charles: Bye, darling.

Camilla: I love you.

Charles: Bye.

Camilla: Hopefully talk to you in the morning.

Charles: Please.

Camilla: Bye. I love you.

Charles: Night.

Camilla: Night.

Charles: Night.

Camilla: Love you forever.

Charles: Night.

Camilla: Goodbye, bye, my darling.

Charles: Night.

Camilla: Night-night.

Charles: Night.

Camilla: Bye-bye.

Charles: Going.

Camilla: Bye.

Charles: Going . . .

Camilla: Gone.

Charles: Night.

Camilla: Press the button.

Charles: Going to press the tit.

Camilla: All right, darling. I wish you were pressing mine.

Charles: God, I wish I was. Harder and harder.

Camilla: Oh darling.

Charles: Night.

Camilla: Night.

Charles: I love you.

Camilla (yawning): Love you, press the tit.

Charles: Adore you. Night.

Camilla: Night.

Charles: Night.

(Camilla blows a kiss.)

Charles: Night.

Camilla: Goodnight my darling . . . love you . . .

Chapter Ten

The Mighty and Their Fall

'The lover thinks oftener of reaching his mistress than does the husband of guarding his wife; the prisoner thinks oftener of escaping than does the gaoler of shutting the door.'

Stendhal (1783–1842)

If they had lived in another age, it would have been a different story. Charles and Diana would have sustained a marriage of convenience in the manner of Edward VII and Queen Alexandra, and Charles and Camilla would have been lovers in the time-honoured tradition of Edward and Mrs Keppel. It was not to be. Nearly a century had passed. The world had changed. The 'gentlemen of the British press', as Queen Victoria once termed them, were no longer gentlemen. (One of them – the most powerful – was actually an Australian, and a republican.) Discretion and deference had gone by the board. And Diana, while she had many of the attributes of her predecessor as Princess of Wales – beauty, presence and a natural empathy for the unfortunate, chief among them – was no Alexandra. She had been brought up in a different age in a different way. She had different expectations of marriage and of life.

Charles, in the late 1980s, was desperately unhappy in his marriage. 'Do not underestimate how painful it is,' the playwright and novelist Michael Frayn said to me recently. 'To be locked into one relationship when, overwhelmingly, you feel the need to be in another, is, quite simply, agony. Have sympathy. And when children are involved, they add to the sense of guilt.' Charles was, indeed, in agony and wracked with guilt. He felt, he said to a friend at the time, 'like a rat in a trap, with nowhere to turn'. He could not, would not, give up Camilla. She was, said a friend, 'his obsession'. According to Michael Blakemore (the director of Michael Frayn's plays that explore the anguish of the married man in the throes of an impossible extra-marital relationship), 'Obsessive love is a little like having one's life permanently scored with a soundtrack of soaring, agonised music. It goes on all day and all night, arresting thought, preventing sleep.' That is *exactly* how Charles felt at this time.

He also felt (to borrow another phrase from Michael Blakemore), 'morally checkmated'. He could not go on with Diana, but he could not escape her. He could not give up Camilla, but he knew the 'indignities' and 'calumnies' to which she was subject as a consequence of their affair. He went doggedly about his duties, but, often, according to friends, he found it difficult to focus because he could not clear his head of what he called 'the impossibility of my position'. One of the reasons he played so much polo at the time – when some courtiers wanted him to cut back on the sport, sensing that it reinforced the image of him as the self-indulgent 'playboy' prince – was simply that on the polo field he could escape his worries. Without his polo at the time, he said, he would have gone 'stark, staring mad'. 'When you are playing polo, nothing else matters,' he explained. 'If you're not concentrating, you come a cropper.'

He came a cropper in any event, spectacularly so, on 28 June 1990, playing in a polo match at Cirencester. Taking a backhanded shot at the gallop, he lost his balance and fell between two ponies. One of the animals then half fell on top of him, kicking his arm in the process. The Prince was rushed to hospital and, over days, then weeks, then months – there was confusion followed by disagreement among the doctors about the best way to treat him – acute physical pain compounded his mental anguish. His right arm was badly damaged. He was treated first at the Cirencester Memorial Hospital and, later, at the Queen's Medical Centre in Nottingham. Diana appeared briefly at both hospitals to show her interest and concern, but the press was more interested in the reported presence at the Prince's bedside of his friend and neighbour, and, as one wag put it, 'his real right hand', Mrs Parker Bowles. According to Charles, Camilla did not visit him in hospital, but, as he says, 'when did the press ever allow the facts to get in the way of a good story?'

The press may have suggested that Mrs Parker Bowles was to be found in places where, in fact, she had never been, but they were not wrong to place her at the heart of Charles's life. He telephoned her as often as he could. He saw her as frequently as his schedule allowed. They met at Highgrove and Balmoral and for weekends and occasional nights at the homes of obliging friends – though only when the children (and nannies) of their hosts were safely out of the way. They even managed a brief holiday in Turkey – on the back of the Prince's official visit to meet the Turkish President in Ankara – and more than once in Italy, in 'magical Tuscany', alongside Balmoral Charles's favourite place on earth. They were organising their lives much as Edward VII and Mrs Keppel might have done: meeting in Britain at the houses of friends who were in the know but would never breathe a word (and who accepted them as a couple, but never discussed the matter with them), and holidaying on the Continent together, taking care, however, always to travel separately to their joint destination.

In Camilla's great-grandmother's day, of course, the press turned a blind eye. Nowadays, they keep a watching brief. From the mid-1980s onwards, Charles, Diana and Camilla were under permanent surveillance – from MI5 possibly, from the world's media certainly. The paparazzi stalked them. The newspapers monitored their every move – or, at least, the moves they managed to detect. Rumour was rife, but the details were sketchy. The most telling accounts of the home life of the Prince of Wales at this time come, not from the journalists, nor from his friends (who confine themselves to saying how 'difficult' it was for all concerned, but how determined Charles was to fulfil his 'duties' come what may), but from the servants.

Paul Burrell, formerly footman to the Queen, then butler to the Prince and Princess of Wales at Highgrove until their separation, when he went to work for Diana alone, and Wendy Berry, housekeeper at Highgrove from 1985 till 1992, have each written compelling – and convincing – accounts of life in the service of the warring Waleses.[180] According to Burrell, after the Prince's polo accident at Circenster, Diana collected her husband from hospital and drove him home to Highrove, planning to remain in attendance 'to nurse and care for him'. According to Burrell (Diana's 'rock', lest we forget), the Prince 'didn't want to know'. Irritated by his pain, he rebuffed her and said he wanted to be alone. The princess, says Burrell, feeling 'utterly rejected' and 'unwanted' in her own house, stayed for less than half an hour and fled back to London in tears:

[180] *A Royal Duty* by Paul Burrell is the better written, but *The Housekeeper's Diary: Charles and Diana Before the Breakup* by Wendy Berry (published in New York in 1995) is equally gripping. It reads like a novelette, and of course it's *hell* when the staff tell tales, but if you have been to the places and met the people, you will agree that Mrs Berry's story rings true.

No sooner had she made her departure than Camilla Parker Bowles arrived. And Prince Charles was pleased to see her. She didn't stay over. In fact, I don't recall her ever staying over.

Camilla Parker Bowles was seen more at Highgrove than ever before but, contrary to established myth, she did not effectively move in or host dinner parties. From being a regular lunch guest, she became a regular dinner guest or day visitor, with her Jack Russell Fred, but over that summer she visited on no more than twenty occasions.

Wendy Berry, the Highgrove housekeeper, takes up the story:

Camilla Parker Bowles, dressed casually and somewhat shabbily in a floral skirt and cotton top, would speed up the back drive and let herself on to the terrace through the Thyme Walk. Charles was always relieved to see her, taking her by the hand and kissing her firmly on the lips every time she arrived. In the early days of his convalescence they were often together with other mutual friends, forming a tightly knit set in which Diana, though invited, never felt at ease.

One day, as Charles waited on the terrace for Nicholas Soames to return from a phone call, Camilla poked her head out of the French windows and, seeing the coast was clear, whispered, 'Hello, darling. How is my favourite little prince today?'

Charles, stripped off to the waist and wearing shorts, looked around in surprise, then, seeing who it was, laughed. The security camera was off. Thick Italian sunglasses hid his eyes. 'Take off your glasses, Charles, I want to see your eyes,' said Camilla softly.

'I am frightened to let you see what my eyes reveal,' said Charles enigmatically. 'They might give too much away.'

And here is the paragraph from Wendy Berry's testimony that, for me, illustrates Charles's devotion to his mistress better than any other. No greater love hath a fastidious non-smoker than to tolerate his partner's addiction to nicotine:

Charles's hatred of smoking was suspended as Camilla puffed away, putting the butts in a collection of ashtrays arranged around the terrace for her benefit. Later on Charles would let her run around after him like a wife as they invited mutual friends over for drinks and meals. Sometimes we were told not to get help, but to stay in the background until everyone had left.

In 1987, Diana was ready to live the lie. 'When we first got married,' she told a group of journalists on a visit to Spain, 'we were everybody's idea of the world's most perfect couple. Now they are saying we are leading separate lives. The next thing is I'll start reading that I've got a black lover.' In 1987 she explained away the impression that she and her husband rarely met, saying: 'It's very simple. My husband and I get around two thousand invitations every six months. We can't do them all, but if we split them up, with him doing some and me doing others, we can fulfil twice as many.'

By 1992, she had a different story to tell. That summer, on 7 June, the *Sunday Times* began to serialise Andrew Morton's book, *Diana: Her True Story*. The book, which delivered on the promise of its title, caused a sensation and brought the crisis in the royal marriage to a head. Essentially, the book told the world that Diana, once full of hope, was now on the brink of despair. It portrayed the beautiful young princess as a wronged woman, locked in a loveless union, psychologically battered by an unfeeling husband who refused to hear or respond to her cries of anguish.

In the publicity surrounding the book, Andrew Morton's sources were acknowledged to be 'Diana's friends'. At Buckingham Palace, however, they suspected Diana herself. They were right to do so. Diana had not come face to face with Morton, but, through a sympathetic intermediary – James Colthurst, an Old Etonian doctor with a soothing bedside manner – she poured her heart out to him at one remove, recording tapes in which she told her story her way and answering any supplementary questions that Morton (via Colthurst) fed back to her. Challenged by her own brother-in-law, the Queen's private secretary, Robert Fellowes, Diana flatly denied any involvement in Morton's book. When the Duke of Edinburgh told her directly that many feared that she had in some way cooperated with the book's author, Diana told her father-in-law, equally directly, that she had not. She lied.

Diana was capable of lying. She could be manipulative and deceitful when it suited her cause. A handful of her closest friends (such as her former flatmate Carolyn Bartholomew) knew of her involvement in Morton's book, because they had been involved, too. Others (such as her own sisters and Rosa Monckton and the Brazilian ambassador's wife, Lucia Flecha da Lima) were taken by surprise. In 2005, Rosa

Monckton told me, 'At the time, we were trying to help her, talking her through her problems, encouraging her to find a way to make her marriage work. We were wasting our time. The explosion was about to happen and we had no idea.' I asked Rosa if she understood why Diana had wanted 'Her True Story' to be told. Rosa said, 'Diana felt she was a victim and she wanted to show herself as the victim.' Did she realise the impact her revelations would have? 'I don't think she had thought through the repercussions. She was so naive. She had no sense of history. She was looking at it all as if she was a teenage girl.'

No book in royal history has had an effect comparable with that of *Diana: Her True Story*. It brought the truth – or, at least, Diana's version of it – into the open. Now, there was no hiding place: Charles and Camilla were caught in the headlights. They did their best to look insouciant, but it was not easy. When, from a distance, an impertinent journalist called out to Charles for a reaction to the book, Charles mumbled 'Fiction, fiction' and hurried on his way. When another reporter managed to corner Camilla during the pre-publication serialisation and asked her for her response, with commendable *sang-froid*, the royal mistress managed to say, 'I haven't read it, but I will with interest when the time comes.'

Camilla kept a cool exterior, but, within, her heart was pounding and her stomach churned. 'God, what she's been through,' says her friend and admirer, Jilly Cooper. 'She's strong that one, she's had to be.' Middlewick House was besieged by the world's media. The Parker Bowleses changed their telephone number. Camilla sought refuge, first in Breconshire, staying with her former brother-in-law (her husband's sister's ex) Nic Paravicini; later, travelling to Venice with her sister, Annabel, for a 'get-away-from-it-all' holiday. She was spotted at the Cipriani Hotel looking 'tired and pale' beneath her parasol as she attempted to sketch a drawing of the Venetian lagoon.

Charles went sketching that summer, too – in the company of his wife, bizarrely. John Latsis, the Greek shipping tycoon (also known as Yiannis Spyridon Latsis), generously offered the Prince and Princess of Wales one of his yachts for a family holiday, and they took it. Sir Angus Ogilvy, who was one of the party (along with his wife, Princess Alexandra, and Lord and Lady Romsey), told me the atmosphere was 'a little strained, though the sun kept shining'. The Buckingham Palace press office advertised the holiday as the Waleses' 'second honeymoon'. In truth, it was the marriage's last gasp. Diana devoted herself to water-skiing. Charles concentrated on his watercolours. Whenever they could, they dined separately. At all times, they slept apart. They were only together at all because of pressure from the Queen and the Duke of Edinburgh.

The tradition of the Prince of Wales having a difficult relationship with his parents is as old as Prince Hal. Edward VII, as Prince of Wales, fell foul of Queen Victoria and Prince Albert. Victoria blamed her son for her husband's premature demise. Edward VIII, as Prince of Wales, disappointed George V and Queen Mary. Edward VIII's abdication in 1937 blighted the rest of his mother's life. The Queen and Prince Philip have their reservations about their eldest son – about his extravagance and tendency to self-pity, in particular – but they recognise his gifts and are grateful for his achievements, and, of course, they love him dearly and wish him well. In 1981, they were delighted with Charles's engagement to Diana and full of hope for the success of the marriage. When it began to go wrong and others said 'I told you so' – Charles's friend Nicholas Soames, Prince Philip's friend Penny Romsey, the Queen Mother's friend Lady Fermoy (Diana's maternal grandmother), among them – the Queen and her husband said nothing. They kept their own counsel. That is their way. When once I asked the Duke of Edinburgh about his children's marital difficulties, he said, emphatically, 'I try to keep out of these things as much as possible.'

The Queen and the Duke knew about Camilla and did not approve. I understand the Queen first learnt that Charles had renewed his relationship with Mrs Parker Bowles from her former private secretary, Martin Charteris, who indicated to Her Majesty that the Prince of Wales was involved with 'a fellow officer's wife' which was 'somewhat against the rules' and 'causing unfortunate talk'. Beyond ensuring that her path and that of her son's mistress never crossed, the Queen did nothing. As Lord Charteris said to me in 1991, 'What could she do?' She certainly did not condone her son's behaviour, but, as Charteris put it, 'Her Majesty's inclination in most matters is not to interfere'. Incredibly, in 2004, Paul Burrell claimed that his late mistress had told him that the Duke of Edinburgh had been 'a collaborating architect in the marriage's downfall' because he had given Charles 'his blessing, with a nudge and a wink, to renew his liaison with Camilla'. Burrell maintained that Diana was told by Charles himself – in the heat of a row – that 'he had always had his father's blessing – from the outset of the marriage – to return to Camilla if the Princess did not make him happy'. Diana was capable of saying many things – and different things on different days – but the idea that Prince Philip would have arranged 'a five year get-out clause' on his son's marriage is risible. Philip told Diana, in terms, what he thought of his son's mistress. 'I cannot imagine anyone in their right mind leaving you for Camilla', he wrote to her, and she believed him.

Charles's parents had their reservations about their daughter-in-law as they did about their son. Indeed, Prince Philip, on more than one occasion, said wryly to friends and older relations, 'I've not been too lucky in my choice of daughters-in-law.' The Queen is reliably reported to have said Diana was 'quite mad' and to have called her 'that impossible girl'. Many in the Royal Family said things of the late princess that were much more disobliging. The Queen was dismayed by the disintegration of her son's marriage and exasperated by the behaviour of both her son and her daughter-in-law, but she was not unsympathetic. She had no time for Camilla. She liked Andrew Parker Bowles, but, according to one of her oldest friends, she said of Mrs Parker Bowles, more than once, 'I do wish she'd go away and leave Charles alone.'

Until the beginning of the serialisation of *Diana: Her True Story* the Queen and the Duke of Edinburgh said little and did nothing. The Queen, I am told by two of her friends, did 'a certain amount of sighing', and the Duke, I know, allowed himself the occasional sarcastic sally. When someone told him that his son was 'in a bad way' and 'much distressed' by the coverage his marital problems were getting in the press because 'he cares so much about the Crown and country', the Duke snorted, 'He's got a funny way of showing it.'

That June, as sales of the *Sunday Times* soared on the back of Diana's revelations, during the week of Royal Ascot the Queen and Prince Philip decided 'something must be done' and sat down with Charles and Diana at Windsor to listen to their woes and talk about the way ahead. According to Diana, the meeting was frank and, under the circumstances, almost friendly. Charles said very little, but Diana laid her cards on the table. Her husband's behaviour was unreasonable, unjust and unfair. She believed the time had come for a trial separation. (She had told Andrew Morton that she thought she would remarry and probably go to live abroad, either in Italy or France.) The Queen and Prince Philip listened sympathetically, but resisted any suggestion of a formal separation. They counselled the unhappy couple to search for a compromise, to think less of themselves and more of others, to try to work together to make their marriage work, for their own sakes, for the sake of the boys, indeed for the sake of Crown and country. The Queen and the Duke were as one. The Prince and the princess were hopelessly at odds. The Queen hoped that the meeting had done something to clear the air and proposed a second meeting on the following day. Diana apparently agreed, but failed to turn up. The Queen, the Duke and Prince Charles remained at Windsor. Diana returned to Kensington Palace.

As his son's marriage teetered on the brink of total collapse, Prince Philip initiated a correspondence with his daughter-in-law that he hoped might prove helpful. The Duke's letters to Diana were typical of his correspondence overall. They were sympathetic, but unsentimental; direct, but to a purpose. He tried to present both sides of the story in the hope that Diana might be able to see them, too. He invited her to examine her own behaviour as well as that of her husband; he reminded her that, while Charles was sometimes difficult, she was not always easy herself. He talked about the canker of jealousy, and the problem of Camilla. He did not condone his son's on-going relationship with Camilla, but he did want Diana to try, at least, to see the situation from Charles's point of view. Her post-natal depression and her irrational behaviour after Prince William's birth had not made her easy to live with. Her constant 'suspicion' of her husband was wearing. In his letters, the Duke confronted his daughter-in-law with some home truths. He invited her to think about her marriage, long and hard. Though much of what he said distressed her, she appreciated the efforts that he made. As Paul Burrell put it, 'Prince Philip did more to save the marriage than Prince Charles.'

It was all to no avail. The game was up. That August – the August of the Queen's '*annus horribilis*'[181] – the *Sun* published a transcript of the 'Squidgygate' tapes and invited readers to telephone a special 'royal hot-hot-HOT-line' to listen in as Diana and her car salesman friend James Gilbey exchanged affectionate intimacies and the Princess of Wales, in no uncertain terms, poured scorn on her in-laws. Some sixty thousand of Her Majesty's subjects paid good money to hear the

---

[181] 'Not a year I shall look back on with undiluted pleasure,' she told guests at a lunch at Guildhall in November. The Latin phrase was suggested by her former assistant private secretary, Sir Edward Ford, and neatly encapsulated a year of grim tidings for Her Majesty which had included her daughter Anne's divorce, her son Andrew's separation, her daughter-in-law Sarah Ferguson's appearance on assorted front pages around the world (topless while having her toes sucked by an admirer), as well as a serious fire at Windsor Castle and the disintegration of the marriage of the heir to the throne.

princess complain: 'Bloody hell, after all I've done for this fucking family . . .' For the Queen, it was the straw that broke the camel's back. 'Enough is enough,' she said.

The announcement came on Wednesday 9 December 1992. I was a member of parliament at the time and, at 3.30 p.m. that afternoon, along with a host of over-excited colleagues, tumbled out of the House of Commons tea room into a crowded chamber to hear the prime minister's 'surprise statement'. That evening, in my diary, I noted the parliamentary reaction to the news:

> We arrived just as the PM [John Major] got to his feet. 'It is announced from Buckingham Palace that, with regret, the Prince and Princess of Wales have decided to separate.' Suppressed gasps and a rumble of sympathy. 'Their Royal Highnesses have no plans to divorce and their constitutional positions are unaffected.' More murmurings. Major elaborated on this: the succession to the throne is unaffected; the Prince of Wales's succession as head of the Church of England is unaffected; there is no reason why the Princess of Wales should not be crowned Queen one day! I find that a little hard to credit.
>
> John Smith [the Labour leader of the opposition, responding] was commendably brief. Paddy Ashdown [the Liberal Democrat leader] less so. Ted Heath [the former prime minister] went way over the top: 'It must be one of the saddest announcements made by any prime minister in modern times.' . . . [Finally,] up popped Dennis Skinner [maverick Labour MP for Bolsover] to tell us 'we don't need a monarchy anyroad', and why should we swear an oath of allegiance to 'the Queen and her heirs and successors' because it's now clear we don't know who they are. He did not catch the mood of the House.

In Wiltshire, at Middlewick House, the mood was uncertain. Besieged by the press, Camilla looked suitably concerned and said, when pressed, 'Obviously if something has gone wrong I'm very sorry for them', adding, somewhat disingenuously, 'but I know nothing more than the average person in the street. I only know what I see on television.' With that, Mrs Parker Bowles climbed into her sister's car and, together, with a police escort, they drove off in the direction of Calne and the refuge of Charlie Shelburne's house, Bowood. I asked a friend of Charles and Camilla – who saw them at the time – if he could recollect their mood that December. Were they elated? 'Far from it,' he said. 'I think the prince was relieved that the separation had been announced, but there was a sense of sadness too. It was a public admission of failure. And he was concerned for his children, of course. I don't believe that either he or Camilla looked on the separation as easing the path to their eventual marriage, if that's what you mean. I don't think they had any idea what the future held in store for them.'

They did not have to wait long to find out. Five weeks to the day after the dignified announcement of the royal separation came the cruel indignity of 'Camillagate'. The worldwide publication of the late-night conversation between the Prince and his mistress – nicknamed 'the Tampax tapes' by those newspapers that wanted to underline the more lurid aspects of their contents – heaped unparalleled humiliation on the unfortunate couple.

'Seven-day wonder,' Nicholas Soames boomed at me at the time. 'Very unfortunate,' murmured John Major, 'but time is a great healer. In the long run, this doesn't affect anything.' Other colleagues at Westminster were less sanguine. A number of them agreed with the stark message of the *Sun* headline: 'LOVE TAPE COULD COST CHARLES THRONE'. Several MPs, including members of the government, expressed the view that an unrepentant adulterer could never succeed as Supreme Governor of the Church of England – forgetting, possibly, that the Church had been expressly created for the convenience of a notorious royal adulterer. One minister appeared in the tea room brandishing a copy of the British Army's General Administrative Instructions opened at the paragraph forbidding illicit relations between serving officers and the spouses of fellow serving officers and making it clear that such 'conduct unbecoming' was a sacking offence. Charles was colonel-in-chief of seven regiments. He was evidently cuckolding a fellow officer. 'It's just not on,' was the minister's line. 'He'll have to go.'

He did not go, of course, but he did retreat. While the furore filled the front pages and the airwaves, Charles went into hiding. He holed up at Sandringham, with his parents, and there he stayed, unseen, for ten days. He tried not to look at the newspapers. They made for grim reading. Even the *Daily Telegraph* (his parents' newspaper of choice) was disobliging, publishing an opinion poll showing that the Prince of Wales's 'approval rating' among the public at large had slumped to an all-time low of 4 per cent. When, eventually, the Prince resumed his public duties – with 'business as usual' as the order of the day – he appeared at a health centre in London's East End where an uncharitable pensioner shouted at him 'Have you no shame?' and grumbled to the attendant newspaper reporters, 'He's a disgrace.'

Many people felt he was, indeed, just that: a disgrace. A number of clergymen voiced their dismay. The Supreme Governor of the Church of England, of course, said nothing in public, and very little in private, either. A member of the Royal Family told me, 'The Queen was distressed, of course she was.' Did she blame Charles? I asked. 'I don't know. She was simply saddened by the whole business. And she will have reflected that if only both of those involved had stuck by their marriage vows none of this would have happened. I do think she felt that Camilla encouraged him.'

In the kitchen at Middlewick House, Camilla was in despair. 'It was hell for her,' said a friend, 'sheer bloody hell. And she didn't have a castle to hide in. She had to face the music alone. She didn't dare telephone Charles because she thought her phone was being tapped. She felt ashamed and humiliated and desperate for her children and for Andrew.' She braved the local shops and was photographed, ashen-faced, coming home carrying newspapers proclaiming her humiliation. She went to a branch of Sainsbury's in Chippenham and was jeered in the car park. A group of angry women threw bread rolls at her. 'It was a low point,' said Nicholas Soames, with masterly understatement.

It was the worst point, her time of trial, the period in her life she least likes to look back on, but, clearly, will never forget. 'She survived it,' says a friend, 'because her family rallied round, her father in particular, and because she's a strong girl.' I imagine her intake of nicotine and gin increased, I said. My witness did not appear amused. 'She lost a lot of weight,' she replied, without a smile. 'It was a beastly time.' And the memory lingers on. Watching Camilla at close quarters in the summer of 2005, taking her first public steps as Duchess of Cornwall, she seemed to me to be more tentative, less assured, as the Prince of Wales's recognised wife than she had been as his official mistress. A year or two ago, co-hosting events with the Prince at Highgrove, Mrs Parker Bowles appeared wholly at home and completely at ease. There was neither diffidence nor defensive body language. In June 2005, at Trooping the Colour on Horseguards Parade and at the Garter ceremony at Windsor, there were both. Her smile was fixed and nervous. She clutched her handbag tightly. Her grooming was immaculate, but she did not look her best because she did not walk tall. She appeared (to me, at least) to be both holding herself back and trying to make herself appear smaller, less conspicuous. 'Yes,' a courtier said to me (he was from Buckingham Palace, not Clarence House), 'she shrinks visibly in the presence of the Queen. Not surprising really.' Riding along the Mall, seated in a horse-drawn carriage on public display for the very first time – an unnerving experience, I imagine, if you are not accustomed to it – the new duchess managed to wave towards the crowds (a little awkwardly, with a large flat hand), but she did not look comfortable. She looked watchful, wary even, as if ready to flinch or duck should a stranger start shouting abuse or hurling bread rolls her way.

In June 2005, Charles and Camilla stood together, proudly, on the balcony of Buckingham Palace. In January 1993, separately, in Norfolk and in Wiltshire, they cowered behind closed doors. When his formal separation from Diana had been announced in December 1992, Charles had said to his friend Nicholas Soames, 'God knows what the future will hold.' Five weeks later, the way ahead looked even more uncertain. The Prince was 'utterly confused' about the prospects for his private life, and, according to Jonathan Dimbleby's account, quite as despondent about his professional achievements too. Dimbleby quotes a letter from Charles, written on 21 January 1993, eight days after the publication of the 'Camillagate' tape, and addressed to the director of the Prince's Trust:

> For the past 15 years I have been entirely motivated by a desperate desire to put the 'Great' back into Great Britain. Everything I have tried to do – all the projects, speeches, schemes etc. – have been with this end in mind. And none of it has worked, as you can see too obviously!

The letter listed Charles's areas of interest and endeavour – from rural communities to the armed forces, from engineering skills to broadcasting standards – before concluding:

> The final point is that I have always wanted to roll back some of the more ludicrous frontiers of the 60s in terms of education, architecture, art, music, and literature, not to mention agriculture!
>
> Having read this through, no wonder they want to destroy me, or get rid of me . . . !

In the event, of course, he was neither destroyed nor got rid of. He was damaged by 'Camillagate', no doubt, and talk of him stepping aside (in favour either of his son, Prince William, or, intriguingly, of his sister, Princess Anne) rumbled on for a month or two, but gradually the dust settled (as it does), the furore abated (as it will), and normal service, more or less, was resumed. 'He got back in the saddle and got on with it,' said Nicholas Soames. 'I struggled on,' says Charles.

Camilla struggled on as well. Initially, she kept her head beneath the parapet, lying low, letting friends bring in the shopping, emerging from her house as infrequently as she could. When sighted – and from this time on, paparazzi became a permanent feature of her life – she appeared thin and drawn. (Some say she lost a stone in weight; others make it two.) But gradually – 'quite quickly, actually', according to one friend – she began to recover her strength and her equilibrium. Winter turned to spring. 'She concentrated on the children and the garden,' says a friend. 'That did the trick.'

Amazingly (at least, to those who did not know the couple) the Parker Bowleses' marriage appeared to be surviving the strain. As spring turned to summer, they made a number of deliberate public appearances together – notably, in May, when, arm in arm, they arrived at the wedding of one of the daughters of their friend, Gerald Ward.[182] At the end of the summer, Camilla joined Gerald Ward's second wife, Amanda, and another mutual friend, Emilie van Cutsem, on a tour of India. Responding to enquiries about his wife's state of health, Brigadier Parker Bowles said, genially, 'She is perfectly all right. She has gone away on holiday with another couple of girls, that's all', adding, for good measure (in case anyone had wondered), 'Everything is all right between us.' Simon Parker Bowles, Andrew's younger brother, also made a statement, reinforcing the agreed line: 'Both Andrew and Camilla have said they will never divorce and, while the relationship is rather eccentric, it appears to work. They get on well.'

They did. They do. They have shared a great deal and they love their children who, to their great credit, both appear to be remarkably well-balanced and engaging individuals. In April 2005, Andrew Parker Bowles, with his second wife, came to his first wife's second wedding, kissing the bride with evident affection and offering the groom an

---

[182] Now Deputy-Lieutenant of Berkshire, a CBE, farmer and industrialist, Gerald Ward was both a friend (and contemporary at Sandhurst) of Andrew Parker Bowles and a friend (and, for a time, extra equerry) to the Prince of Wales. He is one of the small circle of people who have been part of this story from the outset. Famously, in 1972, he was a member of the party at Annabel's nightclub in Berkeley Square when Charles was seen dancing with Camilla Shand for the first time.

apparently warm handshake of congratulation. What, in truth, Andrew Parker Bowles makes of Prince Charles, I cannot tell you. 'Not much,' I am told (predictably), but, in honesty, I do not know for certain because all he appears to have said about the Prince of Wales on record was twenty-three years ago at the time of Charles's marriage to Diana: 'Marvellous leader, marvellous man. Get on any horse and ride well.'

I assume that, during their marriage, Andrew Parker Bowles endured the indignities that went with his wife's ongoing affair with the heir to the throne, partly because he had little choice in the matter and partly because it allowed him free rein to follow his own inclinations. After her divorce from Mark Phillips, he renewed his friendship with Princess Anne. After her divorce from Richard Hambro, he renewed his friendship with Charlotte Soames. At the end of 1993, he told those impertinent enough to ask that his own divorce was 'not on the cards'. At the same time, Buckingham Palace took the same line on behalf of Charles and Diana: 'The Prince and Princess of Wales have no plans to divorce.' 1994 was to change all that.

1994 was the silver jubilee of Prince Charles's investiture as Prince of Wales. To mark the anniversary, and as part of a concerted campaign 'to Tipp-Ex the Tampax' by showing the Prince as a 'thoughtful, sensitive and intelligent' human being, driven by 'a powerful sense of duty and destiny', Charles was persuaded by Jonathan Dimbleby – and by his own eager-beaver private secretary, Richard Aylard – to cooperate in the making of a 150–minute television film and a six-hundred-page book about his life. It was a mistake – not from our point of view (the film was well made and worth watching; the biography is essential reading for anyone interested in the life and work of the Prince of Wales), but from Charles's.

The Prince gave Dimbleby unprecedented access to his private papers, his diaries and his personal correspondence with family and friends. Dimbleby used the material well. The Prince gave the broadcaster something more, however: a sustained lament over the travails of his childhood and a frank admission of his own adultery. The nation was riveted. The Prince's parents were appalled. The Shands and the Parker Bowleses were bemused. What was the point? What was to be gained by it? 'Understanding and sympathy,' had been the hope, according to Richard Aylard. 'A better understanding of the prince, and, in time, a greater sympathy.'

The Prince had thought his candour would do him credit. Instead, the confession of his sins and his public commitment to continuing his relationship with Mrs Parker Bowles – 'she has been a friend for a very long time and will continue to be a friend for a very long time' – broadcast to a television audience of fourteen million earned him renewed opprobrium and scant sympathy. It was the broadcast, closely followed by the book (in which Charles's relationship with Camilla was acknowledged even more fully), that persuaded Andrew Parker Bowles that it was 'time to call it a day' as far as his marriage was concerned and left Camilla little alternative but to agree. In public, the cuckolded husband and the 'outed' mistress said not a word. They left the talking to Andrew's younger brother, Simon Parker Bowles, now the owner of Green's restaurant in Mayfair, once an employee of Major Shand at his wine merchants in South Audley Street. It was Simon who had introduced Camilla to his brother. Simon was on a visit to Australia that autumn and, when asked for a reaction to Charles's revelations, made the family's feelings crystal clear:

> Prince Charles does not have our sympathy at the moment. You can't go back and blame your upbringing, or your parents, as he has done That is wrong and very hurtful. Even if you feel it, you don't go around talking about it, particularly if you are a member of the royal family.

Camilla, said Simon Parker Bowles, had been 'dropped in a heap' by the Dimbleby book. Charles, he concluded, 'is very mixed up. It must be heartbreaking for the Queen, who has really done her job so well.'

Camilla, in her way, was mixed up, too. That summer, on 14 July, her mother, Rosalind, frail for some years as a result of osteoporosis, died, aged seventy-two. Five months later, on 14 December 1994, she and her husband filed for divorce. 'It was a difficult time for her,' said Major Shand, 'all the old certainties had gone.'

The grounds cited for the divorce, mutually agreed, were not adultery by either party but the fact that husband and wife, apparently, had been living apart for more than three years. No one was going to argue about it, and everyone agreed that the divorcing couple's statement, released on their behalf by their solicitors, was a model of its kind:

> The decision to seek an end to our marriage was taken jointly and is a private matter, but as we have no expectation that our privacy will be respected, we issue this statement in the hope that it will ensure that our family and friends are saved from harassment.

Most especially we ask that our children, who remain our principal concern and responsibility, are left alone to pursue their studies at what is clearly a difficult time for them.

Throughout our marriage we have always tended to follow rather different interests, but in recent years we have led completely separate lives. We have grown apart to such an extent that, with the exception of our children and a lasting friendship, there is little of common interest between us, and therefore we have decided to seek a divorce.

The Parker Bowleses' dignified statement was published on Tuesday 10 January 1995. They were right to regard their hope for privacy as quite forlorn. The following Sunday, 15 January, one Ken Stronach, for fifteen years Prince Charles's valet, decided to 'tell all'. 'CHARLES BEDDED CAMILLA AS DIANA SLEPT UPSTAIRS' ran the headline in the *News of the World*. What Dimbleby had sketched out in loose outline, Stronach filled in with graphic detail. He told us when Charles had moved out of the marital bed (immediately following Prince Harry's conception) and when Camilla had moved in (on nights when Diana was in London and the Highgrove intruder alarms had been switched off). He told a lurid tale and supplied plenty of circumstantial detail. Apparently, his duties included scrubbing green grass stains from his master's pyjamas ('They'd obviously been doing it in the open air'), changing the bed linen in his master's bedroom to mislead the rest of the household staff ('It didn't fool anyone for a minute') and – when Charles was away at Middlewick House on overnight manoeuvres – leaving a marked-up copy of the *Radio Times* by his master's chair to mislead Diana into thinking her errant husband had been spending an innocent evening in front of the TV.

At Sandringham, the Queen and the Duke of Edinburgh shook their heads in disbelief. At Kensington Palace, according to her own account, Diana, still Princess of Wales, shook with rage. What appalled her, she said, quite as much as the story, was the photograph that went with it: a photograph of Camilla – apparently taken at Birkhall on the Balmoral estate – with a young Prince William sitting contentedly in the background. Diana did not want to see her husband's mistress and her eldest son together in the same frame. 'He wants it both ways,' she said, 'but he's a fool if he thinks he can mess with me and get away with it.'

Later in the year, on 20 November (the feast day of St Edmund the

Martyr, the ninth-century king of the East Angles who was scourged and spread-eagled as an offering to the gods), Diana proved her point. She gave an interview to Martin Bashir for *Panorama*. It was the most watched television programme in the history of British broadcasting. Twenty-three million viewers tuned in and saw Diana, bashful but brave, dewy-eyed but determined, give the star performance of her life. She had worked on it. She had worked on her look and her lines quite carefully. She said what she wanted to say. She poured scorn on her husband: she held him in open contempt. She confessed to her own adultery, but if there was blame, she knew where that blame should be laid: at her husband's feet – and those of his mistress. The Princess of Wales – now thirty-four, but according to one critic 'never lovelier' – expressed her view that Charles would never become King and then, eyes cast down, modestly, defined the role she sought for herself. 'I would like to be queen of people's hearts,' she announced.

As soon as the broadcast was over, Nicholas Soames, Charles's close friend (and a government minister at the time), gave his verdict. He described the princess's performance as 'toe-curlingly dreadful'. It suggested to him that the unfortunate lady was 'in the advanced stages of paranoia'. Soames spoke for the Prince and his circle – but not for the government or the people. Opinion polls in the days that followed showed public support for Diana running at around 85 per cent. The public loved her. The *world* loved her. Across the globe, two hundred million people watched Diana tell her story. In New York (and New Delhi) she was praised for her candour and pitied for her plight. Newspapers in Catholic countries even forgave her her adultery because she was 'a wronged woman'. In London, the *Daily Mail*, hailing her as 'a heroine', quoted Jane Austen's verdict on the unfortunate Caroline of Brunswick, George IV's wretched queen: 'She was bad, but she would not have become as bad as she was if he had not been infinitely worse.'

Not everyone shared the general opinion. 'She's evil,' said more than one member of the royal household. 'She's wicked,' said at least one member of the Royal Family. The Queen said, 'Enough is enough' – yet again. Her Majesty consulted the prime minister (John Major), the Archbishop of Canterbury (George Carey), her private secretary (Robert Fellowes). She then wrote concisely, unequivocally, and by hand, to both the Prince and the princess giving it as her decided opinion, supported by her husband, that an early divorce was now desirable. Charles apparently welcomed his mother's ultimatum with a line from *Hamlet* (Shakespeare's play about another indecisive prince): 'For this relief, much thanks.'

In fact, the divorce settlement took many months to negotiate. The two sides began a long way apart. The princess's initial demands were said to include the suggestion that any future children she might have by another husband should bear hereditary titles and that she should receive an immediate sum of £50 million. The Palace was inclined to be less generous, both in terms of cash to be given and kudos bestowed. (The Duke of Edinburgh is reported to have proposed that, as well as losing her rank as a Royal Highness, Diana should be downgraded from Princess of Wales to Duchess of Cornwall – the title now enjoyed by her successor.) Charles was said not to want to argue about anything. 'Let her have what she wants' was his line. Diana said all she really cared about were the boys. 'The one thing I was terrified of,' she later told my friend, Anthony Holden, 'was losing the children. Once I knew they were safe, that the royal machine was not going to steal them from me, I didn't really care about anything else.' (Perhaps Nicholas Soames was right: maybe there was a touch of paranoia there. Access to the children was never an issue. Diana's customary complaint was that Charles spent too little time with his sons, not too much, and she never questioned the Queen and Prince Philip's very obviously loving and hands-on commitment to their grandsons.) In the event, Diana sur-rendered her royal status, and agreed to be known as 'Diana, Princess of Wales', in return for a lump-sum payment of £17 million and an annual staff and office allowance of £400,000. And that was that.

Or so they thought. For a while, Charles and Camilla lulled themselves into believing that the years of storm and strife were over.

Charles resumed his duties – and did so with a renewed energy and sense of purpose. (I say that because so many of those close to him have told me this was the case. In fact, my impression is that, in public at least, he remained pretty dutiful and anxious to please even in his darkest hours. On the occasions when I met him in the mid-1990s, through his patronage of the Chester Cathedral restoration fund, I was always impressed. He was invariably well briefed and friendly. You sensed he cared.) He gave more time to his sons and was careful of them. (I am told – on the best authority – that he never said harsh or hostile things about their mother within their hearing.) Knowing that Diana would never be there again, he set about making Highgrove wholly his own home – with Camilla's help, of course.

Camilla had also settled into a calmer way of life. She was said to be one of the myriad 'Names' to have suffered severe losses as an underwriter at Lloyds of London in the early 1990s, but she was not on her uppers by any means. On their divorce, the Parker Bowleses sold Middlewick House and Camilla created a new family home – for her children and her widowed father and her Jack Russell terriers, Freddy and Tosca – at Ray Mill House in the hamlet of Raybridge (once the home of the wonderfully named Snozell family), near Laycock in Wiltshire, just south of Chippenham and twenty minutes from Highgrove. The house cost £850,000 and was bought in trust for Camilla and her children, with the Earl of Halifax (the other Charles, married to the other Camilla Parker Bowles) as principal trustee.

Camilla stabled her favourite hunter, Molly, at Highgrove. Charles did not hide his friendship with Mrs Parker Bowles. Nor did he flaunt it. He allowed 'friends' to quote him to the press as saying, unequivocally, 'I will never remarry.' He was reported to have told the Queen, 'I will always put my duty first. I will reign alone, for the sake of the monarchy.' At the same time, he saw to it that another quotation entered the public domain. The Prince of Wales would not be marrying his mistress, but nor would he abandon her – ever. That was 'non-negotiable'.

Charles and Camilla met at Highgrove; they met at Ray Mill House; they met out hunting; they met at the homes of friends. They were even photographed together at their 'remote Welsh love-nest', Glyn Celyn House, near Brecon, in Powys, the home of Camilla's sometime brother-in-law, Nic Paravicini. Some say that the Prince himself – tired of all the secrecy: 'it looks shabby and tawdry' – was responsible for giving the News of the World the tip-off that enabled them to secure the photograph of Camilla, 'her hair still tousled from the night before', wrapped in a plain white dressing gown, 'taking a lingering look across the valley from the window'. That seems to me unlikely, but what is certain is that gradually, slowly, tentatively, Charles was trying to gain public acceptance of the fact of his relationship with the 'non-negotiable' love of his life. He also wanted the world to see her as he saw her: not as a royal mistress who had blighted the life of a vulnerable princess and undermined the monarchy in the process, but as a woman of quality, compassionate and cultivated, who, through love and loyalty, had sacrificed her own reputation in his cause.

In April 1997, encouraged by Charles, Camilla made the first public appearance of her life: speaking at a press conference as a new patron of the National Osteoporosis Society. (She was wracked with nerves and they showed, but she spoke from the heart and that showed too. Both her mother and grandmother had been victims of the disease.) In July 1997, Charles hosted a spectacular party at Highgrove to mark Camilla's fiftieth birthday, and the press – to their surprise – were told by the Prince's press office where and when to be to secure the best photographs of the arriving and departing guests. Camilla arrived in Charles's chauffeur-driven car wearing his birthday present: a diamond and pearl necklace said to have belonged, once, to Camilla's great-great-grandmother, Alice Keppel. 'Camilla looked absolutely radiant,' reported Jilly Cooper. 'It was a wonderful evening,' she said: 'The most striking memory I have is of the full moon which arrived early and stayed. I think it's a sign.'

Perhaps it was. Six weeks later, Diana was dead. And once Diana was dead, anything was possible.

Conclusion

Darkness and Day

'In a good play, everyone is in the right.'

Friedrich Hebbel (1813–63)

Five years after Diana's death, in the summer of 2002, at a charity dinner at Highgrove, hosted by Prince Charles and his companion, Camilla Parker Bowles, a fellow guest – a naval man, a linchpin in the Prince's Trust – turned to me and said, 'I used to come here when Diana was alive. The atmosphere was always strained. Nobody was comfortable then. It's all so easy now.'

That is the essence of it. Charles and Camilla are comfortable together. They are on the same wavelength: they are kindred spirits; good companions; proper friends. Where Charles and Diana chafed one another constantly, Charles and Camilla rub along just fine.

You can see it when you are together with them. He laughs, then she laughs; he tilts his head and pulls a face, she shakes hers and smiles. Watch them as they circulate among their guests and you see two people at ease with one another and with themselves. The body language says it all. And because they are good together, and because he is, self-evidently, so much happier and easier when she is around, everyone accepts her. Including William and Harry.

On the night of the charity dinner, which was in aid of the British Forces Foundation, Diana's boys – both destined in due course for a stint in the armed services – were also on parade. They were seated together, a fair distance from the top table, with a crowd of their own friends. (The friends were all drinking merrily and smoking fast: William and Harry, conspicuously, were not.[183]) When it was time for

---

[183] When the dinner was over, with Ben Elton (who was providing the cabaret), I descended on the boys. They were larky and effortlessly charming. Ben and I were

286

Charles and Camilla to leave, the Prince led the way, while his mistress, discreetly, slipped around the edge of the room and joined William and Harry at their table. She half knelt between them, said goodnight and something about their plans for the next day. She was easy with them, familiar, but big-sisterly rather than maternal. She was trying, but not trying too hard. And they were friendly and wholly relaxed with her.

In 2005, at the time of Charles and Camilla's engagement, through the spokesperson at Clarence House the boys officially expressed their 'delight' at the news. Unofficially, some among the staff at Clarence House said that William (who was just fifteen when Diana died) has never taken to Camilla. Others said – or were said to have said – that Harry (the recalcitrant adolescent) is the one who finds his stepmother a trial. From all I have seen and heard (and I have talked with many of their family and friends in recent months, and done my share of eaves-dropping), I reckon the boys are not so much 'delighted' by the marriage of Charles and Camilla as 'content' that it has happened. Children are self-referential. They are absorbed in their own world. Camilla does not interfere with that. She does not play the heavy hands-on stepmother. (She has grown-up children of her own, after all: Laura is now in her mid-twenties; Tom, now entering his thirties, is a married man himself.) William and Harry are now of age, as well. They are getting on with their own lives. One of their friends said to me, 'They do not have particularly strong views one way or the other, I know that for a fact.' 'If this is what Dad wants, that's fine by us,' seems to be their line.

What Diana would have wanted is more difficult to say. Diana despised Camilla, resented her and blamed her for the unhappiness and failure of her own marriage to Prince Charles. I met Diana and liked her. She talked about Camilla a great deal. She tended to avoid mentioning her by name, referring to her as 'you-know-who' or 'her' or 'that woman' or 'the third party'. After Camilla's divorce and then her own, Diana talked openly and often about the possibility of Charles and Camilla marrying. Her tune varied with her mood. On one occasion she said, 'Marry her? Over my dead body.' On another, 'Oh, what the hell, let him marry her. Why not? I'm past caring.'

In fact, Diana never truly seemed past caring. To the very end, she seemed to be in open competition with her rival. Because she was younger, more beautiful and an international celebrity, in terms of

avuncular and overfamiliar. I thought at the time, 'Poor lads, they are going to have to endure a lifetime of this.' I thought later how well they handled us.

media coverage Diana could outmanoeuvre and outclass either Charles or Camilla (or both combined) whenever she chose – and she did. Diana would have regarded Camilla marrying Charles as a defeat (I am sure of that), but she claimed not to lose much sleep over the possibility because she was convinced it would never happen. She said she knew the Queen would 'never, *never*' approve of Charles marrying Camilla, 'And he wouldn't without her blessing.'

Diana always maintained she had 'a lot of time' for the Queen. 'She's strong that one', she remarked once, referring to Her Majesty, 'unlike we-know-who' – meaning Prince Charles. The Queen's strength was certainly tested to the limit in the immediate aftermath of Diana's death. In the early hours of Sunday 31 August 1997, when the chauffeur-driven Mercedes in which Diana and her lover, Dodi Fayed, were travelling across Paris at speed, pursued by paparazzi on motorbikes, entered the tunnel at the Place de l'Alma and crashed into a concrete pillar, the Queen was at Balmoral, asleep, on holiday, with her family. At 2.00 a.m. the Prince of Wales and the Queen were woken with news of the accident. At 3.30 a.m., the British embassy in Paris confirmed that Diana, Princess of Wales, was dead.

Charles, 'appalled, simply appalled' and 'numb with shock', broke the dreadful news to his sons and, I am told, held on to each of them hard and fast. Almost immediately, with the boys' agreement, he decided he must travel to Paris to accompany Diana's body back home. For a moment, the boys thought they should go to Paris too, but the Queen, I am told, thinking of the confusion they would find there, and the possibility of press intrusion, said 'Better not'. While Charles flew to Paris, the Queen and Prince Philip kept William and Harry at Balmoral, out of harm's way, as they hoped, and out of the public eye. Some who saw it on television thought it 'heartless' that William and Harry were expected to join the rest of the Royal Family at church on that fateful Sunday morning, almost as if nothing had happened. In fact, the boys wanted to go and the Queen was pleased that they did. There is comfort to be had from familiar hymns and prayers. There is solace to be found in established form and custom.

The Queen viewed Diana's death as a private tragedy for William and Harry. The public displays of grief – worldwide and extraordinary – caught Her Majesty off balance. Her instinct and upbringing had taught her – and her generation – that you keep your tears for the pillow. Crying in public is not something the Queen would allow of herself, or expect of her children and grandchildren. It is not the royal way. It is neither dignified nor necessary – nor helpful. But, on television, in the first week of September 1997, it seemed the whole world was openly weeping and wailing – and baying for Her Majesty to shed some tears, too. 'Show Us You Care' chorused the headline writers.

By the end of the week – some say the most difficult of her reign – she had done just that. On the Thursday night, the Royal Family appeared together at the gates of Balmoral to inspect the field of flowers laid there in Diana's memory. Charles, ashen-faced, walked between his two sons. He held Harry's hand. On the Friday morning, in a gesture of royal respect without precedent, the Union flag was hoisted to the top of the Buckingham Palace flagpole and then lowered to half-mast. On Friday evening, the eve of the funeral itself, the Queen gave a live broadcast that some say was the most effective of her reign. It diffused any hostility towards her and, at the same time, rang true. Diana, she said, was 'an exceptional and gifted human being' whom she admired 'for her energy and commitment to others, and especially for her commitment to her two boys'. She spoke of the 'extraordinary and moving reaction to her death' and the 'lessons to be learnt' from it. She spoke as a queen and 'as a grandmother' – and what she said, and how she said it, simply and directly, with sincerity but without false sentiment, reminded the people who watched that she wasn't such a bad old stick after all.

On Saturday morning, before the funeral, the Queen, with her family, stood at the gates of Buckingham Palace, and Her Majesty led by example, bowing her head slowly as Diana's coffin was driven past. In the formal funeral procession, Diana's former husband and her younger brother, the Queen's son and godson, Prince Charles and Charles Spencer, were due to walk behind the gun carriage bearing her coffin along the route to Westminster Abbey. Prince Harry and, in particular, Prince William were uncertain as to whether or not they, too, wanted to walk behind the coffin. The Duke of Edinburgh, who had not planned to walk (he was merely the ex-father-in-law, after all), said to William, 'If you don't walk, you may regret it later. If I walk, will you walk with me?' As grandparents, the Queen and Prince Philip did their best by their grandsons that week.

As a father, Charles did his best, too. To use a phrase Diana would have understood, he was there for his boys that week. He was very calm with them – remarkably so, given the traumatic circumstances – and, according to those who saw them together, gave them exactly what they needed: unconditional love and a sense of security. One of his family said to me, 'I think the bond between them, already strong, was strengthened further. And deepened. As a family, they came out of it more united, understanding one another better and, in a way, admiring one another more. Charles was very proud of the way William and Harry handled themselves. He was right to be.'

Charles and his sons drew closer to one another in the aftermath of Diana's death. But what about Charles and his public? 'The people's princess' – as the new prime minister, Tony Blair, aptly termed her on the day of her death – was being mourned by the whole world: what were the people going to make of the prince who had married their heroine and then – so it seemed – abandoned her to her fate? Having mourned her death, would they now bay for his blood?

Eight years on, the suggestion seems absurd, but in the week of Diana's death anything seemed possible. Officials at Buckingham Palace, witnessing the waves of grief that appeared to be sweeping the world, were fearful that the grief might turn to anger. They were nervous about allowing the Prince to go out among the crowds. 'They might jeer him,' said one courtier. 'They might lynch him,' said another. Clive James, the Australian writer, said, 'I know him well enough to be sure that since last Sunday he has been on the Cross, and wondering whether he will ever be able to come down.'

Charles was crucified with guilt and with remorse. If he had not married Diana, none of this would have happened. If, somehow, he had made his marriage work, none of this would have happened. If he had not loved Camilla . . . what might have been?

Camilla, a guest at Diana's wedding, did not attend her funeral. Camilla lay low that week – and for many weeks to come. She stayed indoors at Ray Mill House. She cancelled engagements. She was due as guest of honour at a party for her sister's business in Dorset: the event was postponed. She spoke with Charles on the telephone, but agreed they dare not risk being caught in a clandestine encounter. They were both bemused by the overwhelming response to Diana's death. One of their friends called it, 'Mass hysteria, no more, no less'. Charles and Camilla may have agreed, but, if they did, they did not say so. A friend of Camilla's told me, 'She was very circumspect at the time, deeply distressed at what had happened and, of course, concerned for the young princes.'

Prior to Diana's death, Charles had spoken openly to friends about his hopes that his ex-wife might marry again. Only then, he felt, would he begin to be left in peace. If she found another husband, the press might stop harassing him and Diana might stop attempting to outmanoeuvre him in the media at every opportunity. And if Diana married again, happily and well, might not he be able to marry again also – as his sister had done? Possibly, but probably not. He knew that. In the year before Diana's death he was shown an opinion poll indicating that 88 per cent of the British public was against him marrying Camilla – and that 54 per cent felt that, if he did marry her, he would need to renounce the throne. It was a forlorn hope in any event, because Diana showed no inclination to marry. In the opinion of her girlfriends, of Diana's varied post-separation boyfriends and lovers, only Hasnat Khan was worthy of her hand in marriage. He was a heart surgeon, two years older than Diana, intelligent, considerate and kind. Diana visited his family in Pakistan. She said to several people, 'I want to marry him and have his babies.' But it was not to be. Khan, engaged twice before, had reservations about committing himself – and his career – to the most famous woman in the world. After two years together, off and on, in the early summer of 1997 the affair fizzled out. Diana took up with Dodi Fayed. 'Dodi was a fling,' Rosa Monckton said to me, 'another fling. Diana was having her teenage years in her thirties.'

Before Diana's death, Charles had felt that if his former wife had remarried somehow a line would have been drawn that all could recognise. At her death, he was not sure what to feel. How the world felt was self-evident. The world was in mourning. Andrew Morton, Diana's mouthpiece while she was alive, memorialised her in death. That autumn, he rushed out a revised edition of *Diana: Her True Story*, in which he came to this conclusion:

> As historians reflect on her renown and her legacy, they will come to judge Diana, Princess of Wales, as one of the most influential figures of this, or any other, age. For as long as there are poets, playwrights and men with hearts to break, tales will be told of the princess who died across the water and returned home to be crowned a queen, the queen of all our hearts.
>
> Diana, Princess of Wales. She wrote poetry in our souls. And made us wonder.

'Pass the sick bag, Mabel' would, doubtless, have been the reaction of Nicholas Soames had he read Morton's epitaph. However, I doubt that he did. He, too, was keeping a low profile. The Prince's camp – quietly confident earlier that summer that they were making slow but steady advances in the battle to secure the public's respect for their champion – was now in rapid retreat. There was no alternative.

In 1867, Walter Bagehot, the accepted authority on the English constitution, declared, to loud murmurs of assent, 'Above all things, our royalty needs to be reverenced . . .' In 1997, it was Diana, alone of all our royalty, who was reverenced. Alive, she was simply the most famous woman in the world. Dead, she was suddenly a martyr, an extraordinary and bizarre combination of Marilyn Monroe (they were the same age when they died) and Mother Teresa of Calcutta (who died in the same week as Diana): as beautiful as the one, as saintly as the other, more iconic than both.

The aftermath of Diana's death almost eclipsed the coverage of Mother Teresa's passing – but not quite. Several newspapers ran cartoons of Diana and Mother Teresa arriving in heaven together, holding hands. Diana once told me that if she had a role model it was Mother Teresa. (Mother Teresa had told Diana that 'to heal other people you had to suffer yourself' and Diana concurred with that.) Camilla, by contrast, had often joked that her role model was her great-grandmother, Alice Keppel. In September 1997, it appeared that Diana had achieved her apotheosis, and Camilla her destiny: the one as a saint to be reverenced, the other as a royal mistress to be reviled.

Of course, as the political maxim has it, 'Nothing is ever quite as good, or as bad, as it at first appears.'[184] Five years after Diana's death, in Rome Pope John Paul II committed himself to the beatification of Mother Teresa, in Kensington Gardens the Diana memorial fountain spluttered fitfully to life, and, at Highgrove, Charles and Camilla stood side by side, smiling, as, with William and Harry in attendance, they welcomed their guests to the home they evidently shared. 'Time is the great physician.'[185]

In his autobiography, the Duke of Windsor – the last Prince of Wales – wrote of 'the overwhelming love and surpassing need' he had for Mrs Simpson. He said that his 'dream of being able to bring her permanently into his life was, although quite vague, extremely vivid'. When Diana

---

[184] David Davis, my whip, introduced me to the saying when I first arrived at Westminster. Credit for my other favourite political maxim belongs to Arthur Balfour (prime minister, 1902–5): 'Nothing matters very much, and very few things matter at all.'

[185] Another prime minister, Benjamin Disraeli (1868 and 1874–80).

died, Charles did not know what the future might hold for him, but he remained determined that Camilla should be part of it.

Gradually, he set about re-establishing his own credibility; eventually, he brought Camilla out of the shadows. In November 1997, Charles attended the premiere of the film *Titanic* and Camilla's children were spotted among the crowds. In December, William and Harry went hunting with the Beaufort, and Mrs Parker Bowles went too. At the beginning of 1998, Charles set out his stall both as a beneficent single father and as a friend and admirer of the most reverenced man on earth. He took Prince Harry to South Africa to see the Spice Girls in concert and to meet Nelson Mandela in person. His staff monitored the opinion polls and their message was clear: his sons – Diana's boys – were his greatest asset; his mistress – Diana's enemy – remained a liability. 'They've just got to accept her,' said the Prince. 'I don't think they ever will,' said Camilla. 'If only they knew her better they might,' said her admirers. Linda Edwards of the National Osteoporosis Society said: 'It is a sadness that the public has not been able to see Camilla as we have seen her – a warm, sincere, friendly woman. She has been misrepresented and I can't help but hope that out of all this current controversy a kinder picture will emerge of Camilla.'

The first official picture of any kind of Camilla and her prince together showed them emerging from the Ritz Hotel in London's Piccadilly in January 1999. The occasion was a party (another one) in honour of Camilla's sister, Annabel. Charles and Camilla, of course, had attended a number of the same events in the preceding months, but had always taken care – great care – to arrive and leave at different times in separate cars. Now, exactly eighteen months after Diana's death, Charles deemed that the moment had come for them to face the cameras as 'an item', together at last, not yet arm in arm, but definitely side by side. The St James's Palace press office alerted the media to the unique photo opportunity and more than two hundred photographers, camera crews and reporters turned up.

There was one person who did not seem to be as biddable as the British press: Her Majesty The Queen. Elizabeth II is, by instinct and upbringing, conservative. She is, in many ways, behind the times and sees no great harm in that. She is also a religious person. She says, 'The teachings of Christ and my own personal accountability before God provide a framework in which I try to live my life.' (At close quarters, I have watched both the Queen and Camilla in church, at prayer. When the Queen prays it is not a matter of form. Paul Burrell, once her footman, told me, 'The Queen gets up at six in the morning to go into her private chapel to pray at Christmas and Easter.') As a religious person (as a private individual, never mind as Supreme Governor of the Church of England and Defender of the Faith), the Queen takes the marriage vows seriously. She would never divorce. It is not something, whatever the circumstances, she would consider, even for a moment. At the beginning of her reign (lest we forget), no divorcee could be or would be presented to her. In 1949, when Prince Charles was eleven months old, you will recall that she told the Mothers' Union: 'We can have no doubt that divorce and separation are responsible for some of the darkest evils in our society today.' Famously, her grandfather, King George V, one of her role models, once said: 'I am not interested in any wife but my own.' That, from the Queen's point of view, is the correct approach for a man to take towards matrimony.

The Queen did not approve of the heir to the throne's relationship with Camilla Parker Bowles. She did not wish to be seen to be giving it her blessing. For many years, deliberately, in private as well as in public, she avoided the possibility of encountering her son's mistress. Even when Diana was dead and Camilla divorced, her resistance remained.

In 1998, Charles turned fifty. He hoped his birthday might provide an opportunity for his mother to meet the non-negotiable love of his life. In fact, the birthday provided several opportunities. The Queen took advantage of none of them. Prince William and Prince Harry organised a bash for their dad: Camilla came, but Granny stayed away. Camilla herself organised a birthday gala for the Prince at Highgrove: the Queen and the Duke of Edinburgh spent the night at Sandringham. And when, at Buckingham Palace, Her Majesty organised her own reception to mark her son's half-century, Mrs Parker Bowles was not on the list of invitees.

And then, in the summer of 2000, the Queen relented. Why? 'Charles was quite insistent,' a courtier told me, 'and the Queen is no fool. She knows what's going on, even if she doesn't always like it. Divorce is a fact of life. It was three years since Diana's death. I think she simply bowed to the inevitable.' The Duchess of Grafton, Mistress of the Robes and the Queen's longest serving lady-in-waiting, told me that, nowadays, Her Majesty's motto is 'Go with the flow'. The Duke of Edinburgh says that the Queen has 'the gift of tolerance in abundance'.

The Queen bowed to the inevitable, but she did so with reluctance and with care. In June 2000 there were two royal birthday parties. One was hosted by Her Majesty, at Windsor Castle, to celebrate five special anniversaries: the one hundredth birthday of Queen Elizabeth The Queen Mother, the seventieth of Princess Margaret, the fiftieth of Princess Anne, the fortieth of Prince Andrew and the eighteenth of Prince William. Mrs Parker Bowles was not invited to this glittering affair: it was the Queen's party for the Queen's family in the Queen's favourite official residence. (Also, I understand the Duke of Edinburgh surmised that Camilla's presence would hijack the press coverage and take attention away from those who were being honoured on their birthdays.) The second of June 2000, however, marked the sixtieth birthday of ex-King Constantine of Greece[186] and, at Highgrove, Charles laid on a special evening in his cousin's honour. The Queen was invited – and she went, without the Duke of Edinburgh. (Prince Philip had a prior engagement, carriage driving in Hampshire: it was not a snub; he was content with the Queen's decision to go to the party and correct in anticipating the press coverage that would follow. 'QUEEN AND CAMILLA MEET – AT LAST!' was a representative headline.)

The encounter, as I understand it, was pretty perfunctory: a curtsy from Camilla, a smile from Her Majesty, a moment of small talk, and that was that. As meetings go it was not memorable, but it was certainly significant. It enabled the *Daily Telegraph* to report to its readers: 'The Queen has finally recognised Mrs Parker Bowles.' From the summer of the year 2000, Charles and Camilla were swimming towards the open sea.

In 2001 came 'the kiss' – not a sculpture by Rodin, but a photo opportunity masterminded by Mark Bolland, Prince Charles's assistant private secretary charged with enhancing the heir apparent's image. To mark the fifteenth anniversary of the National Osteoporosis Society, a party was given at Somerset House, with Camilla – now president of the Society – as nominal hostess and Charles as guest of honour. His Royal

[186] Constantine II, King of Greece, 1964–73, is the grandson of Constantine I, the older brother of Prince Andrew of Greece, Prince Philip's father. In 1964 he married Princess Anne-Marie, younger daughter of Frederick IX of Denmark and sister of Queen Margarethe of Denmark. In April 1967, when the 'Colonels' junta' seized power in a military coup, he made an abortive attempt to regain control and then fled to Rome that December. He was formally deposed in 1973 and the monarchy in Greece was abolished by referendum in 1974. The ex-king has lived in London ever since and remains close to his many royal cousins. He is delightful company, easy, unstuffy and unpretentious. He has a good word for everybody and, while pleasantly chatty, is effortlessly discreet. (We first met at Jeffrey Archer's lunch table in the 1980s. He gave me a lift home afterwards. As I got out of the car I said, 'Thank you, your majesty.' He said, 'Any time, guv.')

Highness arrived and, to a fusillade of clicking camera shutters and flashing lights, genially bussed the president on both cheeks. As kisses go, they were not memorable, but they were significant. We all knew (thanks to that tape!) what the couple were capable of in private: now we were vouchsafed a decorous touch of public intimacy. Photographs of 'the kiss' were relayed around the world – and the world, curiously, did not come to an end.

Charles and Camilla were now living together openly, and Camilla was now beginning to acquire the look and (according to some) the manner appropriate to a Prince's acknowledged consort. She had smartened herself up considerably: she worked on her figure and her posture, on her fingernails and her hair: she began to dress with a style to which we were unaccustomed. (For 'the kiss', for example, she wore a lilac chiffon dress by Anthony Price and looked a treat.) For the first time in her life, she wore designer clothes on a regular basis – frocks by Paddy Campbell and Robinson Valentine, hats by Philip Treacy, jewellery by royal appointment. Charles took time and trouble (and spent serious money) seeking out pieces of jewellery believed to have been given by Edward VII to Mrs Keppel so that, in his turn, he might present them to Mrs Parker Bowles.

In private, the Prince treated his mistress as his consort and now expected his court to do the same. A friend of mine was honoured (and delighted) to be invited to a weekend house party by the Prince, but was a little taken aback by the grandeur of the occasion, by the formality, and by the way in which it was intimated to him and the other guests that when Mrs Parker Bowles appeared she should be treated with due respect. Whenever Camilla appeared, the company – ladies included – stood to attention. Whenever Camilla rose to leave the room, all rose with her. He told me, 'I found we were bobbing our heads, bowing really, treating her like a princess, simply because that seemed to be what was expected.' I understand that it was around this time that members of Charles's entourage coined a nickname for Mrs Parker Bowles. Among themselves, they began to call her 'La Reine'.

On 30 March 2002, Easter Saturday, Queen Elizabeth The Queen Mother died. Charles was bereft. His grandmother had 'meant the world' to him. Her death, of course, was inevitable and hardly unexpected (she was 101) and brought with it incidental consolations for her favourite grandson: he was able to make Clarence House his London base and he inherited Birkhall on the Balmoral estate as his

Body language: Camilla shows off her engagement ring at Windsor Castle, following the announcement of her engagement to the Prince of Wales, 10 February 2005

First steps: Charles and Camilla emerge from the Guildhall, Windsor, following their civil wedding, 9 April 2005

The bride and groom, the Prince
of Wales and the Duchess of Cornwall,
during the Service of Prayer and
Dedication at St George's Chapel,
Windsor, conducted by the Archbishop
of Canterbury, Dr Rowan Williams,
9 April 2005

Sister and father of the bride: Annabel Elliott and Bruce Shand arrive

First husband and son: Andrew Parker Bowles and Tom in St George's Chapel

Happy families: The Queen, Prince Harry and the Duke of Edinburgh in the foreground, with Major Shand, Annabel Elliott, Peter Phillips and Prince William behind

After Trooping the Colour, marking the Queen's official birthday, Camilla joins the royal family on the balcony of Buckingham Palace for the first time. *L – r*, Prince William, the Duchess of Cornwall, Ella Mountbatten, the Prince of Wales, Prince Edward, Earl of Wessex, the Queen, Sophie, Countess of Wessex, and the Duke of Edinburgh, 11 June 2005

Another day, another first: The Duchess of Cornwall, in an open horse-drawn carriage, leaves the Garter service at St George's Chapel, Windsor, 13 June 2005

The Duchess of Cornwall and the Prince of Wales, aboard HMS *Scott*, at Portsmouth for the International Fleet Review marking the 200th anniversary of the Battle of Trafalgar, June 2005

In 1972 Camilla first claimed her prince on the polo field. Thirty-three years later, in June 2005, she hands out the prizes at the Cirencester Park Polo Club, and kisses her stepson, William, and her husband, Charles

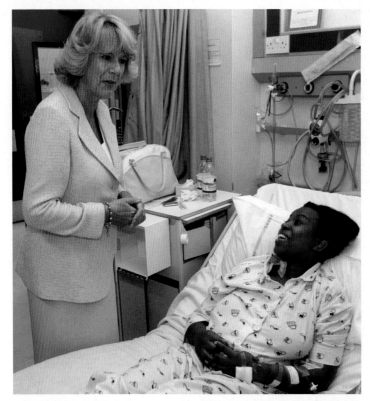

Duty calls: The Duchess of Cornwall at St Mary's Hospital, Paddington, visiting Cynthia Bobb-Semple, one of the victims of the London bombings of 7 July 2005

Back on the balcony: The Prince of Wales, the Duchess of Cornwall and Prince Harry at Buckingham Palace on 10 July 2005, watching poppies drop from a Lancaster Bomber as part of the commemoration of the sixtieth anniversary of the end of the Second World War

Scottish home.[187] He set about refurbishing both – and in some style. From his grandmother he inherited not only the properties but also much of her traditional good taste and her propensity for extravagance – or her liking for things to be done 'properly', depending on your point of view.

Birkhall needed work. It had not been fully redecorated since Elizabeth, as Duchess of York, had it done to her specification in 1931. Clarence House was faded, too. Charles and Camilla's improvements to both have been extensive, and costly. The cost of building Clarence House in the 1820s was £22,232. The cost of refurbishment, following the Queen Mother's death, came to more than £6.5 million. Much of this was borne by the taxpayer: Clarence House is the Prince of Wales's operational headquarters. Some of it was borne by the Duchy of Cornwall – worth, these days, around £460 million. Prince Charles is a rich man. And behaves like one.

His grandmother encouraged him in his extravagances. His wife, I am told, 'understands' them. His parents, I know, do not approve. The Queen keeps her breakfast cereals fresher longer by storing them in Tupperware containers. The Prince of Wales does not. The Duke of Edinburgh has the leanest and most cost-effective office of any of the senior members of the Royal Family. Whenever possible, the Duke travels on commercial flights, usually accompanied by just one aide, and he trundles around London in an environmentally friendly electric taxi cab. The Prince of Wales does not. Charles has a style and taste and panache – and way with money – that reflect his maternal grandmother rather than his parents. Charles has the equivalent of 135

[187] Clarence House has been a royal residence for more than 170 years. Incorporating the south-western corner of the Tudor buildings of St James's Palace, the house was built between 1825 and 1827 to the designs of John Nash for the third son of George III, Prince William Henry, Duke of Clarence (later William IV) and his wife Adelaide. Queen Victoria's son, the Duke of Connaught, lived here until his death, aged ninety-one, in 1942, when the building was taken over for war work, with two hundred staff of the Foreign Relations Department moving in to use Clarence House as the base for maintaining contact with British prisoners-of-war abroad, and administering the Red Cross Postal Message Scheme. In 1949, the house was returned to royal use, as the London home of Princess Elizabeth and the Duke of Edinburgh. From 1953 until her death it was the home of Queen Elizabeth The Queen Mother. Birkhall, an eighteenth-century hunting lodge on the Balmoral estate (acquired by Prince Albert for Queen Victoria in 1851), had been the Highland home of Queen Elizabeth since 1931 when she was Duchess of York. Birkhall is closed to the public, but the refurbished state rooms at Clarence House are open to visitors in the summer – and well worth visiting.

full-time staff, earning £3.8 million a year. Many of them, of course, run his office and his charities, but around thirty work for him personally. His retinue includes a valet, two butlers, two chauffeurs, four chefs, eight housekeepers and eight gardeners. The Queen is reported to have said, 'The amount of kit and staff he takes about – it's obscene.' I think he thinks it is part of the point of being Prince of Wales. At a party at Highgrove, I thanked him for his superb hospitality. 'I believe it's important to do things properly, don't you?' he said. 'Yes, indeed, sir,' I purred, congratulating him (sincerely) on the wonderful way it was all done: the silver, the crystal, the lighting, the flowers – especially the flowers. 'They came from the garden,' he said. 'It's a joy to behold,' I murmured. 'Isn't it?' he said, beaming, 'I'm so glad you like it. I want you to like it. I'm so lucky to have all these lovely things around me. I simply want to share them. I want everyone to love my garden. It is a joy, isn't it? Such a joy.' That, simply, is not the way his parents talk.

When the Prince of Wales entertains, he entertains royally. If he is giving a weekend house party, he hires in extra staff to ensure that every guest has their own maid and valet and, each evening, the setting for dinner, formal and fabulous, does literally take the breath away. If you are unaccustomed to the grandeur, it can be overwhelming. In July 2004, for example, the actor Sir Antony Sher, and his partner, were invited to Charles's annual weekend for members of the arts community. It was held at Sandringham. (The Queen lends her Norfolk home to Charles for the occasion and he transforms it.) 'We were apprehensive,' Sher noted in his diary at the time. 'Turns out all the other guests felt the same.' Sher's account gives a precise and accurate sense of what it is like to be entertained by the Prince of Wales:

> On the first evening – yesterday – I passed Jeremy Paxman in a corridor and he said, 'I've just had a conversation with Prince Charles – about fishing – and everything I said seemed to echo in my head – I sounded like such an idiot.' . . . It's a relief that the other guests include a couple of of mates – the actress Miriam Margolyes and the playwright Peter Shaffer. Then there's one of my heroes, the artist David Hockney, also Lady Solti (the widow of the conductor), Michael Morpurgo (the children's laureate), James Howard-Johnston and Angela Huth (the historian and the writer), Leo de Rothschild (of the banking family), Drue Heinz (of the beans empire), and the Earl and Countess of Gowrie.

This morning all of us accompanied Prince Charles and Camilla to the Sandringham Flower Show – all except Hockney, whom I watched crossing the great lawn at the back of the house with watercolour pad and paints. Then we travelled in a convoy of cars to an informal lunch at one of the log cabins dotted round the estate. The meal was described as a picnic, but was rather sumptuous, on a long table in the shade of a tree . . . This evening there's a formal and very romantic dinner in the garden at Sandringham, under an avenue of lime trees, the long table lit by candles, with night-lights and lantern in the branches and on the surrounding lawn.

By allowing Charles to use Sandringham, knowing that Camilla would be there as hostess, the Queen was giving her son's relationship with his partner her tacit approval. I understand that Her Majesty felt that Charles was 'somewhat precipitate' in moving Camilla so swiftly and so comprehensively into Birkhall following the Queen Mother's death, but was 'pleased' to learn that when he took Camilla with him to Crathie Church at Balmoral for the first time, the party – which included Princess Margaret's daughter, Sarah Chatto, and Camilla's old flatmate Virginia Carington – was given a warm reception by well-wishers waiting outside the church.

In the way he entertains, Charles reflects the extravagant yet elegant taste of his grandmother, Queen Elizabeth, and evokes the golden, bygone age of his great-great-grandfather, Edward VII. It irritates his parents, not so much because his style is not their style, but because they know it lays him – and the monarchy – open to unnecessary criticism. For example, in November 2004, under the headline 'Edwardian? (No, he's just feudal and blissfully unaware of it)' two of the *Daily Mail*'s most experienced (and informed) royal watchers, Geoffrey Levy and Richard Kay, launched a typical attack on the heir apparent:

No man is more hermetically sealed from the realities of modern life; no man lives such a pampered existence without the need to lift a finger to really prove himself; and no man has heard so much praise from fawning gurus that his head has been turned to accept their judgement that he is an intellectual and a man of wisdom.

Those who are hostile to the Prince will relish my revelation that some members of the Clarence House staff have enjoyed calling Camilla 'La

Reine'. In fairness to the Duchess of Cornwall, everyone to whom I have spoken who has known her for more than thirty years says she has not changed in that time. One friend says, 'Maybe people have changed in the way they treat her, now she's with Charles, but she hasn't changed. She goes along with his way of life because she wants to please him. A lot of it she finds a nuisance – the extra security etc. She spends more on clothes and things now because that's what's expected. She isn't personally extravagant. And she isn't grand. She really isn't.'

Camilla may not be extravagant or grand, but nor is she cheap. As Duchess of Cornwall, she performs public duties and can be said to be paying her way. As Mrs Parker Bowles, she had no official standing so that the cost of her upkeep – coming in part from the Duchy of Cornwall, and from the taxpayer, too – was open to scrutiny, and awkward questions. In February 2005, before the announcement of Charles and Camilla's engagement, the House of Commons Public Accounts Committee decided to look into their financial affairs. One of their number said, with a sarcastic edge to his voice, 'The Duchy is a very profitable organisation established with the main purpose of covering the cost of the heir apparent's public and private life. That, as far as I am aware, does not include his live-in partner. It is something worthy of scrutiny.'

What prompted the scrutiny was, in part, the Prince's own openness. In the summer of 2004, he took the unprecedented step of revealing his financial commitment to Mrs Parker Bowles in his first annual review. He did not go into the detail of the precise amounts he was spending on Camilla, but he did reveal that, out of his own pocket, he paid for two part-time secretaries, a gardener and a driver to help her. He also funded the cost of her security guards, grooming and travel, reckoned to be in the region of £250,000 a year. Additionally, inevitably, because his life and hers were shared lives now, Mrs Parker Bowles benefited to some extent from the services of twenty-eight Clarence House staff, including members of the press office.

In 2004, the Prince's private secretary, Sir Michael Peat, insisted that any private expenditure on Mrs Parker Bowles came from 'taxed income'. He said, 'Mrs Parker Bowles doesn't want anyone to suggest she is benefiting from public money.' But, as Sir Michael was speaking up on Mrs Parker Bowles's behalf, MPs were pointing out that Sir Michael himself was engaged to work for the Prince, not his mistress. The Prince's own figures suggested he had never been more prosperous. His annual income from the Duchy had soared from around £3 million in 2003 to nearly £12 million in 2004. His records suggested that he paid £4.4 million on tax, but he only paid tax after deducting millions in 'business expenses', including the cost of staff of all kinds at Clarence House, Highgrove and Birkhall. In addition to his huge income from the Duchy, Charles received a further £4.1 million from public funds to cover the cost of his public duties. How much of all of this was going Camilla's way? And why? And what was the lady doing to justify this expenditure – 'other', as one MP put it to me, 'than pleasuring her prince in the way mistresses are supposed to do'. Happily, with news of the royal engagement, these awkward questions blew away.[188]

In retrospect, Charles's marriage to Camilla seems an inevitability. If it had not happened, and they had chosen to go on living together, as the years went by, and the Queen's eventual demise grew inexorably closer, the awkward questions about the position, role, status and cost of Mrs Parker Bowles would have kept recurring – and been ever more difficult to answer. From the moment that the Queen acknowledged Camilla, and her place in Charles's life, the marriage became a realistic possibility. According to one courtier I spoke to (from Buckingham Palace, not Clarence House), 'Once the Queen had accepted Mrs PB as a fact, as far as the marriage was concerned, it was no longer a matter of "if", but of "when?" For obvious reasons, 2002 was out and 2003, of course, began somewhat inauspiciously.'

2002 was 'out' because it was the year of the Queen's golden jubilee. Coming off the back of the outpouring of national affection shown for her mother (more than one million people lined the route of Queen

[188] Questions are no longer being asked about the cost of Camilla, but MPs continue to show an interest in the cost of the Prince of Wales. In June 2005, Clarence House published the Prince's 'annual report', showing that the Duchy of Cornwall's income had risen to £13,274,00, a figure that included a European Union Common Agricultural Policy subsidy of £680,000 and profits of more than £1 million from the Prince's 'Duchy Originals' brand of organically produced groceries. The report also showed that, in addition to his income from the Duchy, the Prince received £2,381,000 from the taxpayer as a contribution towards running Clarence House, his secretariat and the cost of official travel. (The taxpayer's contribution was lower than in the preceding year because the refurbishment of Clarence House was complete.) Martin Salter, Labour MP for Reading West, gave his reaction: 'I do not object to the Prince of Wales running a successful business, but I have a problem with an operation which generates £13 million a year profit, still takes large sums of money from the taxpayer and claims money from Europe . . . I am not a republican, but it is appalling that the prince is not only taking subsidy in Britain but sticking his nose in the European trough as well.'

Elizabeth's funeral; a billion people were reckoned to have watched the event on television worldwide), the celebrations marking Elizabeth II's fifty years as sovereign were a complete success. (As Lord Snowdon said of the Prince of Wales's investiture at Caernarfon in 1969, 'What went wrong? Nothing went wrong!' Even Camilla was allowed to come to the party: she was invited to the classical concert at Buckingham Palace during the jubilee weekend and seated with the rest of the Royal Family, in the row immediately behind the Queen.) 2003 began 'somewhat inauspiciously' because of the turbulent and murky backwash from the trial of Paul Burrell.

In the aftermath of Diana's death, Burrell was arrested, charged and eventually put on trial at the Old Bailey, accused of stealing 310 personal items belonging to Diana, Charles and their children. The case came to trial because, as Burrell put it to me, 'Charles and the boys had been told by the police that I'd dressed up in Diana's clothes and already sold some of her stuff in America.' The case collapsed because, as the trial was reaching its climax, on 25 October 2002, the Queen and Prince Charles and Prince Philip – travelling together by car to St Paul's Cathedral to attend a memorial service for the victims of the Bali bombings – had a brief conversation in which the Queen, prompted by her husband, told her son that she recalled having had a meeting with Paul Burrell, shortly after Diana's death, at which Burrell confided to her that he had taken some of Diana's possessions from Kensington Palace to his home where he was storing them for safe-keeping.

This revelation – relayed by the Prince to his private secretary who confirmed it with the Queen and then transmitted it to the proper authorities – established that Burrell had had no intention to deceive. The prosecution case crumbled; no further evidence was offered; Burrell was found not guilty. It was a good day for the butler, but an uncomfortable one for the Queen. For a start, the case that collapsed was 'Regina v Burrell' and what brought it to its knees was an intervention from Regina herself. Had Her Majesty really only just recalled her meeting with her former footman? Or had she chosen this moment to mention the matter because she was fearful of what damage might be done if the trial continued and the defence offered evidence about her son and his marriage that might be better left unheard? If her intent was not Machiavellian, then, at best, the eleventh-hour timing of the Queen's contribution illustrated all too clearly how little and how poorly mother and son communicated.

From Charles's perspective, the fallout from the trial of Paul Burrell was considerable and damaging. The case threw up all sorts of unsavoury flotsam and jetsam – notably the accusation that, in 1996, there had been a 'cover-up' of an alleged homosexual rape of one member of Charles's staff by another, and that, over a period of years, other members of staff, with the connivance of the Prince, had been selling on official gifts for personal profit. The accusations sent the press into a frenzy (huge headlines; pages of salacious speculation) and allowed all those with long-held reservations about the Prince to have their day. Patrick Jephson, for example, formerly private secretary to Diana, Princess of Wales, spoke sonorously of 'a kingdom of anxious subjects' in a fever of worry 'that their next king's court was sinking in a mire of dodgy court cases, financial fiddles and sexual depravity'.

Three years on, it all seems like so much water under the bridge. At the time, for Charles – and for Camilla, and for their future prospects – it seemed quite overwhelming. To the media, at the time, almost nothing else appeared to matter. On Armistice Day, 11 November 2002, the newspapers ran photographs of the Queen and the heir apparent laying wreaths at the Cenotaph in remembrance of the fallen, while the headline writers told a less heroic story. 'Charles's aide denies rape claim' declared the front page of the customarily restrained *Daily Telegraph*. Forty-eight hours later the same paper announced 'an unprecedented inquiry into the series of scandals that has engulfed the Royal Family since the collapse of the trial of Paul Burrell'.

The enquiry was conducted by the Prince's private secretary, Sir Michael Peat, with the assistance of a senior criminal barrister, Edmund Lawson QC. They hoped to report their findings by Christmas. In the event, it took them until the following March. They interviewed 159 people and corresponded with 223 more. I have reproduced the summary of their findings in Appendix B on pages 328–32 and recommend a reading of the full report (available online), because, whether or not you agree with its conclusions (and some regard it as a predictable 'whitewash'), the tone and detail of the report give a fascinating flavour of aspects of Prince Charles's world.

The questions the Peat Report, as it came to be known, sought to answer were straightforward. Was there anything improper or remiss in the conduct of The Prince of Wales's Household with respect to the termination of the Burrell trial? Was there an improper cover-up of the 1996 rape allegation made by one of the Prince's personal staff? Had official gifts given to the Prince of Wales been subsequently sold? And did any members of the Prince's household receive improper payments or other benefits?

The first question was easily answered. There was no improper conduct by or on behalf of the Prince of Wales in respect of the termination of the Burrell trial. The Prince had, throughout, serious concerns about the implications of Burrell being tried. He was concerned that both he and Prince William might be called as witnesses and by the prospect of information personal to himself and his family being revealed during the trial – particularly the distress which would be caused to his sons by 'revelations', true or not, about their mother. He would have preferred it if a trial could have been avoided. The Prince was advised, however, that he could not properly intervene, and should not be seen to be interfering with or seeking to influence the prosecution process. He followed that advice. Several opportunities presented themselves during the investigation to intervene and stop the process, and none was taken. The disclosure made by the Queen on 28 October 2002 of her conversation with Burrell was 'properly made'. There was no evidence that the disclosure was made for improper motive, nor was there any evidence that by making this disclosure there could have been an expectation that the trial would be discontinued. Matter closed. Case dismissed.

The matter of the rape allegations was more complicated. The alleged victim in the case was one George Smith, formerly a Welsh guardsman (a survivor of the bombing of HMS *Sir Galahad* during the Falklands war), latterly a member of the Prince's domestic staff. He polished Charles's shoes and found favour with Diana. According to her secretary, Patrick Jephson, 'The princess loved his irrepressibly sunny outlook and the girls in the office never failed to be cheered whenever he visited.' Smith claimed that, in 1989, in London, he had been raped by a member of the Prince's staff; and that, in 1995, in Egypt, accompanying the Prince on an official visit, he had been sexually assaulted by the same man. 'How I wish I could disbelieve him,' said Patrick Jephson. Others had no difficulty in disbelieving him, accusing Smith of being an alcoholic whose word could not be relied on because of his 'poor mental and physical state' caused by post-traumatic stress disorder. The Peat Report came down on the side of the unbelievers:

Q. Was there was an improper cover-up of the 1996 rape allegation made by Mr George Smith in 1996?

A. There was no improper cover-up in the sense that those involved deliberately or dishonestly sought to suppress what they believed might be true. However, the allegation was not dealt with in the best way by The Prince of Wales's Office.

No one in the Prince's household believed Mr Smith's rape allegation. (Well, almost no one.) The Prince gave no credence to it and his staff shared in his disbelief. Hounslow Police decided not to give the allegation credence and chose not to investigate it. Understandably, at the time, a major concern was to avoid publicity being given to what was believed to be a baseless allegation. There was also a concern to follow the Prince's instructions that Mr Smith 'must go', but should be well provided for. (He was given a severance package of £38,000.) Peat concluded that, while there were lessons to be learnt from the poor handling of the matter, there was no dishonest intent on the part of the Prince or his household and, while the settlement with Mr Smith was very generous, it was not so generous as to suggest it derived from an improper motive.

If you read it, you will notice that the summary of the Peat Report fails to mention Diana's involvement in the matter. Diana made and kept a recording of George Smith recounting his allegations of rape and assault – and, according to Smith, of another incident 'involving a member of the royal family and a servant' which, he believed, would deal the monarchy 'a very damaging blow'. Why did Diana make and keep these recordings? She was acting 'with typical concern for a favourite former servant', says Patrick Jephson. He concedes, however, that she might have had an additional 'and equally typical motive': 'she needed a weapon of last resort in her continuing battle with her husband'.

To the best of my knowledge, Diana did not directly accuse Prince Charles of homosexual practices, but she certainly made disparaging remarks about one or more members of his personal entourage and, with little jokes and sly asides, definitely implied that there was a limp-wristed side to her ex-husband's nature. Mixing with some of her circle in the mid-1990s, I heard any number of cheap shots at the expense of Charles's sexuality. A friend of the Prince told me in 2005, 'We knew this sort of talk was going on and that Diana encouraged it. It was wholly without foundation, of course, but the prince was put in an impossible position. Any public denial would only fuel speculation. There will always be people who say "No smoke without fire".'

The Peat Report's final area of investigation concerned the alleged onward sale of gifts given to the Prince and of the role played in this by his personal assistant and former valet, one Michael Fawcett. Mr Fawcett was accused of selling these items, with the Prince's connivance, and of taking a 20 per cent cut for himself. He was found not guilty. The Peat Report, having spent considerable time and effort listing more than two thousand official gifts presented to the Prince, tracing those with a value of £150 or more, concluded that one official gift, and a number of personal ones, had been sold and that 'policies and procedures in this area have been deficient'. The report also found that staff had 'received benefits, gifts, entertainment and discounts from Royal Warrant Holders and other suppliers'. There was a requirement in the terms of employment not to accept presents from firms or tradesmen, and the practice should not have been permitted, but it had been. According to the report, Mr Fawcett was not above reproach, but nor was he, in any serious sense, culpable:

> There is no evidence of financial impropriety on the part of Mr Fawcett. He (as well as others) infringed the internal rules relating to gifts from suppliers, but the rules were generally not enforced and he made no secret of such gifts. Press suspicions were understandably aroused by his involvement in the sale of gifts (which, unknown to the media, were authorised by The Prince of Wales). This has encouraged some to voice rumours as to Mr Fawcett's financial probity, but there is no evidence to justify any finding by us that he has been guilty of alleged financial misconduct.

The press had dubbed Michael Fawcett, 'Fawcett the Fence'. When the Peat Report was published, he became 'Fawcett the Fall Guy'. He left the Prince's full-time employment, bloodied but unbowed. He received a severance package worth a reported £500,000 and the promise of future freelance work as the Prince's 'events and functions manager'. Charles liked Fawcett's style, and likes it still. To this day, he uses Fawcett's company, Premier Mode Events, to organise set-piece social events on his behalf. The Prince's accounts published in June 2005 showed an expenditure of £507,000 on official entertaining in the preceding year, much of it spent under the direction of Michael Fawcett.

Diana did not like Fawcett's style. Diana complained, regularly, about those close to Charles who, in her view, 'oiled up to him', 'fawned on him' and 'did whatever he wanted'. Diana expressed the opinion that Fawcett had 'too much influence' on the Prince and she considered it 'unhealthy'. Patrick Jephson put it like this: 'Unless you have witnessed it, it's hard to comprehend the influence exercised by some apparently minor palace functionaries. I learnt very early in my career that real power in the Royal Household isn't necessarily held by the people with the most medals, biggest offices or smartest cars. It can just as easily be found on the back stairs, among the jealous and competitive servants who see their employers at their most un-Royal moments. Backstairs power beats office power almost every time. In practical terms, this power is usually expressed tacitly. "I squeeze the Prince of Wales's toothpaste" translates as "I am entrusted with his most intimate confidences".'

Diana resented Fawcett most, of course, because she saw him as one of those who facilitated Charles's clandestine meetings with Camilla. 'She thought he was quite poisonous,' one of Diana's girlfriends told me. When 'the war of the Waleses' was at its most ferocious, bitter things were said – and implied – by both sides. Diana's camp characterised Charles as weak-willed, self-indulgent and easily led; she described the atmosphere within his household as 'unwholesome'. Charles's camp characterised Diana as hysterical, deceitful and paranoid. A senior member of the Royal Family, looking back on it all in 2005, told me, 'There was probably a bit of truth on both sides.'

At the time of the publication of the Peat Report, in March 2003, Patrick Jephson described Charles's court as 'a private universe, obsessed by the moods and shifting requirements of the figure at its centre'. That may have been true in Jephson's day (he went to work for Diana in November 1991), but, from my observation, it is much less true today. Having had a taste of both at first hand, I can report that the atmosphere surrounding the Prince of Wales in 2005 is wholly different from that which engulfed him in 1990. Then sycophancy and defensiveness were evident at every turn. Inevitably, there are still traces of both (Charles is the Prince of Wales, after all), but, from all I have seen and heard, I sense that the 'below stairs hothouse' described by Patrick Jephson has cooled considerably, and 'upstairs', the arrival of Sir Michael Peat, as the Prince's private secretary in 2002, and of Paddy Harverson, as his communications secretary in 2003, has brought a new professionalism and openness to the administration of the Prince's affairs.

Sir Michael Peat comes from a long line of royal accountants. His father was a Privy Purse auditor, as was his great-grandfather, William

Barclay Peat, who was a founding partner of the accountancy firm Peat Marwick, now KPMG, where Sir Michael was previously a partner. He spent twenty years in the family business, before joining the royal household in 1990, first as director of Finance and Property Services, then, from 1996, as Keeper of the Privy Purse. In 2002, when he left the Queen's service to join the Prince of Wales, Her Majesty was delighted. She felt (I am quoting her) that Peat was 'just what Charles needs'. 'He may not be that charismatic,' I was told at Buckingham Palace, 'but he is totally straight – in every sense of the word.' (My source was smiling broadly as he said this.) Equally straight – and straightforward – is Paddy Harverson, a former *Financial Times* journalist and director of communications at Manchester United Football Club. He is tall, broad, good-humoured, direct, and a man I can envisage working as comfortably for the Duke of Edinburgh as the Prince of Wales – not something that one could say about many of his predecessors.

In December 2001, having spent the day in the retinue of the Queen and the Duke of Edinburgh as they fulfilled official engagements in Wiltshire, I travelled back from Swindon to London by train in the company of Her Majesty's private secretary, lady-in-waiting and assistant press secretary. By chance, travelling on the same train, in a different compartment, was Mark Bolland, then assistant private secretary and spin-*meister* to Prince Charles. The Queen's team registered the presence of the Prince's man, but made no attempt to greet him. Indeed, from the rather obvious displacement signals they manifested (visibly twitching and then burying their noses in paperwork), I got the distinct impression that Bolland was *persona non grata* and that, as a general rule, for safety's sake, any unnecessary contact with the world of the Prince of Wales was best avoided.

Today, all that has changed. Bolland – smooth, smart, ingratiating, gay: the man behind the first PR campaign to gain credibility for Mrs Parker Bowles at the end of the 1990s – has moved on. He has been replaced by Paddy Harverson, described to me at Buckingham Palace as 'a breath of fresh air at Clarence House'. In June 2005, when I went to Clarence House to meet Mr Harverson, I liked him at once. He came straight to the point. 'The Prince and the Duchess don't want anyone to be writing about their first marriages,' he said. 'But it's going to happen,' I ventured, 'so we might as well get it right.' I assured Mr Harverson – as I had assured Sir Michael Peat and members of the Prince's family and assorted friends of Charles and Camilla to whom I had spoken – that my portrait was intended to be sympathetic. He nodded and said, 'Yes, but there's going to be something in it that whoever serialises it will pick up and put on the front page. There's bound to be something.' Paddy Harverson understands the workings of the modern media completely.

His task is not to dwell on the past, but to look to the future and to do all he can to accentuate the positive. He knows it is not easy. 'I went to Yorkshire with the Prince the other day, visiting all sorts of projects, a range of really interesting things involving his various charities, but the only coverage we got was in the *Sun*. They had a photograph of the Prince with a red mark on his nose and ran a funny piece about how the Duchess was now beating him up.' He laughed and sighed at the same time. 'All that good work going on, and the only coverage of the entire day is a joke about the Prince's red nose!'

We met in the week that the Prince took a leaf out of the contemporary corporate handbook and rebranded his sixteen principal charities under a single name: The Prince's Charities. Together the charities employ more than 1,400 full-time staff and several thousand volunteers. They raise some £110 million per year. On the back of a review by McKinsey & Co., the management consultants, the Prince decided to 'unite but not unify' the charities, explaining to the charities' trustees and staff: 'We are trying to promote more "joined-up" working between you all, more opportunities to learn from one another, better planning, research and intelligence, and the highest standards of good governance and management.'[189]

Sir Michael Peat and Paddy Harverson also hope that the unified brand will help raise the profile of Charles's charitable endeavour. As Sir Michael put it, a little wearily, 'The only thing that never

[189] If the phrase '"joined-up" working' has a New Labour ring to it, that could be because the Prince was speaking to notes drafted by Sir Tom Shebeare, his director of charities, through whom Charles got to know Peter Mandelson in the 1990s. Mandelson and Shebeare had worked together at the British Youth Council in the 1970s and jointly published a pamphlet, 'Youth Unemployment – Causes and Cures'. Shebeare, who has worked for Charles since 1986, is credited with much of the success of the Prince's Trust, which has helped more than 500,000 underprivileged young people since it was established in 1976. Mandelson – formerly New Labour's director of campaigns and communications; latterly, European Trade Commissioner – was for some years quite close to Charles. The story goes that there was a falling out, when Charles asked Mandelson, 'How am I doing?' and Mandelson told him. I have not been able to make this anecdote stand up. Sources close to Charles advise me that Mandelson was 'never *that* close' to Charles.

leaks from Clarence House is the great work that the Prince of Wales does.'

The plan for the future is settled. From the team at Clarence House, all the focus, all the energy, all the attention, will be concentrated on the Prince's good works and on his performance of his public duties. Charles will do his stuff, and, where appropriate, Camilla will be at his side. For example – and I have taken these two days at random from the week in which I happen to be writing this – on 4 July 2005, during the day, together Charles and Camilla launched Veterans' Week in St James's Park to commemorate the end of the Second World War, and, in the evening, on his own, Charles hosted a dinner for the chairmen of the English Regional Development Agencies; on 5 July, together, the Prince and the Duchess hosted a reception for 'kindertransport' evacuees, again as part of the commemoration of the end of the war; later, the Prince, alone, went to the Victoria & Albert Museum in South Kensington to open a new garden there; finally, in the evening, together once more, the Prince and Duchess gave a dinner for the Prince's Drawing School. The Duchess will accompany Charles when there are crowds to be met and photo opportunities to be had, and when the occasion is one that is of interest to her – e.g., as an amateur artist herself, an evening with the supporters of the Prince's Drawing School is inevitably more congenial to Camilla than an evening with the worthies of the English Regional Development Agencies.

Camilla is there to support Charles, to share his burden, not to add to it. 'I just love having her with me,' he says, beaming. I have watched them on parade together: they are a team. 'It's good, isn't it?' says Paddy Harverson. And there is no doubt about their relative authority. Camilla is Charles's companion and consort, not his competition. She will do her own thing, now and again, but not too often – and what she does will reflect her genuine interests, enthusiasms and friendships. For example, to take just one more day at random, on 30 June 2005, while Charles, on his own, spent the morning saluting pioneers of sustainable energy and the afternoon meeting members of the Aberdeen Angus Cattle Society, Camilla travelled, on her own, to Hampshire, to Stratfield Saye, ancestral home of the Duke of Wellington, where, attended by her friend, the Marquess of Douro, she opened the Wellington Farm Shop. It was an informal ceremony and a happy outing. In the evening, Prince and Duchess were together again, but this time, unusually, the event was one in which the Duchess, not the

Prince, took the lead. It was a dinner in support of a local Wiltshire charity of which Camilla is patron: the Bobby Van Trust.[190]

Mention of the Marquess of Douro reminds me . . . On 22 August 1997, at 6.40 a.m., Camilla Parker Bowles took an early morning flight from Stansted airport to join the Marquess of Douro and his family for a summer break at the Wellington estate in Spain. Twelve hours earlier, from the same airport, Diana, Princess of Wales, left England for the last time, travelling to Nice, by private jet, to join Dodi Fayed in France. Camilla and Diana are both part of this story – always were, and always will be. For Charles, there is no escape. As someone said, 'No man is rich enough to buy back his past.'

There is no doubt that Camilla is good for Charles and that he is a happier man and a better Prince of Wales because of her. 'I still can't accept her,' a friend of the family said to me, 'I simply can't. I've not met her. I'm sure she's perfectly nice, but . . .' His voice trailed away. He is of the view, shared by many (including the Queen and the Duke of Edinburgh), that the combined effect of the failure of Charles's marriage to Diana and the fact of Charles's affair with Camilla has been to devalue the currency of the monarchy. A traditionalist at Buckingham Palace told me, regretfully, 'So much damage has been done. What was once a respected institution, genuinely looked up to and admired, has become a joke. Did you know that at the time of the ['Camillagate'] tapes, Mick Jagger appeared on American television [on *Saturday Night Live*] dressed as a palace footman and presented a Camilla look-alike with a box of tampons on a silver salver? It was supposed to be a present from the Prince of Wales. Apparently, the audience thought it hilarious. Twelve years later, Mick Jagger is a Knight Commander of the Order of the British Empire and Camilla is a Duchess and a Royal Highness.'

In his treatise on the role of the British monarchy, Walter Bagehot said, 'We have come to regard the Crown as head of our morality.' Bagehot's contemporary, the American poet and essayist Ralph Waldo Emerson, said, 'Men resemble their contemporaries even more than their progenitors.' Charles and Camilla are not Victorians. They are

---

[190] Bobby Van is not a person, but a vehicle in which two Wiltshire bobbies travel the county carrying out repairs to the doors and windows of properties likely to be targeted by criminals. The householders are the elderly and the vulnerable, including disabled people and victims of domestic violence. The scheme was launched in Swindon in 1998, the first initiative of its kind in the UK, and since then, more than 4,000 calls have been carried out.

creatures of their time. They reflect our world and its morality – not the world of the Queen and the Duke of Edinburgh, let alone that of Queen Victoria and Prince Albert. Charles and Camilla live in an age when many (nearly half) of first marriages fail. As one of Charles's oldest friends put it to me (he, too, is on his second marriage): 'They cannot unmake the past, but they can make a success of the future and they will. Theirs will be a model of a second marriage. Everyone will see how well they get on together – and how well all four of their children get on, with them and with one another.'

Charles regrets the past, but he is no longer brooding about it. 'He's free at last,' one of his family said to me. The ghosts have all gone. He was married three years to the day since the funeral of his beloved grandmother, Queen Elizabeth The Queen Mother. Whether or not she would have given his union with Camilla her blessing is beside the point: she is not here any more. And Diana is dead too.

Diana, when she was alive, both during and after their marriage, undermined Charles and sapped his energy. Sometimes Charles felt his parents undermined him and sapped his energy, too. Not any more. Charles's parents are old people now: the Queen will be eighty in 2006, the Duke of Edinburgh, eighty-five. They are a formidable couple (she is the Queen after all, and he can be alarming), but they have mellowed considerably with age. They are still active (extraordinarily so, given their antiquity), but, inevitably, they are less vigorous than once they were. They are no longer in the ascendant. Indeed, they are visibly in decline. And Charles is not frightened of them any more.

Once upon a time, Charles was the Hamlet of the House of Windsor: the prince who could not make up his mind. He shilly-shallied, he vacillated, he danced – fitfully – to everybody else's tune. When his father said, 'Are you going to marry Diana or aren't you? Make up your mind, man', he did as he was told. When, twelve years later, his mother looked at the shambles of his marriage to Diana and said, 'Enough is enough', he looked wanly into the middle distance and agreed. But that was then and this is now, and, within the House of Windsor, and only relatively recently, the balance of energy and authority have changed. 'He's his own man now' is how one of his siblings put it to me.

He is not yet the boss, of course. The Queen has conceded much in recent months, but by no means everything. On the occasion of the Queen's official birthday, in June 2005, when Camilla made her first appearance on the Buckingham Palace balcony, Her Majesty, coincidentally, made an interesting and telling gesture. She authorised the publication of a new order of precedence relating to female members of the Royal Family. It was an order of precedence without precedent. In the past, the pecking order has always been straight-forward: the sovereign comes first, followed by the wife or widow of the sovereign, followed by the wives of the sons of the sovereign, followed by the daughters of the sovereign, followed by the wives of grandsons of a sovereign, followed by granddaughters of a sovereign. In 2005, the Queen changed all that, giving, for the first time, seniority to the blood relatives of the sovereign.

In 1995, for example, before divorce and death took their toll, the female order of precedence ran like this:

The Queen
Queen Elizabeth The Queen Mother (widow of George VI)
The Princess of Wales (wife of the Prince of Wales, the sovereign's eldest son)
The Duchess of York (wife of the sovereign's second son)
The Princess Royal (the sovereign's daughter)
The Princess Margaret, Countess of Snowdon (the sovereign's sister)
Princess Alice, Duchess of Gloucester (widow of George V's third son, the late Duke of Gloucester)
The Duchess of Gloucester (wife of George V's grandson, the present Duke of Gloucester)
The Duchess of Kent (wife of George V's grandson, the present Duke of Kent, oldest son of George V's fourth son)
Princess Michael of Kent (wife of George V's grandson, the second son of the late Duke of Kent)
Princess Alexandra (George V's granddaughter, only daughter of the late Duke of Kent)

By giving preference in her new order of precedence to the blood line, the Queen secured several neat tricks at a stroke. She rewarded the loyalty and service of her daughter, Princess Anne;[191] she did the same

[191] The Queen has regularly rewarded her daughter for her endeavours. In 1987, Her Majesty accorded Anne the title 'The Princess Royal'; in 1994, Anne became a Lady of the Garter; in 2000, in recognition of her fiftieth birthday and her years of public service, she became a Lady of the Thistle.

for her first cousin, Princess Alexandra, not only moving her to the top of the pack, but in the process enabling Alexandra to leapfrog her sister-in-law, the hapless Princess Michael of Kent (never, alas, a favourite at Buckingham Palace); and, finally, she put the newcomer to the family, very gently, in her place. Her Majesty's top ten in 2005 looks wholly different from that of a decade before:

The Queen
The Princess Royal (the sovereign's daughter)
Princess Alexandra (George V's granddaughter)
The Duchess of Cornwall (wife of the Prince of Wales)
The Countess of Wessex (wife of the sovereign's third son)
The Duchess of Gloucester (wife of George V's grandson)
The Duchess of Kent (wife of George V's grandson)
Princess Michael of Kent (wife of George V's grandson)
Miss Zara Phillips (Princess Anne's daughter, eldest granddaughter of the sovereign)
Lady Sarah Chatto (the late Princess Margaret's daughter, granddaughter of George VI)
Lady Davina Lewis (eldest daughter of the Duke of Gloucester, great-granddaughter of George V)
(You have to be of age to feature in the list, hence the absence at the moment of the Duke of York's daughters, Beatrice and Eugenie.)

When the Queen's new order of precedence was published, those who understand these things absorbed its significance and its subtlety. Her Majesty did not intend to snub Camilla personally or to demote her son's second wife: she simply wanted – in the words of a Buckingham Palace spokesman – 'to clarify the private administrative Precedence for the Palace'. The Queen's document, properly entitled 'Precedence Of The Royal Family To Be Observed At Court', does exactly that. It makes it clear that the Queen, who rarely breaks with tradition, has chosen to do so. The pecking order among the ladies of the Royal Family has been changed.

When the Queen's document, marked 'Private', made its first public appearance, an unnamed spokesman announced that Camilla was 'relaxed about the arrangement'. Indeed, it 'reflected her wishes'. Buckingham Palace insisted: 'This is not a downgrading of the Duchess, but merely reflects that the Duchess is a duchess, not a princess.' This is nonsense, of course. Camilla Parker Bowles, as wife of the Prince of Wales, is Princess of Wales, just as Marie-Christine Troubridge, as wife of Prince Michael of Kent, is Princess Michael of Kent.[192]

The Queen is alive to the niceties of royal protocol. It has been her life, after all. Who sits where at a state banquet is a matter of moment to her – not of great moment, perhaps, but of some moment, certainly. And Camilla is to be seated two places further away from the Head of State than she might have expected as consort to the Prince of Wales.

However, the Queen has already bestowed one signal and significant honour on Camilla. She has made her a Royal Highness. The rank – never bestowed on the Duchess of Windsor, to HRH The Duke of Windsor's lifelong chagrin – is in the sovereign's personal gift. What close observers of the royal scene will be watching for now is the length of time the Queen chooses to take before bestowing further honours on her new daughter-in-law. When it comes to 'gongs for the girls', Her Majesty has two particular orders at her disposal – and she does not dish them out willy-nilly. The Queen does not rush to judgement. What she gives to whom, and when, precisely reflects her considered opinion of an individual's contribution to national life and to the work of the Royal Family.

The Royal Victorian Order was founded by Queen Victoria, in 1896, as a way of rewarding outstanding personal service to the sovereign. The lowlier long-serving royal staff receive the MVO (and become Members of the Order); the Queen's private secretaries get the KCVO (as Knight Commanders); ladies of the royal house get the GCVO (as Dames Grand Cross). Princess Alexandra, the Duchess of Kent and the Duchess of Gloucester all have the Order. Princess Michael of Kent does not have the Order, nor was it offered to Sarah, Duchess of York,

[192] Wives automatically assume their husband's rank. My wife, Michèle Brown, is also Mrs Gyles Brandreth. However, men do not take on the rank of their wives. When Philip Mountbatten RN (formerly Prince Philip of Greece) married Princess Elizabeth in 1947, he was created Duke of Edinburgh and given the rank of Royal Highness and made a Knight of the Garter by George VI. He was not created a Prince of the United Kingdom until 1957. After Antony Armstrong-Jones married the Queen's sister, Princess Margaret, he was created Earl of Snowdon, but not given the rank of Royal Highness. When Princess Anne married Captain Mark Phillips, he got nothing – except a wife. Following the attack on Princess Anne's car in the Mall in 1974, Phillips was awarded the CVO. (Anne received the GCVO and her personal protection officer, who was shot and wounded in the assault, was awarded the George Cross.)

nor Diana, Princess of Wales. The Queen has another, even more personal order at her disposal: the Royal Family Order, created at the beginning of her reign. She has given it to almost every royal lady you can think of: her mother, her sister, assorted cousins and aunts; in 1969 she gave it to the Duchess of Kent and Princess Anne; in 1981 she gave it to the Duchess of Gloucester and the Princess of Wales. Conspicuously, she did not give it to the Duchess of York and has not given it to Princess Michael of Kent, but she has given it to her son Edward's wife, Sophie, Countess of Wessex.

Sophie's ride as a royal bride has not been altogether easy. She married Edward in 1999, when he was thirty-five and she was thirty-four, a fresh-faced, wholesome, blonde public relations executive who appeared to have a sensible head on resolute shoulders. Appearances, however, can be deceptive – as Sophie found to her cost when, in the spring of 2001, on behalf of her PR company, she took a meeting with a potential 'client', an Arab 'sheikh', who turned out to be an under-cover reporter for the *News of the World*. Sophie's small talk, as recorded by the 'sheikh', was hardly treasonable, but it was unfortunate. She referred to the Queen as 'the old dear' and the Queen Mother as 'the old lady' and described the Prince of Wales and Camilla Parker-Bowles as 'number one on the unpopular people list', only likely to be married after the death of 'the old lady'. She was not discreet. Prince Charles was not amused. The Queen was none too pleased, either.

Charles was even more dismayed when his younger brother's ill-starred television production company, Ardent, turned up unexpectedly in Scotland, apparently engaged in making a documentary about St Andrew's University where Charles's son, Prince William, had recently enrolled. The Prince of Wales was reportedly incandescent. (The newspapers said 'the air turned blue' when Charles heard that his own brother was invading his own nephew's privacy. I am told that, in fact, Charles's initial reaction was simply to sigh and say, not for the first time, 'God, he's an ass.') The upshot of these two incidents came in 2002 when the Wessexes agreed to withdraw from commercial life and decided – as the official statement put it – 'to focus their energies more into supporting those organisations, charities, individuals and companies who deserve to be recognised for their effort, initiative and entrepreneurship'.

Sophie now does what she does very well. She turns up; she looks nice; she is very friendly. Essentially, that is all that is required of a royal lady. After a shaky start, happily, the Countess of Wessex has hit her stride. Meeting her is a pleasant experience, akin to meeting Anthea Turner or Elizabeth Hurley.[193] It is not as exciting as it was to meet Diana, Princess of Wales, because Sophie is not so famous and because Diana, incontrovertibly, had a certain magic about her. Meeting Camilla is exciting, too. It is 'an event', because the Duchess of Cornwall has both the glamour that comes with fame and the fascination that goes with notoriety. People are only quite interested to meet Sophie, because they are only marginally interested in Prince Edward. They are very interested to meet Camilla, because they are very interested in Prince Charles. (Let us face it, Prince Edward is to be nothing:[194] the Prince of Wales is to be King.) Besides, because they have heard so much about her, they want to know: what's she really like?

The short answer, to quote one of the Queen's ladies-in-waiting, is that she is 'really, really nice'. I am told that Her Majesty 'would not have expected it to be otherwise'. I am also told (by a member of the Royal Family) that, since April 2005, the Queen has been 'getting on famously' with her new daughter-in-law: 'It has all been much easier than anyone expected.'

The credit for this must go to Camilla. She has done everything that her husband has asked of her, but she has asked for almost nothing in return. With the Queen and the Duke of Edinburgh, she has tried, but she has not tried too hard. The last divorcée to join the Royal Family was Princess Michael of Kent, born Baroness Marie-Christine von Reibnitz and nicknamed 'Princess Pushy' by unkinder members of the House of Windsor. 'I do not believe that Princess Michael would ever have established a cosy relationship with the Queen,' said Lord Mountbatten's secretary (who later also worked for Prince and Princess Michael). 'The royal family is very inward-looking and finds it hard to

[193] Probably more akin to the former than the latter. As a model, Elizabeth Hurley is world-famous, which Sophie Wessex, minor royal, and Anthea Turner, minor TV personality, are not. Not long ago, I escorted Miss Hurley as she toured the stands at the Grosvenor House Antiques Fair and I was struck by the way those she met treated her very much as they would have treated royalty. Three men bowed to her and one lady curtsied. It seems people want princesses in their lives.

[194] In fact, on the death of his father, Edward is to be re-created Duke of Edinburgh. He has already taken on a number of Prince Philip's commitments, notably as the front man for the Duke of Edinburgh's Award Scheme. Philip has always had a soft spot for Edward, somewhat to the surprise and irritation of Prince Charles.

welcome strangers; and the Queen, particularly, finds it very difficult to relax unless she is surrounded by those with whom she feels at home.' The Queen, increasingly, feels at home with Camilla. This is partly because they have so much in common: friends, family, dogs, horses; partly because, generationally, they are surprisingly close (the Queen is twenty-one years older than Camilla, but thirty-nine years older than Sophie); partly, too, because Camilla's manner with Her Majesty – becomingly tentative, at first – is friendly without being overfamiliar (poor Sarah, Duchess of York, was so loud – and so vulgar); and partly, also, because the Queen has seen how well her grandsons get on with their new stepmother and been much reassured by that. (I am told that the Queen, when she attended Prince William's graduation ceremony at St Andrews, was especially impressed by how 'natural' William was with Camilla, chatting to her, and greeting her with a friendly kiss, without any sign of awkwardness.)

Camilla is finding her feet within the Royal Family. Gradually, she is hitting her stride with the public, too. Diana, Fergie, Sophie – each had difficult moments in the immediate aftermath of marrying one of the Queen's sons. As a senior royal put it to me, with a chuckle, 'Camilla has the advantage of maturity.' She behaves like a grown-up because she is one. On the day after the explosion of the terrorist bombs in London in July 2005, she accompanied Prince Charles on a visit to St Mary's Hospital in Paddington to meet some of the survivors. Patients, nurses and doctors alike were impressed by her easy, unforced bedside manner. When Andrew Meyer, a medic who was one of the first on the scene after the explosion at Edgware Road station told her, 'The survivors were so brave, not screaming – they waited in line', she replied, 'It was very, sort of, British, wasn't it?' As I watched her in action that day, I thought, 'She has the tone and attitude of the Queen Mother.' As she left the hospital she said, 'It makes me very proud to be British.' She caught the mood of the moment, perfectly.

'They are a good team,' one of the reporters at St Mary's said to me. 'You can see, they just get on.' Charles and Diana were never a good team. They were never in harness. Absurdly, they were frequently in competition. While Charles and Diana had almost nothing in common, Charles and Camilla share so much. For example, on the Saturday before the London bombings, Bob Geldof staged his star-studded Live8 concert in Hyde Park. Had Diana been alive, she would have wanted to be there, combining duty with pleasure. It was her sort of event, in a way it could never have been Charles's.[195] That Saturday, Charles was where he wanted to be, in Stratford-upon-Avon, with Camilla, combining duty with pleasure, as patron of the Royal Shakespeare Company, attending a performance of *A Midsummer Night's Dream*. It is one of Charles's favourite plays. It contains the famous line, 'The course of true love never did run smooth.'

Another of Charles's favourite plays is *The Madness of King George* by Alan Bennett. It contains the memorable line, 'To be Prince of Wales is not a position. It's a predicament.' While the line is frequently used as an epigraph in books about Prince Charles, in his case I do not find it especially apt. I do not believe Prince Charles has ever been impatient to be King, for example, and for more than thirty years, from his late twenties onwards, he has, without doubt, successfully carved out for himself a distinct and distinguished role as Prince of Wales. Look at Appendix A and consider the range of his interests and achievements. Talk to anyone who has seen him in action at close quarters and, without exception, they will speak of his energy, intelligence, imagination, sympathy and commitment.

His predicament has not been his position so much as his personality. Hugo Vickers, the Queen Mother's biographer, says 'metaphorically, he was born with a headache'. Countess Mountbatten, his godmother, describes him as 'a sensitive soul'. I came across a letter from his sometime guru, Laurens van der Post, to his sometime psychotherapist, Dr Alan McGlashan, that touches on several key aspects of Charles's character. McGlashan had, for a time, been close to Charles, as therapist and friend. In 1995, when he was ninety-seven, McGlashan wrote to van der Post to ask why it was that Charles was no longer in touch with him. Van der Post replied:

> I have never initiated a discussion with [Prince Charles] about your special relationship, and he has never discussed it with me, except from time to time to mention how much he valued knowing you, and how what had been a professional relationship had given him a

---

[195] Charles proclaims that he is 'old-fashioned' and proud of it. Some years ago, when he was still married to Diana, he attended a concert at the Royal Albert Hall given by Meatloaf in aid of the Prince's Trust. The chairman of the Albert Hall told me at the time: 'All of Charles's people were there, all ages, all types, a true cross-section of the British public having a great time . . . And what did HRH do? He put in his earplugs and looked sad. As he left he said, "Dreadful, wasn't it?"'

companionship of heart and mind that he had never met before. You, I am certain better than any of us, know how misunderstood and starved he has been of really spontaneous, natural affection – and, indeed, the respect his own natural spirit deserves. I do not really think you can think of it as you would with normal people because his life in the last few years has meant that he has terrifyingly less time for his 'being', as he calls it, than he has ever had, and his being is something precious to which you are very important . . . Please, please, do not let that be a source of unease. There is nobody he respects more than you, and he would be terribly upset if he felt that he had hurt you . . .

McGlashan and van der Post are both dead now. Kathleen Raine died in 2003. Lord Mountbatten is long gone and Queen Elizabeth The Queen Mother, who seemed immortal, is dead, too. The old men and women who, in their different ways, sustained Prince Charles through his years of travail are no more. Charles remembers them with affection, respect and gratitude, but he does not need them now. He has Camilla, and with Camilla he has that 'companionship of heart and mind' for which he has always yearned. 'At last,' he says, 'I feel complete.'

Laurens van der Post, whom Charles so much admired, once said, 'Nothing expresses the psychology valid to the English political evolution better than the place of the crown . . . The first thing about a crown, of course, is that it is round and that roundness has always been the expression of wholeness, the opposite of that which is angled, slanted and incomplete.' Charles feels complete. And he has come full circle. At last, he has married the woman he should have married more than thirty years ago.

In the popular imagination, Charles and Camilla's first encounter was at a polo match. Thinking of the symmetry, I thought it would be appropriate to conclude my research for this book on the polo field, so, on 7 July 2005, by kind invitation of the commandant, I travelled to the Royal Military College, Sandhurst, to watch Charles in action. In the event, at the last moment, he cancelled.[196] It was the day of the London bombings and duty called.

From now until their deaths, Charles and Camilla, together, will play

[196] Prince Harry played on and played well. It was interesting to watch the game. It certainly calls for skill, courage and the ability to play as part of a team. I can see its attraction for the Prince of Wales: when playing polo, absolute concentration is required. You can think of nothing else.

their parts in the various dramas of our national life. They will visit the sick, they will comfort the bereaved, they will honour the dead. They will do their duty, looking grave, or gay, as the situation requires. They hope, of course, that the personal drama of their own lives will absorb us rather less in the future than it has in the past.

On 23 May 2005, the Duchess of Cornwall, dressed in pink, undertook her first solo engagement since becoming a member of the Royal Family. As president of the National Osteoporosis Society, she visited Southampton General Hospital. She was presented with several posies, including one from two-year-old Emily Forrester who ran up to Camilla, handed over her posy and ran back to her mother before deciding to return to give the Duchess a kiss. The card with the flowers was signed by Emily and her sister Jessica. It said, 'We think you will be a lovely Queen!'

The story of Charles and Camilla has been extraordinary, almost beyond belief. The woman who once cowered in a supermarket car park while strangers threw bread rolls at her, now stands on the balcony at Buckingham Palace waving at the crowds below. You could not make it up. It is the stuff of fairy tale – which, of course, is what we expect of royalty. And, like a fairy tale, for all the hurt and humiliation along the way, it is a story with a happy ending. Charles and Camilla are happy together. There is no doubt about that. And happiness is like sunshine: we warm to it. We will warm to them.

Appendices

A. The Role of the Prince of Wales

The Prince of Wales's title, while ancient, carries no established or formal role. Prince Charles, as the twenty-first holder of the title in 700 years, has tried to create a role for himself, and, as he sees it, this falls into three parts:

(i)   Undertaking royal duties in support of the Queen.
(ii) Working as a charitable entrepreneur.
(iii) Promoting and protecting national traditions, virtues and excellence.

For details of how he attempts to fulfil his role, I recommend a visit to his website: www.princeofwales.gov.uk. It is partial, of course, but impressive nonetheless, and provides a full account of the Prince's many and varied good works, and details of his numerous public engagements. (He carried out 500 in the year to 31 March 2005, including 103 overseas.) The website also provides access to a wide range of his past speeches and to his official Annual Report, as well as details of his own service career and various appointments as a colonel-in-chief.

At the heart of his charitable endeavour are what are now called 'The Prince's Charities', a group of not-for-profit organisations of which Prince Charles is president; fourteen of the sixteen charities were founded personally by him. The group is the largest multi-cause charitable enterprise in the United Kingdom, raising more than £100 million annually. The organisations are active across a range of areas of interest to Charles:

Opportunity and Enterprise

The Prince's Trust
The Prince's Scottish Youth Business Trust
PRIME and PRIME Cymru

Education

The Prince's Drawing School
The Prince's School of Traditional Arts

Health

The Prince of Wales's Foundation for Integrated Health

The Built Environment

The Prince's Foundation for the Built Environment
The Prince's Regeneration Trust

Responsible Business and the Natural Environment

Business and the Community
Scottish Business in the Community
The Prince of Wales International Business Leaders Forum
The Prince of Wales's Business & The Environment Programme
In Kind Direct

The Arts

Arts and Business
The Prince of Wales Arts & Kids Foundation

Charles is also concerned at trends in education which he believes rob young people of their cultural heritage as well as access to fulfilling work. He has founded The Prince of Wales's Education Summer School to give teachers of English and History a chance to debate their subjects with leading academics and writers away from the classroom. He says that the same concern with future generations as well as the current one is behind his work to improve protection of the environment.

He takes a close interest in the running of the Home Farm at Highgrove, which has been converted to organic methods – a reflection of his views on agriculture, and concern about the use of artificial pesticides and fertilisers, with their effect on wildlife.

Through The Prince of Wales's Foundation for Integrated Health, he advocates a more patient-centred approach to health care, with more understanding of complementary therapies.

The Prince is also patron or president of around 360 organisations, whose range of interests and activities include young people, the unemployed, the disabled, the elderly, the problems of the inner cities, education, medicine, the arts, conservation, national heritage, environment, architecture and sport. He claims not to be involved in any organisation simply as a figurehead, and it is worth looking at the full list on the website because it provides a revealing insight to his concerns – and personality.

B. The Peat Report

In the aftermath of the trial of Paul Burrell, Sir Michael Peat, private secretary to the Prince of Wales, assisted by Edmund Lawson QC, looked into a range of uncomfortable questions that had been raised by the case. Their report was published on 13 March 2003 and can be downloaded in full at www.princeofwales.gov.uk/news/2003/03.mar/peatreport.

Here is a summary of the findings and recommendations of the report.

1. Was there was an improper cover-up of the 1996 rape allegation made by Mr George Smith in 1996?

There was no improper cover-up in the sense that those involved deliberately or dishonestly sought to suppress what they believed might be true. However, the allegation was not dealt with in the best way by The Prince of Wales's Office.

No one in the Household believed Mr Smith's rape allegation. The Prince of Wales gave no credence to it and his staff shared in his disbelief. Hounslow Police decided not to give the allegation credence and chose not to investigate it. Perhaps understandably, a major concern was to avoid publicity being given to what was believed to be a baseless allegation. There was also a concern to follow The Prince of Wales's instructions that Mr Smith 'must go' but should be well provided for.

The objectives – right or wrong – were to secure Mr Smith's leaving, without giving him cause to repeat the allegation; and to provide generously for Mr Smith's future.

Conclusions

There was not an improper cover-up in the sense that those involved deliberately or dishonestly sought to suppress what they believed might be true.

However, a serious allegation of this sort should not have been treated so dismissively – even though there was universal disbelief as to its veracity – without full and documented consideration of the decision not to investigate. A lack of appropriate senior management involvement and of an effective personnel department resulted in poor handling of the matter.

The settlement with Mr Smith was very generous, but not to the extent that the conclusion must be that it derived from an improper motive.

Recommendations

Action has been taken since 1996 to improve the Household's personnel systems in line with best current practice.

2. Was there anything improper or remiss in the conduct of The Prince of Wales's Household with respect to the termination of the Burrell trial?

(Sir Michael Peat, who became The Prince of Wales's Private Secretary in August 2002, was involved in some discussions with the Police prior to the Burrell trial, and he was involved in the disclosure of The Queen's conversation made on 28th October 2002 to the Police and CPS. In view of this, this section was the exclusive responsibility of Mr Lawson.)

There was no improper conduct by or on behalf of The Prince of Wales in respect of the termination of the Burrell trial.

The Prince of Wales had, throughout, serious concerns about the implications of Mr Burrell being tried.

He was concerned that both he and Prince William might be called as witnesses and by the prospect of information personal to himself and his family being revealed during the trial – particularly the distress which would be caused to his sons by 'revelations', true or not, about their mother. He would have preferred it if a trial could have been avoided.

The Prince was advised, however, that he could not properly intervene, and should not be seen to be interfering with or seeking to influence the prosecution process. He followed that advice. Several opportunities presented themselves during the investigation to intervene and stop the process, and none was taken.

The disclosure made on 28th October 2002 of The Queen's conversation with Mr Burrell was properly made. There is no evidence that the disclosure was made for improper motive, nor is there any evidence that by making this disclosure there could have been an expectation that the trial would be discontinued.

Conclusion

There was no improper conduct by or on behalf of The Prince of Wales in respect of the termination of the Burrell trial.

3. Have official gifts given to The Prince of Wales been sold?

One official gift has been identified as having been sold (it was thought by The Prince of Wales to have been a private gift) and a few private gifts have been sold. Because of poor record keeping a number of official gifts could not be accounted for. It is not thought likely that they have been sold, but they may have been lent or given to or taken by staff or destroyed. A number of smaller gifts have been given to staff (because it was believed that they would otherwise go to waste). Policies and procedures in this area have been deficient.

A detailed exercise was undertaken for a three year period (1999 to 2001) to try to identify whether official gifts had, using a new broader definition, been sold.

Of 180 traceable official gifts given to The Prince of Wales during the three-year period, with a value of over £150 or more, 19 could not be accounted for. Most had limited realisable value and it is unlikely that The Prince of Wales would have asked for any to be sold or exchanged; it is possible that these have been lent or given to or taken by or destroyed by staff, but we have no evidence to this effect.

The Prince of Wales has not, as a matter of principle, passed on official gifts to staff, unless they are food or perishable items, or items of smaller value. As far as is known, items passed on to staff have never included any non-perishable items given or sent in by members of the public.

The listing of official gifts received during 1999–2001 identified two where replies from Warrant Holders indicated there had been an exchange. In one case it was not realised that the gift was official and in the other it would only be categorised as official using the new definition now being introduced. The replies from Warrant Holders also identified one official gift which had been sold (it was thought to be private) and seven private gifts which had been sold or exchanged.

Conclusion

There was no documented definition of official gifts. The policies and procedures in The Prince of Wales's Household to record and control the receipt, maintenance and disposal of official, and other, gifts including the maintenance of inventory records, have been deficient. This was not intentional, but the result of pressure of work and limited resources. In part it was also because those involved had become accustomed to the practices which were established when the Office was much smaller.

Recommendations

New policies and procedures should be introduced, including a documented and more comprehensive definition of official gifts. No official or private gifts will in future be sold or exchanged, except for private gifts, in exceptional circumstances and with the permission of the donor. No official gift will be given away other than to charity or, for obvious practical reasons, if it is food or another perishable item with a value of less than £50.

4. Have any staff in The Prince of Wales's Household received improper payments or other benefits?

Staff have, in the past and with the knowledge of senior management, received benefits, gifts, entertainment and discounts from Royal Warrant Holders and other suppliers. There was a requirement in the terms of employment not to 'accept presents from firms or tradesmen' and the practice should not have been permitted.

The Review found no evidence of staff selling gifts given to The Prince of Wales without authorisation or taking commissions or 'slices' of the proceeds where authorisation had been given.

There is no evidence of financial impropriety on the part of Mr Fawcett. He (as well as others) infringed the internal rules relating to gifts from suppliers, but the rules were generally not enforced and he made no secret of such gifts. Press suspicions were understandably aroused by his involvement in the sale of gifts (which, unknown to the media, were authorised by The Prince of Wales). This has encouraged some to voice rumours as to Mr Fawcett's financial probity, but there is no evidence to justify any finding by us that he has been guilty of alleged financial misconduct.

Conclusion

Administrative policies and procedures with respect to gifts, discounts and other benefits for staff have been seriously deficient.

Recommendations

Clear guidelines should be drawn up and circulated to all staff setting out the Household's rules in respect of gratuities, gifts, discounts and hospitality and explaining the tax implications. All discounts should be listed, approved and regularly reviewed by senior management. No discount should be accepted if the discount is greater than the supplier offers its own staff.

C. The Wedding Day

The Prince of Wales and Camilla Parker Bowles were married in a civil ceremony at the Guildhall in Windsor on Saturday 9 April 2005. For those who enjoy the details, here they are.

The ceremony was conducted by Clair Williams, the Superintendent Registrar. Prince William and Tom Parker Bowles were the witnesses to the marriage, and Prince William had the responsibility for looking after the wedding rings, hand-made by Wartski in the court style using Welsh gold. The marriage ceremony took place in the Ascot Room within the Guildhall and lasted approximately twenty minutes.

The flowers in the Ascot Room were cut from the gardens at Charles and Camilla's country homes: Highgrove and Raymill. Bunches of lily of the valley also decorated the room. (Traditionally, lily of the valley symbolises the return of happiness.)

Following the civil wedding, there was a Service of Prayer and Dedication at St George's Chapel, for which the music was chosen by the bride and groom and included Bach's Cantata *Nun Komm der Heiden Heiland* and excerpts from Handel's Water Music. Among the musicians who performed at the service were members of the Philharmonia Orchestra, of which the Prince of Wales is patron, and the St George's Chapel Choir. A Russian version of The Creed, set to music by Gretchaninov, was sung by Ekaterina Semenchuk, a young Russian contralto who had been specially flown over as a wedding gift from the Mariinsky Theatre Trust of St Petersburg, of which Charles is both a patron and a benefactor.

At the beginning of the service, a number of organ and orchestral pieces were played, including Farewell to Stromness by the Master of the Queen's Music, Sir Peter Maxwell Davies, and works by Walton, Bach, Handel, Finzi, Grieg and Elgar.

As the Prince of Wales and the Duchess of Cornwall joined the congregation, the orchestra played the Adagio movement of Albinoni's

Oboe Concerto in D minor. During the service, three hymns were sung, all favourites of the royal couple: Immortal Invisible (tune: St Denio), Love Divine All Loves Excelling (tune: Blaenwern), and Praise My Soul The King of Heaven (tune: Goss). After the concluding blessing, a verse of the National Anthem was sung, followed immediately by a specially commissioned 'Celebration Fanfare' by the Welsh composer Alun Hoddinott.

The main decorations in the chapel were mature English-grown flowering trees: Malus Evereste – a flowering crab apple named after Sir Edmund Hillary's conquest of Everest in the coronation year; the Great White Blossom; and Prunus Hai Haiku (each about four to five metres high) in wooden boxes made by a carpenter at Highgrove. These were underplanted with English meadow flowers such as cowslips, fritillaries, camellias, pulsatilla, anemone, violas and narcissi from the Duchy of Cornwall nurseries. (All the trees and plants were later replanted in the gardens at Highgrove and Clarence House as a lasting memory of the day.) Outside the chapel were two banks of jonquils and daffodils, given by the Hosking family of Fentongollan Farm, Tresillian, Truro.

After the service, the couple left St George's Chapel, flanked on both sides by representatives of the regiments with which the Prince is associated, and then met representatives of the charities with which they are associated. For the Prince, there were representatives from many of the 360 organisations of which he is patron or president. The Duchess was greeted by representatives from the Wiltshire Bobby Van Trust and the National Osteoporosis Society of which she is president.

Afterwards, the Queen hosted a reception in the State Apartments at Windsor Castle. The wedding cake was made by Dawn Blundone and Mary Robinson who make cakes for the Highgrove Shop. It was a single-layered, plain white, organic, rich fruit cake, 24-inch square with an octagon dome. The square had detailed lattice-work and a small initial 'C' in the lattice. The corners of the square were decorated with roses, thistles, leeks and daffodils. The octagon was made up of panels with different designs. One panel has a Cipher of The Prince of Wales picturing a coronet, a garter and the three feathers. Another panel featured the Crest of the Duchy of Cornwall and another has the Crest of the Duke of Rothesay. A further panel had a coronet surrounded by a pearl cameo and the initial 'C'. The remaining panels featured roses to represent England, daffodils and leeks to represent Wales and thistles to represent Scotland. The top of the cake featured the Crown of the Heir Apparent.

Charles and Camilla used the Prince of Wales's naval sword to cut the wedding cake. The sword, which originally belonged to the Prince's great-grandfather, King George V, is normally used for Investitures.

The clothes

For the wedding, Camilla was dressed by Robinson Valentine, a firm established in 1986 by Antonia Robinson and Anna Valentine who had met on a pattern-cutting course. They say their 'ethos' is to create clothes that 'capture the mood of the moment and are also timeless'. Anna Valentine has been designing for Camilla since 2001. Work on the 2005 wedding outfit started on 21 February and continued until the final fitting on the Tuesday before the wedding. There were two initial meetings followed by eight fittings.

For the civil ceremony, Camilla wore an oyster silk basket-weave coat with herringbone stitch embroidery and a chiffon dress with appliqué-woven lacquered disc detail. The design team wanted what they called 'a crisp clean look with subtle detailing'. To achieve this, the design team used two fabrics with very different textures. The lacquered discs were made in Switzerland to Robinson Valentine's specifications while the hand-worked herringbone detail on the coat was embroidered in-house using silk thread.

The bride wore an elegant court shoe in pale beige suede, with an almond toe and a five-centimetre heel, designed by Linda Bennett, founder of LK Bennett, who opened her first shop in Wimbledon village in 1990 selling shoes and accessories.

For the civil ceremony, Camilla wore a natural straw hat overlaid with ivory French lace and trimmed with a graphic fountain of feathers, designed by Philip Treacy. (Treacy was born in Ireland in 1967, started sewing at the age of five and moved to Dublin in 1985 to study fashion at the National College of Art & Design, making hats as a hobby. He is now one of the world's most sought-after milliners.)

Camilla's handbag was an East/West clutch bag made from embossed calf leather, lined with suede and made with a half-flap. The inside was imprinted with the Launer name and Royal Warrant and included a matching coin purse and leather-covered mirror.

The bride's hair for the day was prepared by Hugh Green of Hugh

CHARLES & CAMILLA

and Stephen, based at Ebury Road, London, and her make-up was by Julia B.

For the Service of Prayer and Dedication, the new Duchess of Cornwall wore a porcelain blue silk dress with hand-painted ikat design, hand-embroidered with gold thread work. Tones of blue and gold were the favoured colours. The designer's starting point was Mrs Parker Bowles's comment that she liked the style of the velvet dress which they had designed for her to wear for a gala night at the Royal Opera House. Robinson Valentine believed the dress required 'a sense of occasion' and their aim was to create 'a flowing, elegant line, concentrating on proportion, fit and silhouette'. A piece of jewellery which belonged to Mrs Parker Bowles's mother became the inspiration for the fabric design. Robinson Valentine carried out research on embroidery, technique and fabric in the textile collection at the Victoria & Albert Museum and decided that to achieve the desired effect they would need to create their own fabric. To give the dress a light and effortless appearance, the fabric was initially treated to remove any stiffness and give it more fluidity. The hand embroidery combined five tones of gold thread, intended to create 'depth and opulence' – and (in my view) succeeding.

The Duchess wore a court shoe with a soft point toe and a five-and-a-half-centimetre heel in pale grey shot silk, with gold embroidery detail on the toe. The gold-leafed feather headdress tipped with Swarovski diamonds was again designed and made by Philip Treacy.

The media – before her wedding, almost universally critical of Camilla's dress sense – was united in praising her appearance on her wedding day. Prince Charles was also reckoned to have looked his best as well. He wore a black morning suit and grey pinstripe trousers made by Anderson and Sheppard with a grey waistcoat, a stiff-collar shirt with a blue and yellow tie, plus a hellebore from the garden at Highgrove in his buttonhole.

Prince William and Prince Harry wore black morning suits from Gieves & Hawkes with grey and black pinstripe trousers. Harry's waistcoat was grey and William's pale blue. Both princes wore tiepins given to them by the Queen – tiepins that had once belonged to her mother, Her Late Majesty Queen Elizabeth The Queen Mother.

And finally . . . the wedding rings – hand-made in court style by Wartski, using Welsh gold supplied by Cambrian Goldfields Limited. The gold used was from the Clogau St David's mine and the River Mawdach in the King's Forest, where it was recovered from deep pools using sub-aqua equipment. It was then refined and alloyed to pass twenty-two-carat gold standard and hallmarked at the London Assay Office.

In a way, Wartski's is the perfect place to finish. It brings the story full circle. Wartski is a family-owned firm of art and antique dealers, specialising in fine jewellery, gold boxes and works by Fabergé. The firm was founded in North Wales in 1865 by Morris Wartski. The business thrived under the patronage of King Edward VII who regularly went to Wartski when looking for presents to give to his mistress, Mrs Keppel.

Acknowledgements & Sources

I hope this book is accurate. If, on reading it, you find errors of fact, please let me know so that I can make corrections for subsequent editions. If you disagree with my interpretation of the facts, please let me know as well. I would like this 'portrait' to be as true as possible. It has been informed by my encounters – some brief, some extended – with most of the principal characters in the story. It has also been informed by my reading of the work of a range of royal biographers to whom I am much indebted.

Christopher Wilson is the acknowledged pioneer of 'Camilla studies', and, while disagreeing with some of its conclusions, I am particularly indebted to his immensely readable book, *The Windsor Knot: Charles, Camilla and the Legacy of Diana*. I also much enjoyed and benefited from *Camilla: An Intimate Portrait* by Rebecca Tyrrel and *Camilla: Her True Story* by Caroline Graham. Two other books have proved invaluable and essential sources to me (as to every other writer interested in this field): *The Prince of Wales: A Biography* by Jonathan Dimbleby and *Diana: Her True Story – In Her Own Words* by Andrew Morton. I am very grateful to these writers for the way in which their work has assisted mine. I must also acknowledge two other distinguished royal biographers, Anthony Holden and Hugo Vickers, to whose friendship, kindness and scholarship I am much indebted.

Many people have been involved in the creation of this book. I want to thank my literary agent, Ed Victor, for making it happen; and my wife, Michèle Brown, for putting up with me while it did. I am greatly indebted to my publisher, friend and mentor, Mark Booth, and to all the members of the Century team, notably Kate Watkins, Charlotte Bush and Ron Beard and his colleagues in the sales force. Considerable thanks are due, too, to my copy editor, Richard Collins; indexer, Douglas Matthews; and picture researcher, Amanda Russell.

Below I have listed the principal books I consulted during my research. Of course, the blame for any errors of commission or omission should be laid at my door and no one else's.

Alice, Princess Alice of Greece by Hugo Vickers, 1999

Arguments with England by Michael Blakemore, 2004

Behind Palace Doors by Nigel Dempster and Peter Evans, 1993

Blood Royal by Charles Mosley, 2002

Camilla: An Intimate Portrait by Rebecca Tyrrel, 2003

Camilla: Her True Story by Caroline Graham, 2003

Charles, A Biography by Anthony Holden, 1998

Charles, Prince of Wales by Anthony Holden, 1979

Charles: Victim or Villain? by Penny Junor, 1998

Closely Guarded Secret by Ken Wharfe, 2002

Daily Mirror interview with Norman Barson, 1996

Diana: Her True Story – In Her Own Words by Andrew Morton (1997)

Diana: In Pursuit of Love by Andrew Morton, 2004

Diana vs. Charles by James Whitaker, 1993

The Diaries of Sir Henry Channon, edited by Robert Rhodes James, 1993

The Dictionary of National Biography, 1975

Don't Look Round by Violet Trefusis, 1952

Edward VII by Christopher Hibbert, 1976

Edward VII and His Jewish Court by Anthony Allfrey, 1991

Edward VIII by Frances Donaldson, 1974

Edwardian Daughter by Sonia Keppel, 1958

Edwardians in Love by Anita Leslie, 1972

Edwina Mountbatten: A Life of Her Own by Janet Morgan, 1991

Edwy the Fair or the First Chronicle of Aesendune by A. D. Crake, 1874

Elizabeth by Sarah Bradford, 1996

The Fringes of Power: Downing Street Diaries 1939–1955 by John Colville, 1985

George VI by Sarah Bradford, 1989

Highgrove, Portrait of an Estate by HRH The Prince of Wales and Charles Clover, 1993

The Housekeeper's Diary by Wendy Berry, 1995

King Edward VII by Philip Magnus, 1962

The King in Love: Edward VII's Mistresses by Theo Aronson, 1988

The King's Mistresses by Alan Hardy, 1980

A King's Story by The Duke of Windsor, 1951

Kings, Queens, Bones and Bastards by David Hilliam, 1998

Lady Curzon's India: Letters of a Vicerein, edited by John Bradley, 1985

Laughter in the Next Room by Osbert Sitwell, 1949
Letters from a Prince: Edward Prince of Wales to Mrs Freda Dudley Ward, March 1918–January 1921, edited by Rupert Godfrey, 1999
The Little Princesses by Marion Crawford, 1950
Love and War by James Hewitt, 1999
More Memoirs of an Aesthete by Harold Acton, 1970
Mountbatten by Philip Ziegler, 1985
Mrs Keppel and Her Daughter by Diana Souhami, 1996
My Diaries by Sir Wilfrid Scawen Blunt, 1919
Not All Vanity by Agnes de Stoeckl, 1950
Oscar Wilde by Richard Ellmann, 1987
The Oxford Dictionary of Saints by David Hugh Farmer, 1978
Portrait of a Marriage by Nigel Nicolson, 1973
Primo Time by Antony Sher, 2005
Prince Charles & Princess Diana: Portrait of a Family by Michèle Brown, 1984
The Prince of Wales by Jonathan Dimbleby, 1995
The Princes of Wales by Wynford Vaughan-Thomas, 1982
The Private World of the Duke and Duchess of Windsor by Hugo Vickers, 1995
Queen and Country: interview with The Princess Royal for the BBC TV series presented by William Shawcross, produced and directed by John Bridcut (a Mentorn production), 2002
Recollections of Three Reigns by Frederick Ponsonby, 1951
Reminiscences by Horace Walpole, 1925
A Royal Duty by Paul Burrell, 2003
The Royal House of Windsor by Elizabeth Longford, 1974
Royal Orders: The Honours and the Honoured by Hugo Vickers, 1994
Royal Secrets by Stephen Barry, 1985
Royal Service by Stephen Barry, 1983
The Royal Wedding by Brenda Ralph Lewis, 1981
Shadows of a Princess by Patrick Jephson, 2000
Storyteller: The Many Lives of Laurens van der Post by J. D. F. Jones, 2001
To Be a King: A Biography of HRH Prince Charles by Dermot Morrah, 1989
Wallis & Edward, Letters 1931–37, edited by Michael Bloch, 1986
The Windsor Knot by Christopher Wilson, 2002

Picture Credits

Section One

National Portrait Gallery London, Topfoto.co.uk, National Portrait Gallery London, National Portrait Gallery London, Photograph by Chancellor of Dublin/National Portrait Gallery London, © Camera Press London, © Camera Press London, © Hulton-Deutsch Collection/CORBIS, © CORBIS SYGMA, © Camera Press London, Topfoto.co.uk, Photograph by William Vanderson/Fox Photos/Getty Images, © Rex Features, © Time Life Pictures/Getty Images, The Royal Archives © 2005 Her Majesty Queen Elizabeth II.

Section Two

© Popperfoto.com, © Rex Features, © Popperfoto.com, © Desmond O'Neill Features, © Camera Press London, © Camera Press London, © Desmond O'Neill Features, Photograph by Lord Kilbracken/Camera Press London, © Camera Press London, Photography by Arthur Edwards/Camera Press London, Serge Lemoine/Getty, © Desmond O'Neill Features, © Desmond O'Neill Features, © Anwar Hussein/Rex Features, © Desmond O'Neill Features, © Rex Features.

Section Three

© Rex Features, © Desmond O'Neill Features, © Rex Features, © Tim Graham, © Desmond O'Neill Features, © Popperfoto.com, PA/EMPICS, © Getty Images, © Rex Features, PA/EMPICS, © Getty Images, Topfoto.co.uk/UPPA Ltd, © Getty Images, Diana Memorial Fund/Camera Press, London, © Tim Graham, Topfoto.co.uk/Star Images, Camera Press London/ROTA.

Section Four

National Portrait Gallery London, © David Dawson, © Camera Press London, PA/EMPICS, Topfoto.co.uk, © Desmond O'Neill Features, © Rex Features, © Rex Features, © Rex Features, © Rex Features, © Rex Features, Author's own, © Tim Graham/CORBIS SYGMA, © Rex Features, © Rex Features, Photograph by John Stillwell/PA/EMPICS, © Camera Press, London/ROTA, © Tim Graham, Photograph by Christopher Furlong/Getty Images.

Section Five

© Camera Press London, Photograph by Peter Tarry/AP/EMPICS, Photograph by Anwar Hussein/Getty Images, © Tim Graham, Photograph by Kirsty Wigglesworth/PA/EMPICS, Photograph by Chris Ison/PA/EMPICS, Photograph by Toby Melville/PA/EMPICS, Photograph by Bob Collier/AP.EMPICS, Photograph by Hugo Barnand/AP/EMPICS, © Tim Graham, © Tim Graham, © Anwar Hussein, Photograph by Fiona Hanson/PA/EMPICS, AFP/Getty Images, Photograph by Barry Batchelor/PA/EMPICS, © Tim Graham, © Tim Graham, AFP/Getty Images, © Anwar Hussein.

Index

Morton's *Diana: Her True Story*, 270;
Queen's view of, 272; on Charles's
separation from Diana, 274–5; behaviour
at public appearances, 276–7; marriage
relations with Andrew, 278; divorce from
Andrew, 280–1, 284; losses as Lloyds
underwriter, 283–4; moves to Ray Mill
House, 284; relations with Charles after
divorce, 284–5; fiftieth birthday, 285;
easy relations with Charles, 286, 318–19,
321; relations with William and Harry,
287; and Diana's death and funeral, 290;
Charles's commitment to after Diana's
death, 293; organises party for Charles's
fiftieth birthday, 294; Queen meets, 295;
lives together openly with Charles, 296;
financial affairs, 300–1; in royal order of
precedence, 314–15; effect when meeting
people, 317
Cornwell, Patricia: *Portrait of a Killer*, 30n
Cotham, A.V., 12
Coward, Sir Noël, 20n, 173n, 213
Cowes, Isle of Wight, 128
Crawford, Marion ('Crawfie'), 125–6; *The
Little Princesses*, 193n
Crawley family, 256n
Crawley and Horsham Hounds, 106
Crofts, Mary, 24
Cronkite, Walter, 27n
Cubitt family, 68n
Cubitt, Charles, 106
Cubitt, Henry, 75
Cubitt, Jeremy, 75, 93
Cubitt, Jonathan, 68n
Cubitt, Laura, Lady, 69
Cubitt, Rosalind Maud *see* Shand, Rosalind
Maud
Cubitt, Sonia, 207–8, 241n
Cubitt, Thomas, 67–9
Culloden, battle of (1746), 31–2
Curzon, George Nathaniel, Marquess Curzon
of Kedleston, 58n, 59
Curzon, Mary, Lady, 58, 59n
Cust, Frances (*née* Steer; *then* Keppel), 35n
Cust, Lieut.-Col. Peregrine Francis, 35n
Cutsem, Edward van, 6
Cutsem, Emilie van, 6n
Cutsem, Hugh van, 6n
Cutsem, Lady Tamara (*née* Grosvenor), 6

Daily Express: on Charles-Camilla act of
repentance, 16
Daily Mail: on Charles-Camilla engagement,
10; on postponement of Charles-Camilla
wedding, 15; attacks Camilla's presence at
Alamein memorial service, 85–6
Daily Mirror: lampoons Charles and Camilla,
16; on Charles's drinking cherry brandy as
schoolboy, 142
Daily Telegraph, 194, 295, 303
Dalton, Hugh (*later* Baron), 73n
Darlington, Sophia von Kilmansegg,

Countess of, 38
Darnley, James, 22
Darnley, Katherine, 22
Davidson, Jim, 8–9
Davies, Sir Peter Maxwell, 333
Davis, David, 292n
debutantes, 158–61
de Manio, Jack, 135n
Dempster, Nigel, 163; *Behind Palace Doors*,
175–6
de Pass, Philip, 220
de Pass, Robert and Philippa, 220
de Trafford, Sir Humphrey and Cynthia,
Lady (*née* Cadogan), 175
Diana, Princess of Wales (*née* Spencer):
popularity and glamour, 2, 44–8, 282,
288, 292; estrangement from van
Cutsems, 6n; Schaufuss ballet on, 7;
forebears, 22–5, 217n; suggests Charles's
homosexuality, 28; death and funeral, 36,
285, 288–9, 292; marriage to Charles, 40,
44–5, 232; and Charles sartorial
fastidiousness, 49n; public good works,
50; attends Alamein memorial service,
86; and Dodi al Fayed, 100n, 291, 311;
marriage relations, 121–2, 232–5, 237–9,
265, 269, 312, 318; non-glove wearing,
150; on homosexuals in Charles's
entourage, 193n; on Charles's relations
with father, 195; self-centredness, 207;
on having 'marriage with three in it',
214–15; on Highgrove, 215; first meetings
with Charles, 217, 219–21; birth and
upbringing, 218–19; insecurity, 219;
awareness of Charles's feelings for Camilla,
222, 227–30; Charles courts and proposes
to, 222–6; media interest in, 222–3, 267;
Charles's doubts on engagement to, 226,
231; bulimia (eating disorder), 227, 232,
237; moves to Clarence House and
Buckingham Palace, 227; and Charles's
behaviour during engagement, 231–2;
divorce, 232, 283; obsession with Camilla,
235–7, 244, 252, 287–8; on honeymoon,
236; undergoes psychotherapy, 237–8;
devotion to children, 242, 283; beauty,
246; faints in Vancouver, 247; affairs and
romantic liaisons, 248–9, 251–2; marriage
breakdown, 248–51, 272–4; and Charles's
injured arm from polo accident, 266–7;
cooperates with Andrew Morton on book,
269–70; family holiday on Latsis yacht
with Charles, 270–1; Prince Philip's
correspondence with, 273; formal
separation from Charles, 274–5; TV
interview with Bashir, 281–2; records
George Smith's accusations against
Charles, 305; dislikes Fawcett, 306–7;
not awarded GCVO, 316
Dickens, Geoffrey, 253n
Dimbleby, Jonathan: TV film on and
biography of Charles, 118–19, 121, 190,

CHARLES & CAMILLA